LANCHESTER LIBRARY
D0321511

The Media

7

Media studies needs richer and livelier intellectual resources. This book brings together major and emerging international media analysts to consider key processes of media change, using a number of critical perspectives. Case studies range from reality television to professional journalism, from blogging to control of copyright, from social networking sites to indigenous media, in Europe, North America, Asia and elsewhere. Among the theoretical approaches and issues addressed are:

- Critical realism
- Post-structuralist approaches to media and culture
- Pierre Bourdieu and field theory
- Public sphere theory – including post-Habermasian versions
- Actor network theory
- Marxist and post-Marxist theories, including contemporary critical theory
- Theories of democracy, antagonism and difference

Essential reading for undergraduate and postgraduate students and researchers of cultural studies, media studies and social theory.

David Hesmondhalgh is Professor of Media and Music Industries in the Institute of Communications Studies at the University of Leeds. His books include *The Cultural Industries* (2nd edition, 2007), *Media Production* (2006) and *Understanding Media: Inside Celebrity* (with Jessica Evans, 2005).

Jason Toynbee is Senior Lecturer in Media Studies at the Open University. His books include *Bob Marley: Herald of a Postcolonial World?* (2007), *Analysing Media Texts* (with Marie Gillespie, 2006) and *Making Popular Music* (2000).

Culture, Economy and the Social

A new series from CRESC – the ESRC Centre for Research on Socio-cultural Change

Editors

Professor Tony Bennett, Sociology, Open University
Professor Penny Harvey, Anthropology, Manchester University
Professor Kevin Hetherington, Geography, Open University

Book Series Board

Michel Callon, Ecole des Mines de Paris
Mary Poovey, New York University
Andrew Barry, University of Oxford
Eric Hirsch, Brunel University
Antoine Hennion, Paris Institute of Technology
Dipesh Chakrabarty, The University of Chicago
Mike Crang, University of Durham
Rolland Munro, Keele University
Tim Dant, Lancaster University
Sharon Zukin, Brooklyn College City University New York / Graduate School, City University of New York
Timothy Mitchell, New York University
Jean-Louis Fabiani, Ecole de Hautes Etudes en Sciences Sociales, Paris
Randy Martin, New York University
John Law, Lancaster University
Andrew Pickering, University of Exeter
Hugh Willmott, University of Cardiff

The *Culture, Economy and the Social* series is committed to innovative contemporary, comparative and historical work on the relations between social, cultural and economic change. It publishes empirically-based research that is theoretically informed, that critically examines the ways in which social, cultural and economic change is framed and made visible, and that is attentive to perspectives that tend to be ignored or side-lined by grand theorising or epochal accounts of social change. The series addresses the diverse manifestations of contemporary capitalism, and considers the various ways in which the 'social', 'the cultural' and 'the economic' are apprehended as tangible sites of value and practice. It is explicitly comparative, publishing books that work across disciplinary perspectives, cross-culturally, or across different historical periods.

The series is actively engaged in the analysis of the different theoretical traditions that have contributed to the development of the 'cultural turn' with a view to clarifying where these approaches converge and where they diverge on a particular issue. It is equally concerned to explore the new critical agendas emerging from current critiques of the cultural turn: those associated with the descriptive turn for example. Our commitment to interdisciplinarity thus aims at enriching theoretical and methodological discussion, building awareness of the common ground that has emerged in the past decade, and thinking through what is at stake in those approaches that resist integration to a common analytical model.

Series titles include:

The Media and Social Theory
Edited by David Hesmondhalgh and Jason Toynbee

Culture Class Distinction (forthcoming)
Tony Bennett, Mike Savage, Elizabeth Bortolaia Silva, Alan Warde, Modesto Gayo-Cal and David Wright

Material Powers (forthcoming)
Edited by Tony Bennett and Patrick Joyce

Centre for Research on
Socio-Cultural Change

The Media and Social Theory

Edited by
David Hesmondhalgh and
Jason Toynbee

Routledge
Taylor & Francis Group

LONDON AND NEW YORK

First published 2008
by Routledge
2 Park Square, Milton Park, Abingdon, Oxon OX14 4RN

Simultaneously published in the USA and Canada
by Routledge
270 Madison Avenue, New York NY 10016

*Routledge is an imprint of the Taylor & Francis Group,
an informa business*

© 2008 Editorial selection and matter, David Hesmondhalgh and
Jason Toynbee; individual chapters, the contributors

Typeset in Sabon by Keyword Group Ltd
Printed and bound in Great Britain by Biddles Ltd, King's Lynn

All rights reserved. No part of this book may be reprinted or
reproduced or utilised in any form or by any electronic, mechanical
or other means, now known or hereafter invented, including
photocopying and recording, or in any information storage and
retrieval system, without permission in writing from the publishers.

British Library Cataloguing in Publication Data
A catalogue record for this book is available from the British Library

Library of Congress Cataloging-in-Publication Data
   The media and social theory / David Hesmondhalgh and
   Jason Toynbee.
      p. cm.
   1. Mass media–Social aspects. 2. Communication–Social aspects.
   I. Hesmondhalgh, David, 1963- II. Toynbee, Jason.
   HM1206.M389 2008
   302.23–dc22   2007046124

ISBN10: 0-415-44799-2 (hbk)
ISBN10: 0-415-44800-X (pbk)
ISBN10: 0-203-93047-9 (ebk)

ISBN13: 978-0-415-44799-7 (hbk)
ISBN13: 978-0-415-44800-0 (pbk)
ISBN13: 978-0-203-93047-2 (ebk)

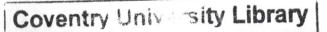
Coventry University Library

Contents

Contributors

Christopher Anderson is completing his doctoral studies in communication at the Columbia University Graduate School of Journalism. He has written extensively on new media technologies, journalistic authority and the sociology of the professions for both scholarly and popular publications. He has contributed chapters to a number of books, including *The Handbook of Journalism Studies* (with Michael Schudson, 2007), *The International Encyclopedia of Communication* (2008) and *Making our Media*. Anderson serves on the editorial board of the *New York City Independent* and has worked as an organiser and editor at the New York City Independent Media Center for the past five years.

Nick Couldry is Professor of Media and Communications at Goldsmiths' College, University of London, where he is also Director of the Centre for the Study of the Global Media and Democracy. He is the author or co-editor of six books, including *Media Rituals: a Critical Approach* (2003), *Contesting Media Power* (co-edited with James Curran, 2003), *Listening beyond the Echoes: Media, Ethics and Agency in an Uncertain World* (2006) and *Media Consumption and Public Engagement: Beyond the Presumption of Attention* (with Sonia Livingstone and Tim Markham, 2007).

John Downey is Senior Lecturer in Communication and Media Studies, Department of Social Sciences, Loughborough University. In 2007 he was Visiting Professor of Sociology at Williams College, Williamstown MA. He has completed projects for the BBC Governors on the BBC's coverage of the Middle East, for the Commission for Racial Equality on media constructions of Britishness, and a comparative study of coverage of the EU constitution. His research interests include the political economy of communication, comparative media analysis and political communication.

Faye Ginsburg is founding Director of the Center for Media, Culture and History at New York University, where she is also the David B. Kriser Professor of Anthropology and Co-director of the Center for Religion and Media which she established in 2003. An anthropologist and film maker, her work over the years has focused on cultural activism, from her early research on women involved in the abortion debate in the United States to her long-term work on the development of indigenous media in Australia and elsewhere. She is the author or editor of four books, most recently *Media Worlds: Anthropology on New Terrain* (edited with Lila Abu Lughod and Brian Larkin, 2002). Her book on indigenous media, *Mediating Culture*, is forthcoming. Her most recent work focuses on the way the media are being taken up as a form of cultural activism among the disabled.

Daniel C. Hallin is Professor at the Department of Communication, University of California, San Diego. Hallin's research concerns political communication and the role of the news media in democratic politics. He has written on the media and war, including Vietnam, Central America and the Gulf War. He has written on television coverage of elections, demonstrating the shrinking 'sound bite' and offering an interpretation of its meaning for political journalism. His new research focuses on comparative analysis of the news media's role in the public sphere, concentrating on Europe and Latin America.

Alison Hearn teaches media theory and cultural studies in the Faculty of Information and Media Studies at the University of Western Ontario, London, Ont. She is co-author of *Outside the Lines: Issues in Inter-disciplinary Research* (with Liora Salter, 1997) and has published in such journals as *Topia: Canadian Journal of Cultural Studies, The International Journal of Media and Cultural Politics*, and *Bad Subjects*. She is completing a book entitled *Real Incorporated: Reality Television, Promotional Culture and the Will to Image*.

David Hesmondhalgh is Professor of Media and Music Industries at the University of Leeds and Co-director (with Justin O'Connor) of the Cultural and Media Industries Research Centre (CuMIRC). He is the author of *The Cultural Industries* (second edition 2007) and editor of *Media Production* (2006), *Understanding Media: Inside Celebrity* (with Jessica Evans, 2005), *Popular Music Studies* (with Keith Negus, 2002) and *Western Music and its Others: Difference, Representation and Appropriation in Music* (with Georgina Born, 2000).

Kari Karppinen is a Research Associate at the Department of Communication, University of Helsinki. His research interests include theories of the public sphere, the media and democracy and media policy. He has published on the controversies involved in the uses and definitions of 'media pluralism' in European media policy.

Purnima Mankekar teaches Women's Studies and Asian American Studies at the University of California, Los Angeles. She is the author of

Screening Culture, Viewing Politics (1999), which won the Kovacs Award from the Society of Cinema Studies. She is also co-editor of *Caste and Outcaste* (with Gordon Chang and Akhil Gupta, 2002). She is working on two books, one on South Asian public cultures, the second on the racial violence faced by South Asians in the aftermath of 11 September 2001.

Toby Miller chairs the Department of Media and Cultural Studies at the University of California, Riverside. He is the author or editor of over thirty books in English and translation. His latest is *Cultural Citizenship* (2007). He edits the journals *Television and New Media* and *Social Identities*.

Philip Schlesinger is Professor in Cultural Policy at the University of Glasgow, where he directs the Centre for Cultural Policy Research. He is working on creative industries policies as well as on a study of literary ethnography. His most recent book is *The European Union and the Public Sphere* (edited with John Erik Fossum, 2007). Fellow of the Royal Society of Arts and of the Royal Society of Edinburgh, and an Academician of the Academy of the Social Sciences, he has held visiting posts in France, Italy, Norway, Spain and Switzerland.

Bev Skeggs is Chair in Sociology at Goldsmiths' College, University of London. She has published *The Media: Issues in Sociology* (1992), *Feminist Cultural Theory* (1995), *Formations of Class and Gender* (1997), *Class, Self, Culture* (2004), *Sexuality and the Politics of Violence and Safety* (with Les Moran, 2004) and *Feminism after Bourdieu* (with Lisa Adkins, 2005).

Annabelle Sreberny is the first Professor of Global Media and Communication in the new Centre for Media and Film Studies at SOAS, University of London. Her interests in media change centre on developments in the global South, particularly in the Middle East and Iran. She tries to establish media as a significant focus for Middle East scholars and to internationalise media studies. Her seminal work *Small Media, Big Revolution* appears on Amazon's best-seller list of books on the Iranian revolution. Her work focuses on the communications dynamics of US–Iran relations and on the Iranian blogosphere. Edited books include *Covering Political Violence* (2006) and *International News in the Twenty-first Century* (2004).

Matt Stahl is an Assistant Professor in the Faculty of Information and Media Studies at the University of Western Ontario. He has published in *Popular Music*, the *Journal of Popular Music Studies* and *Labor: Studies in the Working Class History of the Americas*, as well as the collection *Bad Music: The Music we Love to Hate* on the social relations of animation and popular music production, the place of these relations in the 'new economy', and their representation in film and television. He is currently working on a book entitled *That* Feeling *of a Revolution: Power, Labor and Property in Popular Music Making.*

Jason Toynbee is Senior Lecturer in Media Studies at the Open University. He has written on creativity, ethnicity and copyright, mainly in the context of popular music. Author of *Making Popular Music* (2000) and *Bob Marley: Herald of a Postcolonial World?* (2007), he has also co-edited *The Popular Music Studies Reader* (with Andy Bennett and Barry Shank, 2006) and *Analysing Media Texts* (with Marie Gillespie, 2006).

Helen Wood is Principal Lecturer in Media Studies at De Montfort University, Leicester. She is author of *Talking with Television* (in press) and has published articles on television and audience research in, for example, *Media, Culture and Society, Communication Review* and *European Journal of Cultural Studies.* She is assistant editor of the journal *Ethnography* and has co-edited a collection of the Centre for Contemporary Cultural Studies papers (in press).

Acknowledgements

This book derives from an international conference, 'Media Change and Social Theory', held at St Hugh's College, Oxford, on 7–9 September 2006, and attended by over 200 people. The conference was organised by the ESRC Centre for Research on Socio-cultural Change (CReSC), based at the University of Manchester and the Open University. We would like to thank the conference organisers, Josine Opmeer and Catherine Lillie (still Catherine Austin when we first planned the conference), for their work, and Tony Bennett, CReSC Co-director, for his support and guidance. Our thanks also to Marie Gillespie, Helen Wood and Farida Vis, who helped with the academic co-ordination of the event.

Most of the chapters here represent developed and updated versions of papers presented at the conference. We heard many excellent papers, and wish that we could have published more. In the end we made a selection based on what we heard, aiming for balance across the book. We would like to thank everyone who contributed to the conference.

D.H.
J.T.

1 Why media studies needs better social theory

David Hesmondhalgh and Jason Toynbee

This book derives from the conviction that we need to enrich the intellectual resources being brought to bear on the media and that one valuable way to do this would be for media analysts to engage much more seriously with social theory. There are two broad problems with existing media studies in terms of its theory. The first appears when we consider the major historical questions currently being raised in the field. Should we understand contemporary developments in media (globalisation, the internet, proliferation of media platforms and so on) as marking our entry into a new period characterised by unprecedented forms of mediated social relations? Or rather do these same developments simply make for continuity in the order of social life? There is a growing body of empirical work which presents one or other of these interpretations. Yet our sense is that many attempts in media studies to historicise the present lack a metatheoretical dimension – that is, they do not establish basic premises about the nature of the media in modern society. Except in a rather oblique fashion, they fail to confront issues of *causation*, from, within and to the media; or of *norms*, that is to say how far putative changes in the character of communication bear on social justice, or prospects for a good life for all. Without addressing these questions in a systematic way it becomes difficult to make an assessment of the quality and extent of change in the media and its consequences.

The second challenge has to do with the narrowness of the sources of existing media theory. Now of course media theory has been informed by social theory. Media studies journals are full of names such as Habermas, Bourdieu, Foucault, Castells, Hall, Butler, Žižek, Laclau, Bauman, Beck, Deleuze, Williams and Giddens, all of whom can legitimately be called social theorists.[1] The problem is the way that such theories tend to be mobilised in media theory and media studies. Typically, a single aspect of their work is taken up, rather than the broader social-theoretical agenda that the best of these theorists utilise. So Habermas's notion of the public sphere is either employed or dismissed – one small part of his work, written in the late 1950s, with some later comments. The same is true of very different theorists. It is more usual, for example, to read invocations of

Judith Butler's concept of 'performativity' than to see her concepts analysed in relation to the fundamental principles underlying her work.[2] This has led to a peculiar narrowness, even as media studies has drawn upon a wide range of theorists. It has meant that looking further afield, to reflect on how general problems raised by social theory might be illuminated through consideration of contemporary communications, is rarely attempted.

Two challenges, then. To meet them, we have brought together sixteen authors in order to consider key processes of media change, using a wide array of social-theoretical perspectives. We discuss the chapters and the book structure later on. But to begin, this introductory chapter focuses on a series of intertwined issues which emerge from the challenges we have identified: what we mean by social theory; the state of existing theory in media and communication studies; and how re-engaging with social theory might enrich the broad subject area.

Social theory: principles and dominant positions

The corpus of social theory is large and with a long historical tail, stretching back to the Enlightenment at least. It can clearly be cut up in a variety of ways – by school, in terms of the genealogy of ideas, and according to political stance. (See Benton and Craib 2001 and Delanty and Strydom 2003 for alternative ways of presenting the field.) We have no room to provide our own account here. So, instead, we move straight to establishing a few principles about what social theory is and what it does. Then we set up an opposition between what we take to be the two leading theoretical positions today – constructionism and empiricism – examining some intellectual and political consequences of their dominance.

Social theory is concerned with explaining the experience of social life. Ian Craib (1992: 7) defines theory in general as 'an attempt to explain our everyday experience of the world, our "closest" experience in terms of something which is not so close'. When we undertake social theory, we are attempting to be much more systematic about experience and ideas concerning the social world than in everyday discourse. Indeed, as Craib emphasises, good theory may well involve making propositions that are counter to our direct experience. This is obviously so in the case of explanations of society such as Marxism according to which how life is lived is determined largely by a deep structure which cannot be directly apprehended, and may even be hidden through the operation of ideology. But it is also true of interpretive approaches, those influenced by anthropology for example, where the key goal is to present an account of a particular society according to 'insiders'. Here too a gap opens up between the experience and the account, as James Clifford (1986) forcefully reminds us in his argument about the inevitable partiality of ethnographic work. Clifford raises a social theoretical question then, but significantly he refuses to follow it through. Rather than trying to negotiate the gap between writing about a society and how that society is experienced from within, he moves straight to the conclusion that its invariable consequence is the production of fictional accounts by ethnographers. To attempt to understand a society is actually to write a story about it which is shot through with your own subjectivity and cultural values. Needless to say, perhaps, we reject this radical subjectivism. For us the problem of distance between social experience and social explanation prompts rather than pre-empts social-theoretical enquiry.

If explanation lies at the heart of social theory, a problem arises, namely that such usefulness of theory is not always apparent to people doing the empirical work which it is supposed to inform. As Derek Layder (1993) points out, one of the reasons that theory has a bad reputation is that, to active researchers, it can seem 'speculative and too far removed from the down-to-earth issues of empirical research' (p. 6). This sceptical attitude 'hinders the general development of social understanding by preventing the harnessing of general theory to the requirements and procedures of social research' (ibid.). Layder (1993: 15) suggests a number of ways in which theories can be linked with empirical research: by taking seriously the fact that 'theoretical ideas act as background assumptions to empirical research and that where these are implicit they should be made explicit'; by using theory to contextualise research and to influence outcomes; and by philosophically examining the bases of knowledge and causation that underlie the research process. We need, says Layder (1993: 7), to see theory as partly, but never fully, autonomous of empirical evidence. Such an attitude underpins this book. In some of the contributions to this volume there is an emphasis on social theory itself and on clarifying and making explicit concepts that act as background assumptions in the work of others. In other chapters there is, rather, an emphasis on the authors' own media research, where the focus is instead on how theory might best underpin the particular research questions being asked. In other words, and as our contributors show, theory can be developed by examining the adequacy of already existing ideas, or it can emerge from a 'bottom up' process of abducting general theory from particular empirical cases.

Theory, then, we see as useful abstraction, never too far removed from concretising evidence and experience, yet nevertheless always removed to some degree – it is separation from the domains of the empirical and experiential which provides the conditions of possibility of theory. But what do we mean specifically by *social* theory; what social things is it about? Beyond defining it comparatively via its obvious concerns with society (as opposed to nature, or political institutions) and its attempt to distinguish between, and make generalisations about, different kinds of society (Callinicos 2007), it is perhaps most useful to think of social theory in terms of the defining problems it has generally sought to address. Delanty (2005: 22) for example, identifies three such defining problems in modern social theory: social subjectivity or socialisation, the rationality of knowledge, and the legitimation of power. John Scott (2006) prefers culture, system and socialisation; action, conflict and nature; and modernity and rationalisation. Some emphasise the great theoretical binaries of structure/agency, micro/macro and universalism/particularism, while others have paid close attention to critiquing these binaries and suggesting their redundancy (wrongly, in our view, but at least the debate is worth having). Much depends upon the particular disciplinary area of social enquiry from which the classifier approaches the social: sociologists will tend to see these things very differently from geographers, for example (as Harvey 2005 discusses). Now it probably goes without saying that we think that there are more and less valid treatments of these questions, more and less useful ways of privileging certain of the themes over others. Our claim here though is quite limited, namely that just to address such metatheoretical problems is a necessary first step for social – and therefore also media – enquiry.

Many influenced by post-structuralism and postmodernism will already be troubled by the way we have put things. Out of a desire to avoid essentialism and reduction they would reject this emphasis on central, defining problems of society. For them, such an approach would be just too fixed and fail to be sensitive to the ever changing nature of the social whereby process, or becoming, is all. Alternatively, influenced by Foucault, some might argue that there is simply no position beyond discourse and the social practices in which it is imbricated. With no outside, and therefore no distance from society, there can be no theorising of it; only the identification and enumeration of social practices.[3] Significantly, a great deal of media studies, and its sibling area of enquiry, cultural studies, has been influenced by such perspectives. Indeed, some of our contributors would share this post-structuralist distrust of 'totalising' theory. It is probably worth saying at this point that our own perspective is influenced by our own encounters with post-structuralism and postmodernism. We believe that there are elements of post-structuralist thought that have enhanced social theory, specifically: an emphasis on the importance of identity and its social-psychological formation; the crucial role of language and, more generally, of representation in social life; and a focus on the issue of standpoint in relation to research or knowledge more broadly conceived. Such developments have been absolutely vital to advances in our understanding of the social since the 1970s.

This is not only a matter of our own evaluation. Most significantly, the broadly constructionist approach has grown exponentially since the 1980s and has now begun to challenge the long-standing orthodoxy in social science, namely empiricism. Empiricism is a problematic term, it has to be admitted. Pejorative in tone, it is never used by exponents of the views which are said by its opponents to constitute it. More, many of those who criticise it in the constructionist camp deny that empiricism is a theory at all. Rather, they suggest that what marks out empiricists is their *lack* of theory and reflection on what one does as a researcher. Nonetheless we would suggest empiricism is a useful attribution which does indeed point to a substantive theoretical position. In the first place, empiricism elevates the significance of experience to the extent that society is reducible to it. No knowledge-claims about the social world can be made unless they have been founded on observation or tested through experiment. Second, social scientific laws, like scientific laws in general, describe recurring patterns of events, and as such they have a predictive facility. Third, empiricism poses the complete separation of 'merely' subjective values from objective, factual statements about the social world that are testable (Benton and Craib 2001: 14–22).

Clearly there are serious differences between empiricism and construc-tionism. Yet we would propose that there is also considerable convergence. We can see it in a common emphasis on experience for one thing. Whether through observation and measurement (empiricism), or in forms of knowledge, discourse and so on (constructionism) both camps take the realm of the social to be coterminous with experience. There is nothing, as it were, *beneath* experience – for instance, social structure, causality or more generally conditions of action which cannot be apprehended through the senses, or are not already inscribed in discourse. As for laws and prediction, while among constructionists the advocates of fluidity are clearly opposed to the empiricists' notion of the covering law, Foucauldians take regularities, stable discursive regimes and so on to be the defining characteristics of the social. Finally, in relation to subjective and objective domains the difference is perhaps more apparent than real. Certainly, while empiricists prize 'objectivity' in social science, constructionists tend to celebrate 'subjectivity'. Yet in each case what seems to be at stake is a form of idealism whereby the social world is always limited to our knowledge and experience. What we want to argue, then, is that renewed attention to a particular kind of social theory can help us move beyond these positions and their widespread adoption in media studies. It is not, we hasten to add, that we reject the insights which have been achieved through both approaches. Rather, that in their (often unexamined) metatheoretical assumptions each tends to block the development of a critical social science, and of critical media research, which can address questions of what is and what ought to be, as well as what is known and experienced.

However, alongside these tendencies there now exists a strong tradi-tion of *critical social theory*, where historically informed and systematic exploration of such normative and explanatory questions is far more to the fore. This kind of systematic exploration is apparent, for example, in some of the writers listed earlier, often cited in media studies, but rarely addressed across a sufficient range of their work; writers who are appropriated for particular concepts and problems, such as Habermas, Bourdieu, Giddens, Mouffe and Butler. It is also apparent – perhaps even more apparent – in the work of certain writers who are very rarely referred to in media studies but who have produced what might be called – without too much facetiousness – a 'loose canon' of critical theoretical work. These writers include Axel Honneth, Nancy Fraser, Alex Callinicos, Margaret Archer, Craig Calhoun, Seyla Benhabib, David Harvey, Andrew Sayer, Perry Anderson, Ian Craib and Derek Layder. They are broadly left/liberal rationalists who have a strong sense of the importance of the symbolic and so (though perhaps more by extension) of the media. We have our own preferences among these writers and thinkers, and among the tendencies they represent. But, to reiterate, our point here is not to advocate a particular line, so much as suggest that such critical social theory provides a systematic exploration of normative and explanatory questions that is potentially helpful for social research and for media studies.

The poverty of media theory: parochialism and mediacentrism

In defending an enabling conception of social theory Derek Layder, cited above, was writing in response to a split in sociology, exemplified in the division between university modules on 'theory' and those on 'social structure' and 'methods'. Such divisions are perhaps inevitable; large fields of enquiry will tend to split up into areas of specialism. The issues of concern are whether the different camps speak to each other, and whether a critical mass of researchers is able to combine, for example, theory and empirical work in a satisfactory way. There is certainly an echo of such splits in contemporary media and communication studies, where it is not unusual to find separate modules and textbooks on media or communication theory.[4] Doctoral researchers often apply to programmes in order to investigate a particular area – say, transformations in national broadcasting systems, or the way audiences in different countries respond to reality television shows – and are frequently asked to pay greater attention to what media or communication theory they will draw upon to make these questions of more general interest to the field. In this context 'doing the theory' can be seen simply as an irritating burden which distracts one from the real task in hand. Yet for that very reason examining how theory is taught in media and communication departments may be instructive. For teaching constitutes a disciplinary approach in the Foucauldian sense. If you make people learn things in a certain way you are defining the field in the strongest possible terms.

The most usual way to divide media theory up is according to the classic triangle of production, texts and audiences; see, for example, McQuail's standard mass communication theory textbook (McQuail 2005) or Williams (2003) or Gripsrud (2002). It is built into the Open University's famous 'Circuit of Culture' model (Hall 1997), which extends Stuart Hall's discussion of the differences between encoding and decoding (Hall 1993/1973) by introducing representation, regulation and identity as extra topics.[5] This split makes pedagogical sense, for this is how much research is divided up, with some researchers specialising in textual analysis, some in production analysis and some in audience studies, and with various theoretical interests and sources associated with each. It is also makes some conceptual sense, for this way of thinking about the field at least forefronts the important asymmetry in the media between producers and audiences – however the power relations between these two groups are understood. What gets called 'communication theory' is somewhat different. Here textbooks and modules will often have a more historical bent, usually outlining the early development of the field in the United States, often setting 'administrative research' against the critical theory of Adorno and maybe other members of the Frankfurt school, tracing effects research through the 1950s and 1960s, and in many cases telling a story of how various forms of critical research influenced by cultural theory came along in the 1970s and 1980s to change the field.

These approaches to teaching media theory tend to be ecumenical, then. They discuss what we have been calling empiricism and constructionism together as part of an argumentative family of theories the oldest members of which are now reaching a ripe and respectable age. Such perspectives even at times touch on the kind of critical social theory that we discussed earlier, in the form of Adorno and perhaps Stuart Hall's encounters with Gramsci and Althusser. Certainly this historical framing has some value.[6] The aim of giving students a sense of where their theory comes from is laudable, and history is good for the banal but valid reason that it tells us (in part at least) about how we got here. Yet the conventional history is also remarkably narrow. Indeed, it is striking that, other than in the highly selective way discussed earlier, critical social theory hardly appears in it. Consequently, media theory as it has been enshrined pedagogically is often lacking in philosophical questions of normativity and explanation. Metatheorising is rare.

We get a similar impression if we look at the academic field in another way, according to how it has characterised its central problematic. From this perspective we might say that a focus on media-in-society has progressively given way to forms of mediacentrism and parochialism over the years. Such tendencies can be seen in the trajectory of the 'political economy versus cultural studies' debate which has loomed large in the field. First a caveat; there is a question about whether we should be discussing this debate at all, because media studies really is more complex than the binary suggests. There are many approaches that do not fall easily into the ready-made categories, and many studies that are thought of as belonging to one or the other should not be pigeonholed in this simplistic way. However, the shorthand steadfastly refuses to go away just because it does refer to a significant institutional and intellectual split in the analysis of the media.

Both camps have their origins in the Marxism which constituted a kind of intellectual avant-garde across the social sciences and humanities in the 1970s and early 1980s. But where political economy focused on cultural commodities and the role of the media sector in contemporary capitalism, cultural studies was concerned with the interlinked questions of ideology and representation. To put it in Marxisant terms, the former concentrated on the media as base, while the latter treated the media as superstructure. This difference in identifying what was the central *problem* of the media in capitalist society increasingly turned into a difference about selecting *objects of study*. For political economy the focus tended to be on production, for cultural studies it was texts, and then very quickly audiences and consumption. And in a series of related splits, cultural studies analysed popular culture and entertainment media whereas political economy examined news and factual media. As for the formulation of media policy, it was claimed by political economy while the everyday experience of media belonged to cultural studies.

Several points need to be made about these developments. First, they involved a double, theoretical-empirical carving up of the field. It may well be the case that the kinds of specialisation encapsulated in the split constitute a legitimate academic division of labour. However, what is problematic is the superimposition of such specialisation on to the theoretical and normative divide between political economy and cultural studies. This has greatly reduced the possibility of grounding a theoretical debate between the two camps because each has little knowledge of (or respect for) the media events, processes and experiences investigated by the other.

The division has also been accompanied by a growing theoretical parochialism. Interestingly, as media and culture became increasingly important topics in the social sciences more broadly (the so-called 'cultural turn') so media studies itself grew more inward looking. Perhaps the fact that other disciplines were looking towards this emergent field had the effect of reducing the perceived need to look from inside out. The double theory–topic split surely had an impact too. Both camps in media studies grew more mediacentric, more concerned with justifying which media elements or processes were key, while the bigger question of the media in society, which the debate had begun with, became less important.

As for their political concerns, while political economy and cultural studies originally shared a commitment to human emancipation derived from Marxism, as Marxism lost credibility in the academy so each branch sought new political footings. On the one hand, cultural studies developed a form of (mainly affirmative) identity politics influenced by feminism and black cultural politics, but also post-structuralist thought. Representation of particular group identities in and through the media became the main focus, while the everyday was taken up as the demotic emblem of a populist 'everyone'. On the other hand, by the early 1990s political economy was calling up Habermas's work on the public sphere to justify arguments for public ownership and control of the media in the interests of communicative rationality.

Finally, these crypto-normative rationales have been overlaid onto a persisting dispute about culture and economy. So, whereas political economy emphasised the importance of understanding the economy and polity as primary causal factors in shaping the character of media, researchers in cultural studies emphasised the firstness of culture and the autonomous, constructed nature of all knowledge (see, for example, Hall 1997)

This story of political economy versus cultural studies is worth telling, we think, because while it is a shorthand account of the trajectory of a complex academic field it nevertheless characterises a major dispute between distinct positions. For that reason we cannot agree with those who impatiently snort that the division is entirely redundant and meaningless and we should just move on. Equally, we do not endorse calls for reconciliation based on the smoothing over of substantive issues of difference. This is simply not possible under present circumstances, for the various episodes of the schism, outlined above, now mutually reinforce one another to the extent that dialogue between the camps only deepens the split. The problem, then, is that media studies lacks theoretical frames which might enable synthesis and in turn transcendence of existing entrenched positions. Our view, as should already be clear, is that a more explicit address of critical social theory can help to provide such a frame, and enable dialogue to take place on clearer ground.

From social to media theory

There are two main elements we would want to take from social theory. The first is a much stronger philosophical grounding of normative questions. Media studies thinks of itself as critical, in the broad and often undefined sense that it seeks to draw attention to things that are wrong in the world, especially, of course, in the media. Yet, as we saw in the previous section, incommensurate positions have developed across the field about what the good and the just might be. These, we would argue, are crypto-normative positions, because they do not make clear the basis of their claims. So cultural relativists tend to emphasise the context-specificity of values, and deny the possibility of arriving at ethical judgements outside the parameters of particular cultures. Any attempts to do so are labelled universalist, via the assertion (more than the argument) that such universalism would deny cultures their autonomy. Relativism in media studies has also come in through the work of Foucault, who, as Nancy Fraser puts it:

> vacillates between two equally inadequate stances. On the one hand, he adopts a concept of power that permits him no condemnation of any objectionable features of modern societies. But at the same time ... his rhetoric betrays the conviction that modern societies are utterly without redeeming features. Clearly what Foucault [...] needs

desperately are normative criteria for distinguishing acceptable from unacceptable forms of power.

(Fraser 1989: 33)

Meanwhile, among political economists and their liberal compatriots, universalism persists. Yet, as with the anti-universalism of the relativists, it is not well justified in most accounts. It may be inferred from the materialism of some of the analysis; we all have economic interests and it is therefore possible to evaluate the organisation of the media on the basis of how it relates to questions of distribution. Or else there may be a liberal appeal to communicative reason, the public sphere or simply the need for pluralism. But not only is the normative case very thin in both approaches (why does distribution matter, why is pluralism good, and should everybody have to have it?) the standpoint of the researcher hardly gets addressed. This is important. We would argue that reflexivity about the position from which researchers research is a valuable contribution of postmodernism and a crucial counter to the assumption often made in empiricist research that neutrality is both desirable and possible. Still, such reflexivity need not exclude normative thinking. Indeed, our view is that we need to move beyond the Manichean binaries that prevail in what passes for ethical thought in many parts of media studies.[7] There is no good reason why acknowledgement of standpoint and the particularity of cultures cannot be accommodated along with a universal ethics.

A number of strands in social theory can help us here. As Andrew Sayer suggests, '[h]uman beings are indeed extraordinarily diverse, but we should ask what is it about them which enables them to exhibit such variety?' His answer is that, '[f]or it to be possible for anything to be shaped in a particular way (for example by culture) it must be the kind of thing which is susceptible to such shaping, that is, it must have (or have acquired) the affordances and resistances which allow such shaping' (2004). Human beings, we might say, depend for their very acculturation on a set of shared propensities which then issue in cultural difference. It follows that it is theoretically possible to build an ethics anthropologically, 'up' from what it is that is shared. This argument certainly helps to provide the ontological grounds for an ethics.

To specify what it might consist in we can turn to a growing body of work which would both delineate the normative and relocate it at the heart of social theory. So there is the ongoing debate between Nancy Fraser and Axel Honneth (2003) about whether it is possible to base an ethics solely on the principle of recognition.[8] And we have the 'qualified ethical naturalism' of Andrew Sayer (2005) – 'naturalist in that it considers that the very nature of good and bad cannot be determined without reference to the nature of human social being' (p. 218); qualified because it acknowledges cultural shaping of the interpretation of needs, and even in some cases of those needs themselves (p. 219). Sayer draws here upon the approach of the philosopher Martha Nussbaum (2001), who argues for the central importance of human flourishing in a practical ethics where compassion is key. Compassion involves a sense of social solidarity that is epistemological as well emotional in character. One recognises oneself in the other, one weighs the scale of the other's predicament, one judges that the other person was not responsible for the predicament herself (p. 321).

It is very common in media studies to hear 'universalism' and especially 'essentialism' used as terms of abuse. The problem is that these values remain under-explored. An invocation of Gayatri Spivak's notion of 'strategic essentialism' or Paul Gilroy's 'anti-anti-essentialism' is as far as those media researchers concerned with such issues are likely to go. But the lazy and widespread accusation of essentialism in 'the politics of culture' runs the danger of brushing aside the important search for the characteristic properties of the good. The new attention to practical ethics in social theory, and especially notions of recognition and human flourishing as universal yet non-exclusionary norms, may thus provide an important resource for media studies in all branches.

A second element in critical social theory that might help to renew media theory is the concept of causality, the idea that the significant thing we are trying to find out about in society is why things happen – including, of course, why we have the media that we have. The predominant view in cultural studies is that the social is a matter of representation or discourse. This essentially flat notion does away with cause and depth. Instead there is radical contingency, actually a crypto-normative value because it implies that what's good is the unexpected, and that exciting things happen in culture through discovery and the creative power of chance. Alternatively, as sometimes found in the Foucauldian conspectus, there is a tendency to pose continuity – for example, Foucault's leading question about the history of sexuality: 'Was there really a historical rupture between the age of repression and the critical analysis of repression?' (1990: 10). Ceaseless contingent change or monumental continuity: these seem to be the predominant approaches in cultural studies to the problem of history. Among materialists in the political economy tradition, on the other hand, the driver of history is big business, or an unholy alliance of political and corporate elites. Here there is certainly a big cause, but the danger is that it is treated as overwhelming and unchallengeable.

We would suggest, then, that what is lacking across the board in media studies is reflection on the general problem of social causality. This is an issue which social theory continues to be strongly interested in. At its centre is the long running structure–agency debate in which there have been partisans on one side or the other (for example, the functionalist–interactionist dispute), but also attempts at synthesis which give due weight to both sides. Anthony Giddens's structuration theory is probably the best known of these (Giddens 1984) and indeed it has had some influence in media studies (e.g. Moores 2005). Yet arguably Giddens is guilty of 'elisionism' (Archer 1995: 93–8), that is to say, the running together of structure and agency such that they become inseparable. The possibility that causality arises in the relations between these elements thus disappears. Our preference would then be for a realist theory of structure and agency which insists on their ontological distinctiveness yet mutual impact upon one another across time. This should be coupled with an understanding of society as *deep*, that is to say, consisting in layered structures or generative mechanisms, but where, nevertheless, higher levels are irreducible to lower ones. Some notion of 'emergence' is therefore necessary in order to account for new things and events, and clearly agency itself must be considered as an emergent property of human subjects (Archer 1995; Bhaskar 1998).

Abstract as it is, the enormous advantage of such an approach is that it enables us to think about agency and structure together in ways which not only do justice to the efficacy of both but which may be carried into empirical work to help explain their interrelationship in the world of human experience and events. This connects with the issue of normativity. For agency, emergent from structure, clearly has a strong normative dimension. Nowhere is this more palpable than in the media, where normative questions about the choices made by audiences, the state, companies and individual producers are rightly central to research. Yet without some theoretical means of evaluating the cause of new kinds of interpretation, representation or changing media regimes – that is to say, through discriminating between structure and agency – we have no means of critical analysis, and ultimately no possibility of intervening in the world of the media.

There is one further issue that arises in relation to causality. We accused media studies of parochialism and mediacentrism above. Too much attention has been paid to the media *qua* media, either because the world is considered to be a product of representation, with the media then being the central means of that representation, or else the media are treated as obscurers of the real world, as in pessimistic political economy approaches. (Of course this is a caricature, but as before we are inclined to carry on painting with a thick brush for the heuristic advantages it may bring.) In such a context, theories of causality derived from social theory enable a return to the question of media in society, itself a variant of the culture-and-society problem sketched by Raymond Williams many years ago. We can begin thinking again about how the media do things in society, how society impacts on the media, and indeed how there is complex determination through and between each. Most of all this will call for a certain de-specialisation, a looking outward from the media to social relations in general. But that's what social theory is very good at.

We should, of course, concede that this outline has been one that leans towards critical realism, and away from post-structuralism; that manifests a preference for the argumentative strategies of analytical and post-analytical philosophy over Continental traditions; and that seeks synthesis rather than exploration. No doubt some of our contributors would not share such preferences. However, there are general aims of good theorising that transcend such differences, and which we believe are apparent even in the uses of theory made by chapters far removed from our own inclinations. What's more, at a meta-level we would contend that the differences in this collection point up many of the issues we have been talking about. In other words, the book has a probing, question-raising agenda about kinds of theory and what it is for, rather than a party line.

Undoubtedly, the use of social theory can enrich our understanding of social problems, unmet needs, suffering and dubious beliefs. It can also undermine the cosy assumptions of more abstract philosophy through its role in underpinning the exacting analysis of case studies. These may in turn suggest new avenues of analysis. We identify examples of this kind of more general use of social theory in media analysis in the outline of individual chapters that follows this section. That said, there needs to be a sensible division of labour between those who focus on philosophical underpinnings and those who employ social theory to achieve a more thorough investigation of the social through empirical work. We also recognise that some of the critical social theory that we have been praising here has not done nearly enough to integrate the theoretical with the empirical (this, for example, is still true of critical realism – an observation also made by Baert 2000). So, as usual in the production of knowledge, we can say there is plenty more work to do.

Outline of the book

How then do the chapters of this book use social theory to enrich our understanding of the relations in and between the media and society? We have identified four broad themes of central importance to media theory that our contributors address in the four parts that follow.

The first part is concerned with the theme of 'Power and democracy' that has been so central to much of media studies. Chapter 2, by Kari Karppinen, exemplifies for us the potential benefits of careful attention to critical social theory when it comes to questions of normativity. Karppinen confronts head-on the questions raised by the very widespread commitment to pluralism in media studies and media theory, manifest in the abundant concern with difference, identity and anti-essentialism in the literature. As Karppinen explains, the problem is that the pluralism implicitly invoked by much media studies is a very ambiguous normative principle. It is not unusual to see the work of Chantal Mouffe mobilised to criticise Habermasian approaches to democracy, and Karppinen summarises the debates here. He points out, though, that the radical or agonistic pluralism of Mouffe and others has rarely been applied to the media in the form of institutional proposals or concrete political questions (cf. Born 2006).

In fact, such radical pluralism is more often mobilised in the cause of a naive celebration of mulitiplicity – and Karppinen shows that this is directly at odds with the work of Mouffe. Radical pluralism in fact directs our attention to macro-political concerns that are consistent with the aims of political economy, and potentially provide a much more solid basis for it than Habermasian public sphere theory.

While Karppinen writes in metatheoretical mode, in Chapter 3 Daniel Hallin offers a historical account of media change that draws upon social theory, and contributes to it by enriching our conceptions of a key term in social and political theory of the last twenty years: neoliberalism. Hallin points out that accounts of media marketisation and neoliberalism often rest on vague and simplistic formulations and offers a more adequate version. He does so by painting a fuller picture of the institutions that had previously counterbalanced market logics in the media, namely the strong ties between the media and organised social groups such as political parties, trade unions and churches, and journalist professionalism. Hallin shows how this situation changed through media commercialisation, and through social and political changes. However, Hallin emphasises that these changes involved more than a shift to consumerism and commercialism. The social movements of the 1960s and 1970s counterculture played an integral part in undermining traditional forms of authority and, significantly, journalistic professionalism contributed to and was influenced by the rise of these new social movements. Neoliberalism, then, is not something that can be rigidly opposed to populist anti-elitism and new social movements; they were to some extent mutually reinforcing. Hallin also questions the assumption in some accounts of neoliberalism (such as Wendy Brown's) that neoliberalism has meant the collapse of the liberal democratic values of the 1960s and 1970s. He stresses the importance of holding on to the complexity of the way that market forces have affected the democratic role of the media, without losing sight of the many troubling features of media commercialisation. This, then, is media analysis that shows us the complexity of media/social relations, and suggests to social theory the importance of thinking more adequately about the media.

Like Karppinen, but coming from a rather different direction, John Downey in Chapter 4 wants to move beyond Habermas. He makes the point that while Habermas is referred to constantly in media studies, the Critical Theory of other writers has been virtually ignored. Yet its insights, particularly in the shape of Axel Honneth's work on recognition, have enormous significance for any politically engaged understanding of media. Downey's starting point is an essay by John Corner which attempts to put the concept of ideology to rest. Both imprecise and incoherent in its different versions, ideology is a concept which has had its day. However, Downey disagrees and, calling upon John Thompson's book about ideology, and then Honneth himself on recognition ethics, he argues for a recovery of the concept of ideology and for its central place in media studies. Quite simply, without it there is no way of showing how power is carried symbolically, nor what it is that is systematically devalued and misrecognised in dominant forms of the media. Finally, Downey makes a link between critical media studies and activism, suggesting that renewal in the academy depends not just on the development of ideas but also on re-engagement with 'media construction' – alternative media, media campaigns and ultimately that central part of the struggle for human emancipation which is symbolic.

How do we conceive of social communication in an era of globalisation – or at least of 'globalising tendencies'? As Philip Schlesinger suggests in Chapter 5, this is a vital question for understanding power and democracy in modern societies. Answering it requires 'thick' theories of social communication that encompass culture, everyday life and emotional attachments to place but that also recognise the continuing importance of political institutions. Schlesinger distinguishes between those statists who emphasise the continuing importance of the nation-state and those cosmopolitans who see a degree of political hope in a diminishing role for the nation-state. Many in media studies have tended to take the latter route. By contrast, Schlesinger argues that the European Union demonstrates the fragility of cosmopolitan visions, and he provides a critique of various visions of Europeanness as part of a new cosmopolitan order, including Habermas's 'thin' emphasis on the importance of the European constitution, and Ulrich Beck's failure to address the institutional realities of the European Union. A crucial issue here is that the European Union is both a federation and a regulator. Mediated communication in the form of Europe-focused journalism is strongly geared to the latter. Schlesinger finds that national public spheres remain robust, and there is little immediate prospect of transcending them in the name of a cosmopolitan political space.

Part II moves us on from issues of media and political power, broadly considered, to the question of 'Spatial inequalities'. Here geography and its attendant theoretical problems enter the picture – the mobility of people, capital and communication; but also the fixity of social structures of inequality at a global level, and indeed forms of resistance to them.

We begin with David Hesmondhalgh (Chapter 6), who is concerned to harness theories of imperialism to media analysis in a new and critical way. Arguing against the long-standing concept of cultural imperialism, which he finds both imprecise and simplistic, Hesmondhalgh calls on David Harvey in order to set out a theory of *capitalist* imperialism, one with a strong media dimension. This takes the form of the expansive global copyright regime which, via international treaty and increasingly tough policing by the United States, is bringing poor countries into the ambit of commodified culture. Strong copyright, then, represents a much more clear-cut instance of imperialism than the complex flows (and sometimes benign outcomes) of the old 'cult. imp.' model. More, David Harvey's theory of over-accumulation helps to explain why this massive expansion of the domain of cultural property is happening now. It is nothing less than 'accumulation by dispossession', the latest twist in the long history of strategies through which capitalism has coped, so far at least, with its systemic crises. By commodifying culture and media, via extensions of the term of copyright and strong global enforcement, capitalism rebuilds its economic muscles while at the same time expropriating the symbolic creativity of some of the world's poorest cultures.

Chapter 7, by Annabelle Sreberny, converges in an interesting way with Chapter 6. The writers of both reject the standard critical model of global media organisation, namely 'cultural imperialism'. Sreberny, however, comes from a completely different, post-structuralist direction. Citing Iranian President Ahmadi-Nejad's open letter of May 2006 to US President George W. Bush, she takes Lacan's discussion of Edgar Allan Poe's *The Purloined Letter* as her point of departure. The tale of this fictional letter, object of subterfuge and trickery, is understood by Lacan to show that 'a letter always arrives at its destination'. Sreberny prefers Derrida's alternative reading, though, according to which there is always an excess of meaning in a letter, such that it *never* arrives. How does this metatheorising bear on the missive from Ahmadi-Nejad? The point is that in Bush's refusal to acknowledge it – an ostensible snub – a multiplicity of meanings opens up, a Derridean excess which confounds the power of the global hegemon to control global communications. This is not only a symbolic event, however. Changing material conditions in the shape of the internet and new media channels located outside the Occident have enabled precisely the kinds of challenge to the interpellation of audiences that is represented by the letter and its vicissitudes of reception.

Where Sreberny focuses on resistance to the power of the West, a resistance enabled via new forms of mediated global visibility, in Chapter 8 Faye Ginsburg shows how indigenous peoples are now using media as mirrors to their own cultures, elaborating – yet conserving – traditions. With three case studies from Inuits in the Arctic, indigenous people of the north-west coast of Canada, and aborigines in Australia, Ginsburg develops the concept of 'cultural activism' to point up the way in which such communities are confounding 'Digital Age' theory. Castells and others had announced a paradigm shift (another version of the historicisation of the present which we noted earlier), a shift marked by the advent of the internet and digitisation. But Ginsburg shows that new media technologies have an entirely different meaning in the hands and eyes of cultural activists from indigenous communities. What is at stake here is neither the construction of a wholly new virtual realm, nor the destruction of existing cultural ground, but rather as she puts it, the extension of 'traditional cultural worlds into new domains'. In effect, then, Ginsburg takes the media practice of indigenous peoples as a kind of theory-in-action, and a means of refuting both the extravagantly optimistic Digital Age and the patronisingly pessimistic Digital Divide discourses. These are theories which have to be interrogated in the light of the praxis of others.

The theme of the redemptiveness of media practice is carried forward by Purnima Mankekar. In Chapter 9 she explores how 'mobile media' are transforming not only the sense of time and place experienced by diasporic communities but therefore too the larger world social historical formation. The mobility of media which is involved here derives partly from the way in which diasporas have become the subjects of new forms of media representation. Mankekar discusses an emerging new genre in Indian film that focuses on migrant communities in London and New York. In an important sense, the mobility of these people, their translocation from India to the West, provides the narrative theme. Yet, as Mankekar notes, the experience of mobility and migration is actually just as important for the people who remain, physically, at home. In this way India becomes a 'node' in an imagined, mediated world, and homeland and diaspora – far from being binary opposites – become 'mutually imbricated'. Mankekar is not arguing against what she takes to be dominant theoretical positions, as was the case with Ginsburg. Rather, she suggests, mobile media bear out and extend what anthropologists and social theorists have already been delineating – the greatly increased salience of time–space relations in a globalising world.

The theme of 'Spectacle and the self' forms the motif of Part III. In one of the most important attempts to apply social theory to the media, published in 1995, John Thompson contrasted the relationship between power and visibility characteristic of the contemporary media with those identified by Foucault in his analysis of the panopticon in the following manner: 'thanks to the media, it is primarily those who exercise power, rather than those over whom power is exercised, who are subjected to a certain kind of visibility'. Furthermore, observed Thompson, this modern form of media power was quite different from pre-modern forms of spectacle, for 'the visibility of individuals and actions is now severed from the sharing of a common locale' (both quotations, Thompson 1995: 134).

These questions of power, visibility and spectacle have not become less significant in the era since Thompson's book was published (see Kellner 2003 for a good book-length treatment). Three of our contributors address these issues (alongside other key social-theoretical questions concerning the media) and two of them relate media spectacle to modern subjectivity. For Nick Couldry, in Chapter 10, spectacle represents a starting point for thinking about how a number of key social theories conceive of power and of society. Actor network theory, highly fashionable among many influenced by post-structuralism, Couldry finds, on balance, to be of limited value. One reason given by Couldry echoes our discussion of normativity above. Bruno Latour dismisses the 'totalising' panoramas of theorists, politicians and others, but he can offer no way of sorting out bad panoramas from good or less bad ones. Actor network theory's limited ontology means that it also has little to say about representation – essential to understanding the media's role in society. Couldry instead offers an account of the media based on 'ritual analysis', emphasising questions of belief and legitimation that are sidelined in actor network theory. Couldry is closer here to Durkheimian and Bourdieuan sociology than to Marxist ideological analysis, but he offers a 'deconstructive' version of ritual analysis, which questions the 'myth of the mediated centre' in much media sociology, in its Parsonian-functionalist and other variants. Importantly, though, Couldry aims to deconstruct the social in a very different way from actor network theory and from post-structuralists such as Laclau and Mouffe who from a position of militant anti-essentialism claim there is no object such as society, instead there is only the 'openness' and non-totalisability of discourse. For Couldry this is an 'inverted universalism', an 'absolutism of denial' that undermines the historical claims that Laclau and Mouffe want to make (and, we might add, potentially has strong implications for the way in which Karppinen sees other work by Mouffe as a potential resource in renewing political economy and democratic theory). Couldry turns to the under-explored work of Roy Bhaskar for a more adequate and yet still sceptical account of the notions of 'the social' and society.

Couldry proceeds from the concept of spectacle to interrogate and recon-struct the normative and ontological bases of social theories. In Chapter 11 Helen Wood and Bev Skeggs approach the political dimensions of spectacle from the bottom up, analysing one of the most important media phenomena of the last decade, reality television. Critics who decry the depthless spectacle of reality television miss a crucial aspect of its politics, say Wood and Skeggs. For reality television, centred on representations of working-class people (and especially working-class women), demonstrates in a supremely visible way the way that class is being remade. In particular, there is increasing emphasis in neoliberal societies on self-management, on the responsibility of people to manage their own lives effectively. One problem with this shift is that it downplays the social forces constraining people's ability to make choices and take action and instead implicitly explains social behaviour in individualistic, psychological terms. This shift is dramatised in reality television, which places (working-class) people in situations with which they are unfamiliar, and then assesses their performance and worth on the basis of how well they cope. Wood and Skeggs make the interesting claim that the emphasis on nowness and immediacy in the programmes makes it even more difficult to demonstrate the self-reflexive depth associated with moral worth in modern societies. This is especially true of that sub-genre of reality television that emphasises the modification of behaviour in the name of providing 'useful' advice to audiences. But, more generally, Wood and Skeggs show how reality pro-gramming's use of sensation and emotion, and in particular its combined use of melodrama and documentary genres in its telling of 'intimate stories', produce spectacles that demonstrate and perpetuate new forms of moral inequality. There is a politics of spectacle here, then, but it is not quite the politics that those who mourn the decline of documentary say it is; rather it refers to new forms of selfhood mandated by neoliberalism. Wood and Skeggs therefore draw on the way that social theorists such as Giddens and Beck show how the individual is compelled to make her/himself the centre of her/his own life plan and conduct, but they strongly dispute the downplaying of class in such theorists. Here we see how media theory can challenge and enrich social theory by focusing in much greater depth on questions of representation.

Those same social theories concerning the reflexive project of the self provide Alison Hearn's starting point in Chapter 12 on personal branding and self-promotion, and she too refers to reality television as a manifestation of some troubling dimensions of this project. Hearn connects these ideas with other theories concerning the central role of 'promotionalism' in modern society (Andrew Wernick) and new modes of capitalism. Echoing Wood and Skeggs, and anticipating the next section's discussion of labour (especially Matt Stahl's chapter), Hearn observes how 'the responsibility for self-fulfilment and meaningful community is downloaded on to the individual worker', leading to new forms of working experience and subjectivity. She draws on the work of Mauricio Lazzarato, David Harvey, Luc Boltanski and Eve Chiapello among others to develop these ideas. This new kind of relationship to the self is apparent in various media phenomena: reality television such as *The Apprentice* and *American Idol*, as already mentioned, but also the personal branding movement in management (for Hearn, this movement invokes an image of autonomous subjectivity which actually undermines such autonomy through its instrumentalism) and websites such as 2night.com and social networking sites such as MySpace and Facebook. Hearn is careful to qualify her claims by making it clear that self-promotion is nothing new. But she suggests important new developments in the relationship between power and visibility. We are, she implies, making spectacles of ourselves in socially damaging ways.

The contributors to the fourth and last part of the collection, 'Media labour and production', bring to these familiar topics in media studies a certain theoretical freshness that derives partly from their address of a key question we have been considering throughout this chapter: is the present a new epoch in media structure and practice? At the same time there is also a more properly metatheoretical concern with the nature of media production and its significance *vis-à-vis* reception or consumption. The question here is: does media labour matter and if so why?

Toby Miller tackles both these questions in Chapter 13. Miller sketches out a binary model of existing media studies. Media Studies 1.0 includes the tradition of media effects research which emerges from bourgeois intellectual anxiety about how the masses might be affected by the shock, danger and sheer seductiveness of modern mediated life. Version 1.0 also takes in variants of political economy and critical theory that have scorned popular culture. By way of contrast, Media Studies 2.0 is optimistic, and invests audiences with a hermeneutic power that can emancipate them from the sort of bondage posed in version 1.0. Condemning the narrowness of both (1.0 ignores activity and struggle in the media; 2.0 denies structure and real power relations), Miller advocates 'frottage' between them. The theoretical means of achieving this consist, first, in a rejection of the originary binarism of the Cartesian mind–body duality, a binarism that underpins the Media 1.0 versus Media 2.0 opposition. Instead, Miller insists (with Lawrence Grossberg) on a dialectical shift towards 'politicising theory and theorising politics'. And that in turn suggests paying renewed attention to labour broadly considered, as well as internationalisation of the media. Miller thus concludes with a critical case study of the global 'precariat', a new layer of international labour – insecure, exploited, displaced – located in sectors as diverse as the media and office cleaning.

In an important sense Chapter 14, by Matt Stahl, on 'rockumentary' film, constitutes a case study in this precariousness of media work. Taking the 2004 film *Dig!* as his centrepiece, Stahl suggests that the emerging genre of the rock documentary serves to provide instruction in 'good' creative work. On the one hand, as exemplified in the career of the band the Dandy Warhols, we are shown a form of labour 'that promises to foster autonomy, self-actualisation and de-alienation'. On the other – and this is picked out in the disintegrating career of the Warhols' erstwhile friends and colleagues, the Brian Jonestown Massacre – we are presented with a narrative of self-indulgence, moral decline and financial collapse. It is what happens when you *abuse* autonomy. The moral is clear. If creative labour is a zone of freedom, then it is one which has to be constantly sustained through discipline, focus and, above all, plenty of hard work. Stahl's contribution to theory, then, consists in showing how theses on the cultural construction of work (from Weber to Beck) find corroboration in rockumentaries – these are training manuals for learning to labour in the neoliberal knowledge economy.

Contemporary journalism has little in common with rock music making, we might assume. However, Chapter 15, by Chris Anderson, suggests a strong parallel. Both 'professions' are riven by insecurity, and in both cases there is deep ambiguity about the nature and status of the occupation. Surveying US journalism research since the mid-1970s, Anderson offers a critique, and then a synthesis, of what he identifies as the three key strands in scholarship. Tracing organisational analysis of journalism (mainly from the late 1970s), work on the production of journalistic discourse and interpretive communities (chiefly Zelizer since the early 1990s) and journalism-as-field (a still flourishing Bourdieuian approach), Anderson shows the enormous explanatory power of theoretical integration. For it is only by bringing the three approaches together, he argues, that we can make sense of the current journalistic moment in which, on the face of it, journalistic expertise is being challenged by a new information laity of bloggers and netizens. In this context, then, professional journalists struggle to establish jurisdiction over journalistic expertise while at the same time attempting, as he puts it, 'to control the cultural discourse that both defines them in relation to others and defines the very nature of their expertise'. Organisation, discourse, field – all three theoretical frames are needed to make sense of the present conjuncture, Anderson insists. Or, to put it in the terms we used at the start of this chapter, if you want to historicise the present in media studies you have to develop some kind of theoretical overview of how your medium works.

In the final chapter Jason Toynbee (Chapter 16) returns to the questions concerning the relationship between production, audience and texts raised by Toby Miller. Toynbee's aim is not only to argue for the precedence of production but also to show how critical realist philosophy can provide a much more serious basis for such a claim than existing schools and tendencies – notably empiricism and subjectivism. The media show a fundamental asymmetry between producers and consumers (in spite of the many absurd claims about the effects of 'user-generated content' in social networking sites and the like). So producers have precedence because they control form and content, but this only takes us so far. How is production organised and what shapes its output? Answering these questions, says Toynbee, drawing upon critical realist social theory, requires adequate consideration of structure and agency. On the structure side, critical realism provides an ontology which brings together structures (economic and otherwise), ontological depth and horizontal conjunction. This means we can avoid having to choose between macro- and micro-causality, between inference from text and from causal linkage, but can use both approaches instead, and better reflect the need for multiple perspectives in understanding the complexity of media–society relations. On the agency side, critical realism offers a formulation of agency as intentional, yet also limited by the opacity of social being, which is of fundamental value in understanding media production. For it helps explain how media making can be instrumental – in other words, subject to market control or more broadly influenced by powerful social forces – and yet at the same time can exist as a zone of relative autonomy and counter-intuitive expression. Finally, Toynbee uses critical realism to argue against the tendency in media studies to downplay the *referential* function of the media. The media have a special capacity to represent the world beyond mere hearsay. And of course producers can unknowingly, or more rarely intentionally, make falsely objective texts. For Toynbee, this means that there is a need for textual analysis which will itself be driven by an ethic of objectivity.

Looking back on this chapter-survey, perhaps what emerges most strongly is the sheer variety of theoretical sources being called upon in the field. Earlier we suggested that integration should be a goal of new theoretical work in media studies. And, indeed, the chapters of this book do integrate ideas from within and beyond media studies. Integration generates both intellectual development and lucidity – positions become clearer. The next step, then, might be to move in another direction, dialectically towards strong argument and intellectual struggle between clearly opposed positions, with a view to synthesising and winnowing out the *best* media theory. That will be a difficult conference to organise, and a tough book to edit. We look forward to them, though.

Notes

1 In the broader sense in which we use social theory in this book, to include political theory and cultural theory. Some are perhaps more readily identified as other things – Habermas, Deleuze and Butler as philosophers, Foucault as a historian.
2 Such fetishism is not unique to media theory, of course. In sociology the holy trinity of Marx, Durkheim and Weber have formed the basis of classical social theory for decades. All three of these names occasionally make an appearance in media and communication theory too. But it seems to us that sociologists would tend to make less selective use of this holy trinity than media studies researchers have of the theorists mentioned above.
3 To clarify, this is not to say that Foucauldian work is atheoretical, but rather that its theory either concerns other things than society, or else treats the social as an epiphenomenon of discourse, power–knowledge, governmentality and so on.
4 In our experience, research methods are much less often taught to undergraduates in media, communication and cultural studies than in other social science programmes, but that is another matter.
5 We should own up that we ourselves decided to maintain this division (while acknowledging its limitations) in putting together a new Open University Media Studies course for the 2000s, DA204 'Understanding Media' (see, for example, Evans and Hesmondhalgh 2005).
6 Especially when told with the enjoyable vigour of Scannell (2007) or the rigorous originality of Morrison (1998).
7 We would point, however, to interesting developments in some media studies, involving much greater attention to analytical ethics (see, for example, Kieran 1998 and Couldry 2006) but also John Durham Peters's brilliant unpicking, in his book *Speaking into the Air*, of the normative assumptions that have accrued around the notion of 'communication'.
8 For a discussion see John Downey's chapter in this volume.

Bibliography

Archer, Margaret (1995) *Realist Social Theory: the Morphogenetic Approach.* Cambridge: Cambridge University Press.

Baert, Patrick (2000) *Philosophy of the Social Sciences: towards Pragmatism.* Cambridge: Polity Press.

Benton, Ted and Craib, Ian (2001) *Philosophy of Social Science: the Philosophical Foundations of Social Thought.* Basingstoke: Palgrave.

Bhaskar, Roy (1998) *The Possibility of Naturalism: a Philosophical Critique of the Contemporary Human Sciences*, 3rd edn. Abingdon: Routledge.

Born, Georgina (2006) 'Digitising democracy', in John Lloyd and Jean Seaton (eds) *What Can Be done? Making the Media and Politics Better*. Oxford: Blackwell/Political Quarterly.

Callinicos, Alex (2007) *Social Theory: a Historical Introduction*, 2nd edn. Cambridge: Polity Press.

Clifford, James (1986) 'On ethnographic allegory', in James Clifford and George Marcus (eds) *Writing Culture: the Poetics and Politics of Ethnography*. Berkeley CA: University of California Press.

Couldry, Nick (2006) *Listening beyond the Echoes: Media, Ethics and Agency in an Uncertain World*. Boulder CO: Paradigm.

Craib, Ian (1992) *Modern Social Theory: from Parsons to Habermas*, 2nd edn. New York: Harvester Wheatsheaf.

Delanty, Gerard (2005) *Social Science: Philosophical and Methodological Foundations*, 2nd edn. Buckingham: Open University Press.

Delanty, Gerard and Strydom, Piet (2003) *Philosophies of Social Science: the Classic and Contemporary Readings*. Maidenhead: Open University Press.

Evans, Jessica and Hesmondhalgh, David (eds) (2005) *Understanding Media: Inside Celebrity*. Maidenhead and New York: Open University Press.

Foucault, Michel (1990) *The History of Sexuality: an Introduction*. London: Penguin Books.

Fraser, Nancy (1989) *Unruly Practices: Power, Discourse and Gender in Contemporary Social Theory*. Minneapolis MN: University of Minnesota Press.

Fraser, Nancy and Axel Honneth (2003) *Redistribution or Recognition? A Political–Philosophical Exchange*. London: Verso.

Giddens, Anthony (1984) *The Constitution of Society: Outline of the Theory of Structuration*. Cambridge: Polity Press.

Gripsrud, Jostein (2002) *Understanding Media Cultures*. London: Hodder Arnold.

Hall, Stuart (1993/1973) 'Encoding, decoding', in Simon During (ed.) *The Cultural Studies Reader*. London: Routledge.

Hall, Stuart (1997) *Representation: Cultural Representations and Signifying Practices*. London: Sage/Open University.

Harvey, David (2005) 'The sociological and geographical imaginations', *International Journal of Political and Cultural Sociology* 18: 211–55.

Kellner, Douglas (2003) *Media Spectacles*. London: Routledge.

Kieran, Matthew (ed.) (1998) *Media Ethics*. London: Routledge.

Layder, Derek (1993) *New Strategies in Social Research: an Introduction and Guide*. Cambridge: Polity Press.

McQuail, Denis (2005) *McQuail's Mass Communication Theory*, 5th edn. London: Sage.

Moores, Shaun (2005) *Media/Theory: Thinking about Media and Communications*. London: Routledge.

Morrison, David E. (1998) *The Search for a Method: Focus Groups and the Development of Mass Communication Research*. Luton: University of Luton Press.

Nussbaum, Martha (2001) *Upheavals of Thought: the Intelligence of the Emotions*. Cambridge: Cambridge University Press.

Peters, John Durham (1999) *Speaking into the Air: a History of the Idea of Communication*. Chicago: University of Chicago Press.

Sayer, Andrew (2004) 'Feminism, critical realism and economics: a response to Van Staveren', *Post-autistic Economics Review* 29 (6), article 5, http://www. paecon.net/ PAEReview/issue29/Sayer29.htm (accessed 27 September 2007).

Sayer, Andrew (2005) *The Moral Significance of Class*. Cambridge: Cambridge University Press.

Scannell, Paddy (2007) *Media and Communication*. London: Sage.

Scott, John (2006) *Social Theory: Central Issues in Sociology*. London: Sage.

Thompson, John B. (1995) *The Media and Modernity: a Social Theory of the Media*. Cambridge: Polity Press.

Williams, Kevin (2003) *Understanding Media Theory*. London: Hodder Arnold.

Part I
Power and democracy

2 Media and the paradoxes of pluralism

Kari Karppinen

Theories and concepts, on which normative views of media and democracy build, have generally taken a pluralist or anti-essentialist turn in recent decades. While notions such as 'media quality' or 'public interest' are increasingly contested, pluralism and diversity not only have become indisputable values, but also rank among the few politically correct criteria for assessing media performance and regulation. Hardly anyone would disagree with the idea that citizens need to have access to a broad range of political views, cultural expressions and aesthetic experiences in the public sphere. The meaning and nature of pluralism as a normative principle, however, remain vague and arguably under-theorised.

Much of the confusion surrounding the notions of pluralism and diversity in media studies undoubtedly stems from their disparate uses in different contexts, but there is also a certain ambiguity inherent in the concept of pluralism itself. As Gregor McLennan (1995: 7) has noted, the constitutive vagueness of pluralism as a social value gives it enough ideological flexibility for it to be capable of signifying reactionary tendencies in one phase of the debate and progressive values in the next. Pluralism thus constitutes a highly contentious and elusive principle in political and social theory as well as for evaluating the performance of the media.

Taking some distance from the attractiveness of commonsense pluralism, this chapter focuses on some paradoxical dimensions in the present discussion on pluralism and the public sphere. Reflecting the renewed emphasis on pluralism in political theory, normative models of deliberative democracy and the public sphere have been increasingly criticised for overemphasising social unity and rational consensus. Instead of a singular notion of the public sphere, public use of reason or the common good, theorists increasingly stress the plurality of public spheres, politics of difference and the complexity of ways in which the media can contribute to democracy. As a result, various radical-pluralist theories of democracy that have attempted to develop less rigidly normative conceptions of democracy and the public sphere have gained more and more prominence also in media studies. In contrast to the allegedly rationalistic and monistic thrust of the Habermasian public sphere approach, they are often seen to resonate better with the chaotic and complex nature of the contemporary media landscape.

I discuss the implications and potential significance of the radical-pluralist approach for media studies and media policy here by drawing mainly from the political philosophy of Chantal Mouffe (1993, 2000, 2005), whose model of 'agonistic pluralism' constitutes one of the most prominent alternatives to deliberative conceptions of democracy. The rationale for this is twofold. First, agonistic pluralism provides a fundamental critique of the traditional Habermasian approach to the public sphere and democracy. Second, and perhaps more important, I argue that her ideas also provide an equally strong critique of 'naive pluralism' that celebrates all multiplicity and diversity without paying attention to the continued centrality of the questions of power and exclusion in the public sphere.

As McLennan (1995: 83–4) notes, one of the main problems with any 'principled pluralist' perspective remains how to conceptualise the need for pluralism and diversity without falling into the trap of flatness, relativism, indifference, and unquestioning acceptance of market-driven difference and consumer culture. While Mouffe's approach itself is open to criticism on many fronts, it serves as a good starting point for illustrating some of the problems in debating the value of pluralism in media politics. The purpose of discussing the agonistic approach here is therefore not to argue for more pluralism as such. Instead, it serves to question the inclusiveness of current pluralistic discourses and emphasise the continued importance of analysing relations of power in contemporary public spheres. While the problems of 'naive pluralism' are certainly not foreign to contemporary media policy, the agonistic model of democracy is discussed here as a possible theoretical basis for bringing the current 'ethos of pluralisation' to bear also on the level of media structures and politics.

The ambiguity of pluralism

The idea of pluralism as a crucial social and political value is nothing new. Premised on the impossibility of unambiguously establishing truth, right or good, especially in social and political affairs, pluralism is one of the constitutive tenets of liberal democracy. According to Mouffe (2000: 18), the acceptance of pluralism, understood as 'the end of a substantive idea of the good life', is the most important single defining feature of modern liberal democracy that differentiates it from ancient models of democracy.

At its broadest definition, pluralism can simply be defined as a theorised preference for multiplicity over unity and diversity over uniformity in whatever field of enquiry (McLennan 1995: 25). In this sense, almost all particular discourses could be conceived as reflecting some aspect of the pluralism/monism interface, and for McLennan, rather than as a specific ideology, pluralism is best conceived as a general intellectual orientation, whose specific manifestations would be expected to change depending on the context.

Despite, or perhaps because of, its ubiquitous nature, it can be argued that sometimes pluralism itself has become the new foundation of social theory. John Keane (1992), for instance, has argued that political values of democracy and freedom of speech themselves should be conceived as means and necessary preconditions of protecting philosophical and political pluralism, rather than as foundational principles themselves. While accepting multiplicity and pluralism has become almost endemic to recent social theory, various universal forms of politics have given way to a new pluralist imaginary associated with identity politics and politics of difference (see Benhabib 2002). As Anne Phillips (2000: 238) notes, there has been 'an explosion of new literature on what are seen as the challenges of diversity and difference' – which according to Bonnie Honig (1996: 60) is 'just another word for what used to be called pluralism'.

Instead of the utopia of a rationally based unitary public sphere, many argue that democracy needs to be seen as pluralised and marked by new kinds of politics of difference. For writers like Keane the ideal of a unified public sphere and its corresponding vision of a unitary public of citizens are becoming increasingly obsolete. Similarly, in media studies, Elizabeth Jacka (2003: 183) has argued that, instead of universal visions of the common good, democracy needs to be seen as based on 'pragmatic and negotiated exchanges about ethical behaviour and ethically inspired courses of action', and we need to 'countenance a plurality of communication media and modes in which such a diverse set of exchanges will occur'. Such a pluralist approach would then be inclusive of different genres of media texts and different forms of media organisation, not privileging 'high modern journalism' as a superior form of rational communication.

In the context of the media, the attraction of pluralism would seem to be closely linked to the attacks on universal quality criteria or other unambiguous criteria for assessing media performance. In this sense, pluralism not only constitutes a perspective for assessing the performance of the media but also a form of political rationality that directly concerns media policy. According to Nielsen (2003), the ideas that all forms of culture contain their own criteria of quality have broken the universal basis for defining cultural quality and have led to a 'pluralistic consensus' in media and cultural policy. The notions of quality, cultural value or public interest are thus increasingly conceived in a relativist manner, avoiding the paternalism of the old paradigm of media policy.

The problem with the pluralistic consensus, however, lies in the ambiguity of pluralism as a normative principle. In a general sense, we are all pluralists, but on closer analysis it seems that the emphasis on pluralism and diversity will inevitably create its own pathologies and paradoxes.

Pluralism and diversity may remain inherently good, but, as McLennan (1995: 8) writes, in deconstructing their value we are faced with questions of the following order. Is there not a point at which healthy diversity turns into unhealthy dissonance? Does pluralism mean that anything goes? And what exactly are the criteria for stopping the potentially endless multiplication of valid ideas?

According to Louise Marcil-Lacoste (1992), pluralism entails a certain ambiguity 'between the over-full and the empty': on the one hand, pluralism suggests abundance, flowering and expansion of values and choices, but, on the other hand, it also evokes emptiness. To recognise or promote plurality in some context is to say nothing about the nature of its elements and issues, their relations, and value. Stemming from this, pluralism can combine both critique and evasion. It involves critique of all monisms and it aims to deconstruct their foundational claims. Yet there is also evasion, in terms of its refusal to develop substantive normative positions concerning social, political and economic processes (ibid.).

In many ways, the ethos of evasiveness and vacuousness is not foreign to contemporary debates in media studies and media policy either. Particularly for those concerned with institutional politics and media structures, postmodern anti-foundationalism and particularism have often represented an irrational threat to modern democratic ideals. If there is no rational basis or common standard for evaluating the media, it is feared, relativism will take over and the 'politics of difference' will lead to a 'politics of indifference'. Given that pluralism is a notion that necessarily generates consensus and does not impose any limits, its flip side is that it indicates no specific content and fails to resolve the problems associated with media structure and democratic regulation of the media. For this reason, there is a need to analyse the different levels and meanings of the concept and the problems it involves.

Pluralism and the public sphere

Although pluralism may have a number of other justifications, I will here focus only on the status of pluralism in democratic theory and political philosophy. As mentioned before, liberal theorists of democracy have long seen pluralism and the clash of divergent opinions and interests in various realms of social life as mediating progress (Bobbio 1990: 21–4). Perhaps most famously this point was made by J. S. Mill (1859/1986), who defended freedom of speech by arguing that all opinions, whether true or false, must have their place in public so that their merits can be openly evaluated. The legacy of liberal pluralism for media regulation, however, has been far from unproblematic. Liberal media policy discourses commonly conceptualise pluralism in terms of 'the free market place of ideas' – although the metaphor and its corresponding tenets of minimal regulation and freedom of choice for consumers actually represent rather poorly the original ideas of Mill (see Gordon 1997; Baum 2001; Splichal 2002).

Given the long tradition of critique from the critical political economy of communication, the notion of free choice in the market place has proved a far from adequate framework for conceptualising media pluralism or any other goals for media policy other than economic ones. In response, critical scholars have instead mostly employed the notion of the public sphere as a theoretical framework in which to seek grounding for the value of media pluralism.

In general, it is arguably around the notion of the public sphere that most fruitful interaction between political theory and media studies has taken place in the last decades. While much of the debate on the media and the public sphere draws upon Habermas's early work (1989), the public sphere is also more broadly understood as a general context of interaction where citizens get informed and public discussion takes place. In this general sense of the concept, voicing of diverse views and access to a wide range of information and experiences are rarely questioned as a precondition for citizens' effective participation in public life.

On reflection, however, it becomes evident that the concept of the public sphere also includes an aspect of commonality and unity. The relationship between pluralism and the commonality inherent in the notion of the public sphere has proven to be one of the central points of contention in recent democratic theory. It can be argued that at some point the emphasis on diversity and pluralism runs against the imaginary presuppositions of democracy itself, so that there is an inherent tension between pluralism and 'publicness' (McLennan 1995: 92). Similarly, Mouffe speaks of 'the democratic paradox': how to envisage a form of commonality strong enough to institute a 'demos' but nevertheless compatible with true religious, moral, cultural and political pluralism (Mouffe 2000: 64)? Consequently, the relative status of universal and plural conceptions of the public sphere has also been one of the key sources of contention in theorising the relationship between media and democracy (see Born 2006).

As the theoretical framework that has dominated much of the recent theorising on the role of the media in democracy, the idea of deliberative democracy tries to reconcile this tension by making the discursive formation of the public sphere the essence of political community. In contrast to liberal pluralism or communitarianism, the deliberative approach thus denies the pluralism of fixed differences (individual or community) that lead to either an aggregation model of individual interests or irreducible community identities. Instead, the emphasis on difference is complemented, and qualified, with an emphasis on the strong public sphere of rational-critical deliberation (see Dahlberg 2005).

In the approaches informed by deliberative democracy, the role of the public sphere and the media is then conceptualised in terms of the 'public use of reason' by free and equal citizens. It provides a norm of rational-critical deliberation, which is free from state and corporate interests, inclusive, aimed at understanding and agreement, reasoned and reflexive. As certain social institutions evidently encourage this type of communication more than others, it also provides an explicitly normative framework, which has sparked a wealth of debate on the relationship between the media and democracy.

The ideal of deliberative democracy, however, has not escaped criticism. For many, the rational-critical basis of the public sphere delivers an overly rationalist conception which, despite claims that it makes room for difference, fails to theorise pluralism adequately. Drawing on theorists such as Foucault and Lyotard, critics see that the deliberative emphasis on communicative reason leads inevitably to a support for the *status quo* of exclusions and inequalities, because it fails to acknowledge the normalising tendencies involved in the designation of a particular form of communication as the rational, democratically legitimate norm (see, for instance, Villa 1992; Fraser 1992; Baumeister 2003; Gardiner 2004).

Much of the criticism is arguably based on a rather simplified reading of deliberative democracy and especially Habermas's later work, which can be seen as advocating a much more plural conception of public spheres (see Brady 2004; Dahlberg 2005). Still, the emphasis on rational consensus is commonly seen to underestimate the depth of societal pluralism and the fundamental nature of value conflicts, in terms of cultural difference and structural conflicts of interest. The general thrust of deliberative democracy is thus seen as too dependent on the view that a benign social order must be grounded in the ideal of consensus. While social reality is increasingly conceived as a chaotic situation of diversity and pluralism, the insistence on consensus is seen as too idealised, too unrealistic and too academic (see Rescher 1993).

In short, the stress on consensus and universal criteria of rationality is seen as leading to an over-centralised model of the public sphere that is incompatible with societal pluralism and that inevitably ignores inequalities between social groups and their specific needs. Iris Marion Young (1997: 401) among others has argued that the defining characteristic of a public is plurality and it is irreducible to a single denominator. Therefore a conception of publicity that requires its members to put aside their differences in order to uncover the common good is seen to destroy its very meaning. Or even more bluntly as Bauman (1997: 202) puts it: 'Habermas's "perfect communication", which measures its own perfection by consensus and the exclusion of dissent, is another dream of death which radically cures the ills of freedom's life.'

One of the hallmarks of 'post-Habermasian' political theory, then, seems to be its distancing from the emphasis on rational consensus. As a result, theorising about the public sphere has taken a markedly pluralistic turn in the past decades. The most notable implication of this is the rejection of a universal or singular idea of the public sphere in favour of a plurality of public spheres, conceptualised as a complex field of multiple contesting publics; a revision that even Habermas himself has now largely conceded.

From rational consensus to agonistic pluralism

In light of the above critiques of deliberative democracy, agonistic, or radical-pluralist, theories of democracy have recently emerged among the most prominent alternative imaginaries in democratic thought. Radical-pluralist theories of democracy typically maintain that civil society is not harmonious or unitary but, rather, characterised by conflicts of interest and an irreducible pluralism of values. Consequently, any system of rational consensus is seen as not only utopian, but also dangerous and necessarily exclusive.

If theories of deliberative democracy and the public sphere have essentially tried to reconcile the tension between pluralism and commonality by placing emphasis on agreement among rational inquirers, the agonistic model of democracy advocated by Chantal Mouffe can be seen as its direct antithesis:

> The belief in the possibility of a universal rational consensus has put democratic thinking on the wrong track. Instead of trying to design the institutions which, though supposedly 'impartial' procedures, would reconcile all conflicting interests and values, the task for democratic theorists and politicians should be to envisage the creation of a vibrant 'agonistic' public sphere of contestation where different hegemonic political projects can be confronted.
>
> (Mouffe 2005: 3)

The underlying argument here is that the ideal of rational-critical deliberative public sphere fails to address power and existing forms of exclusion. Furthermore, it has not adequately theorised the themes of plurality, openness and undecidability, and thus inevitably excludes the articulation of difference and conflict outside democratic deliberation. As Mouffe (2000: 49) argues, 'consensus in a liberal-democratic society is – and will always be – the expression of hegemony and the crystallisation of power relations … [and] because it postulates the availability of consensus without exclusion, the model of deliberative democracy is unable to envisage liberal-democratic pluralism in an adequate way'. While Habermas conceives the public sphere as an arena of rational and critical debate leading to a consensus, radical pluralists argue that democracy should be conceived as agonistic confrontation or continued contestation.

Another mistake of liberal rationalism that Mouffe (2005: 6) sees as characteristic of deliberative democracy is to ignore the affective dimension mobilised by collective identifications and passions in politics.

In Habermas's approach, the separation of the private realm, the realm of irreconcilable value pluralism, and the realm of the public, where rational consensus can be reached, is a key distinction. According to Mouffe, what this separation really does is to circumscribe a domain that would not be subject to the pluralism of values and where a consensus without exclusion could be established. In assuming that all differences could be relegated to the private sphere through the construction of a procedurally based rational consensus, deliberative democrats ignore the irresolvable nature of conflicts over political values. They 'relegate pluralism to a non-public domain in order to insulate politics from its consequences' (Mouffe 2000: 33, 91–2).

Agonistic pluralism also requires abandoning the essentialism dominant in the liberal interpretation of pluralism and acknowledging the contingency and ambiguity of social identities. Identities are never fixed, but always contested. An agonistic public sphere is thus not only an arena for the formation of discursive public opinion, or the aggregation of predefined interests, but also a site for the formation and contestation of social identities. Consequently, one of the main uses for the agonistic approach for scholars in media and cultural studies has been to promote a model of the public sphere which takes into account not only rational debate, but also questions of emotion, passion, identity and their importance in media use.

Radical pluralism and media politics

When applied to normative debates on the media, such radical-pluralist critique has obviously found most of its resonance as a critique of the biases and flaws of existing normative frameworks. In a way, this also reflects the division of democratic theories into (1) those oriented to democratising or rationalising the procedures of decision making and (2) those confined more explicitly to the processes of resistance and contestation as inherently valuable. As Bonnie Honig (1993: 2) writes, the radical pluralist approach justifies itself above all as a critique of political theorists that measure their success by the elimination of dissonance and conflict, and thus confine politics to the tasks of stabilising moral and political subjects, building consensus, or consolidating communities and identities. Radical pluralism thereby explicitly aims to shift the emphasis of democratic politics to the processes of dislocation, contestation and resistance.

While both logics may have merits, the role of the media has never been understood so much in terms of direct participation in state power but primarily in terms of a critique of other centres of power. Even Habermas (1996: 359) demoted the public sphere to the status of a 'warning system with sensors that, though unspecialised, are sensitive through society' and has thereby seemingly relieved it from the burden of solving problems or having to produce a rational solution to political questions. In this sense, it is easy to understand why an approach that emphasises the aspects of contestation and dislocation (instead of the utopia of rationalising society through some universal principles) seems particularly attractive in theorising the role of the contemporary media.

The demand for new theoretical perspectives thus seems evident. As Georgina Born (2006) has argued, current debates on media policy have tended not to pay sufficient attention to the implications of pluralism for contemporary media. At the same time, however, she argues that media policy analysts have baulked at the challenge of founding ideas for reform on normative rationales or political philosophy.

The problem seems to be that while the Habermasian public sphere approach has long been mobilised as a normative backbone in debates on media structure and policy, for instance in defence of public service broadcasting, the implications of radical pluralist perspectives for the media have been much less debated. In fact, it seems that a lack of institutional proposals or of interest in concrete political questions is a more widespread feature of postmodern theories of radical difference and pluralism (McLennan 1995: 85). These perspectives have been used more as oppositional discourses or critical tools in questioning various monisms of media studies and political economy, and not as coherent normative theories that would pertain to questions of media structure and policy.

For many critics, this affirms the problems of evasiveness and vacuousness in postmodern and radical pluralist perspectives. While most acknowledge that they often provide valuable critique, they get criticised for their refusal to develop substantive normative positions. This has led some critics to argue that with the emphasis on diversity, difference and the proliferation of identity movements, politics is becoming pluralised to the point of being trivialised.

Just as the 'old pluralism' of liberal individualism and interest group politics was marked by a strategic avoidance of political economy and questions of power (see McClure 1992), it can be argued that the 'new pluralism' of identity politics is similarly marked by indifference and relativism towards broader political and economic structures. In concentrating on the formation of multiple identities it neglects the unequal possibilities open to different groups. Nancy Fraser (1997), for instance, speaks of a divide between politics of redistribution, understood in material, institutional, political-economic terms, and the 'ethos of pluralisation' found on the level of micro-politics and the symbolic realm. In its denial of all universalism and systemic concerns, Fraser argues, the discourse of pluralisation has so far been incapable of dealing with macro-political concerns.

Against naive pluralism

It seems that at times the emphasis on pluralism and complexity echoes the postmodern antipathy towards all kinds of social centralism and planning and leads to a more general critique of all kinds of 'cultural policing', which are seen as attempts to stabilise or stifle difference, to create political closure or to define in other ways the acceptable limits of pluralism from above. In the absence of alternatives, much of the theoretical reflection on media and democracy remains either explicitly or implicitly based on normative models derived from the Habermasian notion of the public sphere, which critics claim is unnecessarily pessimistic and one-dimensional. As a carry-over from the pessimism of Habermas's initial formulations of the public sphere, it would seem that growing social disintegration and cultural fragmentation are inevitably counterproductive to the ideals the media ought to serve, imposing a theoretical frame that one critic calls 'democracy as defeat' (Jacka 2003).

Consequently, radical-pluralist perspectives have been employed mainly as counter-narratives to the Habermasian approach. For authors with a more optimistic outlook, the key development that is supposedly making a more pluralist media system possible is the growth of channel availability that allows ever greater diversity and choice, catering to more and more specialist tastes and needs (Jacka 2003: 188). Pluralistic democracy is then seen to be realised when people can freely construct their identities by choosing from the ever-expanding options in the public sphere.

Following this line of reasoning, John Hartley, for instance, has coined the notion of 'semiotic democracy' to separate democracy from the tediousness of collective action and to re-articulate it with questions of self-realisation and the choices people make for themselves. Interpreting citizenship primarily in terms of identity and difference, Hartley invents the concept of 'do-it-yourself citizenship' as 'the practice of putting together an identity from the available choices, patterns and opportunities on offer in the semiosphere and the mediasphere' (1999: 178). Seeking 'democratisation without politicisation', writers like Jacka and Hartley envisage a shift from political democracy to semiotic democracy, a future of post-political, post-adversarial citizenship that is based on semiotic self-determination – choices people make for themselves – rather than state coercion or paternalism.

Such postmodern anti-paternalism, which leans on the recognition of complexity and plurality, is founded on resistance to any central rationalist planning and the denial of any systematic or integrative metatheories. However, based on such praise of individual cultural autonomy and choice, it is no wonder if the current stress on popular consumption, active audiences and individual creation of meaning is mistaken for the neoliberal idea of consumer sovereignty. It can be argued that the discussion of pluralism in media studies and media policy has often taken a form of naive celebration of all multiplicity, which all too easily converges with the neoliberal illusion of free choice.

My purpose here is to argue that it is precisely this kind of 'naive pluralism' and the evacuation of political economy that the radical-pluralist approach in democratic theory is aimed against. Contrary to the post-modern celebration of pluralism, Mouffe has explicitly argued that radical pluralism must be distinguished from the forms of postmodern politics which emphasise heterogeneity and incommensurability to the extent of valorising all differences. Because of its refusal to acknowledge the relations of power involved in 'constructions of differences', such naive pluralism, Mouffe (2000: 20) argues, is compatible with the liberal evasion of politics, and converges with the typical liberal illusion of pluralism without antagonism. Instead, for radical pluralism to be compatible with the struggle against inequality, one must also acknowledge the limits of pluralism.

Equally critical of ideas such as life politics or subpolitics – which the notion of semiotic democracy would seem to reflect – Mouffe (2005: 54) has explicitly stressed the need to acknowledge the crucial role played by economic and political power in the structuring of the hegemonic order. Instead of standing for dissolution of politics into semiotic democracy, personal therapy, or individual do-it-yourself citizenship, she has stressed that the democratisation of any social institution is above all a political task.

It is by emphasising questions of power and exclusion that radical pluralism therefore takes its distance from both the liberal notion of the free market place of ideas and the postmodern praise of all difference. I argue that, in media studies, the radical-pluralist approach is best interpreted, not as praise of multiplicity as such, but as a call to recognise the aspect of power, exclusion and control inherent in all conceptions of the public sphere. As such, it departs from the political minimalism of liberal pluralism, for, in contrast to the view that pluralism is best protected by restricting politics to its bare essentials, radical pluralists contend that spaces in which differences may constitute themselves as contending identities are today most efficiently established by political means (see Connolly 1991: xi). There is no reason in principle, then, why the radical-pluralist perspective should be incompatible with questions of media policy or political economy.

Rethinking pluralism, choice and regulation

Among the central metaphors through which policies on media pluralism or almost any other public policy are conceived today are the market place and 'choice'. As Zygmunt Bauman (1997: 93) puts it, freedom of choice has become the main stratifying variable in our multidimensionally stratified societies, to an extent that choosing is everybody's fate. The only differences are the ranges of realistic choices and the resources needed to make them.

Of course, in the tradition of critical political economy of the media, models based on free competition and choice have long been criticised for ignoring that choice is always pre-structured by the existing conditions of competition. As Splichal (1999: 291) argues, the 'plurality' of the media as such is not a reliable indicator of a society's level of freedom, since it may create only the illusion of content diversity by hiding the fact that all mass communication processes are restrained by different forms of indirect control exercised by both the state and private corporations, ranging from formal regulation to pressures of advertising and subsidisers. A realistic question is thus not whether there will be forms of political intervention or regulation in the future, but rather what form they should take, what values they are based on and how these decisions are arrived at.

More eloquently, Bauman (1999: 73–8) explains that, throughout modernity, the principal tool of 'setting the agenda for choice' or pre-selection has been legislation, a tool which political institutions are now abandoning. However, this 'liberalisation' does not necessarily mean that the freedom of choice is expanding, but that the power of pre-selection is being ceded to non-political institutions, above all markets themselves. Consequently, the codes or criteria of pre-selection are changing, and, among the values towards which choosers are trained to orient their choices, short-term pleasure, hedonism, entertainment and other market-generated needs come to occupy a privileged place. So, according to Bauman, the late modern emphasis on freedom of choice and individual autonomy has not really increased individual freedom, but has instead led to 'unfreedom', the transformation of a political citizen to a consumer of market goods.

This illustrates the point about how the equation of media pluralism with free choice fails to take into account the wider relations of power in which the media are situated. Contrary to the language of 'the free market place of ideas' where the market is seen as a self-regulating and spontaneous mediator, the market itself is a politically designed institution, not a homogeneous, unstructured and unregulated natural entity (see Keane 1992: 119). The actual shape of the markets must always be crafted by political and legal regulation and it hardly emerges spontaneously as a neutral mediator of civil society. Any market also imposes its own criteria of pre-selection and construction of difference. In other words, every kind of system necessarily limits the range of public choices, yet all of them have a tendency to present this process of pre-selection as neutral or natural while in truth their criteria are inevitably political, in the broad sense of the word.

If structural inequalities and conflicts are ineradicable, as Mouffe argues, the main question regarding the public sphere is then not how to bracket or even eradicate relations of power, but rather to recognise and make them visible so that they can enter the terrain of political contestation. Power relations can be modified and room can be made for a plurality of alternative modes of power. A crucial question for media studies informed by radical pluralism thus remains: what institutional arrangements will best help narrow the gap in participatory parity between dominant and subordinate groups and create a plurality of power structures that are maximally open to democratic contestation (Fraser 1992: 122)?

Based on this, we can understand radical pluralism, not as a postmodern celebration of spontaneous multiplicity, but as a call for attention to institutional restructuring and macro-political concerns that also pertain to the political economy of the media. In this sense it arguably provides even stronger normative framework for media reform than the traditional Habermasian framework. It is due to the separation of the communicative realm from the systemic spheres of money and power that Dryzek (2000: 26), for instance, has concluded that, if it provides no sense of how political and economic structures should be further democratised, it is difficult to regard Habermas's theory of democracy as a contribution to critical theory. While Habermas assumes that participants in ideal public deliberation somehow bracket inequalities and treat each other as equal, his radical-pluralist critics like Mouffe claim that, in practice, the structural inequalities are undistinguishable from the actual communicative practices. In this sense they also conceivably pay more attention to their modification.

In fact the issues here are quite similar to those raised by Nicholas Garnham regarding identity politics. While one form of identity politics is a claim for recognition and toleration, another aspect is a claim on scarce resources, such as access to the media, cultural subsidies or production resources. Yet 'too often there is an attempt to combine a request for recognition and a share of public resources that such recognition brings with it and, at the same time, demonise the very common decision making, the politics, that must inevitably go with such resource distribution' (Garnham 2003: 198).

All in all, I argue that there is no reason why radical-pluralist arguments could not be used to defend concrete institutional arrangements in media policy. (For one of the few attempts to do this see Craig 1999.) Public service broadcasting or support for alternative media structures, for instance, can be seen as key tools in creating a plurality of power structures that are open to democratic contestation and that resist the hegemonic tendencies of the market.

Conclusion

I began by pointing to some contradictions and paradoxes in using pluralism as a catch-all value in media politics. While many current arguments in media policy point back to some of the central problems with pluralism – both philosophically and politically – it is not my purpose to argue that pluralism should not remain an important value in contemporary media policy.

However, it is important to note that, regardless of their popularity, pluralism and diversity have their limits as policy principles. Not only are there limits to pluralism in both political-economic and ethical terms, the concept of pluralism itself does not offer much unambiguous basis for the demands of democratic politics on the media, but rather constitutes itself an object of political contestation. With developments in media technology it is becoming even less clear in which sense it is meaningful to speak of media pluralism, if the media landscape is characterised more by abundance and limitless choice than by scarcity or lack of options.

What I have proposed here, by means of applying the idea of agonistic pluralism to the context of media politics, is that it is not enough to conceive media pluralism in terms of heterogeneity and a diversification of options. Instead, it needs to be analysed in connection with the structural relations of power that define the criteria that guide systems of representation and limit the available choices. Posed as an alternative to both liberal minimalism and to the rationalistic idealisations of deliberative democracy, the radical pluralist approach can thus be understood as an argument for the continuing centrality of question of power in media politics. The danger of what I called 'naive pluralism' is therefore that such questions are veiled or ignored under the illusion of communicative abundance or limitless choice. Unequal relations of power remain crucial in the field of media policy and media institutions and there is no reason to think that technological or any other developments will lead to spontaneous harmony.

This points to the continued relevance of the critical political economy of communication, and its attempts to reveal and analyse structural hierarchies of power that influence and shape our media environment. And as such analysis usually leads to normative questions, it also demands that we continually engage with normative political theory of different orientations to test our normative assumptions.

Bibliography

Baum, B. (2001) 'Freedom, power and public opinion: J. S. Mill on the public sphere', *History of Political Thought* 22 (3): 501–24.

Bauman, Z. (1997) *Postmodernity and its Discontents*. Cambridge: Polity Press.

Bauman, Z. (1999) *In Search of Politics*. Cambridge: Polity Press.

Baumeister, A. T. (2003) 'Habermas: discourse and cultural diversity', *Political Studies* 51 (4): 740–58.

Benhabib, S. (2002) *Claims of Culture: Equality and Diversity in the Global Era*. Princeton NJ: Princeton University Press.

Bobbio, N. (1990) *Liberalism and Democracy*. London: Verso.

Born, G. (2006) 'Digitising democracy', *Political Quarterly* 76 (1): 102–23.

Brady, J. S. (2004) 'Assessing the agonistic critiques of Jürgen Habermas's theory of the public sphere', *Philosophy and Social Criticism* 30 (3): 331–54.

Connolly, W. (1991) *Identity/Difference: Democratic Negotiations of Political Paradox*. Ithaca NY and London: Cornell University Press.

Craig, G. (1999) 'Perpetual crisis: the politics of saving the ABC', *Media International Australia* 95: 105–16.

Dahlberg, L. (2005) 'The Habermasian public sphere: taking difference seriously?' *Theory and Society* 34 (2): 111–36.

Dryzek, J. S. (2000) *Deliberative Democracy and Beyond: Liberals, Critics, Contestations*. Oxford: Oxford University Press.

Fraser, N. (1992) 'Rethinking the public sphere: a contribution to the critique of actually existing democracy', in C. Calhoun (ed.) *Habermas and the Public Sphere*. Cambridge MA: MIT Press.

Fraser, N. (1997) *Justice Interruptus: Critical Reflections on the 'Postsocialist' Condition*. New York and London: Routledge.

Gardiner, M. (2004) 'Wild publics and grotesque symposiums: Habermas and Bakhtin on dialogue, everyday life, and the public sphere', in N. Crossley and M. Roberts (eds) *After Habermas: New Perspectives on the Public Sphere*. Oxford: Blackwell.

Garnham, N. (2003) 'A response to Elizabet Jacka's *Democracy as Defeat*', *Television and New Media* 4 (2): 193–200.

Gordon, J. (1997) 'John Stuart Mill and the "marketplace of ideas"', *Social Theory and Practice* 23 (2): 235–50.

Habermas, J. (1962/1989) *The Structural Transformation of the Public Sphere*. Cambridge: Polity Press.

Habermas, J. (1996) *Between Facts and Norms*. Cambridge: Polity Press.

Hartley, J. (1999) *Uses of Television*. London: Routledge.

Honig, B. (1993) *Political Theory and the Displacement of Politics*. Ithaca NY and London: Cornell University Press.

Honig, B. (1996) 'Difference, dilemmas and the politics of home', in S. Benhabib (ed.) *Democracy and Difference*. Princeton NJ: Princeton University Press.

Jacka, E. (2003) 'Democracy as defeat', *Television and New Media* 4 (2): 177–91.

Keane, J. (1992) 'Democracy and the media – without foundations', *Political Studies* (special issue) 40: 116–29.

Marcil-Lacoste, L. (1992) 'The paradoxes of pluralism', in C. Mouffe (ed.) *Dimensions of Radical Democracy*. London: Verso.

McClure, K. (1992) 'On the subject of rights: pluralism, plurality and political identity', in C. Mouffe (ed.) *Dimensions of Radical Democracy*. London: Verso.

McLennan, G. (1995) *Pluralism*. Buckingham: Open University Press.

Mill, J. S. (1859/1986) *On Liberty*. Buffalo NY: Prometheus Books.

Mouffe, C. (1993) *The Return of the Political*. London and New York: Verso.

Mouffe, C. (2000) *Democratic Paradox*. London: Verso.

Mouffe, C. (2005) *On the Political*. London: Routledge.

Nielsen, H. K. (2003) 'Cultural policy and evaluation of quality', *International Journal of Cultural Policy* 9 (3): 237–45.

Phillips, A. (2000) 'Equality, pluralism, universality: current concerns in normative theory', *British Journal of Politics and International Relations* 2 (2): 237–55.

Rescher, N. (1993) *Pluralism: Against the Demand for Consensus*. Oxford: Clarendon Press.

Splichal, S. (1999) *Public Opinion: Developments and Controversies in the Twentieth Century*. Lanham MD: Rowman & Littlefield.

Splichal, S. (2002) *Principles of Publicity and Press Freedom*. Lanham MD: Rowman & Littlefield.

Villa, D. R (1992) 'Postmodernism and the public sphere', *American Political Science Review* 86 (3): 712–21.

Young, I. M. (1997) 'Difference as a resource for democratic communication', in J. Bohman and W. Rehg (eds) *Deliberative Democracy: Essays on Reason and Politics*. Cambridge MA: MIT Press.

3 Neoliberalism, social movements and change in media systems in the late twentieth century

Daniel C. Hallin

Over the past few decades, many dimensions of social life that once remained at least partly outside the structure of the market have now been incorporated substantially into it. The mass media are among the most important of those social institutions which have been subject to 'enclosure' by the logic of the market in the Age of Neoliberalism. It is common today to build the story of recent social change, and in particular to discuss change in media institutions over the past generation, in terms of the shift to neoliberalism. All too often, however, this way of telling the story of media and social change rests content with vague and simplistic formulations which, I will argue, are far from adequate to understand the changes that have taken place in media and in social systems over this period. Take for example David Harvey's generally very useful little book *A Brief History of Neoliberalism*. This book says curiously little about the media, though it could be argued that changes in the media system are actually rather central to the rise of neoliberalism. This is because market-based media have often displaced non-market forms of social organisation – as political marketing, for example, displaces older forms of political organisation – and because contemporary media are among the 'new apparatuses that integrate subjects into a moral nexus of identifications' (Rose 1996: 57–8) that are crucial to the 'government at a distance' that constitutes what Rose calls 'advanced liberalism'. What Harvey does say is the following (p. 80): 'a few media magnates control most of the flow of news, much of which then becomes pure propaganda'. This analysis is consistent with Harvey's general interpretation of neoliberalism as above all a restoration of the social and political power of economic elites. Many accounts within media studies characterise the shift to neoliberalism in the media sphere rather differently, as a process of depoliticisation, in which media lose their function as institutions of the public sphere and are absorbed into the world of commerce and consumption as mere vehicles for advertising and for a commodified entertainment industry. There are ways in which these two formulations might be reconciled, but they are different enough on the surface to suggest the need for a fairly careful analysis about just what the significance of the shift toward more market-driven media actually is.

One thing that is often missing in accounts of the rise of neoliberalism is a clear analysis of where neoliberalism came from, what the old social order was that it displaced, and why that old order broke down. What I would like to do in this chapter is to trace this historical background more concretely and to show how this can point us in the direction of a more complex understanding of media in the Age of Neoliberalism. Once we begin trying to move the analysis beyond the global concept of neoliberalism, of course, we have to confront the fact that this history is not the same all over the world, though there may be some common elements to it. I will focus here on three areas of the world which I know reasonably well: the United States, Western Europe and Latin America. Parts of the analysis will certainly apply to other parts of the world, other parts may not.

The shift to neoliberalism in media systems and its historical context

The old order: the market, political institutions and media professionalism in the mid-twentieth century

The mass media in the West have always been centrally an institution of the market. Johannes Gutenberg was a goldsmith, and Futz, who bankrolled his enterprise and eventually controlled it, was a lawyer; both were part of the emerging market society of early modern Europe. The early 'print capitalism' of which they were pioneers was then transformed in the nineteenth century with the rise of mass-circulation newspapers, beginning in the United States in the 1830s, and later in the nineteenth century in Europe. The newspaper was one of the first mass-produced commodities, and newspapers were among the largest manufacturing companies in the nineteenth century, at least in the United States and Britain. In the press systems that prevailed in the mid-twentieth century, however, marketplace logic was counterbalanced and modified by two forces. First, and especially important in continental Europe, were the strong ties that existed between the media and the organised social groups that made up the public sphere, and also largely controlled the state: political parties, trade unions, churches and the like (Hallin and Mancini 2004). In terms of Bourdieuian field theory, we could say that these ties, together with the related fact that broadcasting was organised as an institution of the state, meant that the influence of the political field on the media counterbalanced to a significant extent that of the economic field. Koller (2007) argues that Habermas (1989), in his account of the structural transformation of the public sphere, collapses what were actually two structural transformations: the first, in the nineteenth century, involving the development of large-scale mass media tied to mass forms of social organisation, and the second, taking place in the post-World War II period in Europe, involving the displacement of these organisations, which formed part of the political world, by purely commercial media.[1]

The second force, especially important in US news media (where other forces balancing the market were much weaker), but also in slightly different forms in Europe, was journalistic professionalism. Journalistic professionalism has a complex relationship with the market; indeed, it has a complex relationship with all the forces I will discuss in this chapter – the market, the state and political parties, and social movements. Its origins, particularly in the United States and Britain, are closely connected with the rise of the commercial mass press and the specialisation of the reporting function that took place in large commercial newspapers. But it did in crucial ways provide a counterweight to the market. It involved the consolidation of a relative degree of what, in Bourdieu's terms, would be called field autonomy, including a normative order, widely accepted for many decades not only by journalists but also by media owners and by the wider society, which emphasised the responsibility of journalists to wider social goals and not just to their particular employers. It was strong enough that when Herbert Gans (1979) did his classic participant observation study of American news organisations in the 1970s, he found that journalists paid little direct attention to market-based criteria in the production of news. It was institutionalised in the form of professional associations like the American Society of Newspaper Editors and, in Europe, often in strong trade unions, press councils, and sometimes legal regulations or structures protecting journalistic autonomy within the news organisation.

The extent to which professionalism existed in tension with the commercial basis of the press is clear in the kinds of conflict that have arisen as neoliberalism has challenged the autonomy of the journalistic field. A few covers from the *Columbia Journalism Review*, the main professional publication of American journalism, give a sense of the strong reaction of journalists to this challenge: 'Money lust: how pressure for profit is perverting journalism' (July–August 1998); 'Zip it: new pressures from advertisers' (September–October 1997); and 'Cracking the church–state wall ... it's not just Los Angeles' (January–February 1998). In American journalistic ideology the 'church–state wall' has a double meaning, referring to the separation required by journalistic ethics between the editorial page of the newspaper and the news columns (between journalism and politics) and between the business and editorial sides of the paper (between journalism and the market). One of the differences between neoliberalism and the liberalism of the mid-twentieth century is that mid-twentieth-century liberals celebrated professionalism precisely because, in their view, it proved that capitalism did not necessarily leave 'no other nexus between man and man than naked self-interest, than callous "cash payment"' – as Marx (1974: 70) had charged in *The Communist Manifesto*; the rise of professionalism proved that the market could coexist peacefully with other social structures, where other value systems and logics of social action prevailed. This was Talcott Parsons' (1939) view. Neoliberals do not believe, as Parsons did, in 'differentiation' and are contemptuous of the idea that professionals have responsibilities that transcend market values.

Broadcasting, meanwhile, had developed along very different lines than the press: in Europe it remained for the most part outside the world of commerce altogether, governed by varying combinations of political logics and logics of journalistic professionalism and relatively autonomous cultural production. Even in the United States, commercial broadcasting was state-regulated and based on a 'trusteeship model' which imposed public service obligations on broadcasters. Regulation combined with limited competition to mute market pressures, at least where the news divisions of the television networks were concerned (Hallin 2000a).

The balance tips toward market forces

This old order in the Western media system was undermined by a number of forces. One was the commercialisation of the media themselves. As early as the 1950s party newspapers and other forms of representative media were losing ground to the commercial press, and they for the most part died out as a significant force in the last two decades of the twentieth century. Newspaper markets, with their dramatic economies of scale, tend toward concentration, and it became increasingly difficult for party papers to compete with large 'catch-all' commercial papers which de-emphasised political commitments. In the United States party papers were already long dead by the mid-twentieth century. But from about the 1950s to the 1970s two special conditions provided newspapers with limited insulation from market pressures (Hallin 2000a). Most had achieved monopolies in their primary markets, so competitive pressures were minimal. And most were family-owned, meaning that they were not subject to the pressures of Wall Street. It was in this economic context that journalistic professionalism was consolidated in the United States, and newspapers tended to present themselves not as ordinary businesses but as institutions of democratic citizenship. Beginning in the 1970s, however, most newspapers were eventually sold to pub-licly traded companies, and as this happened expectations rose for the profit margins they would return. Readership, meanwhile, was declining, and in recent years advertising revenue has as well. By the 1990s, as the *Columbia Journalism Review* lamented, journalists were increasingly forced to defer to business managers and the market-based logic they enforced.

In broadcasting the change was even more dramatic, with European broadcasting shifting in the 1980s and 1990s from public service systems to systems dominated by commercial broadcasting, while in the United States deregulation largely removed the public service obligations which had been at the heart of the 'trusteeship' model. In both cases, moreover, television markets became vastly more competitive, and a primarily commercial internet sector developed alongside broadcasting.

Latin America, like the United States, always had primarily privately owned, commercial media, though with direct state intervention in certain countries and certain periods. Nevertheless in Latin America market forces were often overshadowed by political forces in the mid-twentieth century. Newspapers, which never had the circulations or advertising bases of their North American or European counterparts, were often dependent on subsidies from the state or were supported by wealthy elites as vehicles for political intervention. Journalists were often integrated into clientelist political networks. And more profitable broadcasting enterprises were often run by owners whose close political ties allowed them to exclude significant competition. In the 1980s and 1990s, however, there was a strong shift to what Waisbord (2000) calls 'market-powerful' media. State-run enterprises, including state-run media, were privatised, broadcast markets grew considerably and became more competitive, for-eign investment increased, politically tied newspapers often lost out to market-oriented ones, and media of all sorts were increasingly integrated into economically powerful multimedia conglomerates, often with strong transnational operations.

The political and social context

The collapse of the mid-twentieth-century media system, and its replace-ment by a media system clearly dominated by market forces, took place in the context of a broader social and political transformation in which key institutions of the political field, particularly the organised social groups that made up the political public sphere, lost their centrality to people's lives and commitments. This transformation began before the rise of neoliberal ideology in the 1980s and 1990s, and is clearly crucial to understanding the latter. It has not, however, been analysed by scholars in nearly the detail it deserves. There is no clear consensus on what to call it; Hallin and Mancini (2004) refer to it as 'secularisation'. Beck and Beck-Gernsheim (2002) refer to it as 'individualisation'. There are, however, large literatures that document parts of the process, for example the decline of political parties and other organised social groups, or, perhaps more precisely, their transformation from organisations intimately connected with the lives and identities of social groups into profession-ally run enterprises that target individual citizens as consumers within political markets (e.g. Dalton and Wattenberg 2000). An important part of the shift, and one which deeply implicated the media, was a shift from more collectivist to more individualist orientations and patterns of communication and association. Swedish researchers, for example, looking at the transformation of journalistic discourse over a period of decades, describe the dominant communication patterns in the 1950s this way:

> A typical communicative situation at this time might show a group in conversation or an audience listening to discussions, lectures and inauguration speeches. A dominating theme is belonging versus loneliness or isolation, in connection with which we find reports about unique, symbolic events: Bridges are being built for the isolated, and ice hockey halls and youth clubs are constructed for the young. Bridges conquer distance and eliminate isolation, and people gather in new halls and clubs.
>
> (Olsson 2002: 69–71)

This activity of social construction was accomplished by collective political institutions, by the state and by organised social groups co-operating with the state. The media identified themselves closely with these institutions and their process of co-operation. By the 1990s the talk show could probably be considered the quintessential forum of political communication, a form in which individual citizens express their particular opinions, and collective political institutions are generally seen as obstacles to the realisation of their ends.

Why this transformation took place remains an open question. Surely, though, one of the basic causes was the incorporation of the mass of the population in Europe and North America into an affluent consumer society and a stable welfare state, in which, for better or for worse, individuals felt they were no longer dependent on their particular group, its organisation and leadership. Koller (2007) also emphasises the importance of the Cold War, which contributed to the deactivation of the ideological and group boundaries that were central to the old political order. Later on, the shift to neoliberalism, and the constraints that shift imposed on what could be accomplished through the political realm, no doubt contributed to finishing off the more collectivist political culture of the mid-twentieth century.

The media themselves were not the prime movers of this social transformation, though they probably did contribute to it in significant ways. Mass media certainly played a role in promoting the growth of the consumer society, most obviously in the Americas, where commercial television dominated, but to a significant extent in Europe as well. And even apart from consumerism, the structure of media audiences increasingly cut across group boundaries, and media discourses were increasingly directed in the second half of the twentieth century to individuals rather than to distinct communities or organised groups. Commercial newspapers expanded their audiences across group boundaries, for example; television allowed political parties to appeal to wider publics beyond their organisationally constituted bases; and these developments helped to transform both culture and social structure.

Critical professionalism, populism and new social movements

Another way in which developments internal to the media contributed to the transformation has to do with professionalism, and here I come to the point where I want to begin to complicate the picture, to develop the argument that there is more to this social transformation than simply the shift to consumerism and eventually neoliberalism. In the 1960s and early 1970s there was an important shift in the news media toward what many analysts have called 'critical professionalism' (e.g. Djerf-Pierre 2000; Neveu 2001, 2002). Journalists who had previously deferred to party and group leaders or to state officials increasingly began to assert their independence and their right to scrutinise elites and established institutions on behalf of their readers and of 'society' or 'the public'. This trend occurred broadly across virtually all of Europe and North America, and to some extent in Latin America as well. One example would be Mexico, where journalists at the leading newspaper *Excélsior* began asserting independence (Leñero 1991; Scherer and Monsiváis 2003), were ousted by the ruling party in 1976, and went on to found what would become a new independent press sector apart from the old corporatist system (Hallin 2000c; Hughes 2006; Lawson 2002). Here is how a Swedish researcher summarises the shift there:

> The new journalism [of the period 1965–85] approached its audience in their role as citizens and aimed to provide them with knowledge and insights which were crucial to mass participation in democratic processes. Underlying the new journalist culture was a conflict perspective on society. This indicated a radical shift in perspective from the ideal of journalism as a mirror and the consensus perspective that had prevailed through the 1950s and early 1960s. One of the prime ambitions of the new journalism was to cast light on injustices and wrongdoing, to expose abuses of power and to examine the underside of society.
>
> (Djerf-Pierre 2000: 254)

The rise of media-driven scandals in this period was of course closely related to this shift (Thompson 2000).

Critical professionalism undermined the authority of the political institutions and weakened their hold on the media and on society and culture more generally. Political elites and their defenders often decried this development. Thus Samuel Huntington, in the section on the United States he prepared as part of a 'Report on the Governability of Democracies to the Trilateral Commission', wrote:

> The most notable new source of national power in 1970, as compared to 1950, was the national media.... There is ... considerable evidence to suggest that the development of television journalism contributed to the undermining of governmental authority. The advent of the half-hour news broadcast led to greatly increased popular dependence on television as a source of news. It also greatly expanded the size of the audience for news. At the same time, the themes which were stressed, the focus on controversy and violence, and, conceivably, the values and outlook of the journalists, tended to arouse unfavorable attitudes toward established institutions and to promote a decline of confidence in government.
>
> (Crozier *et al.* 1975: 98–9)

Huntington exaggerated the extent of the change, ignored the highly deferential baseline from which it began, and obscured the wider social and political context in which it took place – the Vietnam War, the abuses of power revealed in Watergate, etc. But the change he was referring to was very real in many ways.

The rise of critical professionalism in journalism can be understood in part as a development internal to the media, a result of the increasing scale of news organisations and the expansion of the size and social role of the press corps. But it was also closely connected to another important set of social changes that took place parallel to the rise of consumerist individualism: this was the cultural and political rebellion of the 1960s and 1970s, the 'rights revolution', as Schudson (1998) terms it, and the rise of new social movements. These social movements – probably we have to include among them not only the left-wing movements we traditionally associate with this period but also the right-wing populist movements that began to develop, usually a bit later, including the evangelical Christian political movement in the United States – clearly played a very important role in undermining the political institutions that dominated the old order in post-World War II Western society. They relied to a significant extent on an increasingly powerful, autonomous and in some ways 'individualised' media to compete with more established political institutions for access to the public sphere. Critical professionalism was also related to the well documented, though perhaps not fully explained, shift toward what Ingelhart (1971) called 'post-materialist' values (Ingelhart 1990; Abramson and Ingelhart 1995).

Journalistic professionalism contributed to and was also influenced by the rise of new social movements and the populist, 'post-industrialist' political culture. It had a complex relationship with those movements, however, just as it did in other ways with the market and with political authority.

Professionals are authorities; they are part of the structure of power. Journalistic professionals certainly were seen this way by the mass public. Eventually, populist anger at established authorities turned on journalists, undermined their claim to speak for the public, and in a way facilitated the neoliberal attack on the journalists' claim to serve values apart from those of the market. It is also worth adding that, if the 'rise of the media' undermined political authority, the multiplication of media channels also played a significant role in undermining the authority of the professional journalist, as blogs and talk shows produced competing claims to represent the voice of the people and brought the journalists' control over channels of communication into question.

For these and other reasons critical professionalism eventually went into decline. As we saw above, the Golden Age of journalistic autonomy in the post-World War II period in the context of which critical professionalism developed was made possible by particular structural conditions; the media, it could be said, were left isolated or suspended between the two structures that control power and resources in society, the political system and the market. This produced an unusual loosening of constraints and a vacuum of power which the professional journalist was able to fill for a while; but it is not surprising that this situation proved transitory. The activism and independence of 1970s critical professionalism have clearly declined, though it would not be correct to say that the changes of that era were simply erased. To return to the Swedish example and bring it full circle, Djerf-Pierre (2000: 255) describes a journalist culture in the 1990s, following the introduction of commercial television, that combines an 'activist approach towards the dominant institutions and a conformist approach towards the audience ... '

Media, neoliberalism and the democratic public sphere

This brings me to my final set of arguments, about how to understand neoliberalism in relation to the rise of new social movements, populism and the democratic role of the media. It is important to note, first of all, that the rise of neoliberalism was not a separate or entirely opposed development from the growth of populist anti-elitism and of new social movements. These historical forces interacted with one another, and to some extent were mutually reinforcing. Horwitz (1989) has pointed out, for example, that deregulation in the United States, including telecom deregulation, was pushed forward in the 1970s by a coalition of neoliberal activists seeking to roll back state regulation and social activists challenging the 'capture' of regulatory agencies by powerful interests, including media corporations. Lee (2007), meanwhile, shows that, in the field of medical care, a significant shift toward marketplace logic was promoted, in part, by activist groups critical of medical patriarchy. Thus the landmark book *Our Bodies Our Selves* used the language of consumerism to argue for the right of women to confront the physician not in the infantilised status of patient but in the adult status of consumer, and to insist on the right to make decisions about their own health care. As Cohen (2004) and García Canclini (2001) argue, in different contexts, consumerism and citizen activism have never been simply polar opposites, but have often merged with one another.

One way to understand the process of social change in the second half of the twentieth century might be to say that there was a period, as the old political order was breaking down, when divergent possibilities for social change emerged, when we could have gone in the direction of consumerist individualism or of activist citizenship, of market-dominated media or of media serving a more thoroughly democratic public, and that in the end, with the triumph of neoliberalism, the power of capital and of consumerist culture suppressed the possibilities for democratic change. Certainly there is much truth to that view. Neoliberalism was in part a very deliberate effort on the part of economic elites to turn back challenges to their power represented by the new social movements – and by related phenomena like the rise of activist journalism. The very fact that new social movements had to resort to the language of consumer rights to challenge hierarchies of power could be said to reflect the already growing hegemony of consumer culture as they emerged. (It is probably no accident that the strongest examples of the intertwining of citizen activism and consumerism come from the US case.) Neoliberalism, moreover, has been very effective in creating political ideologies that can co-opt and incorporate rhetorics of empowerment and liberation and popular critiques of authority into legitimations of the market. In the media sphere it is clear that market logic has become increasingly dominant and also that management has in many cases reasserted authority ceded to journalists in earlier decades.

Yet I am not convinced by the common narrative that sees a unilinear decline in the state of democracy, and of the democratic role of the media, in the era of neoliberalism. Wendy Brown, for example, in a provocative essay titled 'Neoliberalism and the end of liberal democracy' (2003), argues that neoliberalism should be seen not merely as an economic policy, but as a transformation of the state and the public sphere, and that it has produced an 'unprecedented degree of passivity and political complacency' (para. 1047). Brown's argument implies an historical shift from some period when liberal democracy was healthier compared with today's 'unprecedented' decline. But when would this have been, in the United States, on which she focuses? Presumably not the 1950s. Was it in 1963–65, the years Kennedy and Johnson took the United States to war in Vietnam with no substantial debate? Was it in 1968–72, when Richard Nixon was at the height of his power? Maybe it was in about 1973–74, when he fell – this is plausible, and as far as the media are concerned, this was the height of critical professionalism, and new social movements were certainly active. But this is a pretty short Golden Age. Maybe it was the 1930s – but then it wouldn't be neoliberalism that caused the decline, it would be war and empire. Anyway, the media were hardly a model of democracy in the United States in 1930s; many of the same issues of political intervention by media owners, for example, that are beginning to re-emerge with the decline of professionalisation, were very much alive in that era.

Consider the case of the Iraq war. I have been surprised to hear many colleagues expressing nostalgia for the Vietnam era, saying, 'Why can't the media today be critical and aggressive the way they were during Vietnam?' There's no doubt that after September 11 the American media shifted toward a deferential stance reminiscent of the early 1960s – though never, in truth, quite as extreme. Neoliberalism may have something to do with this, in the sense, for example, that it has made journalists more conformist in relation to their bosses and to market forces, though the constriction of democracy in this period really has more to do with the ascendancy of neoconservatism, a rather different ideological current.[2] But the path the American media and public opinion have followed in the case of the Iraq war is really not very different from the path they followed in Vietnam (Hallin 1986); support for US policy in Iraq has declined at least as rapidly – or as slowly, depending on one's point of view – as it did in the case of Vietnam. The increased centrality of market forces in the American media no doubt had something to do, for example, with CNN's instructions to its personnel, during the Afghan war, to de-emphasise civilian casualties; its principal competitor, Fox, was using patriotism as a marketing vehicle. But market forces probably also had something to do with the strong emphasis on the human costs of the war later on; contemporary news culture – a joint product, I would argue, of the growth of market forces and the influence of the cultural and political anti-elitism of the 1960s to 1980s – easily lends itself to heavy dramatisation of dead and wounded American troops and their families. (The actual American casualty rate is much lower in Iraq than it was in Vietnam.)

If we turn to Latin America, it is even more clear that we cannot simply assume that the rise of neoliberalism means the decline of liberal democracy. The shift to neoliberalism has been quite dramatic in Latin America, where state-centred 'import substitution industrialisation' was the prevailing economic policy through the early 1980s. Neoliberalism was in a sense first put into practice in Chile, during the Pinochet dictatorship. But the dictatorships that prevailed across most of the continent in the 1970s collapsed, and liberal democracy, for all its limitations – some of them certainly imposed by neoliberalism – is obviously much stronger there than it was a generation ago: not only have competitive electoral systems emerged or re-emerged but social movements, for example among indigenous populations, have proliferated and often gained unprecedented influence, and elites have lost much of the immunity they once had from public scrutiny.

The media field in Latin America is increasingly dominated, as Waisbord puts it, by 'market-powerful' media.

> Fueled by technological innovations and laissez-faire legislation, major media companies sought horizontal and vertical expansion. There has been a decline in the number of newspapers and readers. Yet the expansion of the television audience, privatization of broadcasting stations, and the explosion of cable and satellite television, have made the media industry highly dynamic and extremely profitable for powerful conglomerates. The politics of economic stabilization also benefited large media companies as advertising revenues have increased while inflation is under control and there is economic growth.
>
> (Waisbord 2000: 71–2)

What is the effect of intensified market forces on the democratic role of the media? It is clearly complex. In important ways, market forces have contributed toward more independent media, less prone to control by the state or to instrumentalisation by particular political interests, more open in the coverage of both electoral politics and competing social interests, more professionalised and more oriented toward serving readers and viewers, rather than particular narrow interests. More independent media have in many cases outcompeted 'officialist' media aligned with the old regime, competition has forced the abandonment of propagandistic reporting styles and the adoption of populist political stances, and market power has, in certain cases, emboldened media to crusade for political change (e.g. Brazil's *Folha de São Paolo* in the mid-1980s) or to engage in investigative reporting, which has become increasingly common across the continent (Waisbord 2000; Lawson 2002; Hughes 2006; Porto 2003; Matos 2008). Market forces alone, however, would never have brought about democratic change in Latin American media. In many cases, for example, the pioneers of change were not large commercial media but more marginal news organisations driven as much by journalistic or political idealism as by market forces (*La Época* in Chile, *Pagina/12* in Argentina, *Proceso* in Mexico). And neoliberal restructuring of Latin American media can clearly have strongly negative effects for democracy as well, producing, for example, extreme levels of sensationalism in television news (Hallin 2000b) – a familiar phenomenon in much of the world – or concentrations of media power that make the media themselves a threat to democracy. The ability of Mexico's broadcasters, including the television giant Televisa, to block an initiative by legislators and citizen groups to write a new media law and rewrite it to serve their particular interests is a clear example.

Conclusion

Over the past few decades a dramatic change has clearly taken place in the structure and social role of the media. This change involves, very centrally, a shift in the balance of power between political institutions and the market, an increased dominance of market forces within the media and to some extent increased power of the media themselves, now firmly rooted in the market, relative to social institutions that once controlled or influenced them. The enclosure of the media by market forces is a troubling development, as many have argued (e.g. Croteau and Hoynes 2001; Herman and McChesney 1997; Franklin 1997). Market forces do not guarantee that the media will serve their non-economic function as institutions of the democratic public sphere, and in many ways the breakdown of the forces that counterbalanced market forces has already taken its toll on the quality of democratic media, producing lowered investment in the production of news, sensationalism and other ethical problems, biases in the segments of society served by the media, and in some cases potentially dangerous concentrations of media power. Certainly media policy needs to be centrally focused on mechanisms that might prevent the media from being absorbed more fully still into market mechanisms.

Commercialisation, however, is not the only process of social change that has shaped the contemporary media, nor is it entirely simple or consistent in its effects. The media culture that prevails today is a contradictory joint product of several currents – growing commercialisation, yes, but also important legacies of the shift toward critical professionalism in journalism and toward a more populist political culture where social movements and ordinary citizens demand and often get a public hearing. Many of the specific changes that have taken place and the specific genres or practices that have emerged are quite complex in their implications for democracy. One example would be the increased personalisation of public communication, the focus of media on 'private' life and on individual experience. This can be seen in some ways as a depoliticisation of public communication, and hence a shrinking away of the public sphere which increases the power of elites by leaving important areas of social life outside the arena of public debate. This is far from a consistent pattern, however, and in other ways the erosion of established boundaries between 'public' and 'private' (and between information and entertainment)[3] represents an opening to actors previously excluded from the institutionalised public sphere (see e.g. Leurdijk 1997) and a politicisation of areas of social life not previously subject to political contestation, from the experience of individual soldiers and their families to the field of medical care (Briggs and Hallin 2007).

The process of change that has led us to where we are today is a complex process. If we are to understand it, we need to avoid dichotomous understandings in which the forces discussed here – the market, new social movements, individualisation and secularisation, professionalism – are placed neatly into the camps of good and evil. The market is not consistently pro- or anti-democracy; neither is journalistic professionalism; neither are social movements or the political culture of populism: they are all deeply ambivalent in their relation to democracy, in part because of the ways they have mutually shaped one another. We also need to avoid the trap of assuming that a critical analysis needs to posit a Golden Age and then to analyse social change as a unilinear decline from that Golden Age – a view, in other words, that stands old-fashioned modernisation theory on its head. The position of the media in structures of power and political participation has been restructured; how that restructuring has affected the democratic public sphere is clearly open to debate, and a sophisticated answer to the question is likely to be fairly complex, with somewhat different answers for different aspects of social and political life, different kinds of conjuncture and different regions.

Notes

1 Koller argues that the United States went through the second structural transformation earlier, near the beginning of the twentieth century. His analysis of the two structural transformations, however, is more persuasive for continental Europe than for the United States, or indeed, to some extent, for all the systems Hallin and Mancini (2004) term Liberal systems. US media were indeed partisan in the nineteenth century, but market forces were always very strong after the 1830s, and the media were never integrated into a political field of organized social groups the way they were in continental Europe.
2 The one aspect of the neoliberal state that probably has the greatest impact on public activism in wartime is the 'volunteer' – or market-based – army. It is hard to imagine the Iraq war being fought with drafted military forces, given the changes in American political culture that occurred in the later part of the Vietnam War. If indeed elites could not fight a war with draftees today as they did in the 1960s, of course, this reinforces the point that the rise of neoliberalism is only one of several social changes that have affected contemporary democracy.
3 Some important interventions in the debate about the political implications of 'infotainment' include Sparks and Tulloch (2000), Brants (1998) and Baum (2003).

Bibliography

Abramson, Paul R. and Ingelhart, Ronald (1995) *Value Change in Global Perspective*. Ann Arbor MI: University of Michigan Press.
Baum, Matthew (2003) *Soft News goes to War: Public Opinion and American Foreign Policy in the New Media Age*. Princeton NJ: Princeton University Press.
Beck, Ulrich and Beck-Gernsheim, Elisabeth (2002) *Individualization: Institutionalized Individualism and its Social and Political Consequences*. Thousand Oaks CA: Sage.
Brants, Kees (1998) 'Who's afraid of infotainment?' *European Journal of Communication* 13: 315–35.

Briggs, Charles and Hallin, Daniel C. (2007) 'Health Reporting as Political Reporting: Biocommunicability and the Public Sphere', paper prepared for presentation at the annual meeting of the International Communication Association, San Francisco, 24–8 May.

Brown, Wendy (2003) 'Neo-liberalism and the end of liberal democracy', *Theory and Event* 7: 1.

Cohen, Lizabeth (2004) *A Consumers' Republic: the Politics of Consumption in Postwar America*. New York: Vintage.

Croteau, David and Hoynes, William (2001) *The Business of Media: Corporate Media and the Public Interest*. Thousand Oaks CA: Pine Forge Press.

Crozier, Michel J., Huntington, Samuel P. and Watanuki, Joji (1975) *The Crisis of Democracy*. New York: New York University Press.

Dalton, Russell J. and Wattenberg, Martin P. (2000). *Parties without Partisans: Political Change in Advanced Industrial Democracies*. New York: Oxford University Press.

Djerf-Pierre, Monika (2000) 'Squaring the circle: public service and commercial news on Swedish television, 1956–1999', *Journalism Studies* 1 (2): 239–60.

Franklin, Bob (1997) *Newzak and News Media*. London: Arnold.

Gans, Herbert (1979) *Deciding What's News: a Study of* CBS Evening News, NBC Nightly News, Newsweek *and* Time. New York: Pantheon.

García Canclini, Néstor (2001) *Consumers and Citizens: Globalization and Multicultural Conflicts*. Minneapolis MN: University of Minnesota Press.

Habermas, Jürgen (1989) *The Structural Transformation of the Public Sphere: an Inquiry into a Category of Bourgeois Society*. Cambridge MA: MIT Press.

Hallin, Daniel C. (1986) *The 'Uncensored War': the Media and Vietnam*. New York: Oxford University Press.

Hallin, Daniel C. (2000a) 'Commercialism and professionalism in the American news media', in J. Curran and M. Gurevitch (eds) *Mass Media and Society*. London: Arnold.

Hallin, Daniel C. (2000b) '*La nota roja*: popular journalism and the transition to democracy in Mexico', in Colin Sparks and John Tulloch (eds) *Tabloid Tales*. Lanham, MD: Rowman & Littlefield.

Hallin, Daniel C. (2000c) 'Media, political power and democratization in Mexico', in James Curran and Myung-Jin Park (eds) *De-Westernizing Media Studies*. London: Routledge.

Hallin, Daniel C. and Paolo Mancini (2004) *Comparing Media Systems: Three Models of Media and Politics*. Cambridge: Cambridge University Press.

Harvey, David (2005) *A Brief History of Neoliberalism*. New York: Oxford University Press.

Herman, Edward and McChesney, Robert (1997) *The Global Media: the New Missionaries of Corporate Capitalism*. London: Cassell.

Horwitz, Robert Britt (1989) *The Irony of Regulatory Reform: the Deregulation of American Telecommunications*. New York: Oxford University Press.

Hughes, Sally (2006) *Newsrooms in Conflict: Journalism and the Democratization of Mexico*. Pittsburgh PA: University of Pittsburgh Press.

Ingelhart, Ronald (1971) 'The silent revolution in Europe: intergenerational change in post-industrial societies', *American Political Science Review* 65: 991–1017.

Ingelhart, Ronald (1990) *Culture Shift in Advanced Industrial Society*. Princeton NJ: Princeton University Press.

Koller, Andreas (2007) 'The Second Structural Transformation of the Public Sphere'; paper presented at the annual meeting of the International Communication Association, San Francisco, 24–8 May.

Lawson, Chappell H. (2002) *Building the Fourth Estate: Democratization and the Rise of a Free Press in Mexico*. Berkeley CA: University of California Press.

Lee, Nancy (2007) 'Curing Consumers: How the Patient became a Consumer in Modern American Medicine', Ph.D. dissertation, University of California, San Diego.

Leñero, Vicente (1991) *Los periodistas*. México: Joaquín Mortiz.

Leurdijk, Ardra (1997) 'Common sense versus political discourse: debating racism and multicultural society in Dutch talk shows', *European Journal of Communication* 12 (2): 147–68.

Marx, Karl (1974) *The Revolutions of 1948: Political Writings* I, ed. David Fernbach. New York: Vintage.

Matos, Carolina (2008) 'Journalism and political democracy in Brazil', Lanham, MD: Lexington Books.

Neveu, Erik (2001) *Sociologie du journalisme*. Paris: La Découverte.

Neveu, Erik (2002) 'The four generations of political journalism', in R. Kuhn and E. Neveu (eds) *Political Journalism: New Challenges, New Practices*. London: Routledge.

Olsson, Tom (2002) 'The right to talk politics in Swedish journalism, 1925–1995', in M. Hurd, T. Olsson and P. Åker (eds) *Storylines: Media, Power and Identity in Modern Europe. Festschrift for Jan Ekecrantz*. Stockholm: Hjalmarson & Högberg.

Parsons, Talcott (1939) 'The professions and social structure', *Social Forces* 17 (4): 457–67.

Porto, Mauro P. (2003) 'Mass media and politics in democratic Brazil', in Maria D'Alva Kinzo and James Dunkerley (eds) *Brazil since 1985: Economy, Polity and Society*. London: ILAS.

Rose, Nikolas (1996) 'Governing "advanced" liberal democracies', in A. Barry, T. Osborne and N. Rose (eds) *Foucault and Political Reason: Liberalism, Neoliberalism and Rationalities of Government*. Chicago: University of Chicago Press.

Scherer García, Julio and Monsiváis, Carlos (2003) *Tempo de saber: presnsa y poder en México*. México: Aguilar.

Schudson, Michael (1998) *The Good Citizen: a History of American Civic Life*. Cambridge MA: Harvard University Press.

Sparks, Colin and Tulloch, John (eds) (2000) *Tabloid Tales*. Lanham, MD: Rowman & Littlefield.

Thompson, John B. (2000) *Political Scandal: Power and Visibility in the Media Age*. Cambridge: Polity Press.

Waisbord, Silvio (2000) *Watchdog Journalism in South America: News, Accountability and Democracy*. New York: Columbia University Press.

4 Recognition and the renewal of ideology critique

John Downey

John Corner's obituary for the concept of ideology in which he argues that we should not mourn its passing too much and begin to move on is premature (2001: 525–33).[1] At the risk of appearing melancholic, I argue that the revival of the concept is of importance (no less) for the future of emancipation in general and the future of media studies as a politically engaged, critical field of study. The striking absence of the concept in current media studies, in contrast to its ubiquity in the 1970s and 1980s, is symptomatic both of the disturbingly widespread assumption of the theoretical and political exhaustion of the Enlightenment project and of the deeply unfortunate narrowness of media studies at the present time (itself a consequence of the otherwise desirable drive towards professionalisation of the field). There are, however, no compelling reasons for either to be the case. Indeed, the reverse is true. Persistent and indeed widening economic, social and political inequalities locally and globally mean that it is ethically imperative to breathe new critical life into media studies as media institutions are not only part of an economic system that prevents human flourishing, but also often present such a state of affairs as either inevitable or, indeed, desirable. The disheartening political situation should not sanction a turning away from critical intellectual engagement. There are, moreover, intellectual resources available for this enterprise that have been left untouched by media studies scholars.

The decline in the concept of ideology, Corner agrees, is indicative of a broader decline in the fortunes of Western Marxism but the fall is also due, he contends, to internal problems in the way that the concept has developed. This is evident in three attempts to revive a concept of ideology in the 1990s – those of John B. Thompson, Terry Eagleton and Teun van Dijk (Thompson 1990; Eagleton 1991; van Dijk 1998). While Corner's critiques of Eagleton and van Dijk are sound (and will not be discussed here), he fails to do justice to Thompson, who is much the hardest target of the three to hit. Thompson's work has been largely overlooked in media studies and this has less to do with internal problems of the concept developed (although there are some) than with an unwarranted disconnection between media studies and younger generations of critical theorists working within or influenced by the Frankfurt school tradition, such as Axel Honneth and Nancy Fraser, that may be referred to as the third generation of Critical Theory. (One could also argue that there is a broader disconnection between media studies and a good deal of both classical and contemporary social theory and sociology.) While media studies for a time drew heavily, if very crudely, upon the work of the first generation of the Frankfurt school, who were the fall guys for cultural populism, one could be forgiven for thinking that, with a few laudable exceptions, its acquaintance with second and subsequent generations begins and ends with Habermas's early work on the public sphere (Habermas 1989). Not all the blame for this disconnection should, however, be laid at the door of media studies. Within Critical Theory there has also been a turn away from media and cultural critique towards legal and moral philosophy, political theory, and commentary on the work of Critical Theorists themselves. What is required is a renewal of the acquaintance between media studies and the Frankfurt school. While Thompson's concept of ideology is itself in need of some repair work, it does mark a conceptual step forward for ideology critique that should be more widely taken up in empirical research and is thus a good place from which to begin to renew the acquaintance.

Corner's major problem with Thompson, it seems, is that Thompson simply reiterates, without perhaps realising that he is doing so, much of the established literature in media studies (for example, on the problem of 'reading off' audience responses to media texts) and so, far from being new, Thompson does not have much to tell media studies. It is true that Thompson does not appear to be as well versed in the media studies literature as he might be (an irritating blindness shared by other social theorists – for instance, Manuel Castells and Pierre Bourdieu). The value of Thompson's work, however, lies in a lucid and, in particular, a systematic development of theory rather than in original applications of the concept. (One might argue, however, that this represents a reasonable division of academic labour between social theory and media analysis.) Corner reaches this 'not much new' judgement because he fails to unpack sufficiently his acknowledgment that Thompson's typology of ideological devices 'has suggestive force for all thinking on this topic' (2001: 528).

Corner does not mention internal problems within Thompson's concept. While there are some, primarily the 'problem' lies in that his concept has rarely been picked up and applied. This has to do with internal problems within media studies as well as a broader exhaustion of Western Marxism. The internal problems of media studies may be conceived in terms of its narrowness that may be related to the growth of media studies *qua* discipline (for example, lack of engagement with both classical and contemporary social theory) and to much more deep-seated uncertainties and confusions concerning questions of ethics, epistemology, and political praxis. In the following I will first outline what I take to be Thompson's modest, but none the less significant, conceptual advance and will then discuss three problem areas with his work and suggest how they might be repaired under the headings: ethics, explanation and political praxis. To repair Thompson I will draw on the work of Axel Honneth and Nancy Fraser.

Thompson's advance

Thompson is unusual in current sociology in that he defends a pejorative concept of ideology. To study ideology is 'to study the ways in which meaning serves to establish and sustain relations of domination' (1990: 56). Thompson is thus making ethical and epistemological claims. Domination is 'bad', symbolic forms that serve to establish or sustain domination are 'bad'. We can also, according to Thompson, identify the operations of ideology and how they relate to relations of domination, i.e. we can say something true about the social world. Although Thompson wishes to reduce the 'epistemological burden' of ideology critique it is difficult to see clearly that he is successful in the endeavour (1990: 56). For example, consider the concept of reification that means the presentation of a mutable thing as a fixed thing. In order to recognise reification we need first to be able to recognise the mutable thing. The use of a pejorative concept of ideology demands robust theories of truth and of the good which serve to underpin critique.

The tendency in the humanities and social sciences to shy away from such ethical and epistemological claims goes a long way towards explaining the demise of the concept. Any pejorative concept of ideology has to substantiate these ethical and epistemological claims. I will put these to one side for the moment in order to outline Thompson's conceptual advance that concerns the systematic way in which he categorises different modes of operation of ideology.

These general modes and strategies are not, it should be noted, ideological in themselves. As a mode of thinking 'legitimation' may or may not be ideological. It becomes ideological when an attempt is made to legitimate domination (Table 4.1). Now there is nothing new or even unexpected about the presence of these strategies. They are commonly commented upon in a variety of works in semiotics, linguistics, discourse analysis, critical discourse analysis and so on. They belong to a standard conceptual toolkit. They are the bread-and-butter of media analysis that has, however, become disconnected from broader ethical, explanatory and political concerns.

What is new in Thompson's work is showing how these different strategies fit together and may be systematically related to a critical concept of ideology. It is not particularly difficult to apply these concepts. The fact that Thompson's concept has not been taken up and developed through empirical work, through ideology critique *per se*, then has nothing to do with this aspect of his work. It must lie in that either his work has

Table 4.1 Thompson's modes of operation of ideology (1990: 60)

General modes	Some typical strategies of symbolic construction
Legitimation	Rationalisation
	Universalisation
	Narrativisation
Dissimulation	Displacement
	Euphemisation
	Trope
Unification	Standardisation
	Symbolisation of unity
Fragmentation	Differentiation
	Expurgation of the other
Reification	Naturalisation
	Eternalisation
	Nominalisation/passivisation

not been read and/or it has not found resonance because the ethical and epistemological claims that he must make are at present intellectually unpalatable. What is needed is: first, the reconnection of the vocabulary of analysis to the idea of a 'good life'; and, second, the reconnection of symbolic analysis to an analysis of the economic and political practices that they help to reproduce.

Ethics: from participation to recognition

The justification for critique goes to the heart of the contemporary problems of critical social science. Why is domination 'bad'? Without an idea of a better place or the 'good life' the notion of critique becomes nonsensical. While Thompson criticises Habermas's premature jettisoning of the concept of ideology and claims to be going back to Marx's notion of domination in his reworking of the concept of ideology, the justification for critique that Thompson posits is *implicitly* based on Habermas's discourse ethics. Thompson does not give reasons for why domination is 'bad' (and this is a problematic absence) but we can work this out if we consider the way in which Thompson writes about how interpretations may be justified:

> In supposing that an interpretation is justifiable, we presuppose that it could *not* be justified by being *imposed*. We presuppose, in other words, that there is a distinction between justifying an interpretation and imposing it on others, or having it imposed on ourselves. To justify is to provide reasons, grounds, evidence, elucidation; to impose is to assert or reassert, to force others to accept, to silence questioning or dissent. To justify is to treat the other as an individual capable of being convinced; to impose is to treat the other as an individual who must

be subjected. This distinction suggests that an interpretation would be justified only if it could be justified without being imposed, that is, only if it could be justified under conditions which included the suspension of asymmetrical relations of power. I shall call this *the principle of non-imposition*.

(1990: 321)

Thompson goes on to outline other principles that hang together with non-imposition (such as self-reflection and non-exclusion).

It should be clear that this is close to, if not exactly the same as, Habermas's account of the universal presuppositions of language. To enter into debate is to presuppose the possibility of justification that entails recognising individuals as equal participants in the dialogue and with equal power to determine the outcome of the dialogue. The critique of domination is thus ultimately grounded in the character of language.

This neo-Kantian discourse ethics is one possible way of seeking to justify ideology critique. In certain respects it is very similar to Nancy Fraser's Habermasian justification of 'participatory parity'. It is undoubtedly true that a dissatisfaction with this attempt to ground critique helps to explain the decline in fortunes of Critical Theory as an intellectual enterprise.

Dissatisfaction with this neo-Kantian approach is also discernible, however, within the third generation of Critical Theory and is most clearly articulated in the work of Axel Honneth (although there is a tendency within Anglo-American social theory to see Honneth as a follower of Habermas). Honneth moves away from an attempt to justify critique through reference to a discourse ethics and towards a justification of critique based upon a reworked Hegelian concept of recognition. This is both an important new avenue of enquiry for Critical Theory as a whole and also for the notion of ideology critique as this allows us to reconceptualise such critique.[2]

Honneth, drawing on the early work of Hegel, argues that recognition is essential for individual self-realisation, for human flourishing. Individuals recognise themselves as subjects by being recognised by others as subjects:

> The individual learns to grasp his or her self as both a full and a particular member of a social community by being gradually assured of the specific abilities and needs constituting his or her personality through the approving patterns of reaction by generalized interaction partners.

(2004a: 354)

The I is a social I that flourishes through being recognised by others. Mutual recognition, where individuals recognise each other as full and equal participants, is the condition that permits human flourishing to its greatest extent. While the starting point for Honneth is Hegel's speculative account of recognition in his Jena work before *Philosophy of Spirit*, he seeks to develop the notion of recognition through the work of Mead on socialisation and refers to psychoanalytical currents of thought on identity formation and the intersubjective turn that again are rarely referred to in the copious media studies literature that is influenced by psychoanalysis (Honneth 1995; Benjamin 1990, 1995; Winnicott 1965). There are also potentially here a number of interesting links via Mead between the third generation of Critical Theory and the pragmatist tradition in the United States that has recently seen a considerable intellectual revival.

If recognition is essential for human flourishing (Honneth refers to this as a 'quasi-transcendental interest' in recognition) then the moral course of action is to attempt to extend the conditions of recognition to all and this necessarily involves critique of modes of thinking that misrecognise. As well as ideology critique, then, recognition may help to furnish criteria of judging political action: if such-and-such happens, will it bring about circumstances of greater recognition or not?

According to Honneth there are three principles of recognition in modern societies that should form the basis of a plural theory of justice: those of love, equality and merit. Societies are to be judged according to how well they perform with reference to these criteria. Indeed, social struggles and social actions are to be judged according to whether they seek to advance or obstruct relationships of recognition in these domains.

After justifying the notion of critique, the task of Critical Theory is to explain the trajectory of societies: why is recognition advancing or retreating? The specific task of ideology critique in this project is to show how and why misrecognition occurs and how it is produced and reproduced materially through institutional and everyday practices.

Honneth, drawing on Habermas, argues that it is only in the sphere of modern law that clear progress has been made in terms of recognition via the principle of equality (universal suffrage, for example). That is not to say that Honneth sees this process as being complete or irreversible (for example, the continued discrimination against homosexuals, the greater restrictions placed upon migrants and asylum seekers, rolling back the 'welfare' state in an era of rapid globalisation and socio-technical change).

In contrast, very little progress has been made in terms of self-esteem and the recognition of merit. Honneth argues that the notions of merit and achievement have been largely colonised by a capitalist value or status system. This is true both in the fields of production and consumption. Some certain forms of work (for example, work that concerns the caring for or nurturing of others which one could claim is fundamental to establishing the conditions for recognition and human flourishing) are systematically devalued. 'Merit' is related to profit rather than to the broader social consequences of work either for the producers (their misrecognition at work as mere instruments of the production process rather than as equal participants) or for those affected by production (for example, those affected by the ecological consequences of production). Status in consumption is related either to quantity or perceived quality of that consumed (hence brands and their symbolic importance for establishing and sustaining relations of inequality) rather than the consequences of consumption for other citizens, for producers and for those affected by consumption. In late capitalist societies, then, ideology critique means a critique of the capitalist status order as well as of national, racial and gender status orders. From the standpoint of an ethics of recognition that emphasises the conditions that must be met in order to permit human flourishing, the development of these status orders appears to be pathological serving to legitimate economic and political inequality within and between societies.

Ideology critique thus has a central role both in the critique of current status orders and in the construction of rivals based upon principles of recognition. The implications of Honneth's work is that the capitalist status order needs to be replaced by a status order based on merit, i.e. on the contribution that individuals make to human well-being rather than say a notion of merit based on an individual's performance in a capitalist market. The idea of meritocracy that is widely embraced by politicians of the centre left and right in contemporary polities is one that is a prime candidate for ideology critique. 'Merit' here often means the equal opportunity to be successful in the capitalist market place, which is naturalised as a measurement of merit. (This understanding of misrecognition in terms of unjustified status inequality should remind us of the potential importance of Max Weber's work for media and cultural analysis, a point made by Fraser 2004: 377. Weber again is a major sociological figure whose work presents a largely untapped source for media studies.)

Now while Fraser, Thompson and Honneth may be divided over whether it is best to attempt to justify critique in a neo-Kantian or a neo-Hegelian way, in shallower philosophical waters they agree about the importance of recognition and the critique of status orders. The sort of society they wish to achieve is very similar – based upon equal participation, the absence of imposition, inclusion – their disagreement is about how this is best justified. In one sense, one must decide about which side of the argument is more compelling, but in another the implications of the disagreement for the actual conduct of ideology critique are minor as long as one accepts the arguments of one side or the other. A Fraser supporter and a Honneth supporter locked in a room with a copy of the *Financial Times* would produce, I suspect, a similar ideology critique. Before we dump the concept of ideology we should at least convince ourselves that neither of these options satisfies us. I do not see this debate occurring in media studies or indeed see many references to the fact that a debate is occurring in political philosophy.

If we take recognition rather than domination to be foundational we can reformulate the meaning of the study of ideology:

> To study ideology is to understand and explain the ways in which misrecognition (*Missachtung*) occurs and how this is related to the operation of economic and/or political power.

Here misrecognition refers both to the presentation of unwarranted superiority as well as to unwarranted subordination. They are the recto and verso of ideology.

In his recent work on developing a plural conception of justice it has become increasingly evident to Honneth that he needs to account for misrecognition in institutional contexts:

> What I can see is that I was not always aware enough of the fact of institutional forms of recognition, ideological forms of recognition. This for me is a difficult problem which I still have to resolve ... what I have to do is to preserve the conceptual means to make a distinction between these false forms of recognition which are definitely there and forms of justified recognition, in that sense correct recognition.
>
> (2004b: 388)

Earlier I referred to a reasonable academic division of labour. If we must rely on Honneth to regenerate Critical Theory via a reading of the young Hegel and help us see the ethical importance of distinguishing between recognition and misrecognition, then it is surely reasonable for media studies scholars to help Honneth out through providing accounts of how and why misrecognition occurs in our limited field of analysis.

At this point we can usefully reintroduce Thompson's work on the modes of operation of ideology and strategies of symbolic construction to help Honneth resolve this problem and provide a link between Honneth's recasting of critical theory and the practice of ideology critique in the field of media studies. We can, without much ado, bolt Thompson's modest conceptual advance on to Honneth's theory of recognition. The problem is less a theoretical one than one of actually simply doing the analysis.

Explanation: from interests to understanding social pathologies

That is not to argue, however, that all is resolved by adding Thompson to Honneth. Thompson suffers from a lack of engagement with the psychological. Thompson in his reconstruction of the concept of ideology goes back to Marx of the time of the *Preface to a Critique of Political Economy* that he sees as the beginning of a more systematic discussion of ideology in his work. Ideology is, for Marx, a way of expressing and sustaining class interests. Now Thompson wishes to amend this in two ways that are relatively uncontentious today. The first way is to argue that class domination is not the only form of domination in contemporary society and, therefore, ideology critique should be extended to cover a greater range (gender, 'race', nation, sexuality and so on). The second is to question the base–superstructure metaphor and see the symbolic as 'constitutive of social reality' rather than as an appendage (1990: 58). The problem comes in the area where Thompson does *not* amend Marx in that ideologies are still seen as representing the 'interests' of a dominant class, sex or 'race'.

Thus Thomson devotes all of his energy to understanding how ideologies are produced and reproduced symbolically and institutionally, while the explanation for why there are ideologies is assumed. What is present here, black-box, is the *de facto* naturalisation of a will to power or a will to dominate, a Hobbesian war of all against all. If we work with this simplistic model of human actors, we not only fail to explain the existence of ideology but also are doomed to fail to account for the desire to live in an egalitarian world. The opposition to ideology could only be an attempt to assert another ideology by a new group of actors. What is needed, therefore, as well as an understanding of how ideology operates, is an explanation of why ideology operates – why, to use Honneth's expression, social pathologies occur – that admits the complexity of human actors. The Marx of the *Preface* does not help us in this respect. The notion that ideologies reflect interests brings explanation to an unjustifiably abrupt end. 'Interests' here are a *deus ex machina*. Why does misrecognition occur? Why is there a desire to dominate? Why is there also a desire to justify one's domination to both the dominators and the dominated? Thompson's account of the how of ideology needs to be accompanied by an explanation of its existence. In this task, social psychology must take its place beside political economy, social-historical and formal analysis of media texts in ideology critique without substituting psychological for economic reductionism. Slavoj Žižek argues that psychoanalysis can play a central role in 'providing the missing support of the Marxist theory of ideology (or, more precisely of accounting for the very lack in the Marxist theory that becomes visible apropos of the deadlocks of the theory of ideology)' (1994: 29), citing as evidence for this Freud's social psychology that he sees as compatible with a form of Marxism. Whatever the relative merits of Žižek's work, here he succinctly points to some necessary repair work in the concept of ideology.

The popularity of Lacanian psychoanalytic theory in media studies, however, has contributed to the relative neglect of *intersubjective* currents of psychoanalytic thought that may be more helpful here bearing in mind the importance placed on recognition as a source of moral and political struggle (Winnicott 1965; Benjamin 1990, 1995; Kohut 1971; Billig 1999; Whitebook 1995).

There is no question that this is an immensely difficult task to achieve but even furnishing thick descriptions of human actors and their motivations, enabled and constrained by institutions, is immeasurably better than the provision of explanations based on crude assumptions about the character of human action marked either by economic or by psychological reductionism. As well as intersubjective psychology another untapped resource for media studies is neo-institutional analysis of the kind practised by Paul DiMaggio and Walter Powell. This may well be helpful in embedding an analysis of symbolic meaning within a broader institutional analysis that is essential if ideology critique is to be more than a disembodied analysis of texts (1991). If Thompson's work may be thought of as moving the concept forward in terms of systematising symbolic analysis, then his failure to engage with psychological thought represents a step backwards in contrast to the first generation of the Frankfurt school. In addition to the well known work of Bourdieu, the development of neo-institutional modes of analysis could prove to be a fruitful resource for media scholars wishing to situate the analysis of symbolic meaning within a broader materialist analysis.

Political praxis: from affirmative to transformative strategies, from identity politics to emancipation

If Honneth is correct to argue that the experience of economic exploitation is phenomenologically secondary in character to the experience of misrecognition, disrespect and humiliation, then this serves to highlight the central political importance of ideology critique in political struggle (2004a: 352). What Honneth means by this is that struggles over redistribution of power become important once subjects feel misrecognised, and therefore struggles over redistribution are part of, not separate from, a struggle for recognition. This highlights the central importance of ideology critique.

It would be wrong here, however, to jump from the fact of unequal status and economic and political inequalities to the assumption of 'false consciousness', the acceptance of misrecognition. The notions of false and true consciousness simply do not make sense, as they suggest the presence of two incommensurable conceptual schemes that would logically be closed to one another. Rather than think about it in this rather crude way, it is better to conceive of the situation as a dialectical struggle between misrecognition and recognition, as a complex, uneven process. It makes sense to talk of false beliefs and false sets of beliefs but not of false consciousness. In order to explain the presence of such beliefs, however, we need to consider not only the presence of ideological operations and strategies but also the circumstances of reception, the how and why of acceptance, rejection or negotiation of such operations.

If the relationship between ideological operations and acceptance is not simple then the relationship between rejection and political action is similarly complex. An absence of overt political struggle may not be the consequence of an acceptance of misrecognition. A critique of misrecognition is a necessary but not sufficient condition for enlightened, progressive political action. Other factors, such as perceived prospects for success dependent upon the balance of forces, are clearly important. However, the importance of recognition implies the centrality of ideology critique to political struggle. What role should it play?

The relationship between ideology critique as a form of political praxis and other forms is not an issue that is developed systematically by Thompson. There are a few remarks concerning ideology critique as an 'intervention' but further political implications are not teased out (1990: 323). There is nothing internal, however, to Thompson's theory that prevents this, but its absence from Thompson's work is symptomatic of an unfortunate separation between critical theorists and political activists.

Although both Fraser and Honneth adopt the concept of recognition they both reject identity politics, with which the concept of recognition has been recently associated. They criticise identity politics on the grounds that it seeks to win recognition for particular group identities. Fraser and Honneth are universalists, they wish to win recognition for individuals as human beings, as full and equal participants, rather than for a particular group. Fraser links identity politics to a strategy of affirmation (where the cultural characteristics of a particular group are valorised) whereas she advocates a strategy of transformation where hitherto distinct identities undergo a transformation in order that individuals from groups previously considered to be distinct are seen as individuals within the same community of equals. Ideology critique is thus a crucial component of political praxis, as it is the means by which the construction of individual and group identities is understood if not transformed. It is a necessary but not sufficient part of a political praxis that seeks to establish relations of recognition.

Nancy Fraser has discussed the relationship between her political philosophy and political struggle. She argues that there are basically two political strategies: the affirmative and the transformative. Affirmative strategies have two problems. First, they tend to 'reify collective identities' that 'lend themselves all too easily to separatism and repressive communitarianism' (2004: 76). Second, 'they often provoke a backlash of misrecognition', adding 'the insult of disrespect to the injury of deprivation' (2004: 76–7). Transformative or deconstructive strategies, in contrast, 'aim to destabilise invidious status distinctions', seeking to replace 'overweening master dichotomies, such as black/white or gay/straight, with a decentred congeries of lower-case differences' (2004: 77).

Clearly then Fraser prefers transformative strategies. Such strategies sit very comfortably with Thompson's concept of ideology and the critique of the various modes of operation of ideology. It also sits well with Honneth's universalism. Recognition means first of all being recognised as a human being, not as a particular sort of human being. On that universal basis struggles can be fought concerning what particular individuals or groups require in order to be recognised in practice.

This universal-transformative use of the concept of recognition and of ideology thus serves to encourage the bringing together of political movements potentially seen as disparate. Their struggles for recognition are seen as the same moral struggle that deserve mutual support, as integral parts of an unfinished Enlightenment project of emancipation. Their struggles against misrecognition are struggles against similar ways of thinking and acting that establish and sustain status difference and economic and political inequality. Such a transformative strategy is not only ethically and epistemologically right but also politically pragmatic. An advocate of affirmation may argue that such strategies are the ones most likely to appeal to oppressed groups but equally the transformationist might argue that it is politically the most pragmatic position because it encourages the development of an upper-case Emancipatory movement made up of individuals with lower-case differences. That this is at odds with the supposedly progressive affirmative politics of identity and multiculturalism testifies to the importance of reviving ideology critique.

Can we fix it? Media theory, praxis and the critical imagination

Michael Burawoy in his 2004 presidential address to the American Sociological Association called for the reinvention of 'public sociology', a sociology that explicitly attempts to engage the public or publics as well as academic audiences and contribute through the exercise of critical imagination to creating a better world (Burawoy 2005). As well as more public sociology, we are in need of some public media studies where the critical imagination returns. Given media studies' public image in the United Kingdom, it is tempting either to retreat to the ivory tower (or at least office tower block) or only to come out in public wearing a white coat and large spectacles. The passionate debate about the nature of the discipline that Burawoy's address provoked should be had in the field of media studies too.

For the hopelessly melancholic there is the commitment to Marx's call to arms in his eleventh thesis on Feuerbach: philosophers have only interpreted the world, the point is to change it. This raises the question of how the principle of recognition can be applied to social struggles. Which struggles are spurned and which supported? This is a matter not only of moral evaluation but also of political efficacy:

> The turn to the normative becomes necessary as soon as we are no longer discussing how present-day social struggles are to be appropriately analysed theoretically, but turn to the question of their moral evaluation. It is obvious that we cannot approve of every political uprising as such, nor hold every demand for recognition to be morally legitimate or defensible. Rather, in general we judge the objectives of such struggles to be positive only when they point in the direction of a societal development that we can grasp as coming closer to our notions of a good or just society. Naturally, in principle, other criteria can also play a decisive role here; criteria related more with the aims of societal efficiency or stability, but these too then only reflect value decisions made at a higher level about the normative meaning and purpose of a societal order.
>
> (Honneth 2004a: 353)

A subset of these political decisions and actions relates to media and cultural institutions: media scholars now by and large see themselves as professional interpreters of media institutions rather than as media activists. While professionalisation has merits it also means that we may be losing sight of broader ethical and political concerns that were central to both media and cultural studies in the 1970s and 1980s. Can 'recognition' help to renew this lost dimension? How are we best to act in order to create media institutions that more closely correspond to our notions of a good or just society? We must, of course, first have some idea of what media institutions would look like that are founded in the principles of mutual recognition. Such a vision not only enables critique but is also a necessary condition of successful political action.

One noteworthy attempt to bring together social scientists who share a commitment to emancipation has been the Real Utopias project led by Erik Olin Wright (http://www.ssc.wisc.edu/~wright/RealUtopias.htm). The focus of this project is less to analyse the current state of affairs than to think through how certain ideas for political action might be developed that will lead in the direction of emancipation. Conferences and books have considered the issues of developing more participatory and deliberative forms of democracy, how market socialism might work, how pension funds could be used to control the capitalist economy, and how legislation might lead to emancipatory change in gender relations. Attention has recently turned to the idea of a basic income or a citizens' income, a guaranteed minimum income that everyone receives irrespective of income or volition to work (Cohen and Rogers 1995; Roemer 1996; Bowles and Gintis 1999; Fung and Olin Wright 2003; Ackerman *et al.* 2006). There are plans to hold a conference led by Robert McChesney and produce a book on how media institutions might be changed to further emancipation.

Given the emphasis in media studies on critical scholarship, it is surprising that, to the best of my knowledge, no similar group of scholars exists that seeks to produce a blueprint of what a media system would look like that would further emancipation, or at least to respond publicly to the way that media institutions are at present organised. The abundance of critical scholarship has not been matched by an increase in political engagement. There is a disjoint between media theory and analysis and media political praxis. As well as media critique there is a need for media construction. Recognition can play a central conceptual role both in critique and in construction and thus is fundamental to bringing together theory and praxis. Long seen as one of the backwaters of media studies, some scholars of alternative media have been particularly 'public' in recent years. The Our Media/Nuestros Medios network was set up in 2000 and now has over 500 members in forty countries. It aims to bring together scholars and activists both virtually and otherwise; to democratise the media through encouraging the production of grass-roots media; and, to influence media policy in support of citizens' media. One of the most impressive aspects of the Our Media/Nuestros Medios network is that it is not entirely dominated by North American and Western European scholars. Spanish is used to communicate as well as English and there have been conferences in South America and Asia as well as richer geographical regions (www.ourmedianet.org). The avowedly activist and cosmopolitan agenda of this network is worthy of emulation by other specialisms within mainstream media studies.

Conclusion

The absence of the concept of ideology in media studies is not, contrary to Corner's essay, something to be welcomed but rather is indicative of a lack of philosophical and political ambition on the part of media studies. This should be understood in the context of broader intellectual and political movements as well as the growing maturity of the field. Perhaps it is now time for the increasingly robust and professionalised field to look outward once again in order to reconnect with social theory, on the one hand, and political praxis, on the other? As well as the third generation of Critical Theory, work in the fields of neo-institutional analysis and intersubjective psychology could surely help to inform media analysis that seeks to understand society as a totality and contribute through guiding praxis to the emancipatory goals of critical social science.

Corner concludes his obituary by arguing that the concept of ideology as frequently used in media studies inhibited research because 'it suggested a theoretically precise grasp of mediation processes that was simply not present'. As a result 'it would be better to hope that we are coming to the end of attempts at repair. We might then be in better shape to pursue further research and argument about the interconnections of meaning, value, social structure and power' (2001: 532). In place of the grandiosity of ideology we need careful and precise analysis of the process of mediation in its complexity.

In contrast to Corner, it has been argued here there is nothing about the concept that necessarily inhibits a precise analysis that admits complexity. More, without such a concept embedded in a critical understanding of the social sciences it is likely that we will lose track of the importance of value and power and consequently the desirability of changing the world, the very things Corner paradoxically wishes to keep in sight.

Notes

1 Even some theorists sympathetic to Marxism have argued that ideology as a concept has outlived its usefulness. Pierre Bourdieu, for example, claims that the concept of ideology (with some justification) 'has been so used and abused that it does not work any more' (1994: 266). I argue that the concept can be repaired and made more politically useful and can avoid the problems of Bourdieu's competitor notions such as 'symbolic power' that tend to skate over the substantial difference between the symbolic and the exercise of economic and coercive power in that the symbolic works through persuasion rather than force (see Lukes 2004). This is important because Bourdieu's work has had considerable influence upon media studies.
2 The present-day Institute of Social Research at Frankfurt has developed a vibrant empirical research programme based around Honneth's philosophical work, see www.ifs.uni-frankfurt.de/forschung/schwerpunkte.htm.

Bibliography

Ackerman, B., Alstott, A. and van Parijs, P. (2006) *Redesigning Redistribution: Basic Income and Stakeholder Grants as Cornerstones of a more Egalitarian Capitalism*. London: Verso.

Benjamin, J. (1990) *The Bonds of Love: Psychoanalysis, Feminism and the Problem of Domination*. London: Virago.

Benjamin, J. (1995) *Like Subjects, Love Objects: Essays on Recognition and Sexual Difference*. New Haven CT: Yale University Press.

Billig, M. (1999) *Freudian Repression: Conversation creating the Unconscious*. Cambridge: Cambridge University Press.

Bourdieu, P. (1994) *Language and Symbolic Power*. Cambridge: Polity Press.

Bowles, S. and Gintis, H. (1999) *Recasting Egalitarianism: New Rules for Accountability and Equity in Markets, States and Communities*. London: Verso.

Burawoy, M. (2005) 'For public sociology', *American Sociological Review* 70: 4–28.

Cohen, J. and Rogers, J. (1995) *Associations and Democracy*. London: Verso.

Corner, J. (2001) '"Ideology": a note on conceptual salvage', *Media, Culture and Society* 23: 525–33.

DiMaggio, P. and Powell, W. (eds) (1991) *The New Institutionalism in Organizational Analysis*. Chicago: University of Chicago Press.

Eagleton, T. (1991) *Ideology: an Introduction*. London: Verso.

Fraser, N. (2004) 'Recognition, redistribution and representation in capitalist global society: an interview with Nancy Fraser', *Acta Sociologica* 47 (4): 374–82.

Fraser, N. and Honneth, A. (2003) *Redistribution or Recognition? A Philosophical-political Exchange*. London: Verso.

Fung, A. and Olin Wright, E. (2003) *Deepening Democracy: Innovations in Empowered Participatory Governance*. London: Verso.

Habermas, J. (1989) *The Structural Transformation of the Public Sphere*. Cambridge: Polity Press.

Honneth, A. (1995) *The Struggle for Recognition: the Moral Grammar of Social Conflicts*. Cambridge: Polity Press.

Honneth, A. (2004a) 'Recognition and justice: outline of a plural theory of justice', *Acta Sociologica* 47 (4): 351–64.

Honneth, A. (2004b) 'From struggles for recognition to a plural concept of justice: interview with Gwynn Markle', *Acta Sociologica* 47 (4): 383–91.

Kohut, H. (1971) *The Analysis of the Self*. New York: International Universities Press.

Lukes, S. (2004) *Power: a Radical View*. Basingstoke: Palgrave.

Roemer, J. (1996) *Equal Shares: Making Market Socialism Work*. London: Verso.

Thompson, J. B. (1990) *Ideology and Modern Culture*. Cambridge: Polity Press.

Van Dijk, T. (1998) *Ideology: a Multidisciplinary Approach*. London: Sage.

Whitebook, J. (1995) *Perversion and Utopia: a Study in Psychoanalysis and Critical Theory*. Cambridge MA: MIT Press.

Winnicott, D. W. (1965) *The Maturational Processes and the Facilitating Environment: Studies in the Theory of Emotional Development*. London: Hogarth.

Žižek, S. (ed.) (1994) *Mapping Ideology*. London: Verso.

5   Cosmopolitan temptations, communicative spaces and the European Union

Philip Schlesinger

The concept of the 'public sphere' is of central importance to media research and integral to thinking about both political culture and popular culture.[1] While the relations between mediated communication and publicity, publics and public opinion have been on the agenda from the very start of analytical reflection on mass communication (Splichal 1999), it would be true to say that for recent generations of scholars, Jürgen Habermas's (1989) classic formulation of the structural transformation of the public sphere has constituted a decisive starting point for debate and investigation – whether one is in agreement with or in dissent from his views (Calhoun 1992). The discourse on the public sphere is proving to be one of the most fruitful contemporary conjunctions between political theory and media research and has become indispensable to how we think about the communicative conditions of a democratic polity and politics.

Currently, there is extensive debate over how to conceptualise the public sphere at a time of globalising tendencies (albeit highly uneven ones) in the economy, international relations and cultural flows, while also taking into account the far-reaching effects of the present digital revolution. In the era of the modern state, the principal space of political communication has been commonly equated with the territorial boundaries of a national community. However, for contemporary cosmopolitans, by contrast with the trope of a national home, communicative space is potentially global in scope. Consequently, so cosmopolitans argue, the key stage for much political action (and relevant forms of discourse) is now properly transnational.

But states – long considered to be the modal, modern frameworks of political communication and the idealised homes of national cultures – have not yet been transcended as the principal controllers of citizenship, the purveyors of key collective identities, or the deliverers of a myriad of services and demands that shape the everyday lives and experiences of their inhabitants. Nevertheless, from a cosmopolitan viewpoint they have been relativised as communicative spaces and containers of political action. Cosmopolitans, therefore, as opposed to national citizens, are involved (potentially, if not actually) in a global conversation about the good society.

Thus, when it comes to conceptualising the public sphere, two broad per-spectives – the statist and the cosmopolitan – are the polar grand variants in play. True, this dualistic characterisation simplifies and dramatises, but it does offer us a clear entry point into the arguments that follow.

If, respectively, the state and the globe describe distinct conceptions of political space, polities that are neither clearly the one nor the other rightly become objects of considerable analytical interest and present a conceptual challenge. In a binary framework their troubling ambiguity simply cannot be resolved. The European Union is such an anomaly. Less all-embracing than the globe, it is also more far-reaching than the state.

So how might we think through the scope and scale of the public sphere and what this might signify for the politico-cultural identities and cohesion of different kinds of collectivity? Whether we frame the problem in terms either of an international system of states and nations or of a global community *in statu nascendi* is highly relevant. Each conception differs radically in how it imagines the spaces of political action, addresses their significance and locates processes of communication. Each, moreover, conjures up diverse views of human possibility and the political constraints within which this unfolds.

What I wish to emphasise here is the continuing analytical importance of political institutions as the bedrock for our understanding of the public sphere. The EU is an intergovernmental, regulatory polity that might yet become a federal system (Fossum and Schlesinger 2007: 1–19). Because the Union's overall character as a polity remains unresolved this has major consequences for the organisation of communicative spaces – and therefore for the possibility of cosmopolitanism.

Social communication and the state

It is precisely the European nation-state, addressed as a political commu-nity, which Jürgen Habermas's (1989) early theory took as its framework for the public sphere. But how are we to think of publicness in the multi-level complexity of the EU? Both national and 'European' discourses and institutions coexist. The EU's policy making is a constitutive part of member states' domestic political agendas and also of their legal and economic frameworks. Yet the Union also occupies a different political level and is often represented as an external locus of decision making. Herein lies the essential ambiguity of the European public sphere. The evolution of the EU has ensured that the state-bounded context no longer completely defines the political scope of communicative communities. Consequently, to analyse emergent European communicative spaces, the focus needs to shift outwards to the transnational arenas centred on the political capital, Brussels, and to consider how these try to address their constituent publics. The challenge, therefore, is to develop a social communication theory capable of addressing the European Union's complexity, by which is meant 'the number of elements in interaction and the number of different states that those interactions can give rise to' (Boisot 1999: 5).

Social communication encompasses the gamut of distinctive signifying practices, values and collectively held beliefs that defines and delimits a communicative community, operating within the framework of a broadly anthropological idea of a culture as a 'distinct whole way of life' (Williams 1981: 13). It is more extensive in scope than political communication, although political institutions and mediated communication about these do have a focal importance for our contemporary understanding of social communication. Arguably, a European public sphere presupposes a theory of social communication because the relations it entails go beyond how citizens *qua* citizens interact with political institutions. Civil society is to be conceived only in part as operating in the political domain. It is also simultaneously a socio-cultural hinterland and a realm of everyday life. Thus a theory of social communication encompasses 'thick' social relations – not least those productive of a sense of belonging and emotional attachments – that continue to be integral to national life, despite its conflictual dynamics.

In this connection, we should consider one line of inquiry that is deeply rooted in the *longue durée* of European experience. Karl Deutsch (1966) first explicitly outlined a social communication theory of nationalism half a century ago, although its origins doubtless lie further in the past. Some fifty years before Deutsch, the Austro-Marxist theorist Otto Bauer (2000) wrote a seminal account of the 'national question' that is the likely precursor of Deutsch's theory. Together, Bauer and Deutsch have exercised a remarkable – and virtually unacknowledged – influence over some of the more significant recent theorising about the communicative dimension of the nation (and therefore of the public sphere). Such now venerable Austro-Marxist thinking is of more than passing interest. Finding a pluralistic solution to communicative complexity inside the European Union has a strong family resemblance to Bauer's wish to give due recognition to national cultural autonomy in a multinational empire. The intimate connection between nationality and 'culture and language' (broadly understood as social communication) was central to his analysis; not least the passions and emotions that competing linguistic and cultural claims could – and did – generate within a creaking imperial order.

Bauer (2000: 34) contended that a modern democratic nation should be seen as a 'community of culture'. In contemporary conditions, it is more common to think in terms of a community of cultures.[2] Bauer also famously observed that the nation was a 'community of fate' (*eine Schicksalsgemeinschaft*) engaged in 'general reciprocal interaction' (ibid.: 100), thereby sharing a common language and culture. He remarked:

> The culture's sphere of influence extends only as far as the communicative possibilities of the language. The community of interaction

is limited by the scope of the linguistic community. Community of interaction and language reciprocally condition each other.

(Bauer 2000: 102)

The nation *qua* linguistic community, then, is conceived as culturally self-contained or, at the very least, as tending towards communicative closure. This was an early statement of a social communication theory of the nation. It came from trying to think through a strategy for ensuring cultural autonomy within a wider political order. This effort to address the *Kulturkämpfe* of the declining years of the Austro-Hungarian Empire has left its conceptual imprint on contemporary theorising about the public sphere in the European Union.

Bauer's line of argument was carried forward by Karl Deutsch – appropriately enough, an early theorist of European union – who contended that nations and nation-states are strongly bounded by their patterns of interaction: 'People are held together "from within" by this communicative efficiency, the complementarity of the communicative facilities acquired by their members' (Deutsch 1996: 98). Social communication, in other words, is held to produce collective cohesion and identity: we are invited to share a common fate. Bauer and Deutsch, therefore, had a fundamentally similar approach to how communicative and cultural practices and institutions (to which language is central) might strengthen the collective identity of a national group by creating and maintaining boundaries.

This simple – but compelling – idea is reproduced in a number of influential theories of nationalism. Ernest Gellner's (1983) view that culture is 'the distinctive style of conduct and communication of a given community' and that it is 'now the necessary shared medium' of the nation is likewise at root a social theory of cohesion. Cultural boundaries become defined by national cultures, which diffuse a literate 'high culture', in which the key agency is the national education system. Media are seen as sustaining that political community, providing it with its deep codes for distinguishing between self and other. For his part, Benedict Anderson (1991) has contended that mechanically reproduced print languages have unified fields of linguistic exchange, fixed national languages and created idiolects of power. So, by going to Gellner's schools, cultured nationals may acquire the competence to read Anderson's novels and newspapers, and thus enter the public sphere endowed with cultural capital. For each of these writers, the collective consumption of mediated communication (based on a common 'national' language) creates and sustains a sense of common belonging. Michael Billig (1995) has endorsed and extended this broad argument. As nationals, he suggests, we live less in a state of perpetual mobilisation than one of the banal assimilation of everyday symbolism and categorisation through knowing about flags and anthems, making distinctions between home and foreign news, absorbing national histories and languages, and having a particular sense of political geography. National identity – outside of crises – is unremarkably reproduced in the routines of everyday life. Culture holds us together: it both conditions and informs our conceptions of national identity. Whereas social communication theorists may differ on the key mechanisms or processes that produce cultural cohesion, all nevertheless agree that some or other dimension of communication is central to how the nation should be conceived.

The above discussion merely underlines the obvious – that no culture is an island. In the theories outlined above, the emphasis is on the place – the territory – occupied by the nation. However, national systems of communication are influenced by what lies outside. National cultures are usually permeable, however much they may be censored and controlled, and in the age of the Internet, mobile devices, and satellite broadcasting, such relative openness is necessarily greater than ever before.

I have argued elsewhere (Schlesinger 2000) that the main thrust of classical social communications theory is to concern itself with the interior of the national culture and communication, with largely endogenous explanations of what makes us what we are, with how boundaries are drawn around us. Look at Bauer's *Fragestellung* and such interiority is not at all surprising: it is congruent with the assertion of the right to have a national communicative space within a wider imperial constitutional framework of competing national cultures. It represents both the quest for, and the defence of, cultural territory.

But it is obvious that such a neatly demarcationist theory of social communication and public space is no longer tenable. It is especially the case, in a 'globalised' world, that its limitations are thrown increasingly into relief by the rapid development of new forms of public electronic connectedness through information and communications technologies, although the emergence of networked spaces does not mean we should now regard the continued shaping role of the state in social communication at the national level as irrelevant (Hjarvard 2001; Street 2001; Sinclair 2004). Nevertheless, as autarchy is utterly *passé* under globalising pressures, statist ideas of communication sovereignty – and therefore of the public sphere – have been forced to shift from 'the unilateral to the consensual, the negotiated, and the multilateral' (Price 2002: 230).

Otto Bauer's century-old problem has been posed afresh by the evolution of the European Union: how may many diverse national, ethnic, linguistic and other cultural communities achieve autonomy within a single, overarching political framework? The old Habsburg empire had to adjust to nationalist claims to autonomy from below and it did not survive these.[3] By contrast, the EU is an importer of already formed nations shaped by (more or less well) established states.[4] If Bauer was trying to find a solution to nationalist demands within an overarching framework, current cosmopolitan writers emphasise the transcendent potential of the emergent European framework to connect a new global order that needs a public sphere to match.

The gradual emergence of a transnational formation such as the EU (as a distinctively developed instance of wider trends towards supranational governance) has unsettled how we might now conceive of established communicative relations between national publics and state-centred systems of power. It has made us intensely aware of the diverse levels at which publics might form, the horizontal ties that bind across state boundaries, and how our communicative competence needs to make appropriate adjustments.

If the EU is engaged in a form of state building, then it lacks one of the key components of a common public sphere, a European intelligentsia. As Abram de Swaan (2007) has pointed out, the EU does not – as yet – have the supporting apparatus of journals, academies, prizes, career opportunities and a common, synchronous debate about key matters of public concern. As he also notes, there are indeed multiple interrelations at the expert level – in short, particular micro-publics do exist – but there is nothing that equates to the routine general debate that still characterises the national public sphere. De Swaan contends that the EU's linguistic diversity – alongside the *de facto* rise of English as 'the vehicular language of Europe' – has continued to underpin the pull of the national. The material underpinnings of a new 'cultural opportunity structure', he suggests, are now needed to counteract the continuing robustness of state systems. Thus, according to this argument, the necessary conditions for sustaining a European public sphere are not yet in place. Whether the micro-publics created by the problem-oriented theorising, empirical research and consultancy that have accompanied the growth of European institutions will in time constitute part of a cosmopolitan, European intelligentsia is still an open question.

While, at present, linguistic diversity at the level of the member states and a fragmented intelligentsia do stand in the way of the formation of a common public sphere, the question of cultural complexity extends much further. First, the EU's member states are not monolingual or monocultural national formations. Regional or minority languages, often with supporting institutions and media systems, operate at a sub-state level, perhaps most potently in regions that are also self-consciously 'stateless nations'. Publics exist at the sub-state level, and are constituted there on the basis of linguistic, cultural or national distinctiveness (Cormack and Hourigan 2007; Moragas Spà *et al.* 1999).

Aside from this, continuing migration and diasporic links have ensured that, as elsewhere, non-indigenous forms of linguistic and cultural diversity – in part sustained by transnational media consumption – are inescapably part of the contemporary landscape of the EU's member states

(Jouët and Pasquier 2001). The consequences are complex. For instance, Asu Aksoy and Kevin Robins (2000: 358) have argued – in the case of Turkish migrants in Western Europe who are consumers of a diverse range of Turkish television programmes – that such consumption initiates a process of 'thinking across spaces, with all the possibilities that this then opens up for thinking beyond the small world of imagined communities'. However, the evidence of such emergent post-national identities is ambiguous. We may ask, for instance, whether diasporic connections sustained via the media crystallise new cosmopolitan possibilities or instead sustain 'long-distance nationalism'.

But these are not mutually exclusive alternatives, as Thomas Hylland Eriksen has observed. Basing his argument on the uses of the internet by a wide range of migrant groups, he writes that:

> Some are content to strengthen and confirm a particular cultural or religious identity in the context of their country or residence; some prioritise interpersonal links with their country of origin; while others – presumably a minority – use the Internet to actively promote the political cause of a territorial nation, real or prospective, in a dispersed diaspora, which is brought together as an abstract community only because of the Internet.
>
> (Eriksen 2007: 7)

Eriksen (2007: 16) goes on to point out that the transborder social cohesion and cultural integration afforded by the internet is inherently unstable; it is faced by the contradictory pull of the 'territorialising forces of the nation-state and the deterritorialising forces connecting people to a nation which is elsewhere or perhaps only in cyber-space'.

The complexity of communicative spaces in the EU sketched above has been added to by the Union's enlargement eastwards and southwards. This has meant that national questions held in check during the Cold War are increasingly the inheritance of the EU to manage (as are relations with Russia). Post-communist Europe has become – in Rogers Brubaker's (1996) phrase – a space of 'nationalising states'. These legacies – which involve contested ideas about the nation – are an inherent part of the discussion within new and aspirant member states about how a European public sphere might evolve (Heller and Rényi 2007). In many cases, national minorities without citizenship of the new nationalising state constitute a significant component of a neighbouring state or states.[5] The implosion of Yugoslavia has left residual ethno-national problems that might be resolved by eventual accession for the successor states. And there is the moot question of Turkish accession to the EU, embroiled in the recurrent debate over whether or not the Union should underline its Christian heritage as an integral part of its identity, a question more political than religious (Schlesinger and Foret 2006).

Towards a cosmopolitan communicative space?

The debate over how to address Europe's religious heritage has been
conducted in the EU's institutional heartlands, involving the European
Commission and the European Parliament, and was part of the discussion
over the Constitutional Treaty in 2002–4 (Foret and Schlesinger 2007).
It has also been widely disseminated – albeit unevenly – through media
coverage (Koenig *et al.* 2006). This example illustrates that, in the
struggle over collective identities in the EU, it is impossible to avoid
institutional politics. On this score, cosmopolitans divide into two main
camps: institutional and post-institutional.

Institutional cosmopolitans use the language of rights and duties and
take seriously the means by which these might be enforced. Habermas's
rights-based, supranational conception of the EU connects to a global
perspective. He portrays the public sphere as potentially unbounded, as
shifting from specific locales (such as the nation) to the virtual co-presence
of citizens and consumers linked by public media. Habermas (1997: 373–4)
argues that communicative space is to be understood in terms of 'a highly
complex network [that] branches out into a multitude of overlapping
international, national, regional, local and subcultural arenas'. He envisages
that 'hermeneutic bridge-building' will occur between different discourses.
A European communicative space conceived in open network terms has
become the new political playground (ibid.: 171). A European public sphere
would therefore be open-ended, with communicative connections extending
well beyond the continent.

What this leaves unresolved is whether or not convergent communicative
practices might in the end produce some kind of cultural cohesion, resulting
in a European community of fate. Habermas's answer to that question
is to propose that EU citizens become 'constitutional patriots'. This post-
nationalist, rule-bound form of identification implies an order of preference
and (however fluid) at least some distinction between an 'us' and a 'them'.
It still carries inescapable echoes of an older, inter-state, conception of
political order. If a social communications approach to the public sphere
insists on the 'thickness' of what sustains the political culture, constitutional
patriotism presumes 'thin' relations – however, it also presupposes affinities
with other patriots. So the EU's cosmopolitan potential is still anchored in
a web of affiliations.

Habermas (2004) emphasises the importance of a European constitution.
This demarcates a distinct political space and provides a common value
orientation. Constitutionalism remains central to how a European public
sphere might be imagined: linked upwards to more general structures of
governance and downwards to more particular ones. Habermas has argued
that the 'the making of such a constitution represent[s] in itself a unique
opportunity of transnational communication' (ibid.: 28). He has stressed
the key role of a 'European-wide public sphere' and 'the shaping of a

political culture that can be shared by all European citizens' (ibid.: 27). Quite how this is to be achieved is still a moot point. We may question whether the constitutional process was an effective form of transnational communication. More striking was the national framing of the debate and how national considerations played into rejection of the Constitutional Treaty in France and the Netherlands in May and June 2005 (Dacheux 2005: 129).

The ratification process ran into the sands and only in 2007 did major new moves take place under the German presidency to recover the lost momentum. A constitutional framework remains of key importance for the development of the EU's political identity. Aside from its directly legal and political significance, a constitution also defines the limits within which 'European' patterns of political culture and communication may be encouraged to emerge at the EU level.

Habermas's attempt to navigate between the free flight of cosmopolitan potential and the gravitational pull of institutions is akin to Manuel Castells's (1998) approach. For Castells, the new communication technologies contribute to the formation of a novel kind of society, the 'informational'. He sees the EU as a precursor of a new political order, of new forms of association and loyalty. The emerging European polity epitomises what Castells terms 'the network state'. The EU is imagined not only as a political-economic zone but also as a specific kind of communicative space. Castells focuses on how networks, facilitated by information and communication technologies, transcend borders, thus in effect providing an infrastructure for cosmopolitanism.

The boundaries of the putative European communicative space – and therefore the potential public sphere – are produced by the nexus of political institutions that constitute Union Europe, the dealings between them, and growing 'subsidiary' horizontal links across the member states (Castells 1998: 330–1).[6] Castells argues that the EU has different 'nodes' of varying importance that make up a network. Regions and nations, nation states, EU institutions, together constitute a framework of shared authority.

Castells suggests that complex interconnected 'communicative complementarities' – as Deutsch once put it – may emerge out of the informal processes of making the union. The potentially globalising pull of communications technologies is countered by emergent patterns of social interaction in the European Union's space.

With a different emphasis, David Held (2004) has sketched an institutionally oriented cosmopolitan conception of citizenship and the kind of public sphere that accompanies this. He envisages a citizenship that goes beyond 'exclusive membership of a territorial community' to:

> an alternative principle of world order in which all persons have equivalent rights and duties in the cross-cutting spheres of decision-making which affect their vital needs and interests. ... Citizenship

would become multilevel and multidimensional, while being anchored
in common rules and principles.

(Held 2004: 114)

To think of the political community as no longer bounded by the sovereign
nation state is highly pertinent to the EU, which Held – like many
others – sees as an example of the 'reconfiguration of political power'
(ibid.: 87). Political communities, he suggests, no longer 'correspond in any
straightforward way to territorial boundaries' (1995: 225). In consequence,
'[t]he cultural space of nation-states is being rearticulated by forces over
which states have, at best, only limited leverage' (ibid.: 126). Held argues
for an international order based on cosmopolitan democratic public law
(ibid.: 227) because 'the regulative capacity of states increasingly has to be
matched by the development of collaborative mechanisms of governance at
supranational, regional and global levels' (2004: 15).

In this vision of a 'social democratic multilateralism' we find a distant
echo of Otto Bauer, since for Held the world consists of 'overlapping
communities of fate' (2004: 107). Such diversity requires the establishment
of 'an overarching network of democratic public fora, covering cities,
nation-states, regions and the wider transnational order', working along
the lines of rational deliberation, argued for by Habermas (ibid.: 109). That
is why in Held's argument the EU is just another node in the institutional
network envisaged, and not a principal focus of interest. One challenge to
this variant of cosmopolitanism, therefore, is to ask what the significance is
of particular fora. For Held it is the articulation between fora (more or less
institutionalised communicative spaces) that is emphasised over the internal
elaboration of territorially bounded spaces. Understandably, therefore, the
detailed workings of a European public sphere will be a matter of relatively
minor interest.

This echoes the outlook of post-institutional theorists of cosmopolitanism who argue that it is essential to think of Europeanness as evolving
beyond the limiting institutional framework of the EU; instead we need to
locate it in a global context.

For Ulrich Beck (2006: 164), the EU's struggle with its political future
is actually an 'institutionalised failure of the imagination' that does not
live up the cosmopolitan dreams of its founding fathers. The Union, he
maintains, lacks political pragmatism and radical openness. The present
tensions between the regulatory and federal models, which are actually
of vital explanatory importance, are swept aside by Beck (rather oddly)
as denying Europe's diversity (ibid.: 171–2). Instead, Beck argues, 'The
political union must be conceived as a cosmopolitan union of Europe, in
opposition to the false normativity of the national' (ibid.: 167). Indeed,
the prospect held out is variously that of a 'cosmopolitan state' or a
'cosmopolitan co-operative of states'. But beyond these slogans it is not
at all clear how power would be exercised, how post-territorial politics

would function or how space for ethno-cultural diversity might be secured. Thus, while I would not dissent at all from Beck's view that European states must co-operate to survive in the context of global risks, there is little but exhortation in his analysis – and certainly little realistic engagement with institutional politics.

For instance, according to Beck, the EU has inaugurated 'a struggle over institutions with the aim of confronting European horror with European values and methods'. Thus, after World War II and the Holocaust, he believes, one of Europe's most positive achievements is to stand for the protection of human rights. He further asserts that commemoration of the Holocaust is an institutional foundation for the EU's identity and indeed for a wider Europe. However, Beck's position takes no account of Holocaust denial, or of the way in which opposition to acts of official commemoration is now connected with the politics of the Middle East, or of the differences between official acts and popular sentiment, or indeed, of present-day competition over victimhood throughout Europe.

Gerard Delanty and Chris Rumford (2005: 20), taking an even more radically post-institutional line, maintain that 'the state does not define a people's imaginary. New conceptions of peoplehood can be found in the cosmopolitan currents that are a feature of Europeanisation' and the emergent social construction of Europe should be understood in the wider context of globalisation. The conception of identity here is 'thin' and dialogical and rooted in 'a system of relations and a capacity for communication' (ibid.: 68). The argument is a boundary-transcending and transformative one, taking its distance from political science models, so that Europe is seen as a space of possibilities for new cosmopolitan attachments in which the challenge for the EU is to 'create spaces for communication'.

Communication is judged valuable principally in articulating connections beyond the EU, rather than in building the Union into a political community or a collective identity. The 'emerging' European public sphere is characterised as 'European-wide forms of communicative competence, discourses, themes and cultural models and repertoires of evaluation within different national contexts'. Its uniqueness is held to be 'based on certain common issues and interconnecting debates in which the community of reference becomes increasingly diluted and, as it does so, reconfigured ... it is a medium in which new expressions of cosmopolitanism are taking place' (ibid.: 103–4). From this point of view, the European public sphere is not so much an institutionalised space that might democratise the Union – and also deal with Europe's chequered past – as a post-institutional launching pad for a new orientation to the world that increasingly sheds its European cast.

However, bounded relations surely still remain important, because, as Christer Jönssen *et al.* (2000: 184–5) argue, 'social communication is most effective between individuals whose mental worlds have been "formatted" analogously over lengthy periods of time'. Strikingly congruent with

Deutsch's principle of communicative complementarity, the argument is that 'human thought requires boundaries', based in proximity, likeness and linkage, so that 'place, neighbourhood and region will continue to play important roles as realms of experience and epistemic communities'. This, in turn, 'fosters local anchorage and regional identity' so that even '[i]n the age of electronic networking, conversation therefore continues to have a major role, as does the face to face meeting' (ibid.).

In an analysis of such meetings Catherine Neveu (2000, 2002) adopted a processual approach to 'becoming European', exploring the internal dynamics of Euro-networking. Investigating what happens when European institutions invite various categories of people to participate in transnational activities, she suggests that the resulting acculturation may have a 'return effect' once participants go back to their places of origin. Involvement in networks and exchanges are seen as building an important path to the formation of a European public sphere. Interaction with European institutions constitutes a kind of 'training process' that may impact on people's notions of citizenship and identity. Neveu's anthropological approach reveals how background models and representations grounded in national discourses come into play and are modified. It remains an open question whether such encounters can build up a common sentimental basis for a nascent cosmopolitanism.

To sum up: the development of a European public sphere may be conceived as based in interaction between Euro-institutions and Euro-networks. In an echo of Norbert Elias's thought, Keith Middlemass (1995: 684–5) has written of the 'Euro-civilising aspect' as informally shaping a community over time. Arguably, the EU is developing a special interactive intensity that in some sectors of public life favours internal communication and creates an internally differentiated referential boundary. Not all institutions have the same centrality; not all networks have the same intensity of interaction. Although a relatively weak, transnational public space has indeed evolved around the policy-making actors in the EU institutions, states, nations and regions remain crucially important as locales for debate and sources of identity. Castells's Euro-networker has not completely forgotten how to wave Billig's national flag and it is plain that the EU's citizens do not yet conform *en bloc* to Habermas's ideal of constitutional patriotism.

'Europeanness', the public sphere and mediated communication

It is no surprise, then, that Juan Díez Medrano (2003: 5) has argued that the 'international variation in support for European integration' continues to be rooted in how and why the EU is differently interpreted in the member states. His empirical research into the production and reproduction of diverse cultural 'frames' in national news media, among political elites and at the level of popular opinion concerning the European Union documents the profound ambiguities of perceptions of European integration. Although the integration project can certainly be likened to a state-building process, eventual EU statehood is by no means an ineluctable outcome.

Because EU policy making and political direction impinge increasingly on member states, the European dimension impacts on the agenda of the mediated political discourse of national polities. However, a fault line runs through contemporary theorising about how political communication impacts on citizenship, collective identity and patriotism. Are these now shifting from their long-standing and often exclusive alignment with the member states (and nations) into a more inclusive cosmopolitan 'European' citizenship, collective identity and constitutional patriotism? Or – and this is the view espoused here – does the Union's liminal status between regulator and federation mean that our analysis necessarily needs to be grounded in ambivalence?

Some have argued for a kind of spill-over effect, in which the dissemination of argument and diverse perspectives across national borders stimulates a wider, European level of political engagement through a collective learning process (Eder 2007; Trenz and Eder 2004). As noted, the constitutional debate has been seen as offering educative content for the building of a common citizenship but so far these hopes have not been realised. Even at key constitutional moments, coverage is framed principally in terms of national politics (Dacheux 2005; Gleissner and de Vreese 2005).

Within the national public spheres, 'Europeanisation' appears to be uneven in impact. Ruud Koopmans and Jessica Erbe (2004) have shown how specific policy arenas covered by the German press are diversely exposed to European themes and perspectives. Paul Statham (2007) has suggested that although 'Europeanisation' means that (to varying degrees) certain EU policy issues are now routinely reported, in France debate about Europe is directly connected with the EU level whereas in the UK it remains far more distanced and self-contained. Such analysis underlines the continuing weight of national political systems in shaping the scope of debates in the public sphere.

While news media in the EU may address similar issues at the same time in different member states, this does not necessarily equate to the widespread distribution of a shared European perspective. And even if the distribution of media content were uniform that would not stop it from being diversely interpreted.

In as much as a media-sustained, transnational communicative space is emerging because of EU integration, this is class-inflected and predominantly the domain of political and economic elites, not yet that of a general European public. Examples of transnational media include *The Economist*, the *Financial Times*, the *International Herald Tribune* and in the audio-visual sphere Euronews and Arte. Traditional print journalism centred on Europe has not easily transcended national boundaries, as the short life of

The European (London) and the much briefer one of *l'Européen* (Paris) have shown (E. Neveu 2002; Schlesinger 1999).

European journalism is geared to the EU's intergovernmentalism, to its continuing role as a regulatory rather than federal entity. In the member states, national editorial values shape coverage of European themes and issues (Kevin 2003: 179), not least because established source–media relations underpin the national discourse. National governmental sources are still of paramount importance for journalists covering EU issues (Morgan 1999) even if other voices are also gaining access to news agendas. Research in Brussels suggests that some weakly transnational forms of exchange have developed at the EU level between journalists and their sources. Christoph Meyer (2000) has argued that there is an increasing tendency for transnational investigative journalism to emerge, thereby contributing to the accountability of the institutions. Occasionally, but not so far systematically, this can have political effects, particularly in the exposure of scandal and corruption. But such alliances still appear to be a transient rather than a systemic feature of the Euro-political scene. Olivier Baisnée (2002) also refers to the co-operative context of Brussels reporting. Although he claims that journalists have been socialised into being 'Europe's only real public' (ibid.: 112, 115) diverse orientations and patterns of coverage prevail in British and French news media, with the EU seen as not very newsworthy (Baisnée 2003). Similar divergences were apparent in the row triggered by European Council president Silvio Berlusconi's address to the European Parliament in 2003. His insult to a German member of the European Parliament was widely reported as 'a clash of (ethnic) nations' rather than triggering European deliberation (Downey and Koenig 2006: 184).

If we are attentive to the cosmopolitan potential of social interaction, we certainly should not discount the transnational relations and negotiations that have become part of the everyday reporting experience. But nor should we overestimate it. European journalism remains divided by diverse national ideas of professionalism, serving domestic markets and principally meeting nationally rooted audience expectations. These still hold the key to career success. The continuing national pull of journalistic practice and frameworks of reference explains the sheer difficulty of developing journalism either for a Europe-wide general public or indeed a particular public oriented to the European Union contained within a given member state. This is a microcosmic illustration of the tensions that still persist between the national principle and Europeanness. Theorising the evolution of the EU requires simultaneous recognition of the relative robustness of national public spheres and of the relative fragility of the cosmopolitan, transnational dimension.

States, nations and regions remain crucially important as locales for debate and as sources of identity. Europeanisation is itself a profoundly ambiguous process. Who now – and who in the future – will be permitted to be a 'European' is an increasingly intense focus for struggles between inclusion and exclusion both within member states and at the borders of the EU itself. Because Europeanisation is a boundary-defining process as well as a transnationalising one, it does not of itself necessarily point to a cosmopolitan outcome.

Notes

1 This chapter is a substantial revision of Schlesinger (2007), itself a major revision of a text first published as Schlesinger (2003).
2 Although, that said, since 9/11 multiculturalism itself has increasingly come under pressure as questions of social cohesion and political loyalty rise up the agenda.
3 With the 2004 and 2007 enlargements, and those still in prospect, the EU is incorporating more and more of the old Habsburg lands.
4 This is an oversimplification, of course. It is certainly not the case that all EU states are to be regarded as homogeneous, as is evident from the politics of devolution and/or separatism in, for instance, Belgium, France, Italy, Spain and the United Kingdom.
5 The Hungarian minority in Romania and Slovakia is a well known case in point, but many more examples could be cited.
6 Castells's more recent work has moved beyond this position. However, his utopian vision of an 'Internet Galaxy' as a zone of citizen freedom still has to contend with a world of states that combine to regulate threats to their control over information (Castells 2001: 178–85).

Bibliography

Aksoy, Asu and Robins, Kevin (2000) 'Thinking across spaces: transnational television from Turkey', *European Journal of Cultural Studies* 3 (3): 343–5.

Anderson, Benedict (1991) *Imagined Communities: Reflections on the Origin and Spread of Nationalism*, 2nd edn. London: Verso.

Baisnée, Olivier (2002) 'Can political journalism exist at the European level?', in R. Kuhn and E. Neveu (eds) *Political Journalism*. London: Routledge.

Baisnée, Olivier (2003) 'Une actualité "invendable": les rédactions françaises et britanniques face à l'actualité communautaire', in G. Garcia and V. Le Torrec (eds) *L'Union européenne et les médias: regards croisés sur l'information européenne*. Paris: Harmattan.

Bauer, Otto (2000 [1907]) *The Question of Nationalities and Social Democracy*. Minneapolis MN: University of Minnesota Press.

Beck, Ulrich (2006) *Cosmopolitan Vision*. Cambridge: Polity Press.

Billig, Michael (1995) *Banal Nationalism*. London: Sage.

Boisot, Max (1999) *Knowledge Assets: Securing Competitive Advantage in the Knowledge Economy*. Oxford: Oxford University Press.

Brubaker, Rogers (1996) *Nationalism Reframed: Nationhood and the National Question in the New Europe*. Cambridge: Cambridge University Press.

Calhoun, Craig (ed.) (1992) *Habermas and the Public Sphere*. Cambridge MA and London: MIT Press.

Castells, Manuel (1998) *End of Millennium*. Malden MA: Blackwell.

Castells, Manuel (2001) *The Internet Galaxy: Reflections on the Internet, Business and Society*. Oxford: Oxford University Press.

Cormack, Mike and Hourigan, Niamh (eds) (2007) *Minority Languages Media: Concepts, Critiques and Case Studies*. Clevedon, Buffalo NY and Toronto: Multilingual Matters.

Dacheux, Eric (ed.) (2005) *Comprendre le débat sur la constitution de l'Union Européenne*. Paris: Publibook.

De Swaan, Abram (2007) 'The European void: the democratic deficit as a cultural deficiency', in Fossum and Schlesinger (eds) *The European Union and the Public Sphere*.

Delanty, Gerard and Rumford, Chris (2005) *Rethinking Europe: Social Theory and the Implications of Europeanization*. London and New York: Routledge.

Deutsch, Karl, W. (1966) *Nationalism and Social Communication: an Inquiry into the Foundations of Nationality*, 2nd edn. Cambridge MA: MIT Press.

Díez Medrano, Juan (2003) *Framing Europe: Attitudes to European Integration in Germany, Spain, and the United Kingdom*. Princeton NJ and Oxford: Princeton University Press.

Downey, John and Koenig, Thomas (2006) 'Is there a European public sphere? The Berlusconi – Schulz case', *European Journal of Communication* 21 (2): 165–87.

Eder, Klaus (2007) 'The public sphere and European democracy: mechanisms of democratisation in the transnational situation', in Fossum and Schlesinger (eds) *The European Union and the Public Sphere*.

Eriksen, Thomas Hylland (2007) 'Nationalism and the Internet', *Nations and Nationalism* 13 (1): 1–17.

Foret, François and Schlesinger, Philip (2007) 'Religion and the European public sphere', in John Erik Fossum and Philip Schlesinger (eds) *The European Union and the Public Sphere: a Communicative Space in the Making?* London and New York: Routledge.

Fossuum, John Erik and Schlesinger, Philip (eds) (2007) *The European Union and the Public Sphere: a Communicative Space in the Making?* London and New York: Routledge.

Gellner, Ernest (1983) *Nations and Nationalism*. Oxford: Blackwell.

Gleissner, Martin and de Vreese, Claes H. (2005) 'News about the EU constitution: journalistic challenges and media portrayal of the European Union constitution', *Journalism* 6 (2): 221–41.

Habermas, Jürgen (1989 [1962]) *The Structural Transformation of the Public Sphere*. Cambridge: Polity Press.

Habermas, Jürgen (1997) *Between Facts and Norms*. Cambridge: Polity Press.

Habermas, Jürgen (2004) 'Why Europe needs a constitution', in E. O. Eriksen, J. E. Fossum and A. J. Menéndez (eds) *Developing a Constitution for Europe*, London and New York: Routledge.

Held, David (1995) *Democracy and the Global Order: From the Modern State to Cosmopolitan Governance*. Cambridge: Polity Press.

Held, David (2004) *Global Covenant: the Social Democratic Alternative to the Washington Consensus*. Cambridge: Polity Press.

Heller, Maria and Rényi, Ágnes (2007) 'EU enlargement, identity and the public sphere', in Fossum and Schlesinger (eds) *The European Union and the Public Sphere*.

Hjarvard, Stig (2001) 'News media and the globalization of the public sphere', in Stig Hjarvard (ed.) *Media in a Globalized Society*. Göteborg: Nordicom.

Jönssen, Christer, Tägil, Sven and Törnqvist, Gunnar (2000) *Organizing European Space*. London: Sage.

Jouët, Josiane and Pasquier, Dominique (eds) (2001) 'Médias et migrations', thematic issue of *Réseaux* 19 (107): 9–237.

Kevin, Deirdre (2003) *Europe in the Media: a Comparison of Reporting, Representation and Rhetoric in National Media Systems in Europe*. Mahwah NJ: Erlbaum.

Koenig, Thomas, Mihelj, Sabina, Downey, John and Gencel Bek, Mine (2006) 'Media framings of the issue of Turkish accession to the EU: a European or a national process?' *Innovation* 19 (2): 149–69.

Koopmans, Ruud and Erbe, Jessica (2004) 'Towards a European public sphere? Vertical and horizontal dimensions of Europeanized political communication', *Innovation* 18 (2): 97–118.

Meyer, Christoph, O. (2000) 'Towards a European public sphere? Transnational investigative journalism and the European Commission's resignation', in Barbara Baerns and Juliana Raupp (eds) *Information and Transnational Communication in Europe: Practice and Research*. Berlin: Vistas.

Middlemass, Keith (1995) *Orchestrating Europe: the Informal Politics of European Union, 1973–1995*. London: Harper Collins.

Moragas Spà, Miquel, Garitaonandía, Carmelo and López, Bernat (1999) *Television on Your Doorstep: Decentralization Experiences in the European Union*. Luton: University of Luton Press.

Morgan, David (1999) *The European Parliament, Mass Media and the Search for Power and Influence*. Aldershot: Ashgate Publishing.

Neveu, Catherine (2000) 'Citizens of Europe and European citizens: exploring European citizenship', in I. Bellier and T. Wilson (eds) *An Anthropology of the European Union: Building, Imagining and Experiencing the New Europe*. Oxford: Berg.

Neveu, Catherine (2002) 'Devenir Européen : entre individualisme et emprise des cadres', *Anthropologie et sociétés* 26: 127–38.

Neveu, Eric (2002) 'Europe as an 'Un-imaginable Community'? The failure of the French news-magazine l'*Européen*', *Journal of European Area Studies* 10: 283–300.

Price, Monroe E. (2002) *Media and Sovereignty: the Global Information Revolution and its Challenge to State Power*. Cambridge MA: MIT Press.

Schlesinger, Philip (1999) 'Changing spaces of political communication: the case of the European Union', *Political Communication* 16 (3): 263–79.

Schlesinger, Philip (2000) 'The nation and communicative space', in Howard Tumber (ed.) *Media Power, Professionals and Politics*. London: Routledge.

Schlesinger, Philip (2003) *The Babel of Europe? An Essay on Networks and Communicative Spaces*, ARENA Working Paper, Oslo: ARENA.

Schlesinger, Philip (2007) 'A fragile cosmopolitanism: on the unresolved ambiguities of the European public sphere', in Fossum and Schlesinger (eds) *The European Union and the Public Sphere*.

Schlesinger, Philip and Foret, François (2006) 'Political roof and sacred canopy? Religion and the EU constitution', *European Journal of Social Theory* 9 (1): 59–81.

Sinclair, John (2004) 'Globalization, supranational institutions, and media', in John Downing, Denis McQuail, Philip Schlesinger and Ellen Wartella (eds) *The Sage Handbook of Media Studies*. Thousand Oaks CA: Sage.

Splichal, Slavko (1999) *Public Opinion: Developments and Controversies in the Twentieth Century*. Lanham MD: Rowman & Littlefield.

Statham, Paul (2007) 'Political communication, European integration and the transformation of national public spheres: a comparison of Britain and France', in Fossum and Schlesinger (eds), *The European Union and the Public Sphere*.

Street, John (2001) *Mass Media, Politics and Democracy*. Basingstoke: Palgrave.

Trenz, Hans-Jörg and Eder, Klaus (2004) 'The democratising dynamics of a European public sphere: towards a theory of democratic functionalism', *European Journal of Social Theory* 7 (1): 5–25.

Williams, Raymond (1981) *Culture*. London: Fontana.

Part II
Spatial inequalities

6 Neoliberalism, imperialism and the media

David Hesmondhalgh

Globalisation and imperialism

The term 'globalisation' appears to be rapidly falling out of fashion.[1] George W. Bush has hardly ever used it, and on the political right it is increasingly felt to refer to a 1990s agenda, associated with the Third Way politics of Clinton and the first period of Blair's government, one where the benefits of Free Trade would power capitalist expansion, reaping fruits that would supposedly be shared by everyone. On the left, globalisation is still a widely used concept, but the events of the early twenty-first century and changes in intellectual fashion have brought a different political vocabulary to the fore: that of empire and imperialism.

This is not just a matter of the neoconservative venture in Iraq. It is true that the Second Gulf War and its appalling aftermath brought to the surface a set of concerns that had been strangely submerged during the 1990s, and that the war in Iraq reunified some sections of the radical left (at least those parts of it concerned about geopolitics) by making clear, even to some who supported earlier interventions in Kosovo and Afghanistan, the malign nature of the US state. But the returns of the concepts of empire and imperialism preceded the election of George W. Bush. Hardt and Negri's book *Empire*, published in 2000, found a ready audience among radical thinkers and activists. And the rising interest in imperialism has been shared by liberal and conservative intellectuals. In 2002 the *New York Times* magazine famously gave up its entire front page to the words 'The American empire. Get used to it' and inside the Canadian commentator and politician Michael Ignatieff extolled the virtues of an enlightened US hegemony (Ignatieff 2002). Jan Nederveen Pieterse (2004: 31) has noted other such apologies for 'enlightened' empire and remarks that, until recently, 'imperialism was a left-wing term, but now empire has become a mainstream theme and makes a comeback in everyday language'.

This shift from globalisation to imperialism has a particular resonance in the social sciences. For those engaged in the study of international communication, in the 1990s globalisation replaced cultural imperialism as the term most widely used in debates in that sub-field. In social theory, globalisation was very often used to denote something quite different from its meaning among left activists and centrist political strategists: *global interconnectedness* rather than the hidden coercions of free-trade economics. For example, the most developed critique of the notion of cultural imperialism in social theory, by John Tomlinson, explicitly contrasted imperialism with this social science sense of globalisation: 'The idea of imperialism contains, at least, the notion of a purposeful project: the *intended* spread of a social system from one centre of power across the globe. The idea of "globalisation" suggests interconnection and interdependency of all global areas which happens in a far less purposeful way' (1991: 175). Yet this still leaves hanging questions about the role of intention, strategy and the serving of interests in the global system, on the part of businesses, nation-states and international institutions. The ready embrace of concepts of empire and imperialism may well reflect a sense that the term 'globalisation' by social theorists evades such questions.[2]

This is not to say that globalisation is a completely redundant term. However, it may now be a term that has been used in such a variety of ways that its analytical purchase has become limited. It has been used too often to speak simplistically about a transition to a new era of 'complexity' or 'connectivity', and in a way that somehow downplays inequality, exploitation and injustice. Of course, there are many poor analyses of imperialism too, but the recent work of David Harvey suggests that this concept still has some potential for understanding the contemporary world, as long as it is used in a way that is sensitive to historical change, and to social theory. So in this chapter I argue that, handled correctly, imperialism can be a useful concept for understanding the relations between economics, politics and media culture in our times. Marxians may embrace such a claim, but others will find it harder to accept. Still more controversial is a second claim that I seek to defend here: that the most useful way to think about imperialism in relation to culture in the present conjuncture is via the notion of copyright.

Here is how I go about trying to justify these two claims. An invocation of the term 'imperialism' in relation to a critical analysis of the media is likely to be confused in many quarters with adherence to the concept of *cultural imperialism*. In the next section, I briefly differentiate my argument from advocates of 'the cultural imperialism thesis'. (My distance from globalisation theory will already be clear, I assume, from my earlier comments.) Let me be explicit, then. I am not advocating a return to those modes of media theory that have tended to be labelled 'cultural imperialism'. On the contrary, I outline my view that those approaches to the media that have adopted the term cultural imperialism do not in general provide adequate conceptual means for thinking through relations between economics, politics and culture.

In the third section I then proceed to argue that an essential (though not sufficient) condition for understanding political, economic and cultural relations in the present conjuncture is a theoretical and historical analysis of *neoliberalism*, and I outline what I think are the most promising uses of this term. Drawing upon Harvey's work, I see neoliberalism as a restructuring of strategies for dealing with the recurring problems of over-accumulation that afflict capitalism, in the interests of the most powerful and wealthy corporations and individuals, and away from social benefits.

The fourth section then addresses the second claim above, regarding copyright. I show that a new nexus of state and financial power under-pinned by neoliberalism is now becoming increasingly tied to the global governance of symbol production and consumption. I then argue that international developments in copyright provide a very significant example of this trend. Copyright is significant in this respect both because of its practical importance (it provides the basis by which culture is made into property) and because its strengthening under neoliberalism has important political and ethical consequences.

The fifth section provides further key elements in justifying the two main claims outlined above, and again David Harvey's recent work is a resource. For Harvey's concept of *accumulation by dispossession* (a revision of Marx's notion of primitive accumulation) in his book *The New Imperialism* (2003) helps to provide an explanation of why neoliberalism has made its own 'cultural turn'. In other words, it helps to explain why there has been an increasing emphasis on information, knowledge and culture in neoliberal discourse. In a nutshell, forms of creativity and knowledge which were not previously conceived as ownable are brought into the intellectual property system, making them available for the investment of capital and the making of profit, and helping to avoid the perennial problems of over-accumulation which haunt capitalism. Capitalism drives further into relatively uncommodified domains and its same restless expansion also leads its drive into new geographical territories. A final section then considers the implications of the arguments in the chapter for understanding the relations between imperialism and culture, and the potential rewards for media analysis, and social theory, if these relations are properly thought through.

Cultural imperialism theory and its problems

Critics have over the years pointed to a number of problems with work carried out under the banner of cultural or media imperialism (or cultural dependence and other variants of the approach): that it operated with an overly simplistic dualism between 'West' and 'non-West'; that it assumed the homogenisation of culture, in the face of evidence of complex multi-plication and hybridisation; and that it tended to assume certain effects for Western cultural exports rather than investigating the ambivalent ways in which they were incorporated into other spaces.[3] I agree with many formulations of these criticisms. I think that capitalist culture is more complex and contradictory than many cultural imperialism writers were able to recognise.

Yet, even if we do not return to these particular and problematic operations of the concept, it might be argued in response to such criticisms that cultural imperialism serves as an 'evocative metaphor', in Annabelle Sreberny's (1997) words, for global processes of (cultural) inequality. (Sreberny's fine piece was not advocating this, but was rather pointing to the way the term has generally been used.) To use the term in this loosely metaphorical way would in my view be a mistake, because we need greater clarity about the relations between imperialism and culture. Vivid metaphors are important but, as David Harvey remarks, 'imperialism is a word that trips easily off the tongue' and 'has such different meanings that it is difficult to use it without clarification as an analytic rather than a polemical term' (2003: 26). There are good reasons to be interested in the concept of imperialism but I believe we need to take the term imperialism more seriously than did the vast majority of writers who used the term cultural or media imperialism.

'Imperialism', for example, was often used in this literature simply to designate the domination of people in some countries by people in another, or of some states by others. Herbert Schiller, who many in media and communication studies would name as the leading exponent of the idea of cultural imperialism, tends to use cultural domination and media/cultural imperialism more or less interchangeably. Schiller's definition of imperialism was 'a system of exploitative control of people and resources' (1991: 17). The problem is that this could just as well serve as an equally loose definition of capitalism. And this points to a crucial issue in understanding international cultural flows in the present historical moment: the relationship between capitalism and imperialism. In the modern world there may be a number of types and definitions of imperialism, but the type that is generally agreed to matter, whether on the left, the right or in the political centre, is *capitalist imperialism*. It seems reasonable to infer that any adequate understanding of imperialism needs to involve a developed consideration of contemporary political-economic processes – and vice versa. Consequently, if we want to think about culture in relation to imperialism it is also surely important to address the way in which contemporary capitalism operates in relation to culture – and here I mean culture in the specific sense of the production and consumption of symbols. This then means thinking about how the cultural industries fit – and don't fit – with developments in capitalism as a whole.

Explaining neoliberalism

Writers of all political persuasions agree that growth is fundamental to capitalism, because only through growth can profits be assured. Stagnation *is* crisis in capitalism. All economic systems are inclined to cycles of expansion and crisis but the systems we call capitalist are especially so. A characteristic of leftist political-economic analysis is to oppose conservative and postmodern complacency about such cycles by seeking to understand how they come about. Some see these periods as crises of over-accumulation, whereby opportunities for profitable investment cannot be found for capital and stagnation therefore sets in. This is what happened in the 1930s and 1970s. Such crises are registered in a variety of forms: gluts of commodities; idle production capacity – including vast numbers of 'unemployed' women and men; and surpluses of money capital lacking outlets. One of David Harvey's major contributions to social and political theory has been to analyse how capitalists, and the nation-states and financial institutions linked to them, attempt to resolve this recurring problem. For Harvey there are two main ways to absorb excess capital. The first is temporally, via long-term capital investment. This could be directly profit-seeking (such as a new drug, or a new film) or it might take the form of social expenditure (such as new schools). The second is spatial, via the opening up of new markets, the creation of new production capacities, or the seeking of new resources, including labour, land and raw materials. In practice the two are combined, in what Harvey calls 'spatio-temporal fixes'. In other words, these are attempts to fix or solve the over-accumulation problem through spatial and temporal means (Harvey 1982, 1989).

The policies of national states, and of international organisations such as the IMF, have a huge impact on the forms these spatio-temporal fixes take, and on which regions and nations benefit from them and which do not. In his more recent work (notably 2003, 2005) Harvey has explored the profound shift that has taken place since the 1970s in how states manage national and international economic processes, beginning with experiments in Chile and Argentina but consolidated in the United States and the United Kingdom in the 1980s. Of course the term generally used for this new conception of political-economic management is *neoliberalism*. Harvey portrays neoliberalism as a response to the worldwide economic crisis of over-accumulation in the 1970s. In the first instance, comments Harvey, it is 'a theory of political economic practices that proposes that human well-being can best be advanced by liberating individual entrepreneurial freedoms and skills within an institutional framework characterised by strong private property rights, free markets, and free trade' (2005: 2). While advocates of such neoliberal theory portray free trade and private enterprise as the means to revivify stagnant economies, they also assume – importantly for the present context – the continuing existence of extremely powerful oligopolies and nodal points of state power, especially the United States.

But how have these theories have been implemented in policy? Harvey (2005) argues that neoliberalism has involved an important historical shift. The social concessions that were achieved in the post-war period by the working classes in advanced industrial economies have been overturned in some cases and remain under threat in others. Neoliberal policy has directed over-accumulated capital away from social expenditure in the interests of social justice and towards ventures that have been hugely profitable for a new international class of chief executive officers and investors. Just as important to neoliberalism as changes in government policy, though less publicly acknowledged, has been the 'deregulation' of international finance capital. This has resulted in a massive increase in the transnational power and activity of finance. Wall Street and to a lesser extent the London 'City' have become the main centres of global finance. The US Treasury and Wall Street have a considerable influence over the regulation of this transnational financial activity, and over the key global economic institutions, the IMF and World Bank, which force vulnerable states to open up their borders for 'free trade' and financial flows.

So the worldwide spread of neoliberalism has created a networked world of financial flows of surplus capital with vast concentrations of power (both reflecting and reinforcing the constant tendency in capitalist competition towards oligopoly). These surpluses can be used up by investment in 'productive' though often extremely harmful activities (dams in India and China, for example) but also by devaluing assets in vulnerable countries, such as Thailand and Mexico. The Wall Street–US Treasury nexus controls global capital values through its ability to control the value of the international currency, the dollar. In effect, then, neoliberalism has re-established the United States as the global hegemon, a position that seemed in doubt to many as recently as the early 1990s. This position may not be secure in the long term, and it never could be, given the fragile stability of the international financial system.[4] However, this dominance, along with the use by the United States of military force as a central plank of its foreign policy, has helped to reinvigorate discussion of imperialism.

Neoliberalism in the symbolic realm: copyright and TRIPS

Neoliberalism, then, is a useful – indeed, essential – overarching term to describe what have emerged as the central guiding principles of economic thought and management in advanced industrial countries – and increasingly in developing and least developed countries too – over the last three decades.[5] It can also be understood as providing the basis of a new variant of capitalist imperialism, based on the Treasury–Wall Street nexus and the political-economic (as well as military) might of the United States. But how have neoliberal policies been manifested and implemented in the domains of media and culture? The key term is marketisation – the process by which market exchange increasingly comes to permeate media and cultural sectors. This involves a number of processes, most notably privatisation of government-owned enterprises and institutions, the lifting of restraints on businesses so that they can pursue profit more easily, and the expansion of private ownership. Various rationales had underpinned the involvement of the state in cultural markets, including the view that telecommunications needed to be understood as a public utility, along the lines of transport or the electricity system; the view that broadcasting was a limited, national resource that governments needed to parcel out; and also the belief that broadcasting had a particular social power, which needed controlling. Elsewhere (Hesmondhalgh 2007: 105–36) I have analysed how each of these rationales was undermined in the 1980s and 1990s, leading to four waves of marketisation. The first wave took place in the United States from the early 1980s onwards, and this then, in a second wave, had an important influence on changes in other advanced industrial states. A third wave in the early 1990s saw a number of countries with authoritarian traditions of state control and ownership, including the Stalinist regimes of Eastern Europe, initiate policies of communications and media 'liberalisation'. Finally, a further round of policy changes involved paving the way for supposed convergence between telecommunications, media and computers in the 1990s and 2000s.[6]

Two factors provided important legitimation for this neoliberal marketisation in the realm of culture and communication. The first was the idea of the information society (and variants such as the 'knowledge economy', more recently reinvented as the 'creative economy') – that information, knowledge, culture, etc., were the main growth areas of national and international economies, and therefore the basis of future or present prosperity. The second was the exploitation of understandable anxieties about government intervention in personal, cultural and political expression. As in all of the different realms of economies where neoliberalism has had an impact, international policy agencies – whether supranational unions of states such as the European Union (EU), trade blocs such as North America Free Trade Agreement (NAFTA) or international trade organisations such as the World Trade Organisation (WTO) – have had an important role to play.

These changes have contributed to considerable change in the cultural industries since the late 1980s, including the further growth of massive conglomerates, and even greater international flows of culture than before. To put the point bluntly, capital has shown an unprecedented interest in culture – and I consider the reasons for this below. As we have seen, 'globalisation' and 'cultural imperialism' theories differ considerably in their interpretations of the intensified and accelerated flows of culture that the world has been witnessing. Here, though, I want to focus on a dimension of neoliberalism that these theories have not really dealt with, one which – to recall Harvey's concise definition above – advocates and develops 'strong private property rights'. In the realm of culture (understood here as the production and consumption of symbols) the most important way in which private property rights are constructed and protected is via copyright. It is worth noting in passing that this fact has been neglected to a remarkable degree in analysis of international communication, including 'cultural imperialism' theory, and indeed in media and cultural studies in general. This is odd, because, as I will explain, cultural property rights (especially copyright) are a critical factor in the relationship between imperialism and culture.

An important sign that culture, information and knowledge are becoming more central to capitalism than ever before is to be found in the implementation of the WTO treaty. A crucial development was the 1994 signing of TRIPS (Trade Related Aspects of Intellectual Property Rights Agreement), one of the twenty-eight agreements or 'chapters' that came out of the Uruguay round of world trade negotiations. Another agreement set up the WTO and the WTO administers TRIPS. The intellectual property standards in TRIPS are therefore obligatory for the (currently) 149 members of the WTO who must – with small provisos and delays – change their national laws and practices to conform to these standards. Christopher May (2004) has shown how developing countries are receiving extensive technical support in training legislators and administrators from a variety of international, government and non-governmental organisations. This is double-edged. It means that developing countries will have more expertise which they can use to take advantage of flexibilities in TRIPS. But it also undoubtedly involves the spread of what we might call cultural neoliberalism. At the policy level, compliance with TRIPS means huge adjustments in countries that have no notion of intellectual property in the sense in which it is enshrined in 'Western' copyright law. While many creative artists in developing countries welcome copyright because they believe it will protect their work from exploitation, by others within their own society and by Western corporations, in fact the spread of TRIPS means the normalisation and legitimation of a fundamentally 'Western' notion of culture across the world. This vision sees copyright as a necessary incentive for artistic or symbolic creativity (and patents as the necessary incentive for scientific creativity). Individual compensation is portrayed as the main driving force of human cultural activity. My main argument, then, is that these various developments need to be interpreted as a form of imperialism in relation to culture. Powerful interests in certain nation states in certain parts of the world are exercising their political-economic power over those elsewhere, in order to extend their power and influence.

The justificatory rhetoric of cultural neoliberalism claims that the globalisation of intellectual property rights embodied in TRIPS will bring more investment and innovation, for the benefit of all. But there is no doubt that the main beneficiaries of TRIPS so far have been based in the United States.[7] One important question for understanding the relationship between imperialism and culture therefore becomes: how did this happen? How did this significant international agreement enhance the United States' (and to some extent the EU's) dominant position in terms of intellectual property, including copyright? Drahos and Braithwaite's authoritative account (2002) shows how a small number of US companies 'captured the US trade agenda-setting process and then, in partnership with European and Japanese multinationals, drafted intellectual property principles that became the blueprint for TRIPS .... The resistance of developing countries was crushed through trade power' (p. 12). This, they argue, was a failure of democracy, and a vital one because of the way in which property rights confer authority over resources, and the way in which informational and cultural resources are important to so many people. They give the examples of information in the form of chemical formulae, the DNA in plants and animals, the algorithms that underpin digital technologies and the knowledge in books and electronic databases. (See Sell 2003 for another valuable account of TRIPS, using realist social theory.)

As Dave Laing (2004) has outlined, the changes to national legislation regimes around the world that have been brought about by TRIPS are complemented by the actions of the United States Trade Representative (USTR), who under Special Provision 301 in the 1988 Omnibus Trade and Competitiveness Act can blacklist countries whose intellectual property practices are harmful to the US copyright industries. This list is announced each year, and the USTR draws heavily on information provided by the International Intellectual Property Alliance (IIPA), which is effectively a lobbying arm of the major US cultural industries (Laing 2004). The relevance of all this to debates about links between imperialism and culture should now be clear. The wealthiest and most powerful countries have used their privileged position to further ensure dominance of a rapidly growing area of modern production and consumption.

The negative implications of this are not just about inequality, they also concern a danger to basic rights posed by new kinds of intellectual property regulation, involving what Drahos and Braithwaite call 'a quiet accretion of restrictions' (2002: 4). Changes to national legislation that have taken place in the wake of the policy atmosphere generated by TRIPS have accelerated the long-term trend towards stronger copyrights. The key elements here are longer terms of existing rights, fewer exceptions to the restrictions on users embodied in those rights (most important, a reduction in 'fair use' or 'fair dealing') and in many cases the creation of new rights. There is no space here to deal with these issues in depth, but Siva Vaidhyanathan (2001: 25) provides an outline of how, in the United States itself, copyright terms have been extended:

1709 Fourteen years.
1831 Twenty-eight, renewable for fourteen more.
1909 Twenty-eight, renewable for twenty-eight more.
1976 Until fifty years after the author's death.
1998 Until seventy years after the author's death.[8]

Such strengthenings of copyright have prevented vast numbers of works from passing into the public domain. This has significant implications for human freedom in the realm of culture. It is important that, against romantic and individualist theories of creativity, we understand that 'significant difference is not made out of the internal resources of the creative subject'; rather, as various writers including Roland Barthes have suggested, such difference is 'generated through the selection, combination and revoicing of what is already there' (Toynbee 2001: 8). Creativity, in other words, is *social* and *intertextual*. If this is the case, then to place radical restrictions on this 'selection, combination and revoicing' through limitations on the public domain is ethically problematic.

My main focus in this chapter is on what international developments in copyright tell us about the relations between imperialism and culture. Earlier, in discussing David Harvey's account, I argued that an adequate social-theoretical account of these relations (one which would throw light on potential connections between economics, politics and culture) needs to consider the problem of *capitalist* imperialism. What does the international strengthening of copyright tell us about this?

One way to begin to answer this question is to see the strengthening of cultural property rights, exemplified here in the internationalisation of the copyright aspects of TRIPS, as a manifestation of a wider trend: the increasing encroachment of private ownership on knowledge and culture. The spread of copyright, along the lines defined in TRIPS and in the visions of advocates of stronger copyright, both within advanced industrial countries and in other societies, means that in more and more places the prevailing conceptions of what constitutes creative or cultural work begin to shift towards the individual property model, and away from a notion of social or collective creativity. And while Western copyright law in theory protects the individual author, in practice copyrights tend to be owned by corporations (which in a bizarre twist are defined as individuals for the purposes of law). This then feeds into a vicious spiral by which cultural corporations become more powerful and more effective in lobbying governments, which then increases corporate power still further.[9]

How is all this connected to the earlier discussions of neoliberalism and capitalist imperialism? TRIPS would simply not have been possible without the geopolitical-economic developments described above, which have reinforced the economic and political powers of the United States, and to a lesser extent the EU. As I indicated briefly in the previous section, neoliberalism can be seen as a set of principles underlying the restructuring of strategies for dealing with the recurring problems of over-accumulation that afflict capitalism, in a way that systematically favours the interests of the most powerful and wealthy corporations, states and individuals. If it is valid to understand neoliberalism as linked to a new form of capitalist imperialism, based around the US Treasury–Wall Street nexus, and the political-economic might of the United States, then here I think we begin to see important connections between contemporary capitalist imperialism, on the one hand, and culture on the other. For the copyright aspects of TRIPS and their implementation over the last decade suggest that the rise of a new nexus of state and financial power underpinned by neoliberalism is now becoming increasingly tied to the global governance of symbol production and consumption, with marked effects on how creativity is conceptualised and practised. There is of course a curious irony here. Neoliberalism, widely presented by its advocates as a limiting of oppressive government intervention, in the cultural realm as elsewhere, actually depends upon state regulation and control. In cultural markets this takes the form of intellectual property statutes, agencies and policing (and other forms too).

Cultural accumulation by dispossession?

However, this leaves an important issue still unresolved. Why has neoliberalism made its own 'cultural turn'? Why the increasing emphasis on information, knowledge and culture in neoliberal discourse, and in contemporary capitalism?

To begin to answer this, we need history. The transition from feudalism to capitalism in Europe is generally taken to have happened between the fifteenth and eighteenth centuries. How did capitalists first get hold of their capital *as* capital? This earth-shattering shift was made possible by what Adam Smith called 'original' or 'primitive' accumulation. Building on Smith, Marx outlined in Part VIII of Volume One of *Capital* the major forms of primitive accumulation. These included the expulsion of the peasants; the appropriation of assets; monetisation of exchange and taxation; the commodification of labour power and the suppression of alternatives; usury, national debt and the credit system; the slave trade; the conversion of common, collective, property rights into exclusive private property rights; and the suppression of rights to the commons.

Hannah Arendt's account of late nineteenth and early twentieth-century European imperialism (published as the second part of *The Origins of Totalitarianism*, but also as a separate volume, Arendt 1968) saw it as rooted in the need for the newly dominant bourgeoisie to expand their economic control beyond the increasingly inadequate territorial boundaries of the nation state. David Harvey in *The New Imperialism* follows Arendt's cue in opposing explanations of imperialism based on under-consumption (such as those provided by Lenin and Rosa Luxemburg). Harvey's emphasis instead is on the thrust by capitalists to deal with the ever-present problems of accumulation via expansion, or by the use of space, and he ties this to an important argument about primitive accumulation. Taking the view that primitive accumulation may in fact have remained central to capitalism, rather than disappearing with its secure establishment in Europe, and in order to avoid the connotations of 'primitive', Harvey coins the phrase 'accumulation by dispossession'.[10] If we accept Harvey's view of the continuing relevance of these processes, then it seems to me that, of the variants of 'accumulation by dispossession' discussed by Marx, two are particularly pertinent to understanding capitalist imperialism in the context of culture and knowledge in the present period: the conversion of common, collective, property rights into exclusive private property rights; and the suppression of rights to the commons.

The term *commons* – used to refer to the common land available to all in the settlements of feudal Europe – is especially interesting here. 'Enclosure' is a term used historically to refer to the process, which in the case of England took place mainly between the fifteenth century and the eighteenth, by which the medieval commons became the private property of landowners.[11] But the term commons has been increasingly used by critics of intellectual property law and practice as a metaphor for that part of our lives which should be a sharable resource for the benefit of all, and the term enclosure has been applied to the increasing encroachment on such commons of private ownership of culture and knowledge (e.g. May 2000; Boyle 2003).

This use of 'commons' will probably be familiar even to those who do not follow copyright debates closely. But the concept of 'accumulation by dispossession' allows us to understand both the original acts of enclosure in the transition from feudalism to capitalism and what James Boyle calls the 'second enclosure' movement, involving the private appropriation of culture and knowledge, as more than just metaphorically linked: they are part of the same long-term global march of capitalist relations into ever more areas of life.[12] This then can provide at least part of an explanation for capitalism's turn to culture, knowledge and information. Forms of creativity and knowledge which were not previously conceived as ownable are brought into the intellectual property system, making them available for the investment of capital and the making of profit, and helping to avoid the perennial problems of over-accumulation which haunt capitalism. Importantly, this applies not only to culture, which is commodified primarily through copyright, but also to other ways in which previously inalienable products are made the object of ownership, including nature and the person, where patent is the crucial instrument. John Frow, for example, has analysed the intellectual property issues and their implications for contemporary culture of the significant and ever-growing trade in bodily organs, and in the use of the biodiversity of developing countries in the agrochemical and pharmaceutical industries (Frow 1996: chapter 3).

But how does this fit more specifically with an understanding of *imperialism* or capitalist imperialism (rather than of capitalism more generally)? Harvey argues, drawing on earlier work by Giovanni Arrighi, that an understanding of imperialism needs to take account of two distinct but intertwined logics, which take different forms and relations in different imperialist projects: the political state-driven logic of territorial expansion, and the economically driven logic of capitalist expansion. Imperialistic practices involve, from the point of view of this second, economically driven logic, 'exploiting the uneven geographical conditions under which capital accumulation occurs' (Harvey 2003: 30) and taking advantage of asymmetries in exchange relations. This, then, is what we see in the spread of intellectual property across the world: increasing opportunities for profit for Western-based corporations, and the commodification and privatisation in developing countries of aspects of culture, nature and personhood previously conceived of as outside the market.

Imperialism and culture

In this final section I want to consider the implications of this discussion for a renewed account of the relations between culture and imperialism, and for the study of media and international communication.

An implication of my approach here for media studies of international communication is that we need to move beyond a certain *impasse* in the cultural imperialism literature. It is probably unfair for critics to claim that concepts such as active audiences and cultural hybridity demolish the notion of cultural imperialism. After all, there was more to the idea of cultural imperialism than functionalist assumptions about the effects of texts. But we can accept the view that the effects of imported content are much more complex and ambivalent than many critical scholars were initially prepared to accept, and still develop a critical account of international communication. As I have implied in this chapter, I think that one extremely important part of such a critical account (though not, of course, the only one) needs to be based on an understanding of *the commodification of culture as accumulation by dispossession*. I argued above that this is clearly manifested in attacks on the cultural commons enshrined in the strengthening and spread of copyright and more generally of Euro-American notions of intellectual property.

This attention to copyright has other advantages for a critical account of the media. It raises fundamental issues about where the money from symbol making comes from and where it goes, and this could serve to make questions concerning *cultural labour* more central than they have been in media studies (see Part IV of this book). But it also potentially links up debates about the international governance of the cultural industries with other debates, such as those about the control of pharmaceutical and agricultural patents. The connection is the notion of intellectual property, of the ownership of ideas, of knowledge, of culture. While 'ownership and control' have rightly been a very important element of political economy research, a somewhat intellectually impoverished notion of ownership has been at work there. To improve on this, we need to relate debates about the ownership of companies to the more fundamental idea of what it means to treat knowledge and culture as *property*. For this raises important questions about control over who has the right and the power to speak, make images, sing and so on, forms of control which often exacerbate more general patterns of inequality, linked to class, ethnicity and gender.

I have also argued for the value of imperialism as a concept with real relevance for understanding the media. There are implications here for those versions of social theory that see globalisation as an essentially undirected process of increasing global complexity. At one level, such theory is right to point to problems in identifying some directive, intentional force. There is no committee of the ruling class dictating strategies of accumulation by dispossession. It is the product of hundreds of businesspeople and financiers making decisions about how best to achieve a good return on investment. But, at another level, there is no doubt that many of the changes discussed here *are* the result of concerted activity in the interests of particular groups of people – especially the owners and executives of the large corporations that dominate the production and distribution of culture, and particularly in the United States. And these actions are underpinned by racist systems of thought, which hold that the cultural outputs of other peoples are ultimately lacking in value, and that their systems of production and consumption need to be brought into line with the way things are done in the West.

This has implications for activism – but they are not easy ones. Accounts based on the idea of 'cultural imperialism' lacked an explanatory account which could locate the commodification of culture across the world within the broader context of capitalist accumulation. The version here, based on Harvey, is only part of such an explanatory account but the notion of accumulation by cultural dispossession helps to draw links with other similar forms of accumulation, including environmental depletion. Perhaps what is needed in the short term is a kind of radical cultural fair-trade movement, which attempts to develop alternative forms of licensing systems appropriate for different developing countries (see Drahos and Mayne 2002 for an important collection of analyses of these issues); perhaps what is needed in the longer term is to persuade everyone on the left to recognise the importance of intellectual property in the modern world, and to build a widespread commitment for a more robust notion of the cultural commons. At the same time, however, this fight against accumulation through dispossession in culture needs to be allied to a critique of the romantic celebration of pre-capitalist relations. We need a dialectical understanding of the development of capitalism. Marx was famously disparaging about the social relations that capitalism displaced; even imperialism was better than feudal poverty and ignorance. We do not need to take this Marxist line to recognise that capitalism can bring positive changes in its wake. We cannot argue for keeping cultural institutions in developing countries at the level of often exploitative local entrepreneurship (though the fact that criminals become so involved in cultural production in such countries is itself a product of dubious copyright regimes). There are no easy solutions. Yet it seems clear that those committed to a public conception of culture, rather than a privatised, individualised one, need to work to resist the spread of neoliberal intellectual property regimes.

Notes

1 This chapter is based on papers that I gave at conferences in Evora (Portugal), Helsinki, Taipei, Cairo and London in 2006. I'm grateful to the various organisers and to those who commented on those papers at these events, plus Des Freedman, Nick Stevenson and, as ever, Jason Toynbee. An earlier written version appeared in Finnish in *Tiedotustutkimus* 29: 2 (2006).

2 Among the thousands of social theory publications on globalisation, probably the leading account was Giddens (1990), where it is coupled with that other great social theory concept of the 1990s, modernity. Jan Nederveen Pieterse (2004: 31–9) has addressed explicitly the relations between globalisation and empire. He is right to say that globalisation does not equal imperialism, but his differentiation between the two terms, which he ends up equating with different eras, seems to me to be dubiously overstated. The era of 'contemporary globalisation' may have seen some multiplicity and diffusion of power but there has also been recentralisation and greater inequality.

3 The most thorough and intelligent critical treatment is Tomlinson (1991), already mentioned above. Lee (1979) also provided some useful systematic treatment of earlier accounts.

4 The economic historian Giovanni Arrighi believes that the rise of East Asian economies will destabilise US hegemony (see Arrighi 2005). That may be the case in the medium term, but for now the United States has ridden all the successive shocks and crises of the last fifteen years, and continues to prosper.

5 Some critics would claim that neoliberalism is too broad a term to be useful. (This is strongly implied by Larner 2003, for example.) But the fact that neoliberal theory is applied in different forms in different nation states in no way invalidates the notion that there is something that can usefully be labelled 'neoliberalism' that they share in common.

6 In his chapter in this book Daniel Hallin further unpacks neoliberalism and marketisation in relation to the media.

7 'No one disagrees that TRIPS has conferred massive benefits on the US economy, the world's biggest net intellectual property exporter' (Drahos with Braithwaite 2002: 12).

8 It is worth noting that 'authors' are very rarely the owners of rights with any value; such rights are nearly always assigned to corporations. Also, there is a separate set of rights in most countries, for those works created out of corporate authorship, such as films. The US Copyright Term Extension Act of 1998 extended corporate authorship from seventy-five to ninety-five years.

9 As May points out, 'while mechanisms exist at the national level to ameliorate problems that the right to private rewards might produce, few mechanisms exist at the global level. There is little way for developing countries to meaningfully factor in the national social costs of strong IPR laws' (p. 833). While May is mainly thinking of patents here, the same is true of copyright law.

10 The emphasis in Marx's account (in *Capital*, Volume I) is on coercion rather than abstinence, and this is a key difference from Weber and other non-Marxian accounts of the rise of capitalism. Harvey, as a good neo-Marxist who has read his Gramsci, accepts that we need to understand the way that consent is mobilised for such changes as well as the use of force and violence

to achieve them. There are numerous debates within and outside Marxism about the adequacy of Marx's conception of primitive accumulation. Maurice Dobb argued, like Marx, that contradictions in pre-capitalist relations were the primary motor of change, with the rise of commerce as just the main catalyst for break-up, rather than the primary cause in itself, whereas Paul Sweezy saw exchange as the basis of the breaking up of pre-capitalist relations. See the essays collected in Hilton (1976).

11 The injustices of the original enclosures have been discussed, among many others, by Polanyi (2001/1944: 36 ff.). See Travis (2000) for a detailed comparison of the original enclosures with 'enclosures' of intellectual property.

12 Boyle's article (2003) contains a discussion of the concept of commons in relation to intellectual property, and a comparison of the idea with that of the legal concept of the 'public domain'. One reason he gives for preferring the notion of the commons to that of the public domain is that phenomena such as free or open-source software, although often understood as belonging to the public domain, are actually outside it, and are better understood in terms of the long-standing debates in the legal and political science literature on 'governing the commons'. This is helpful, but Boyle remains silent on the historical forces driving changes in intellectual property.

Bibliography

Arendt, Hannah (1968) *Imperialism*. New York: Harcourt Brace.

Arrighi, Giovanni (2005) 'Hegemony unravelling – 2', *New Left Review* 33: 83–116 (second series).

Boyle, James (2003) 'The second enclosure movement and the construction of the public domain', *Law and Contemporary Problems* 66: 33–74.

Drahos, Peter, with Braithwaite, John (2002) *Information Feudalism: Who owns the Knowledge Economy?* London: Earthscan.

Drahos, Peter and Mayne, Ruth (eds) (2002) *Global Intellectual Property Rights*. Basingstoke: Palgrave/Oxfam.

Frow, John (1996) *Time and Commodity Culture*. Oxford: Oxford University Press.

Giddens, Anthony (1990) *The Consequences of Modernity*. Cambridge: Polity Press.

Hardt, Michael and Negri, Antonio (2000) *Empire*. Cambridge MA: Harvard University Press.

Harvey, David (1982) *The Limits to Capital*. Oxford: Blackwell.

Harvey, David (1989) *The Condition of Postmodernity*. Oxford: Blackwell.

Harvey, David (2003) *The New Imperialism*. Oxford: Oxford University Press.

Harvey, David (2005) *A Brief History of Neoliberalism*. Oxford: Oxford University Press.

Hesmondhalgh, David (2007) *The Cultural Industries, second edition*. London and Los Angeles: SAGE.

Hilton, Rodney (ed.) (1976) *The Transition from Feudalism to Capitalism*. London: Verso.

Ignatieff, Michael (2002) 'Nation-building lite', *NYT Magazine*, 28 July.

Laing, Dave (2004) 'Copyright, politics and the international music industry', in Simon Frith and Lee Marshall (eds) *Music and Copyright*, 2nd edn. Edinburgh: Edinburgh University Press.

Larner, Wendy (2003) Guest editorial, *Environment and Planning D: Society and Space* 21: 509–12.

Lee, Chin-Chuan (1979) *Media Imperialism Reconsidered*. Beverly Hills CA: Sage.

May, Christopher (2000) *A Global Political Economy of Intellectual Property Rights*. London: Routledge.

May, Christopher (2004) 'Capacity building and the (re)production of intellectual property rights', *Third World Quarterly* 25 (5): 821–37.

Nederveen Pieterse, Jan (2004) *Globalization or Empire?* New York: Routledge.

Polanyi, Karl (2001/1944) *The Great Transformation: the Political and Economic Origins of our Time*. Boston MA: Beacon Press.

Schiller, Herbert I. (1991) 'Not yet the post-imperialist era', *Critical Studies in Mass Communication* 8: 13–28.

Sell, Susan K. (2003) *Private Power, Public Law*. Cambridge: Cambridge University Press.

Sreberny, Annabelle (1997) 'The many cultural faces of imperialism', in Peter Golding and Phil Harris (eds) *Beyond Cultural Imperialism*. London: Sage.

Tomlinson, John (1991) *Cultural Imperialism*. London: Pinter.

Toynbee, Jason (2001) 'Creating problems: social authorship, copyright and the production of culture', Pavis Papers in Social and Cultural Research 3. Milton Keynes: Open University.

Travis, Hannibal (2000) 'Pirates of the information infrastructure: Blackstonian copyright and the First Amendment', *Berkeley Technology Law Journal* 15 (777 [*sic*]).

Vaidhyanathan, Siva (2001) *Copyrights and Copywrongs: the Rise of Intellectual Property and how it threatens Creativity*. New York: New York University Press.

7 A contemporary Persian letter and its global purloining

The shifting spatialities of contemporary communication

Annabelle Sreberny

I start with a small communicative event, a letter from one person to another, and try to explore with and through it the ramifications for media analysis.[1] I want to use the letter that President Ahmadi-Nejad of Iran sent to President George W. Bush of the United States in May 2006 to think about the multiple, intertwined, forms of communication that constitute the contemporary mediascape; the way it functions to erode the boundary between private and public space; and about how and which people are 'interpellated' by contemporary forms of communication. The forms and efficacy of contemporary international diplomacy, specifically the volatile relationship between the United States and Iran, will be only briefly touched upon here.

It is often said that the letter as a form of communication is dead, replaced by e-mail and mobile telephony, and that collectively we will leave a poor paper trail for future historians to excavate. And yet a rather ancient form of political letter still exists within diplomatic relations, despite the availability of a plurality of other forms of communication. On the one hand, this was a private exchange of letters between two men; on the other hand, it partakes of a long history of diplomatic letters that inhabit a quasi-public status, especially as historical documents.[2] So the dynamics of private–public communication were foregrounded. I will use the work of John Durham Peters (1999) to explore these issues.

Another issue became apparent when the one person to whom the letter was addressed did not answer it while others, both professional commentators and ordinary members of the public in many countries, responded in an abundant profusion of serious and satirical ways. This raises the question of who exactly is 'interpellated' or hailed by a message, which of course does not have to be the 'intended recipient'. I explore this issue by examining the arguments raised by Lacan (1988) in relation to Edgar Allan Poe's short story *The Purloined Letter* and Derrida's dispute with Lacan.

This line of argument has two broad consequences. One is to open up once again an analysis of interpellation from Althusser on. His model seems to imply both a linear process – those who are hailed accept the hailing – but also that those who are 'hailed' are hailed only once by their hegemonic national ideological apparatus. His model of ideological interpellation seems to see effects as direct, univocal and potent, essentially a pre-media studies position, but also as framed within a national polity by the ideological state apparatus. So, in a globalising environment, with messages wilfully paying no heed to boundaries, where actually is hegemony located and indeed can it be/should it be spatialised? Lacan and Derrida offer a more open and ambivalent understanding of response, while Laclau resolves hegemony into practices of articulation and thus offers the possibility of unending antagonism but also continuous change, since counter-articulations are always being constructed.

The second issue, which is directly linked to the first, is the complex and difficult task of actually trying to think about media within a global, or transnational, frame of reference and to acknowledge that audiences as self-selecting agents accept or respond to 'hails' from many and varied messages, not all of which were intended for them. An overly glib approach in media and cultural studies and beyond is to see the United States as global hegemon by virtue of its expansive media conglomerates, an interesting elision from political articulation to economic influence. Indeed, there is an odd crossover in right and left perspectives in the assumption of a seamless 'empire' (Hardt and Negri 2000) into which everyone is entangled, while the 'clash of civilisations' (Huntington 1997) at least has the merit of recognising some ongoing struggle for hegemony.

Here it is particularly pertinent that this letter comes from the Iranian President to the US President; indeed, it is quite over-determined. The Islamic Republic of Iran has been framed in the West as the instigator of Islamic radicalism since its emergence in 1979 and has indeed maintained its own radical critique of Western cultural imperialism and US attempts at hegemony. In 2008 it appears that Iran is actually gaining credibility and support among numerous populations as a global counterweight to US hegemony.

Thus my final strand of analysis is about the meaning of the letter as an overture to dialogue between the Islamic Republic and the United States, which have been frozen in an icy silence since the hostage crisis of 1979. Here my focus is on the shift in the power dynamics of letters when the sending and receiving are visibly played out on a global stage, and on the consequences for the phony propaganda war in which the two nations are caught up. This is simply a taste of the complex set of issues around 'hard' and 'soft' power that undiplomatic relations makes problematic.

Thus, while I start with a small communicative event, the theoretical issues became complex. The letter can be seen as a brilliant counter-articulation to the United States' attempt to present itself as hegemonic. In the way the process played out, the letter worked to puncture US pre-tensions to listening and dialogue and actually revealed the rather clumsy nature of purported hegemony. I hope this approach has the merit of providing an actually existing example of the blurring of boundaries between private/closed and public/open communication that was played out transnationally; of the difficulties of thinking about hegemony and interpellation in a context of convergence among different forms of communicative technologies that cut across national borders; and of an instance of globality, or global reception, when spontaneously produced responses occur across transnational divides.

A letter, addressees and responses

On 8 May 2006 President Ahmadi-Nejad of the Islamic Republic of Iran sent President George W. Bush of the United States a letter. The US President did not reply, while vociferous responses echoed around the world.

For all the whirling talk of 'democracy' Ahmadi-Nejad probably enjoys a larger electoral majority than Bush, with the contestation about hanging chads and voter misregistration, although it is true that the choices put before the Iranian electorate had already been highly filtered. Relations between the two countries have been formally frozen since the post-revolutionary hostage crisis of 1979. Amidst a looming international controversy around Iran's desire for nuclear energy, and many internet whispers about the US desire for and preparations toward 'regime change', the eighteen-page letter was delivered by Swiss intermediaries.

As John Durham Peters has eloquently reminded us in his wonderful book *Speaking into the Air* (1999), the notion of the posted letter as a 'private, specifically addressed message' was quite late in development. In the mid-1850s in the United States postmasters were privy to local news and gossip, and were monitors of who was reading what, since local post offices kept logbooks of who purchased postage for what mail, as payment was typically made by the recipient, not the sender. It was the innovations of the mid-nineteenth century – which included the pre-paid postage stamp (1840, Great Britain), patents for envelopes that sealed off the contents from any kind of inspection (1849, United States) and the arrival of the street postbox – that heralded the convention of mail as a secure private channel, giving the sender control over their letter and making the address circuitry more focused. It is thus perhaps not such a surprise that Edgar Allan Poe's short story *The Purloined Letter* was written in 1845, before the privatisation of the post, when the receipt of a letter triggered all kinds of responses. I can't explain more than the gist of the story here:

The Queen receives a letter and, while being visited in her boudoir by the King, her evident embarrassment and attempt to hide the letter are seen by the Minister, who contrives to replace the letter with a substitute, to the knowledge of the Queen, who can do nothing for fear of attracting the King's attention. After eighteen months of frustrated police attempts to find the letter, Dupin, the detective, arrives at the Minister's office, only to discover the letter is in the most obvious place, hanging in front of the mantelpiece, whereupon he substitutes for it another letter, unknown to the Minister. However, Dupin's letter includes a message in his own handwriting that will make his act known to the Minister if and when he opens the letter. The obvious plays are on who sees what, who has power over whom, about interpersonal politics and the deceits that are performed.

Lacan presented his seminar on *The Purloined Letter* in 1955, as part of his weekly seminar on Freud's *Beyond the Pleasure Principle*, and it formed the first essay in *Ecrits*, a collection of his writings published in 1966 (and republished in 1988). His focus is twofold. He explores the anomalous nature of the letter, which serves as the 'true subject' of the story, since the reader knows very little about the actual content of the letter nor about the sender. He also explores the pattern of intersubjective relationships in the story where the visible monitoring of the actions of the other characters, their interchange around the letter, generates the principal interest. Lacan's seminar ends with the famous phrase 'a letter always arrives at its destination' (Lacan 1988: 53).

In 'Le facteur de la verité' Derrida takes on Lacan's reading of *The Purloined Letter*, mainly to question Lacan's claim that 'what the "purloined letter", that is, the not delivered letter [*letter en souffrance*], means is that a letter always arrives at its destination' (1987: 443–4). Derrida argues that 'a letter can always *not* arrive at its destination', the point being that not only can a letter always not arrive, but rather that 'it belongs to the structure of the letter to be capable, always, of not arriving' (1987: 444).

As Žižek (2001) points out in his reply to Derrida, the point of this claim is not that a letter will always reach 'the empirical other, who may receive it or not' but rather to '[lay] *bare the very mechanism of teleological illusion*', to point out that in fact that the 'true addressee' is 'the big Other', the symbolic order itself, which receives it '*the moment the letter is put into circulation*' (2001: 10). That is to say, at one level its meaning is already predefined. Žižek objects to Derrida's critique and accuses him of 'misread[ing] the Lacanian thesis', with what Žižek describes as the 'primordial response of common sense' argument that 'a letter can also miss its destination' (2001: 10). However, it is probably Žižek who has performed the misreading. While Žižek argues that the letter always arrives in the symbolic order, Derrida points out that the letter 'can always be fragmented without return, and the system of the symbolic, of castration, of the signifier, of the truth, of the contract, etc., always attempts to protect the letter from fragmentation' (1987: 444), an attempt that by its very existence demonstrates the acknowledged possibility of fragmentation.

While the various authors involved in this debate are keen to accuse others of misreadings, it seems quite clear on sustained reflection that what is at stake here is a more fundamental conflict of ideas. Derrida in fact, in his critique of Lacan, is taking on more than just the 'seminar on *The Purloined Letter*' and is developing a critique in line with a large portion of his work. As he says, precisely at the moment 'Dupin and the seminar find' the purloined letter, 'when they believe that it is here or there as on a map, a place on a map as on the body of a woman, they no longer see the map itself: not the map that the text describes at one moment or another, but the map [*carte*] that the text "is"' (1987: 443). That is to say, despite the attempts of character or reader to consign the letter to one place in a symbolic order, there is always an excess meaning, a remainder that cannot be so defined.

So how does this debate over the possibilities of a letter relate to our own quite particular case of a letter from Iran? Precisely in the emphasis placed by Derrida on the surplus of meaning that is denied by theorists of symbolic order. It is belief in the overriding dominance of a particular symbolic order, a belief that subsumes all facts and realities, convenient or not, into its own overriding logic that drove the US administration to reject this letter, to view it as nothing more than a cheap, transparent piece of propaganda, *Realpolitik* clear and simple. And it is not that there is no element of truth in their argument; but to advance only this far, to stop here, is to miss out on so much as well. As Derrida would point out, there is always more: there is always a remainder. Indeed, an acknowledgement that 'a letter can not arrive' may be an acknowledgement of the other with a different value system and set of interpretative lenses. Finally, here, Žižek's position, that a letter 'always arrives at its destination, since its destination is wherever it arrives' (Žižek 2001: 10) may be explained through his reformulation of Althusser's (1977) interpellatory call: the call is meant for whoever turns round and recognises it as a call.

But I am also suggesting that there is a further analytic step to be taken around issues of interpellation that works with and thinks through the nationcentric boundedness of the notion. In a globalised environment, where messages, ideologies, interpellations do not remain within nationally bounded space, where then is the location of hegemony – indeed, does hegemony have a location? Althusser has been read differently by subsequent theorists. While Hall (1989) retains a sense of locus, of hegemony being monolithic, massive and oppressive, Laclau and Mouffe (1985) treat hegemony as much more labile and less firmly situated. They resolve hegemony into practices of articulation and so the occasion for unending antagonism but continuous change (even if not apparent), because counter-articulation is always taking place.

The letter can be seen as a challenge to a putative US hegemony, a counter-articulation on the part of a far less powerful country. The manner in which the United States itself responded and the responses of commentators, at home and abroad, to which I turn, show the agonistic – or antagonistic – international politics at work.

Intended recipient, interpellated audiences

Thus we have here, triggered by a nineteenth-century essay about a purloined letter, an early and fascinating argument among the contemporary psychoanalytic and deconstructionist greats about the intention of communication and 'actual' versus intended audiences.

The actual Persian letter invited just such a real debate on an erudite academic e-mail list that focuses on the Middle East. Precisely such arguments were to be found as experts sought to disentangle the motivation behind Ahmadi-Nejad's letter. Weren't the Iranians 'simply playing politics?' I heard a realist specialist in international relations argue, so positioning Ahmadi-Nejad into a pre-fixed set of 'knowledgeable' positions about wily Iranians. Others wondered if the letter was really intended for Bush. Wasn't Ahmadinejad trying to speak to the American public over Bush's head? Didn't the letter 'really' summon 'international public opinion'? Wasn't Ahmadi-Nejad 'really' speaking to his Iranian publics? It could even be asked if he himself had reckoned that the failure to reply would be so revelatory. The intention of the sender and second-guessing the intended audience were the focus of debate, and the letter itself was not taken seriously as a communication, let alone positively imagined as an invitation, an opening up of possible dialogue, nor as possibly addressing multiple audiences simultaneously.

The White House immediately dismissed the letter as containing nothing new or of consequence. Bush stayed silent.

Some actual responses

Diplomatic letters are more like medieval letters patent, which were not personal but open ones. This letter was made public both by the Iranians and, translated, by the Americans some days after its delivery, and posted on the web.[3] If the intention of the letter's sender remained obscure, the actual responses to this letter were vivid. Exploring the actual responses is a large research project. Here I can only sketch some of the findings and focus on the analytic issues raised. In short, it seemed that almost everyone *except* the person to whom the letter was addressed had something to say. There is an obvious division of respondents: those who do this for a living and those who do not, so-called 'experts' and 'commentators' of various kinds and ordinary people.

The professional commentators are interesting both for the specific logics of argument but almost as much for their interlinkages; one right-wing commentator is connected to another while one Iranian diasporic voice links to many others such voices and to more liberal Western commentary.

US liberal commentators, for example, saw it as an opening that Bush should take up, as indeed did Henry Kissinger and Madeleine Albright. George Perkovich (2006), of the Carnegie Endowment for International

Peace, on 9 May 2006 said the letter raised questions about American 'justice', questioned whether the United States or Iran is more righteous, and suggested that the letter should be answered in kind by the Bush administration. 'You know, liberal societies, liberal democracies, have a whole lot to say on their behalf in terms of justice, and we ought to have that discussion, and take it frontally,' says Perkovich. 'We ought to take up the challenge'.

Fred Kaplan (2006) at Slate.com, in a piece on 10 May 2006 entitled 'Dear Mahmoud', noted the polite terms of address used. 'It may be worth noting that his letter opens, "Mr George Bush, President of the United States of America" (as opposed to, say, "Supreme Devil of the Land of Infidels"). Twelve times in the course of the letter Ahmadi-Nejad begins a new thought with a respectful "Mr President …". Twice he calls Bush "Your Excellency"'. Kaplan remarked that never, in the twenty-seven years since Ayatollah Khomeini's revolution, has an Iranian head of state addressed an American president directly – and so cordially – and argued that Bush should publicly respond to the letter, at length and in detail:

> Daffy as the letter is, it does contain one clue that Ahmadinejad might really be seeking a dialogue. More to the point, many people and governments in the world, especially (but by no means exclusively) in the Muslim world, are taking the letter seriously and believe that it deserves a reply …. In short, it provides a perfect opportunity for Bush to do what he should have been doing for the last few years – to lay out what America stands for, what we have in common with Muslim nations, and how our differences can be tolerated or settled without conflict.

David Limbaugh (2006), a right-wing commentator, on 11 May 2006 realised the Catch 22 that Bush was in by not replying. Ahmadi-Nejad's letter was seen as a positive step by many nations and media around the world. It was broadly welcomed by the Arab 'street'. The Indonesians, the Malaysians and the Chinese all urged Bush to respond and to negotiate with Iran. The world saw the delivery of the letter. The silence and lack of response were also seen, and spoke as loudly.

Satirical interventions abounded. On Iranian.com, a post on 16 May 2006 (http://www.iranian.com/Shorts/2006/may2006.html#9b) read:

> At the White House, aides said that writing a letter of such length to President Bush, who is known for his extreme distaste for reading, was the most provocative act Mr. Ahmadinejad could have possibly committed. 'Everyone knows that the last book the president read was *My Pet Goat*,' one aide said. 'Expecting him to read an eighteen-page letter is really asking for it, and that Iranian dude must have known that!'

Cartoonists, increasingly in public view because of the controversy over the Danish cartoons as well as Ahmadi-Nejad's proposal to solicit cartoons of the Holocaust, in an exhibition that went on show in Tehran in autumn 2006, offered condensed visualisations of this 'moment'.

The public(s)' responses

W. Philips Davidson many years ago (1984) argued about the impossibility of conceiving of global public opinion, since there were no forms through which it could be expressed. By now there are journals and articles about it, and PEW Research Center (http://pewresearch.org) studies regularly present the world with a statistically accurate sample of 'global public opinion' which is essentially a collection of national samples compiled together and not really then a measure of 'global' public opinion.

A more interesting way to conceive of and to study global public opinion is the diverse ways in which an event – here the letter – is picked up through inter-media commentary and internet debate. There are many cyberspatially distributed sites where discussion about the letter has taken place, where individuals who feel themselves somehow 'interpellated' by the letter engage in discussion about it, its meaning and its ramifications. These discussions about the letter, its intention, meaning and possible responses appeared in many languages on many web sites. The Iranian press and web sites were buzzing, including diasporic voices. A number of discussion forums were located in the United States. The *China Daily* ran an extensive debate in English, as did the *Asia Times* online.

There are many hermeneutic pitfalls in trying to understand these lists. One can't assume that people posting to a list in China are Chinese or live in China. But *China Daily* posts clearly included Chinese who had visited Iran, enjoyed their stay and felt that Iran had a legitimate case in relation to nuclear energy. *Asian Times* posts also raised questions about US power in that region. What is significant is that these fora exist at all, that they took the letter and Iran–US relations as a topic for their discussions.

I would make two points here. One is that here we have a specific example of 'globality' in action, the term coined by Roland Robertson (1992) that suggests that the world is increasingly seen as a single place and that people around the world feel 'interpellated' by a variety of events a long way away and have something to say about them. And second, in response to Philips Davidson, the way in which the net allows for such spontaneously occurring public opinion around the world as well as for exploring the main political lines of arguments evident in different lists is one way to think about and examine something we might start to call 'global public opinion'.

Furthermore, much work on the internet examines how pre-existing groups – diasporas and other social collectivities – extend themselves in cyberspace. By following the links between commentators and opinion formers we can see new networks emerging, evidence of the real global extensivity of the net. Thus a supposedly small interpersonal, perhaps bilateral, event became global. Everyone had an opinion about the letter and voiced it, except for the person to whom it was addressed. Of course, most everyone has an opinion on everything, but while there's lots of crackpot stuff out there, analysts and ordinary folk alike become able to watch the movement of opinions.

Responses as already always mediated

Here comes the other literary figure who lurks in my title, Montesquieu, whose *Persian Letters* (1977) are an early staging of the encounter between Orient and Occident in the form of fictitious letters by two Persian travellers coming to seek enlightenment in the West and the manner in which the discipline in their harem back home collapses. While more nuanced than many, it stands within a tradition of orientalism identified by Said, of the East defined and represented by the West. However, this purported hegemony of Western representations of the other and the 'power' of Westerm media channels is being profoundly challenged by a range of articulations coming from within the 'Middle East', not least from Iran itself. No longer only recipients of external representations, Arabic media channels in the period since the 1991 Gulf War have seen massive investment, with new channels launched such as al Jazeera (Qatar) and al Arabiyya (Saudi Arabia), but also external broadcasting in English (Al Jazeera English, launched in 2006). The state broadcasting system of the Islamic Republic broadcasts in Arabic and Azeri, and in 2007 launched its own English-language news channel, PressTV. Hence, once again, any attempt to claim Western cultural hegemony has to explain, or explain away, these other voices and positions.

Any 'opinions' we may find on the net are always already mediated in many ways, by competing historical narratives and sedimented understandings; by specific national media coverage of an event; by the domestic and international broadcasting of the two countries concerned; and by the diffusion of this content over countless other media sites. A question about the real object of media studies can be raised. No longer, if ever, can we utilise a framework that recognises only and simply 'national' media. But there are not yet fully global media, that is, channels with ubiquitous reach, nor indeed is there a fully 'global' system, since many populations remain without access and the requisite linguistic background. Rather there exists a huge meshing of transversal 'flows' (a terrible term from hydraulics but one that serves some purpose) of images and information, receivable through an array of communications technologies: an enormous hall of mirrors, material being reflected and refracted in countless ways. How do we make an intelligent cut into all of this to gain a picture of what's happening?

Within this complex system, the United States and Iran appear to be unequal protagonists. English has far greater reach than Persian. There is the well documented range and penetration of US channels. The United States seems to have determined the discourses on their conflict, its constant mention of 'Iran's nuclear weapons' creating a linguistic 'fact' evidenced in almost two million Google hits while the new trope of 'Islamic fascism' is picked up in countless stories. A somewhat sedimented media analysis of the relative cultural and political strengths of the United States and Iran would produce such argument.

Yet even a cursory reading on internet posts about the letter revealed far more nuanced and fine-grained positions posted on e-lists. Many of these acknowledged Iran as a signatory to the NPT treaty while the Iranian desire for nuclear energy was seen by many as a legitimate right of developing nations; noted the lack of attention to, even recognition of, Israel's nuclear weapons; and noted the hypocrisy of the United States in itself not recognising international agreements such as the Kyoto protocols. Further, a PEW study conducted in the period after the Ahmadi-Nejad letter had been made public explored which country people in fifteen countries feared the most. It triggered a large headline in the British *Guardian* newspaper that the United States was feared more than Iran. At least in this ongoing propaganda war, the obvious imbalance of mediatic power is *not* producing the expected global response. Indeed, if anything, the reverse seems to be the case, in that kudos attaches to Ahmadi-Nejad as simply 'standing up' to the United States.

In media studies we are faced with a significant conundrum that, despite the prevalence of US channels, it appears that many populations are escaping the iron hand of American propaganda. Our crude arguments leave us some explaining to do. Indeed, there is mounting evidence that the Americans themselves recognise this problem, in the growing debates about the failure of public diplomacy and the intended 'export of democracy' which are readily to be found in Rand Corporation papers (e.g. Bernard 2004). The commitment of $65 billion of armaments to 'friends' in the region is also an implicit sign that US 'soft power' through propaganda channels in Arabic and Persian has not worked.

I do not wish to argue that the net debate presages a global public sphere of rational debate. Much of the debate is raucous, ill informed, naive and plain scary. But by interrogating it we get a sense for which populations are 'hailed' by specific political events and the logics of their arguments. It also becomes possible to explore the dynamics whereby previously *unconnected* people build networks through citations and linkages. The emergence of varied epistemic communities *through* communication is one of the key potentials of the net, and one that we need to take more seriously.

Also, if contending ideologies and articulations of the world are increasing accessible to more people, a model of hegemony or interpellation bounded by the nation-state makes no sense. The globalisation of neoliberal economics is increasingly faced with an expanding anti-globalisation movement. The vast structure of US military, financial and ideological power finds itself bogged down in unwinnable wars and losing face to a country it has tried to construct as a pariah state. Perhaps 'audiences' constitute themselves and select which 'interpellations' to hear.

The letter and US–Iran relations

Let me return to the dynamic of the letter as a symbol of US–Iran relations, frozen in an icy silence for over a quarter of a century since the taking of hostages in the US embassy immediately after the 1979 revolution.

As with gifts and other forms of interaction, the power dynamics in letters – even e-mail – are fascinating. Much analysis would suggest that power means not having to reply. Here is a locking of horns between competing males and their mails: Bush and Ahmadi-Nejad. Bush treats Ahmadi-Nejad like a typical unequal and shows his power by not replying.

But given the global 'publicness', *pace* John Thompson (1995), of the letter, by not replying and being seen not to reply Bush looked churlish and the one to refuse dialogue. This process was noticed by many US newspapers from the first press conference on the topic. In a context of increasing global visibility of some events, the dynamics of 'purloining' become more complex. Perhaps the commentators and bloggers all play the role of Dupin the detective, 'finding the letter' and leaving a substitute?

So did the Iranian overtures make it the 'weaker' party? Not necessarily. Ansari (2006) has argued that the old and prevalent orientalist image of the wily Persians has real roots in so far as historically Iranians have been bad at and have not enjoyed war; indeed, from the nineteenth century Russia, France and Britain exploited Iranian military weakness. He argues that Iranians will use all sorts of 'political' methods at their disposal to avoid war. In comparison, it could be argued that the United States is good at war, that it likes to test its investment, technologies, organisation and training, and, by default, that it is bad at politics. This may well be far too crude a binary but it merits some thought.

Beeman (2005) offers a different binary optic for viewing their relationship. He suggests that the United States and Iran utilise different typologies of interaction. Broadly, he argues that the United States assumes egalitarian structures *within* the country, of an increasingly classless society, but as the global hegemon it anticipates a hierarchical structure *between* countries, here between the United States and Iran. Iranian culture is the obverse. It assumes hierarchical structure *within* its own community, that produces complex patterns of responsibility and reciprocity, but egalitarian structures between countries, i.e. between the United States and Iran. Hence the stand-off: while Iran seeks recognition and engagement as an equal on the world stage, the United States rebuffs Iran as a minor player, albeit on the 'axis of evil'. Yet the burden of global visibility – that includes the nightly visibility of news about chaos in Iraq, ongoing conflict in Afghanistan and the instability of Pakistan – suggests that for the United States at the moment this is a failing option.

As I have indicated already, there are indications that Iran's political communicative practices are more effective externally than the Americans' at this point in their propaganda war. The brutal violence that has broken out in Iraq, partly but not solely to be understood along factional lines, and the increasing volume of rhetoric about a 'Sunni–Shi'ite split' has meant that Iran is suddenly seen as a key player and possible mediator in Iraq. Thus it was that US ambassador Ryan Crocker and Iranian ambassador Hassan Kazemi Qumi talked in Baghdad in May 2007. There has been little follow-up. Indeed, Ahmadi-Nejad's visit to the United States to address the United Nations were marked by refusal to let him visit the World Trade Center site and by the aggressive newspaper headlines marking him as 'evil'. The political stand-off between the two countries continues even as the political contradictions inside Iran grew more evident. While Ahmadi-Nejad has started his own blog internally Iran is clamping down again on newspapers and bloggers. Over the spring and summer of 2007 the Islamic Republic imprisoned a number of visiting Iranian-Americans whom it condemned as complicit in US manoeuvres to destabilise it: probably a crude warning to its own people not to be too resistant.

Toward an ending

Some weeks after the delivery of the letter, at the end of May 2006, Condoleeza Rice appeared, or rather was seen on the scene, a bit like Dupin, but she does not actually visit Iran. (Perhaps sending Rice to Iran would be like sending coals to Newcastle!) Again, the Swiss were used as messenger to communicate with the Iranians. The US statement started with the words 'The pursuit by the Iranian regime of nuclear weapons represents a direct threat to the entire international community,' hardly a positive invitation to dialogue. In the Lacanian reading of the Poe story, the letter questions the Queen's honourable relationship with the King, situating her in a chain of signifiers. The notion of 'purloining' suggests that there is a diversion or misplacement and that the signifier has a proper course, the structure of repetition, the letter of the law. By not closing down the webs of signification earlier the world has interposed its varied meanings and US hegemony looks weakened.

Noticeable in all of this, both in the purloined Poe and in responses to the Ahmadi-Nejad letter, is that little attention is paid to the actual content of the letter. The letter from Iran warrants some analysis in its claims to a shared logic by the monotheistic Abrahamic religions and a shared religiosity between Ahmadi-Nejad and Bush. But even such ecumenism falls on deaf ears.

So, starting with a letter, and using the Lacan–Derrida debate, and probing Althusser's notion of interpellation, I have tried to explore the blurring of private–public boundaries produced by the extensive visibility of contemporary global communications. I suggest a different notion of audience, as those people who actively respond to events, who choose and create themselves. Clearly different addressees can be interpellated in different ways to different ends at the same time. Meaning always overflows structure or intention. It is time to reconsider interpellation critically within a more global frame and ask whether that has not also been subject to hegemonic closure. In short, how the interpellated accept their interpellation remains almost totally unconsidered. I have proposed here that one way to explore the phenomenon of globality is by examining the events that do trigger global reactions, even if those are varied, antagonistic and dissonant, and to suggest that counter-articulation is always present alongside any momentarily dominant articulation.

I have also suggested that one way to examine the tangled mesh of US–Iranian relations is by analysing their communicative modes. The letter was in some ways an oddly direct mode of address for Iranians, who often prefer to find a *parti-bazi*, or third person, to put forward an important case. Bush's refusal to engage – indeed, the dismissal of the letter as not containing anything of interest – was a rebuttal of Iranian national standing and its growing regional significance, itself a by-product of the failed strategies in Iraq and elsewhere.

There are obvious ironies. A United States that trumpets democracy and freedom of speech is seen not to respond and to close down communication while the Islamic Republic of Iran, known for its censorship, tries to engage. A society that believes it is good to talk doesn't take an overture to dialogue seriously. An essential element of US hegemony consists in recognising dialogue only on its own terms, already slanted to its frame of reference. The play of issues around openness versus cover-up, transparency versus deceit, is the very stuff of political communication, so there is plenty of analytic work to be done, not least about how to think beyond the enduring frame of the 'national' toward transnational responses in varied parts of the world, and among quite different, even unexpected, populations.

I have tried to suggest that an apparently simple and unimportant 'gesture' by a leader of a Third World, indeed Muslim (therefore backward), country, which was largely dismissed by those in power, raises much broader questions about the whole nature of communication, its addressees and what is at stake in interpellation, including its spatiality. A key issue is: who determines who is supposed to be included in interpellation? The trap in interpellation is that, being pre-media studies, it assumes the relationship between the source of an interpellation and the various potential addressees is relatively uncomplicated. However, *pace* Derrida, there is a more radical rupture between producers and recipients, with undecidability as the central outcome.

Here the original analysis of the purloined letter is significant once again, because it is essentially about visibility, who sees whom did what? It is about interpersonal surveillance and a shifting balance of power between characters. In a media and communications environment of complex geospatial extensivity it is a certainty that 'others' will see what 'we' do and react. This new communicative spatiality must become more central to the study of the media.

I have tried to reflect in a comparative-historical way on the multiple interconnecting levels in which public political communication takes place, and to acknowledge how little we still understand about these processes in a context marked by a global internet system and global power struggles. Focusing on a letter as a form of communication which has only recently lapsed in Western cultures, and now is suddenly hoiked out into the global arena again, is a good way of relativising the all-too-easy assumptions we make, especially in the West, about the technological procedures of public communication, diplomacy and readerships/audiences.

Durham Peters completes his analysis of the emergence of the private, addressed letter with an analysis of the 'Dead Letter Office', the material evidence of letters that never arrive, of missed communication, 'the dump for everything that misfires', and asks, 'What is the meaning of the letter buried in the Dead Letter Office whose writer does not know it is lost and whose recipient does not know it was ever sent?' (1999: 171).

In *The Purloined Letter* lost matter is settled back into place. Dupin hands the letter to the police, who supposedly return it to the Queen.

In this case, an important letter was delivered. It's never too late for a reply.

Notes

1 I would like to thank Anghad Chowdhry, who first pointed me toward the debates around *The Purloined Letter*, and Chris Roberts, who worked with me along the way and who will find echoes of his voice in the text. I have also benefited from generous comments from John Downing, Mark Hobart, Ron Inden, Jason Toynbee and Gillian Youngs. The weaknesses are all my own.
2 Three sets of letters with Middle East foci are al-Jabarti's interrogations of Napoleon's proclamations, Gobineau's remarkable correspondence with de Tocqueville (de Tocqueville 1959) and Kennedy's correspondence with Nasser (Bass 2003).
3 As with Ahmadi-nejad's speech about the Holocaust, there are differences in translated texts which have become the subject of analysis themselves.

Bibliography

Althusser, L (1977) 'Ideology and ideological state apparatuses', in *For Marx*. London: New Left Books.
Ansari, A. (2006) *Confronting Iran: the Failure of American Policy and the next Great Conflict in the Middle East*. London: Hurst.

Bass, W. (2003) *Support any Friend: Kennedy's Middle East and the Making of the US – Israel Alliance*. New York: Oxford University Press.

Beeman, W. (2005) *The 'Great Satan' vs. the 'Mad Mullahs': How the United States and Iran demonize each Other*. Westport, CT: Praeger.

Bernard, C. (2004) *Five Pillars of Democracy: How the West can promote an Islamic Reformation*. Santa Monica CA: Rand Corporation, http://www.rand.org/publications/randreview/issues/spring2004/pillars.html (accessed 12 October 2007).

Derrida, J. (1987) 'Le facteur de la verité', in *The Post Card*. Chicago: University of Chicago Press.

De Tocqueville, A. (1959) *The European Revolution and Correspondence with Gobineau*, trans. J. Lukacs. New York: Doubleday Anchor.

Durham Peters, J. (1999) *Speaking into the Air*. Chicago: University of Chicago Press.

Hall, S. (1989) 'Ideology and communication theory', in B. Dervin, L. Grossberg, B. J. O'Keefe and E. Wartella (eds) *Rethinking Communication* I, *Paradigm issues*. London: Sage.

Hardt, M. and Negri, T. (2000) *Empire*. Cambridge MA: Harvard University Press.

Hobart, M. (2000) 'The end of the world news: television and a problem of articulation in Bali', *International Journal of Cultural Studies* 3 (1): 79–102 (unpublished postscript).

Huntington, S. (1997) *The Clash of Civilizations and the Remaking of World Order*. New York: Simon & Schuster.

Kaplan, F. (2006) '"Dear Mahmoud": how Bush should respond to the Iranian President's letter', *Slate*, 10 May, www.slate.com/id/2141589/(accessed 12 October 2007).

Lacan, J. (1988) 'Seminar on "The Purloined Letter"', in J. P. Muller and W. J. Richardson, *The Purloined Poe*. Baltimore MD: Johns Hopkins University Press.

Laclau, E. and Mouffe, C. (1985) *Hegemony and Socialist Strategy: Towards a Radical Democratic Politics*. London: Verso.

Limbaugh, D. (2006) 'Fatherly lessons from President Ahmadinejad', 11 May, http://www.davidlimbaugh.com/mt/archives/2006/05/new_column_fath.html (accessed 12 October 2007).

Montesquieu, C. L. de S. (1977) *Persian Letters*, trans. C. J. Betts. Harmondsworth: Penguin.

Muller, J. P. and Richardson, W. J. (1988) *The Purloined Poe*. Baltimore MD: Johns Hopkins University Press.

Perkovich, G. (2006) 'Bush should engage Bush in dialogue, not back away', Carnegie Endowment for International Peace Council on Foreign Relations interview, 9 May, http://www.carnegieendowment.org/publications/index.cfm?fa=view&id=18322 (accessed 12 October 2007).

Philips Davidson, W. (1984) 'Global public opinion', in G. Gerbner and M. Seifert (eds) *World Communications: a Handbook*. New York: Longman.

Robertson, R. (1992) 'Globality and modernity', *Theory, Culture and Society* 9 (1), 153–61.

Thompson, J. (1995) *The Media and Modernity*. Cambridge: Polity Press.

Žižek, S. (2001) *Enjoy your Symptom!* London: Routledge.

8 Rethinking the Digital Age*

Faye Ginsburg

In March 2005, the United Nations inaugurated a long-awaited programme, a 'Digital Solidarity Fund', to underwrite initiatives that address 'the uneven distribution and use of new information and communication technologies' and 'enable excluded people and countries to enter the new era of the information society' ('From the Digital Divide ...', 2005).[1] What this might mean in practice – which digital technologies might make a significant difference and for whom and with what resources – is still an open and contentious question. Debates about plans for the Fund at the first meeting of the World Summit on the Information Society (WSIS) in December 2003 are symptomatic of the complexity of 'digital divide' issues that have also been central to the second phase of the information summit, held in November 2005 in Tunisia.[2]

In this chapter, I consider the relationship of indigenous people to new media technologies that people in these communities have started to take up with both ambivalence and enthusiasm over the last decade. To give a sense of that oscillation, let me start with three quotes that articulate the range of stakes. The first – a statement leaning toward the technophilic – is from Jolene Rickard, a Tuscarora artist, scholar, and community leader, introducing an online project, called CyberPowWow,[3] that began in 1996 in order to get more Native American art on the web:

> Wasn't it the Hopi that warned of a time when the world would be circled by a spiders' web of power lines? That time has come.... There is no doubt that First Nation peoples are wired and ready to surf and chat. It seems like a distant memory when the tone of discussion about computers, interactivity, and aboriginal people was filled with Prophetic caution. Ironically, the image of Natives is still firmly planted in the past. The idea that Indians would be on the frontier of a technology is inconsistent with the dominant image of 'traditional' Indians.
>
> (Rickard 1999)

The second, more sceptical, quote is from Alopi Latukefu, regional manager of the Outback Digital Network,[4] a digitally based broadband network that began in 1996, linking six Aboriginal communities in Australia:

> So seductive is the power of the ICT medium that it might only appear to remove centralised control out of the hands of government and into the hands of the people, giving them the notion of ... empowerment. While ongoing struggles for self-determination play a complex role in the drive to bring the Information Age to indigenous communities in Australia and around the world, it can be argued that self-determination within one system may well be a further buy-in to another.
>
> (Latukefu 2006: 4)

Latukefu continues:

> The issue that needs to be raised before any question of indigenous usage of the Internet is addressed is: whose information infrastructure or 'info-structure' determines what is valued in an economy – whether in the local community or the greater global economy which they are linked to? ... Associated with this is the overarching issue of who determines knowledge within these remote communities and for the wider indigenous populations throughout Australia and beyond?
>
> (Latukefu 2006: 4)

The third quote is from the 2003 indigenous position paper for the World Summit on the Information Society, which states, 'Our collective knowledge is not merely a commodity to be traded like any other in the market place. We strongly object to the notion that it constitutes a raw material or commercial resource for the knowledge-based economy of the Information Society.' Like some of their corporate counterparts, international indigenous representatives want to limit the circulation of particular ideas, knowledge and cultural materials. They 'strongly reject the application of the public domain concept to any aspect related to our cultures and identities' and further 'reject the application of IPR [intellectual property rights] regimes to assert patents, copyrights, or trademark monopolies for products, data or processes derived or originating from our traditional knowledge or our cultural expressions ...' (Indigenous Position Paper, 2003).

The issues raised in these quotes echo those I have heard in my own research with indigenous media makers, positions that are not necessarily in contradiction. Fundamentally, they ask who has the right to control knowledge and what are the consequences of the new circulatory regimes introduced by digital technologies. Rickard articulates a desire, as an indigenous artist, to work with digital technologies in order to link indigenous communities to each other on their own terms, objecting to stereotypes that suggest traditional communities should not have access to forms associated with modernity. Latukefu cautions that one must take into account the power relations that decide whose knowledge is valued, while the statement of the Indigenous People's Working Group offers a strong warning against the commodification of their knowledge under Western systems of intellectual property.

Why are their concerns barely audible in discussions of new media? I would like to suggest that part of the problem has to do with the rise of the term 'the Digital Age' over the last decade and the assumptions that support it. While it initially had the shock of the new, it now has become as naturalised for many of us – Western cultural workers and intellectuals – as a temporal marking of the dominance of a certain kind of technological regime ('the Digital') as is 'the Palaeolithic's' association with certain kinds of stone tools for palaeontologists. This seems even more remarkable given certain realities: only 12 per cent of the world is wired (according to statistics from the January 2005 World Economic Forum in Davos), and only sixteen people in every hundred of the world's population are serviced with telephone land lines.[5] Digerati may see those numbers and salivate at the possibilities for entrepreneurship. But, for an anthropologist who has spent a good portion of her career looking at the uptake of media in remote indigenous communities, the unexamined ethnocentrism that undergirds assumptions about the Digital Age is discouraging; indeed, the seeming ubiquity of the internet appears a facade of First World illusions. I am not suggesting that the massive shifts in communication, sociality, knowledge production, and politics that the internet enables are simply irrelevant to remote communities; my concern is with how the language smuggles in a set of assumptions that paper over cultural differences in the way things digital may be taken up – if at all – in radically different contexts and thus serve to further insulate thinking against recognition of alterity that different kinds of media worlds present, particularly in key areas such as intellectual property.

In this chapter, I examine how concepts such as the Digital Age have taken on a sense of evolutionary inevitability, thus creating an increasing stratification and ethnocentrism in the distribution of certain kinds of media practices, despite prior and recent trends to de-Westernise media studies (see Curran and Park 2000). Work in new (and old) media that is being produced in indigenous communities might expand and complicate our ideas about 'the Digital Age' in ways that take into account other points of view in the so-called global village.

A history of digital debates

Let me turn to my first task by briefly reviewing some of the recent debates around the rhetoric of the Digital Age – for certainly I am not alone in my concern, though mine may be shaped in a particular way. Within the ranks of those who have been writing and worrying about 'Cultural Production in a Digital Age' and its global implications, there is some contestation as to 'whether it is appropriate, given unequal access to advanced technologies (let alone more basic goods)' in different parts of the world that the term 'the Digital Age' be used to define the current period (see Klineneberg and Benzecry 2005). This debate occurs in tandem with that attached to the Digital Divide, the phrase invented to describe the circumstances of inequality that characterise access (or lack of access) to resources, technological and otherwise, across much of the globe. Even as it wants to call well intentioned concern to such inequities, the term nonetheless invokes neo-developmentalist language that assumes that less privileged cultural enclaves with little or no access to digital resources – from the South Bronx to the global South – are simply waiting, endlessly, to catch up to the privileged West. Inevitably, the language suggests, they are simply falling farther behind the current epicentre, whether that be Silicon Valley or the MIT Media Lab.

Some exemplary cases that have made it to the *New York Times* and the *Wall Street Journal* provide charming counterpoints of hopeful possibility, stories of far-flung villages 'catching up' to the West. For example, in a *New York Times* article, James Brooks (2004) describes the work of Bernard Krisher, representing both MIT's Media Lab and the American Assistance for Cambodia group in O Siengle, Cambodia, a village of less than 800 people on the edge of the forest that is emblematic of life for the millions of Asians who live on the unwired side of the Digital Divide. Through the Motoman project, the village connects its new elementary school to the internet. Since they have no electricity or phones, the system is powered by solar panels, and, as Brooks (2004) describes it:

> An internet 'Motoman' rides a red motorcycle slowly past the school [once a day]. On the passenger seat is a gray metal box with a short fat antenna. The box holds a wireless Wi-Fi chip set that allows the exchange of e-mail between the box and computers. Briefly, this schoolyard of tree stumps and a hand-cranked water well becomes an Internet hot spot [a process duplicated in five other villages]. At dusk, the motorcycles [from five villages] converge on the provincial capital, Ban Lung, where an advanced school is equipped with a satellite dish, allowing a bulk e-mail exchange with the outside world.[6]

Tellingly, this story was in the Business Section of the *Times*, suggesting that part of its charm is the possibility of new markets, the engine that drives even such idealistic innovation in consumer technologies; computers and the internet are hardly exceptional.

This techno-imaginary universe of digital eras and divides has the effect, I argue, of reinscribing on to the world a kind of 'allochronic chronopolitics' (to borrow a term from Johannes Fabian's 1983 *Time and the Other*), in which the 'other' exists in a time not contemporary with our own. This has the effect of re-stratifying the world along lines of a late modernity, despite the utopian promises by the digerati of the possibilities of a twenty-first-century McLuhanesque global village. For the last two decades, scholars have argued about (and mostly for) the transformative power of digital systems and their capacity to alter daily life, democratic politics, and personhood. That sense of a paradigm shift is perhaps most evident in Castells's 1996 classic *The Rise of the Network Society*. The premise of his work, of course, is that the internet has more or less created a new era by providing the technological basis for the organisational form of the Information Age: *the network*. In *The Internet Galaxy* (2003) Castells's scale seems to have expanded from society to the cosmos. While he celebrates the internet's capacity to liberate, he also cautions us about its ability to marginalise and exclude those who do not have access to it and suggests that we need to take responsibility for the future of this new Information Age.

Taking the critique a bit farther, no less a luminary than Bill Gates, founder of Microsoft and once the personification of new media evangelism, has become an outspoken critic of that attitude. Initially, he was part of the group of American executives who, at the 1998 World Economic Forum in Davos, dedicated themselves to closing the gap on digital equity. By 2000, however, in a speech at a conference entitled 'Creating Digital Dividends', Gates demonstrated a remarkable change of heart, offering blistering criticism of the idea of the Digital Divide and its capacity to blind people to the reality of the condition of the globe's poorest people. As he put it at the time:

> OK, you want to send computers to Africa, what about food and electricity – those computers aren't going to be that valuable. The mothers are going to walk right up to that computer and say, 'My children are dying, what can you do?' They're not going to sit there and, like, browse eBay or something. What they want is for their children to live. They don't want their children's growth to be stunted. Do you really have to put in computers to figure that out?
>
> (Quoted in Verhovic 2000: A1)[7]

His apparent disdain for the notion that the world's poorest people constitute a significant market for high-tech products has had an impact. The priorities of the $21 billion Bill and Melinda Gates Foundation are with health care, in particular the development and distribution of vaccines. At the January 2005 World Economic Forum meeting, while technology guru Nicholas Negroponte was marketing a mock-up of a $100 laptop computer, hoping to capture China's 220 million students as possible consumers of digital technology, Gates was reported to be 'in the thick of plenary discussions ... considering ways of eliminating poverty and disease that do not encompass information technology' (Markoff 2005).[8] 'I think it's fascinating,' Gates commented, 'that there was no plenary session at Davos this year on how information technology is changing the world' (Markoff 2005).[9]

The internet, of course, has been met with some optimism by those sharing concerns of broader access for freedom of expression and social movements. Manuel Castells in *The Power of Identity* (1997) noted the range of dissident social actors, such as the Zapatistas in Mexico. Today, we would add to that list an array of groups, from the grass-roots leftist political sentiments organised by moveon.org to right-wing Christians and militant Islamists to the Falun Gong in China. These and scores of other groups have used the internet to shape what some call 'the network logic' of anti-[corporate] globalisation movements and smart mobs, as well as its uptake by loosely linked Islamic terrorists. Additionally, a number of researchers have noted how the internet has in many cases reduced the 'price of entry' into a cultural field, creating openings for actors and organisations who were previously unable to get their work into the public, as the inclusion and impact of bloggers during the 2004 US presidential campaigns (Massing 2005). Clearly, then, digital networks can enable the global dispersion of creative and political activity.

In its 12–18 March 2005 cover story, no less an advocate for the spread of free enterprise than *The Economist* features a rethinking of the term (and terms of) 'The Real Digital Divide', along with a compelling photo of a young African boy holding an ersatz cellphone made of mud to his ear. Its lead opinion piece states that:

> the debate over the digital divide is founded on a myth – that plugging poor countries into the internet will help them to become rich rapidly.... So even if it were possible to wave a magic wand and cause a computer to appear in every household on earth, it would not achieve very much: a computer is not useful if you have no food or electricity and cannot read.
>
> ('Technology and development' 2005)

Ideas about what the Digital Age might offer look different from the perspective of people struggling to manage to make ends meet on a daily basis. As *The Economist* notes, research suggests that radio and cellphones may be the forms of digital technology that make the difference, once basic needs are addressed (Norris *et al.* 2001). My concern here, however, is to ask whether terms like the Digital Divide too easily foreclose discussion about what the stakes are for those who are out of power. Rather than imagining that we know the answers, clearly, we need to keep listening to the large percentage of the earth's population that is on the unwired side of the so-called digital divide.

Going digital: indigenous internet 'on the ground'

So what does the 'Digital Age' feel and look like in indigenous communities in remote regions of the world where access to telephone land lines can still be difficult? As Kyra Landzelius asks in her 2006 collection, *Native on the Net*, 'Can the info-superhighway be a fast track to greater empowerment for the historically disenfranchised? Or do they risk becoming "roadkill": casualties of hyper-media and the drive to electronically map everything?' (2006: 1). Recent developments give some insight into what it might actually mean for indigenous subjects. As Harald Prins (2001) has argued regarding the place of indigenous people in 'cyberia':

> Although indigenous peoples are proportionally underrepresented in cyberspace – for obvious reasons such as economic poverty, technological inexperience, linguistic isolation, political repression, and/or cultural resistance – the Internet has vastly extended traditional networks of information and communication. Greatly enhancing the visibility of otherwise marginal communities and individuals, the information superhighway enables even very small and isolated communities to expand their sphere of influence and mobilize political support in their struggles for cultural survival. In addition to maintaining contact with their own communities, indigenous peoples also use the Internet to connect with other such widely dispersed groups in the world. Today, it is not unusual for a Mi'kmaq in Newfoundland to go on the Internet and communicate with individuals belonging to other remote groups such as the Maori in New Zealand, Saami in Norway, Kuna in Panama, or Navajo in Arizona. Together with the rest of us, they have pioneered across the new cultural frontier and are now surfing daily through Cyberia.

Clearly, Prins points to the circumstances in which use of the internet – and more broadly the cross-platformed use of digital technologies – is being taken up in indigenous communities on their own terms, furthering the development of political networks and the capacity to extend their traditional cultural worlds into new domains (Anderson, no date). It is that latter enterprise that I address in the following examples.

Recent initiatives demonstrate what some of these possibilities look like in three very different parts of the world: Inuit regions of Nunavut through the work of Igloolik Isuma; the work of Arrernte living in town camps in Alice Springs, central Australia, creating an innovative interactive project called 'Us Mob'; and a digital animation project by Canadian-based northwest coast Aboriginal artists and storytellers who have created an animated version of *The Raven's Tale*. All are exemplary of community-based groups collaborating with a number of agencies to indigenise the use of digital technologies in the interests of storytelling as a way to generate broader understandings of their histories and cultures, for wider audiences but, most important, for their own cultural futures.[10]

Igloolik Isuma and Sila.nu

During the 1970s, as satellite-based television made its way into the Canadian Arctic, Inuit people began exploring the possibilities that these combinations of media forms offered for local productions that could be distributed over the vast expanses of Canada's north. Zacharias Kunuk, a young Inuit man at that time, had the vision to turn these technologies into vehicles for cultural expression of Inuit lives and histories, forming a media production group called Igloolik Isuma.[11] Kunuk worked with friends and family members, creating a remarkable team of non-professional actors who recreated the stories of the transformations of their own lives over the last century, starting with works such as *Qaggig* in 1988 and quickly moving on to create the remarkable television series entitled *Nunavut*, which is also the name of the recently formed Inuit-controlled territory where Kunuk's home settlement is located. The series *Nunavut* was a staple not only of TV Northern Canada (the pan-Arctic satellite station that preceded the current first national indigenous cable television station, Aboriginal Peoples Television Network), but it also screened at MoMA in New York and the Pompidou Centre in Paris.

Fast-forward to 2001 and the premiere at the Cannes Film Festival of Kunuk's first feature, the epic recreation of a well known Inuit legend, *Atanarjuat, the Fast Runner*,[12] at the Cannes Film Festival. There, this first film ever made by an Inuit director in the Inuktitut language received the coveted Camera d'or award for best first feature and went on to stunning critical and theatrical success, picking up many more awards along the way. In 2005, Kunuk and his crew shot their second feature, a Danish co-production entitled *The Journals of Knud Rasmussen*, based on the writings of the famous Inuit-Danish explorer who travelled throughout the Arctic in the 1920s exploring the transformations of Inuit life that were occurring in the early twentieth century, when Inuit shamans first encountered Christian missionaries. The journals provide the storyline for a film that provides an Inuit perspective on that fateful historical encounter.

But, never content to think conventionally, Kunuk and company established an incredible web site from the film's production location (http://www.sila.nu/live) that allowed us to follow what was happening on the film set on a daily basis while also sending us back to Rasmussen's journals and the key characters he met in his journeys through the Arctic.[13] Daily blogs by an 'embedded' journalist and (of course) their own anthropologist provided different perspectives, while QuickTime movies showed us how multiple languages (English, French, Inuktitut, Danish) were negotiated, as well as how props and food were managed in this remote Arctic locale. Pop-ups offered a linked glossary for foreign or more arcane words. Background bios on key personnel – on and off screen – illuminated the community-based approach to film making that Kunuk and his partner Norman Cohn have perfected. (My personal favourite was the interview with the lead sled dog, Tooguyuk, who 'described' the trials of learning commands in both 'Greenlandic' and 'Igloolik' and talked about looking forward to his 'girlfriend having puppies, so I'm excited to be a daddy'.) Inuit web site producer Katarina Soukup explained the project and its origins:

> Isuma has wanted for a long, long time to use the Internet to connect the remote Arctic with people around the world, a way to bring people to Igloolik without the extreme expense and inconvenience of traveling here, as well as to allow Inuit to remain in their communities and out on the land without losing touch with the twenty-first century. One dream is a nomadic media lab/television station out on the land connected to the Internet. It just has not been technically possible until now, thanks to a high-speed data satellite phone and wireless broadband in Nunavut, making remote, nomadic computing much less expensive. The goals with the educational website are to connect people to Inuit culture through the Internet and our films. We have been creating materials for the educational market for about two or three years (e.g. the Isuma Inuit Culture Kit), and the site is another step in this direction. The project employs an innovative technical infrastructure to deliver to the world priceless Inuit cultural content, such as interactive e-learning activities, video-on-demand, customisable teacher resources, and Inuktitut language lessons. It is a platform for North–South communication and collaboration. In addition to educating the public about Inuit culture, another goal of the site is to develop a youth and educational market for our films.
>
> (Quoted in Ginsburg 2005b)

The site was beautifully designed in every sense. The project had two teams, one in the Arctic at Igloolik and another in Montreal. In Igloolik the team was made up of about nine members: three videographers, an audio reporter, a photographer, and three writers who did the daily blogs, as well as eight youth trainees from the community who were learning about media production. The Sila web site presented a remarkable demonstration of how this technology might be successfully 'indigenised' to help Inuit school kids, college students in New York, Maori colleagues in New Zealand, and many others, learn about their film making, the Arctic, indigenous lives, missionisation, and new ways of 'understanding media' (McLuhan 1964/1994) and their possibilities in the twenty-first century.

Us Mob, central Australia

A digitally based project has been developed by the activist lawyer and documentary maker David Vadiveloo in collaboration with Arrernte Aboriginal youth living in Hidden Valley, a town camp outside of Alice Springs in central Australia. *Us Mob* is Australia's first Aboriginal children's television series and interactive web site. On the site, users interact with the challenges and daily lives of kids from the camp – Harry, Della, Charlie, and Jacquita – following multi-path storylines, activating video and text diaries, forums, movies, and games that offer a virtual experience of the camp and surrounding deserts, and uploading their own video stories. The site, in English and Arrernte, with English subtitles, was launched at the Adelaide Film Festival on 25 February 2005 and simultaneously on ABC television and ABC online.[14]

The project had its origins in requests from traditional elders in the Arrernte community in central Australia to David Vadiveloo, who first worked with that community as their lawyer in their 1996 historic Native Title claim victory. Switching gears since then to media activism, Vadiveloo has made six documentaries with people in the area, including the award-winning works *Trespass* (2002), *Beyond Sorry* (2003), and *Bush Bikes* (2001). Us Mob is the first indigenous project to receive production funding under a new initiative from the Australian Film Commission and ABC New Media and Digital Services Broadband Production Initiative (BPI); it received additional support from the Adelaide Film Festival, Telstra, and the South Australian Film Corporation.

The Us Mob project was motivated by Vadiveloo's concern to use media to develop cross-cultural lines of communication for kids in the camps. As he put it:

> After ten years of listening to many Arrernte families in Town Camps and remote areas, I am trying to create a dynamic communication bridge that has been opened by the Arrernte kids of Alice Springs with an invitation extended to kids worldwide to play, to share, and to engage with story themes that are common to all young people but are delivered through Us Mob in a truly unique cultural and physical landscape.
>
> (Quoted in Ginsburg 2005a)

In keeping with community wishes, Vadiveloo needed to create a project that was not fictional. Elders were clear: they did not want community members referred to as 'actors' – they were community participants in stories that reflected real life and real voices that they wanted heard. To accomplish that, Vadiveloo held workshops to develop scripts with over 70 non-actor Town Camp residents, who were paid for their participation. The topics they raised range from Aboriginal traditional law, ceremony, and hunting to youth substance abuse and other Aboriginal health issues. Building bush bikes is the focus of one of the two Us Mob games, while the second one requires learning bush skills as players figure out how to survive in the outback. Producer Heather Croall and Interactive Producer Chris Joyner were integral partners for Vadiveloo. Apart from raising finance, they wrote the project together with Vadiveloo; then, final scripts were written by indigenous screenwriter Danielle McLean. Camera work was by Allan Collins, the indigenous award-winning cinematographer and Alice Springs resident. The final project has been approved by traditional owners and the Indigenous organisation Tangentyere Council.

In creating this project, Vadiveloo hoped to create a television series about and by Aboriginal youth, raising issues relevant to them, as well as an online programme that could engage these young people to spend time online acquiring some of the skills necessary to be computer-literate. He was particularly concerned to develop an alternative to the glut of single-shooter games online and the constant diet of violence, competition, and destruction that characterise the games they were exposed to in town. 'When kids play and build together,' Vadiveloo explains, 'they are learning about community and consequence, and that is what I wanted to see in the project' (quoted in Ginsburg 2005a). And, rather than assuming that the goal is that Aboriginal children in central Australia catch up to the other side of the Digital Divide, based on someone else's terms, he wanted to help build a project that dignified their cultural concerns. This is charmingly but emphatically clear in the first encounter with the Us Mob home page that invites you in but, as it would be if you visited them in Alice, notifies you that you need a permit to visit:

> Everyone who wants to play with us on the full Us Mob website will need a permit. It's the same as if you came to Alice Springs and wanted to visit me and my family, you'd have a get a permit to come on to the Town Camp. Once you have a permit you will be able to visit us at any time to chat, play games, learn about Aboriginal life and share stories.
>
> We love going out bush and we're really looking forward to showing you what it's like in Central Australia. We'll email you whenever we add a new story to the website. We really hope you can add your stories to the website cos we'd love to learn about your life too.[15]

Us Mob and Hidden Valley suggest another perspective on the Digital Age, one that invites kids from 'elsewhere' to come over and play on their side.

Raven Tales, north-west coast of Canada

Raven Tales: How Raven stole the Sun (2004) is the first of a series of experiments in digital animation by Simon James (Kwakwaka'wakw) and Chris Klentz (Cherokee) that create new versions of centuries-old stories to be shown across Canada on that country's Aboriginal People's Television Network. This work reworks famous north-west coast myths from Kwakwaka'wakw, the Squamish, and Haida peoples – in particular the Raven trickster figure, along with Eagle, Frog, and the first humans. It includes voices ranging from well known native actors such as Evan Adams of *Smoke Signals* (Chris Eyre 1998) fame to the voice of hereditary chief Robert Joseph. Cutting across both centuries and generations, it uses the playful spirit of animation to visualise and extend the lives of these myths. These stories and the distinctive look of north-west coast design have been proven, as producer Simon James joked during the Q&A at the New York premiere of this work in the fall of 2004, by '10,000 years of local market research' (quoted in Ginsburg 2005c).

Spicing up these stark and complex traditional stories with some contemporary humour and the wonders of digital animation is always a risk. But clearly it was a risk worth taking, when the murky darkness of the Myth Time is suddenly (and digitally) transformed from barren smoky greys to brilliant greens, the result of the Raven's theft of the gift of light and its release into the world.[16]

At the New York premiere, animator Simon James's father, a Kwakwaka'wakw artist and elder, came on stage with his drum, embellished with the distinctive raven design. Inviting other Native media makers who were present to join him on stage, he sang 'Wiping the tears' to remember those who have come before and are gone and to praise the work of this new generation. When Pam Belgarde, a Chippewa woman who had produced another work shown in the session, came up, he dressed her in the traditional black and red regalia, a stunning full-length button cape with appliqués of wild roses and a regal fur hat. As he draped the cape across her shoulders he explained, 'When we meet someone we are honored to meet, we dress them to show that we are willing to go cold in order to keep our guests warm.' Simon began to beat the drum and asked us to look at the empty seats in the theatre and think of those who came before; the media producers on stage lowered their eyes. At the conclusion of his song, he addressed the audience and said, 'All our ceremonies need witnesses. And as witnesses we ask you to be part of that tradition, and go and share with others what you have seen today.'

In each of these cases, digital technologies have been taken up because of the possibilities they offer to bring in younger generations into new forms of indigenous cultural production and to extend indigenous cultural worlds – on their own terms – into the lives of others in the broader national communities and beyond who can serve, in the way that Simon James expressed, as virtual witnesses to their traditions, histories, and daily dilemmas.

Conclusion

To return to the concern that motivated this chapter, I want to underscore the way that the term Digital Age stratifies media hierarchies for those who are out of power and are struggling to become producers of media representations of their lives. It is an issue that is particularly salient for indigenous people, who, until recently, have been the object of other people's image-making practices in ways that have been damaging to their lives. And, unlike other minorities, questions of the Digital Age look different from the perspective of people struggling to control land and traditions that have been appropriated by now dominant settler societies for as long as 500 years.

In an effort to underscore what their work is about, I use the term *cultural activist* to describe the conscious way in which they are – like many other people – using the production of media and other expressive forms as a way not only to sustain and build their communities but also as a means to help transform them through what one might call a 'strategic traditionalism' (to borrow from Bennett and Blundell 1995). This position is crucial to their work but is effaced from much contemporary cultural theory addressing new media that emphasises dislocation and globalisation. The cultural activists creating these new kinds of cultural forms have turned to them as a means of revivifying relationships to their lands, local languages, traditions and histories and articulating community concerns. They also see the media as a means of furthering social and political transformation by inserting their own stories into national narratives as part of ongoing struggles for Aboriginal recognition and self-determination.

Increasingly, the circulation of these media globally – through conferences, festivals, co-productions, and the use of the internet – has become an important basis for nascent but growing transnational network of indigenous media makers and activists. These activists are attempting to reverse processes through which aspects of their societies have been objectified, commodified, and appropriated; their media productions and writings are efforts to recuperate their histories, land rights, and knowledge bases as their own cultural property. These kinds of cultural production are consistent with the ways in which the meaning and praxis of culture in late modernity have become increasingly conscious of their own project, an effort to use imagery of their lives to create an activist imaginary. One might think of media practices as a kind of shield against the often unethical use or absolute erasure of their presence in the ever-increasing circulation of images of other cultures in general, and of indigenous lives in particular, as the indigenous position paper for the World Summit on the Information Society makes clear. At every level, indigenous media practices have helped to create and contest social, visual, narrative, and political spaces for local communities and in the creation of national and other kinds of dominant cultural imaginaries that, until recently, have excluded vital representations by First Nation peoples within their borders. The capacity of such representations to circulate to other communities – from indigenous neighbours to NGOs – is an extension of this process, across a number of forms of mediation, from video and film to cyberspace (Danaja and Garde 1997).

Indigenous digital media have raised important questions about the politics and circulation of knowledge at a number of levels; within communities this may be about who has had access to and understanding of media technologies, and who has the rights to know, tell, and circulate certain stories and images. Within nation-states, the media are linked to larger battles over cultural citizenship, racism, sovereignty, and land rights, as well as struggles over funding, air space and satellites, networks of broadcasting and distribution, and digital broadband, that may or may not be available to indigenous work. The impact of these fluctuations can be tracked in a variety of places – in fieldwork, in policy documents and in the dramas of everyday life in cultural institutions.

I explore the term Digital Age because it so powerfully shapes frameworks for understanding globalisation, media, and culture, creating the 'commonsense' discourse for institutions in ways that disregard the cultural significance of the production of knowledge in minoritised communities, increasing an already existing sense of marginalisation. Rather than mirroring the widespread concern over increasing corporate control over media production and distribution, and the often parallel panic over multiculturalism (Appiah 1997), can we illuminate and support other possibilities emerging out of locally based concerns and speak for their significance in contemporary cultural and policy arenas? Institutional structures are built on discursive frameworks that shape the way in which phenomena are understood, naturalising shifts in support for a range of cultural activities. In government, foundations, and academic institutions, these frameworks have an enormous impact on policy and funding decisions that, for better or worse, can have a decisive effect on practice.

Other scholars who recognise, more generally, the significance of locally situated cultural practices in relation to dominant models point instead to the importance of the productions/producers who are helping (among other things) to generate their own links to other indigenous communities through which local practices are strengthened and linked. For example, Rob Wilson and Wimal Dissanayake point to such processes as part of 'an aesthetic of rearguard resistance, rearticulated borders as sources, genres, and enclaves of cultural preservation and community identity to be set against global technologies of modernisation or image-cultures of the postmodern' (1996: 14). Indeed, simultaneous to the growing corporate control of media, indigenous producers and cultural activists are creating innovative work, not only in the substance and form of their productions, but also in the social relations they are creating through this practice, that can change the ways we understand media and their relation to the circulation of culture more generally in the twenty-first century.

Such efforts are evidence of how indigenous media formed over the last decades now find themselves at the conjuncture of a number of historical developments: these include the circuits opened by new media technologies, ranging from satellites to compressed video and cyberspace, as well as the ongoing legacies of indigenous activism worldwide, most recently by a generation comfortable with media and concerned with making their own representations as a mode of cultural creativity and social action. They also represent the complex and differing ways that states have responded to these developments – the opportunities of media and the pressures of activism – and have entered into new relationships with the indigenous nations that they encompass.

I conclude on a note of cautious optimism. The evidence of the growth and creativity of indigenous digital media over the last two decades, whatever problems may have accompanied it, is nothing short of remarkable. Formations such as these, working out of grounded communities or broader regional or national bases, offer an important elaboration of what the Digital Age might look like, intervening in the 'left behind' narrative that predominates. While indigenous media activism alone certainly cannot unseat the power asymmetries which underwrite the profound inequalities that continue to shape their worlds, the issues their digital interventions raise about the politics of culture are on a continuum with the broader issues of self-determination, cultural rights, and political sovereignty, and may help bring some attention to these profoundly interconnected concerns.[17] Indigenous media offer an alternative model of grounded and increasingly global relations created by indigenous people about their own lives and cultures. As we all struggle to comprehend the remapping of social space that is occurring, indigenous media offer some other co-ordinates for understanding. Terms such as 'the Digital Age' gloss over such phenomena in their own right or as examples of alternative modernities, resources of hope, new dynamics in social movements, or as part of the trajectory of indigenous life in the twenty-first century. Perhaps it is time to invent new terms to remind us of the issues of power at work from a position that interrogates the hegemonic order implied in the language of the Digital Age.

Notes

* This chapter is an expansion of a piece of work that is being published elsewhere: Ginsburg, F. (2008) Rethinking the Digital Age, In *Global Indigenous Media*, Pam Wilson, Michelle Stewart (eds). Duke University Press.
1 I would like to thank the following people for the ongoing conversations that helped me to write this chapter, in particular Leo Hsu, David Vadiveloo, Katrina Soukoup, and Barbi Zelizer. The piece grew out of a column first written for the

online journal *Flow*, in January 2005, and a lecture of the same name delivered 22 February 2005 at the Annenberg School for Communication at the University of Pennsylvania in their Scholars Programme series. Thanks to Pam Wilson and Michelle Stewart for encouraging me to write this piece, and to Jason Toynbee for his insights.

2 For information on the 2005 WSIS see http://www.itu.int/wsis/index-p1.html.

3 As the site's founders explain at http://www.cyberpowwow.net/about.html, 'The CyberPowWow project, conceived in 1996, is part web site and part palace – a series of interconnected graphical chat rooms which allow visitors to interact with one another in real time. Together the web site and palace form a virtual gallery with digital (and digitized) artworks and a library of texts ...'

4 See the web site at http://www.odn.net.au/.

5 For discussion of these statistics at the 2005 World Economic Forum see http://www.weforum.org/site/knowledgenavigator.nsf/Content/   New+Technologies. For an excellent discussion of the complexity of accounting for telephony statistics see Shirky (2002).

6 The system, developed by First Mile Solutions, based in Boston MA, uses a receiver box powered by the motor cycle's battery. The driver need only roll slowly past the school to download all the village's outgoing e-mail and deliver incoming e-mail. Newly collected information is stored for the day in a computer strapped to the back of the motor cycle.

7 Thanks to Leo Hsu for passing this reference on to me.

8 Thanks to B. Ruby Rich for this reference.

9 My citation of Bill Gates – one of the world's wealthiest men, who has only recently adopted such a stance – is meant to some extent as a provocation, but also to point out that there are indeed different positions within the world of the digerati that are worth taking seriously for those of us interested in finding a wedge in the discursive and political fields.

10 For other examples see Landzelius (2006), Prins (2002), and Christen (2005).

11 See their web site at http://www.isuma.ca.

12 See http://www.atanarjuat.com for the film's web site.

13 See http://sila.nu/swf/journal and http://www.sila.nu/live. The web site is financially supported by Telefilm Canada's New Media Fund, Government of Nunavut (Department of Sustainable Development), Nunavut Community Economic Development, Heritage Canada (Canadian Studies Programme), National Research Council (Industrial Research Assistance Programme). Nunavut Independent Television Network (NITV) is a collaborating partner, along with sponsorships from Ardicom Digital Communications, SSI Micro, and Stratos Global Corporation.

14 For web site see http://www.usmob.com.au.

15 Us Mob web site at http://www.abc.net.au/usmob.

16 *Raven Tales* premiered in Los Angeles in 2005 at the National Geographic's All Roads Film Festival (http://www.nationalgeographic.com/allroads), which gave the project completion funds, the only digital animation in that project. It was slated to air on Canada's APTN aboriginal television network in 2005.

17 My thanks to Jason Toynbee for his helpful reminder to keep those connections alive.

Bibliography

Anderson, J. (no date) 'The imaginary politics of access to knowledge: whose cultural agendas are being advanced?' *Unpublished manuscript.*

Appiah, K. A. (1997) 'The multiculturalist misunderstanding', *New York Review of Books* 44 (15): 30–6.

Bennett, T. and Blundell, V. (1995) 'First peoples', *Cultural Studies* 9: 1–24.

Brooks, J. (2004) 'Digital pony express links up Cambodia', *New York Times*, 27 January, p. E1.

Castells, M. (1996) *The Rise of the Network Society*. London: Blackwell.

Castells, M. (1997) *The Power of Identity: the Information Age*. London: Blackwell.

Castells, M. (2003) *The Internet Galaxy: Reflections on the Internet, Business, and Society*. Oxford: Oxford University Press.

Christen, K. (2005) 'Gone digital: aboriginal remix in the cultural commons', *International Journal of Cultural Property* 12: 315–44.

Curran, J. and Park, Myung-Jin (eds) (2000) *Dewesternizing Media Studies*. New York: Routledge.

Danaja, P. and Garde, M. (1997) 'From a distance', in C. E. Smith and H. Burke (eds) '1997 Fulbright Symposium: Indigenous Cultures in an Interconnected World' (pre-circulated papers).

Fabian, J. (1983) *Time and the Other*. New York: Columbia University Press.

'From the digital divide to the need for a worldwide solidarity movement' (2005) *Digital Solidarity Fund*, http://www.dsf-fsn.org/en/02–en.htm (accessed 12 October 2007).

Ginsburg, F. (2005a) 'Rethinking the Digital Age', *Flow: a Critical Forum on Television and Film* 1 (8), http://flowtv.org/?p=651 (accessed 12 October 2007).

Ginsburg, F. (2005b) 'Move over, Marshall McLuhan! Live from the Arctic!' *Flow: a Critical Forum on Television and Film* 2 (4), http://flowtv.org/?p=447 (accessed 12 October 2007).

Ginsburg, F. (2005c) '10,000 years of media flow', *Flow: a Critical Forum on Television and Film* 1 (4), http://flowtv.org/?p=673 (accessed 12 October 2007).

Ginsburg, F., Abu Lughod, L. and Larkin, B. (2002) 'Introduction', *Media Worlds: Anthropology on New Terrain*. Berkeley CA: University of California Press.

'Indigenous position paper for the World Summit on the Information Society' (2003) *Indigenous peoples and the Information Society*, draft version. Geneva, http:// www.un-ngls.org/WSIS%20-%20Indigenous-PositionPaper-EN. rtf (accessed 12 October 2007).

Klineneberg, E. and Benzecry, C. (2005) 'Introduction: cultural production in a Digital Age', *Annals of the American Academy of Political and Social Science*, special issue, 597 (1): 6–18.

Landzelius, K. (ed.) (2006) *Going Native on the Net: Indigenous Cyber-activism and Virtual Diasporas over the World Wide Web*. London: Routledge.

Latukefu, A. (2006) 'Remote indigenous communities in Australia: questions of access, information, and self-determination', in K. Landzelius (ed.) *Going Native on the Net: Indigenous Cyber-activism and Virtual Diasporas over the World Wide Web*. London: Routledge.

Markoff, J. (2005) 'Taking the pulse of technology at Davos', *New York Times*, 31 January, http://cel.media.mit.edu/press/mirrors/NYT100DollarPC.html (accessed 12 October 2007).

Massing, M. (2005) 'The end of news?' *New York Review of Books*, 52 (19), 1 December, http://www.nybooks.com/articles/18516 (accessed 12 October 2007).

McLuhan, M. (1964/1994) *Understanding Media: the Extensions of Man*. Boston MA: MIT Press.

Norris, P., Bennett, W. L. and Entman, R. (2001) *Digital Divide: Civic Engagement, Information Poverty, and the Internet Worldwide*. Cambridge: Cambridge University Press.

Prins, Harald (2001) 'Digital revolution: indigenous peoples in Cyberia', in W. A. Haviland (ed.) *Cultural Anthropology*, 10th edn. Fort Worth TX: Harcourt.

Prins, H. (2002) 'Visual media and the primitivist perplex: colonial fantasies, indigenous imagination, and advocacy in North America', in F. Ginsburg, L. Abu-Lughod and B. Larkin (eds) *Media Worlds: Anthropology on New Terrain*. Berkeley CA: University of California Press.

Rickard, J. (1999) 'First Nation territory in cyberspace declared: no treaties needed', *CyberPowWow: an Aboriginally Determined Territory in Cyberspace*, http://www.cyberpowwow.net/nation2nation/jolenework.html (accessed 12 October 2007).

Shirky, C. (2002) 'Sorry, wrong number', *Wired* 10 (10), 10 October, http://www.wired.com/wired/archive/10.10/view.html?pg=2 (accessed 12 October 2007).

'Technology and development' (2005) *The Economist*, 10 March, http://www.economist.com/opinion/displaystory.cfm?story_id=E1_PSQNRTS (accessed 12 October 2007).

Verhovic, S. (2000) 'Bill Gates turns skeptical on digital solution's scope', *New York Times*, 3 November, pp. A1–A18.

Wilson, R. and Dissanayake, W. (1996) 'Introduction', in R. Wilson and W. Dissanayake (eds) *Global/Local: Cultural Production and the Transnational Imaginary*. Durham NC: Duke University Press.

9   Media and mobility in a transnational world

Purnima Mankekar

My objective in this chapter is to sketch the contours of a theoretical framework that explores the relationship between media, mobility, and transnationality. For several decades now, transnational connections between different parts of the world have been strengthened by the relative ease of international travel, the globalisation of capital and labour, and the transnational proliferation of communication technologies (Appadurai 1996; Appadurai and Breckenridge 1988; Glick Schiller *et al.* 1994; Gupta and Ferguson 1997; Hannerz 1996; Harvey 1989; Morley and Robins 1995; Ong 1999). In my ongoing research, I construct a feminist ethnography of how transnational public cultures mediate the social relationships, imaginations, and desires of gendered subjects at two nodes in a global circuit of images, texts, and commodities, New Delhi and the San Francisco Bay Area.

Building on feminist scholarship on space, migration, travel, and location, as well as on feminist media studies on the relationship between media and subjectivity, I examine the role of transnational public cultures in the discursive (re)production, transformation, and gendered mediation of 'India' and 'Indian culture' in these different, but interconnected, sites. By transnational public cultures I refer to mass media that traverse national and geographic borders (popular film, television, and print media), as well as public expressions of community such as protests, cultural festivals, and ethnic grocery stores. My objective in this larger project is to formulate a transnational analytics (Grewal *et al.* 1999) that goes beyond the conceptualisation of home and diaspora as discrete sites by examining the relationship between media, placement, and displacement. For instance, a number of Hindi films have focused on Indians in the diaspora. How do discourses of gender and sexuality shape these portrayals and, additionally, how do they mediate the dynamic constitution of Indianness and national belonging both within India and its diasporas? What do these representations tell us about changing experiences of nationhood and identity in a transnational world?

I engage 'India' as an optic rather than as a pre-given political and cultural fact: I am interested in tracing how modes of longing and belonging, affiliation and disaffiliation, and identification and alienation might exceed and, on occasion, subvert the interpellatory claims of the contemporary Indian nation-state both within India and among diasporic communities. As several scholars have pointed out, transnationalism does not, in any way, render national or regional cultures obsolete (for instance, Appadurai 1996; Gupta and Ferguson 1997; Ong 1999): transnational cultural formations are frequently accompanied by the emergence or consolidation of parochial, regional, and national identities. I am concerned with how transnational public cultures, and mobile media in particular, not only link but, more important, help discursively *construct* the homeland and diaspora.

Texts-in-motion

Mobility, feminist theorists teach us, is a thoroughly social process. Ahmed *et al.* insist that not only are the forms and conditions of movement highly divergent, they also necessarily exist in relation to similarly divergent configurations of placement and of feeling 'at home' (2003: 1). Furthermore, it seems egregiously presentist to assume that mobility is unique to the present moment: while it is obvious that the ease of travel has resulted in an acceleration of the physical mobility of some individuals and communities, the imposition of border patrols, immigration checks, indeed the birth of the modern nation-state might well have circumscribed the ability of people to move. Finally, mobility cannot be conceived as separate from location. In her discussion of location and travel, Caren Kaplan posits that 'transnational subjects are produced through location as well as mobility, certainly, as national economies dictate who moves to obtain work and who stays put' (2003: 220). Just as the mobility of peoples is shaped by their location along axes of difference and inequality, such as, gender, race, class, and sexuality, so too is the cultural work of mobile media refracted by their embeddedness in larger landscapes of affect, desire, and consumption. At the same time, media create and participate in social fields that shape, circumscribe and, in many ways, constitute the mobility of peoples, texts, and commodities.

Fundamentally, media function through as well as enable the circulation of signs. Further, to the extent that culture is formed, at least in part, through semiosis, media play a central role in the construction of culture itself: hence, to speak of the 'cultural context' of mass media is to fall back on a substantialist notion of culture that is ostensibly unmediated by semiosis or outside the reach of media. Media spur mobility in all its forms, ranging from physical mobility to imaginative travel and virtual migration. In my research, I have worked with heterogeneous communities of people who moved from India to the United States: these ranged from new immigrants and members of long-established diasporas to temporary workers on special work permits such as H1B visas and 'undocumented' men and women. At the same time, I have also been concerned with the relationship between media and the mobility of people within India: these include people who have been displaced because of religious violence or persecution; workers in a new sector of the Indian economy, the business processing outsourcing (BPO) industry, chiefly call centre employees who performed what sociologist A. Aneesh has termed 'virtual migration' (2006) through their interaction with clients abroad; and last, but not least, with women and men who do not physically move but, through their consumption of transnational public cultures, engage in forms of imaginative travel.

I take as my foundational premise that mass media are themselves constituted through mobility. Indeed, mobility is an intrinsic characteristic of mass media which, by definition, circulate across space and over time: after all, it is through circulation that media acquire social significance. It is not surprising, then, that much of media theory is predicated on implicit, albeit frequently unexamined, assumptions about circulation, circuits, and 'flows' of media. From some of the earliest paradigms dominating media theory, such as the so-called hypodermic model of media effects, to more nuanced models that explain the social significance of media (for instance, Stuart Hall's encoding and decoding paradigm) circulation and circuitry emerge as crucial premises. Recent theories about globalisation and transnational media similarly depend on the notion of the 'flow' of media from points of production to points of reception. Notions of flow seem to me to be misleading because, evidently, transnational mass media do not all flow uninterrupted from one part of the world to another. Rather than conceptualise the traffic in media as mechanistic 'flows' from one culture to another, it seems more accurate to analyse media in terms of their bumpy and uneven trajectory as emerging from, converging with, and even bypassing multiple sites across the world.

Brian Massumi has suggested that social analysis must acknowledge the primacy of movement as a way to theorise processes of identity formation and social change (2002). Drawing on Massumi's insights that (1) all movement occurs in time, and (2) movement is a crucial component of temporality, I would like to begin by examining the relationship between media, mobility, and temporality. Two obvious but undertheorised aspects of media are that media exist in and through mobility, and that the work of media occurs not just across space but, equally important, in time. Examining the cultural work of media, therefore, implies tracing not only their spatial dimensions (as in Appadurai's 1996 notion of scapes; see also Mankekar and Schein 2004) but also their temporal dimensions. While foregrounding the materiality of media, the diverse forms through which they function, their textuality and modes of enunciation, it is also important to remind ourselves that media work within and through historical context. To begin with, media are not just reflective of particular socio-historical formations but are constitutive of them. For instance, during the late 1980s and early 1990s, state-run Indian television played a critical role in the production of middle-class subjectivity, the formulation of discourses of Indian womanhood, and in the consolidation of Hindu nationalism as a political formation; at the same time, viewers' interpretations of what they watched on television were refracted by the specific socio-historical conjuncture in which they were situated, as well as by their positions along axes of class, gender, and religious affiliation (Mankekar 1999).

Media and temporality are intimately connected in other ways as well. Our very experience of time can be structured through our consumption of media. For instance, in my previous research with lower middle-class and upwardly mobile men and women in New Delhi, it became clear to me that my informants structured their household routines around their favourite television shows, so that viewing television literally punctuated the everyday rhythms of their family lives. My informants would plan their mealtimes, rush home from work or social events, and organise their daily lives around the telecast of their favourite television programmes. This continues to be the case now that cable and satellite television have introduced a plethora of channels into people's homes and lives: the rhythms of family life, indeed of domesticity, function in tandem with habits of viewing and consumption.

Finally, media shape how people experience the passage of time – how they remember (or forget) aspects of the past, how they interpret and live in the present, and how they imagine the future. In fact, rather than conceptualise the past, present, or future as *a priori* or autonomous realms of experience, it makes sense for us to think of the ways in which media enable the very constitution of past, present, and future through, for instance, the mediation of memory, contemporaneity, and futurity. This has come up for me time and again in my current work. My informants in the San Francisco Bay Area, for example, sometimes experience India as a 'homeland' that belongs in the past, filtered through memories of their lives there. These memories are often soaked with affect – whether that of nostalgia, ambivalence, or antagonism.[1] Frequently, these affect-laden memories of the past are refracted through the consumption of mass media like Bollywood films, including films that represent an authentic, albeit phantasmic, 'Indian culture' as 'vanishing' in the face of an allegedly invasive modernity (Ivy 1995). These films participate in the creation of a sense of temporal rupture for diasporic subjects, especially new immigrants, for whom the homeland becomes a place 'left behind' in the past.

However, media participate in the creation of a phantasmic past in the so-called homeland as well. For many of my informants in India, spectacular renditions of Hindu religious serials like the *Ramayana* and the *Mahabharat* on television form an archive of collective memory: these serials, the *Ramayana* in particular, depict 'the national past' in terms of the 'Golden Age' of Hinduism. These representations shape the construction not only of the national past but also of contemporaneity and futurity. The phantasmic past represented in these serials functions as a foil for representations of the present as contaminated by westernisation, modernity, or, most perniciously in the discourses of Hindu nationalism, Islam. These depictions of the glorious Indian past are also deployed as a blueprint for the formation of the nation of the future. These constructions of temporality – in terms of the collective national past, present, and future – have had devastating political implications. Accomplishing a slippage between (upper-caste) Hindu and Indian culture, they have facilitated the growing hegemony of Hindu nationalist discourses of cultural purity predicated on the marginalisation, if not demonisation, of Islam and Christianity, and the exclusion of lower-caste struggles for social justice.

Media and world-making

I have focused so far on the relationship between media, mobility, and temporality. In this section I'd like to analyse the ways in which, in a transnational world, media participate in world-making through the production of affect and desire. I turn now to how the affective connections created by mobile media enable the reterritorialisation of space. Drawing on Massumi (2002), other theorists of affect (for instance, Deleuze and Guattari 1987; Ahmed 2004), and on my own previous research on the role of state-run television in the production of nationalist affect (2000), I do not conceive of affect as located within the domain of the psychic, the cognitive, or the subjective; it is not, therefore, tied to tropes of interiority. Massumi (2002) argues that affect is distinct from feeling (the domain of individual subjectivity) and emotion (the domain of the social and the linguistic). Drawing on the work of C. S. Peirce, affect can be described in terms of abduction – a sense of intensity that exists prior to its capture by language.

Media create intersectionalities of affect and social structuration by enabling the circulation of affect within and across communities. In such instances, affect is generated and *mobilised* by transnational media to produce webs of relationality between subjects (see Ahmed 2004: 119 for a similar discussion). Put another way, affective economies (to borrow the term from Ahmed 2004) generated by mass media enable the suturing of individuals into interpretive communities. At the same time, as we know, these interpretive communities are neither homogeneous nor monolithic and are, instead, often rife with internal hierarchies and differences based on socio-economic status, gender, sexual orientation (to name a few). As I will argue below, any analysis of media-generated forms of affect must, hence, trace how affective economies articulate with prevailing social formations and axes of power.

Ahmed *et al.* point out that 'The affectivity of home is bound up with the temporality of home, with the past, the present, and the future. It takes time to feel at home. For those who have left their homes, a nostalgic relation to both the past and home might become part of the lived reality in the present' (2003: 9). By generating and circulating a range of affective economies, mobile media frequently blur the boundaries between location and migration, stasis and movement, homeland and diaspora.[2] Media like Bollywood cinema and satellite television enable the reterritorialisation of space through the construction of a phantasmic India which cannot, ultimately, be located in a specific place. As an extra-geographic entity, this phantasmic construction of India is inscribed with particular kinds of affect. Bollywood cinema, for instance, participates in the constitution of homeland and diaspora by generating a *range* of affect spanning nostalgia and longing, as well as disaffection, alienation, and, at times, antagonism – as in the case of minorities placed at the margins of Indian nation-state. For instance, a family of Sikhs with whom I worked closely during my fieldwork in New Delhi were unequivocal about how alienated they felt from some of Bollywood's portrayals of 'Indian tradition'. Speaking, in particular, of the 1990s blockbuster *Hum Aapke Hain Kaun* (dir. Sooraj Barjatya, 1994), a saga of an upper-class family of orthodox Hindus, they insisted that Bollywood cinema participated in the conflation of Indian and Hindu culture by representing Hindu traditions, rituals, and customs as quintessentially Indian. Films like *Hum Aapke Hain Kaun* indexed to them *their* location at the margins of the Hindu/Indian nation, and reinforced their sense of alienation and disaffection. Here again we see the relationship between mobile media and the location of particular social subjects.

Several of my informants in the San Francisco Bay Area, including those who felt extremely antagonistic towards the Indian nation-state, described how watching Indian television programmes on satellite television enabled them to feel connected with India. Watching these programmes produced memories of 'the homeland' shot through with a complex range of affect that was, in turn, shaped by their social locations. In some cases, watching satellite television was suffused with longing; for instance, one woman claimed that she subscribed to satellite television because 'it brings India into my home in California'. However, in contexts where memories of India were painful, as in the case of another woman who left India in order to flee the homophobia of her family and community, satellite television enabled her to feel an entirely different kind of affective connection – this time, of ambivalence shot through with relief – with the India she had 'left behind'. The affective economies created by satellite television inflected these diasporic subjects' experiences of temporality in terms of how they remembered the past, lived in the present, and imagined the future and, in so doing, forged links between the past, contemporaneity, and futurity.

Media play a critical role in processes of emplacement. Media rework place through affect and, to this extent, make spaces into particular kinds of places (cf. Gupta and Ferguson 1997; see also Massey 1993).

Much has been written about how media represent the homeland to diasporic subjects. However, I am equally interested in how media represent and, to this extent, constitute 'the foreign' as a particular kind of place for viewers residing in India. I turn, once again, to the example of Bollywood. There is a long tradition of representing the foreign in Bollywood films – either as *mise-en-scène* for romantic fantasy or as the setting for stories about the lives of Indians settled abroad. In the Bollywood imaginary, London has often been represented as the locus of the foreign and, more specifically, of *vilayat*. Thus, although Switzerland, France, the United States and now, increasingly, Australia and New Zealand have become settings for the 'picturisation' of romantic songs, London has historically been the location of choice for stories about the lives of expatriate Indians. In many of these films, London is usually represented as a place peopled by other Indians. But, perhaps more important, it is the place where the clash between 'Indian' and 'Western' culture (symbolising tradition and modernity respectively) is staged. In recent films, however, London has been depicted not only as the stage for the battle between tradition and modernity, East and West, but has also become a place where Indians can (and do) live with the supreme confidence of those who are no longer bystanders but are participants in the new globalised economy.

Hence, in Bollywood films about Indians living in 'the West', London and, more recently, New York become specific kinds of places. This is particularly the case in films made after the early 1990s, when the Indian economy was 'liberalised'. These post-1990s films are noteworthy in how they represent the relationship between travel and mobility, on the one hand, and culture and national identity on the other. In years past, Indians who lived abroad were depicted in Bollywood film as somehow less authentic, less Indian than those living in India; they were represented either in terms of 'brain drain' or a betrayal of their homeland. After the 1990s, when the Indian state constructed a new category of identity for upper-class Indians settled abroad, that of the Non-Resident Indian, or NRI, Bollywood cinema's portrayals of expatriate Indians changed subtly but profoundly. Instead of being culturally impure or inauthentic, the NRIs of many of these films were depicted as more authentic, more Indian than even their compatriots in India. The film that spearheaded this change in the portrayal of NRIs was *Dilwale Dulhaniya Le Jayenge*, or *DDLJ*, as it is known among English-speaking Indians (Mankekar 1999).

In *DDLJ*, as in many other such films, NRIs were depicted as male and upper-class, with the capital to invest in India. Not only do these films represent the experiences of those who travel but, in a more profound way, they constitute the experience of travel through their depiction of the lives of (select segments of) Indians residing in the West. It is also important to note that these films have an enormous market among audiences all over the world – in many ways they represent the diaspora to itself. But, as my interviews with several young men and women in the San Francisco Bay Area indicate, these films also constitute the experience of being in diaspora by providing these viewers with a language, a discourse, a mode of representing their own struggles, aspirations, and identities. Thus, for instance, in the words of one South Asian fan of Bollywood cinema that I interviewed, *DDLJ* enabled her to 'see, clearly, how as an immigrant I have to cope with intergenerational conflict'. This young woman was not alone in articulating how Bollywood films like *DDLJ* literally produce a particular vision of their subject positions as second-generation immigrants in the United States. As suggested by these discourses, films like *DDLJ* enabled them to experience being in diaspora largely in terms of intergenerational conflict (rather than by their positionalities along axes of class, race, gender, or sexuality).

Moreover, the texts of mobile media themselves become spaces of intimate habitation for many people who do not physically move. In such instances, mobile media forge practices of imaginative travel and, thereby, participate in processes of world-making by enabling viewers and spectators to inhabit worlds that are, at once, phantasmic and intimate. Thus, for example, despite the fact that they had never set foot outside India, several of my informants in New Delhi could imaginatively navigate the streets of London (or, for that matter, New York City) through their consumption of films about Indians abroad. To the extent that they enable subjects to inhabit other worlds and experience other forms of existence, these forms of imaginative travel are neither marginal nor epiphenomenal to the constitution of subjectivity.

For many young men and women that I worked with in New Delhi, media also played a crucial role in inciting the desire to travel. Transnational mass media, such as television shows produced in India and abroad, films, advertisements, and the internet generated a range of fantasies about 'life in the West', and played a crucial role in producing in these young men and women the desire to try to go abroad in search of a better life, upward mobility, financial security, or a more cosmopolitan lifestyle. Some of my lower middle-class and middle-class informants wished to move overseas to make a life for themselves, in large part because they were driven by their desire to acquire the commodities they saw flashing on their television screens, on billboards all over the newly configured landscapes of New Delhi, and in films. For, even though commodities had begun to flood the Indian market after the liberalisation of the Indian economy, most of my informants believed that the commodities they so fervently desired would be more readily accessible in the West: in their fantasies of upward mobility through travel, these commodities became icons of (an easier, happier, more successful and, at times, more glamorous) life in the West. As Appadurai points out, 'the images, scripts, models, and narratives that come through mass mediation (in its realistic and fictional modes) make the difference between migration today and in the past. Those who wish to move, those who have moved, those who wish to return, and those who choose to stay rarely formulate their plans outside the sphere of radio and television, cassettes and videos, newsprint and telephone' (1996: 6).

Mobility and the politics of mobility

As Doreen Massey (1994) and several other feminist scholars have pointed out, mobility through space is shaped by larger social fields.[3] For one, the physical mobility of individuals and communities is mediated by their locations along axes of class, gender, sexuality, race, national origin and, now in the post-9/11 world, religious affiliation. Furthermore, states remain crucial regulators of the mobility of peoples, commodities and, perhaps to a lesser extent, of capital. Additionally, as we know, even when social and political factors are productive of mobility, they are not always so in ways that are empowering or liberatory but, instead, might even be violent or coercive – as in the case of economic refugees fleeing the structural violence of poverty and inequality, political refugees and asylum seekers whose mobility is produced by the coercive power of states, as well as those fleeing more intimate forms of violence such as domestic violence, homophobia, or sexual assault. In such instances, the mobility of individuals and communities is a measure not of their empowerment but of their dislocation or displacement (Clifford 1997; Mankekar 1994).

The imaginative travel engendered by media is also inflected by relations of power. Our capacity to imagine, even to fantasise, is shaped by our structural locations in social fields. Although I remain sceptical of the suggestion that the social role of the imagination is unique to the contemporary era, I draw here on Arjun Appadurai's ground-breaking conceptualisation of the imagination as a social practice. Appadurai points out that 'the imagination has become an organised field of social practices, a form of work (in the sense of both labor and culturally organised practice), and a form of negotiation between sites of agency (individuals) and globally defined fields of possibility ...' (1996: 31). Therefore, against the notion of the unfettered imagination, I locate it firmly within the socius: how and what we imagine is shaped by our structural locations which, in turn, refract the discursive horizons of our imagination. Here we see, once again, that the cultural work of mobile media is refracted by our locations in particular social fields.[4]

Media have also enabled a new form of migration for some recent entrants into the global economy. Preliminary research conducted by Akhil Gupta and myself with young men and women employed in the information technology industry in India suggest the myriad ways in which media play a central role in the creation of new kinds of labouring (and fantasising) subjects. These young men and women, who hail largely from middle-class families in cities and small towns, frequently work for multinational companies that outsource their customer care departments to call centres and business processing outsourcing industries (BPOs) in India. These workers are trained to act *as if* they live and work in the West – ostensibly, so they can better serve their Western clients. Hollywood films, television shows, and other media produced in the West are central components of their 'training' as they are taught to take on not only Western names – so that Nandita might become Nancy, and Abhijit becomes Alex – but, equally important, to adopt Western (usually American) accents and ways of speaking. (These impersonations of Nancys and Alexes are primarily designed to stave off concerns among clients living in the West about the supposedly negative effects of outsourcing on the national economies of the United States and the United Kingdom.) In these contexts, media enable a new form of travel termed 'virtual migration' (Aneesh 2006).

The circulation of signs enabled by media plays a critical role in not just producing but also constraining mobility. In the aftermath of the tragic events that we now memorialise as '11 September 2001', media have been centrally implicated in the proliferation of the semiotics of fear and hate through the transnational circulation of the semiotic chain Muslim/Islamic fundamentalist/*jehadi*. The semiotic slippage from Muslim to militant *jehadi* has become ubiquitous through its travels back and forth across the world. This chain of signifiers has taken on a life of its own as it circulates via transnational media between India, where the militant *jehadi* is materialised in the form of the Kashmiri militant or the Muslim fundamentalist, and the United States, in the person of the Al Quaida terrorist. The transnational circulation of this cluster of signs has facilitated the immobility of Muslims (and those perceived to be Muslim) in many parts of the non-Muslim world – ranging from deportations and incarcerations and restrictions on travel by so-called random checks at airports to the constraints experienced by most of Muslims, Sikhs, and others perceived as Muslim who now feel imprisoned by the threat of racial and xenophobic violence.

Conclusion: theorising media in a world of movement

I would like to sum up by reflecting on how we may theorise media in a world of movement. As I note above, theorising media entails unpacking the relationship between mobile texts, on the one hand, and socio-political processes of emplacement and displacement on the other. I have been concerned with how media participate in our experience of time as well as space, place-making and displacement, and in shaping fantasies as well as itineraries of travel.

Although global interconnections are neither new nor unprecedented, the speed at which images, texts, capital, and people currently travel represents shifts that are quantitative as well as qualitative. One important qualitative shift stems from the ubiquity and density characterising the circulation of mass-mediated texts and images around the world (Appadurai 1996;

Hannerz 1996). At the same time, in many contexts capital, texts, and images move faster than people, thus highlighting the uneven speed at which global traffic occurs (Grewal *et al.* 1999: 655). As argued above, transnational media such as film, video, and the internet play a crucial role in not just representing but in constituting the experience of travel, migration, and 'dwelling-in-travel' (Clifford 1997) – both for those who move, as well as for those who do not. Grewal *et al.* argue that 'Transnationalism cannot be charted in a unitary and definitive fashion' (1999: 653). By focusing on the circulation of television programmes, films, commodities, images, and texts between India and the United States I reverse dominant notions of the transnational, according to which commodities, texts, and images 'flow' from the West to the rest of the world. Thus, India emerges not as a 'local' site for the reception of mass media, but as a node where transnational public cultures are both produced and consumed.

Furthermore, mobile media constitute homeland and diaspora not as binary opposites but as mutually imbricated. Diaspora is sometimes conceived as transgressing or exceeding the boundaries of the nation-state and, to this extent, problematising conceptions of national belonging. Yet, where transnational media generate and circulate longing and nostalgia as nationalist affect, they may, for some diasporic subjects, reinscribe the nation as phantasmic fetish: as several diasporic nationalisms have shown us, nationalist affect is particularly potent when experienced at a physical distance from imagined/imaginary homelands. Hence, the webs of affect generated by transnational media suggest that diaspora is neither inevitably 'post-national' nor does it necessarily undermine hegemonic conceptions of the singularity of nationalist identity.

Engaging the relationship between media and mobility entails not only unpacking the binary of homeland versus diaspora but, also, a rethinking of the relationship between movement and stasis, mobility and location. I've been interested in the role of media in shaping, if not producing, different forms of mobility: the physical movement of individuals within and across national borders; the movement of commodities, texts, images, and capital; the impersonations and 'virtual migration' of young men and women in New Delhi as they interact with clients abroad; and the imaginative travel of those who, ostensibly, 'stay put' but are able to inhabit milieux and worlds at a distance. Furthermore, as noted above, media also participate in the constraining of movement. In the post-9/11 era, transnational media have participated in the proliferation of the semiotics of fear by facilitating the circulation of the sign of the terrorist, resulting in the physical and symbolic incarceration for many communities. Several Sikhs, Muslims, and those perceived as Muslim/Middle Eastern have been hampered in their mobility because of the hostility generated through media-generated spectacles of terror. The containment of their mobility has been enacted, in large part, by the circulation of signs that have been generative of specific kinds of affect such as fear and hate.

Despite all the hyperbole about the hypermobility of modern and postmodern subjects, while some forms of movement have been accelerated, others may have become increasingly circumscribed. For, if transnationality is about the transgression of national borders and sovereignties, it is also about the reinstatement of other kinds of boundaries and governmentalities. And if transnationality is about the dizzying circuits constituted by the movement of capital, texts, and commodities, it is also about the formation of certain kinds of subjects who are resolutely located in a particular place and a particular time. As they participate in the construction of desire and identity in the face of particular regimes of power, the most mobile of media are embedded in contexts of both location and dislocation, and displacement and emplacement.

Notes

1 I will elaborate on the relationship between media and affect shortly.
2 Although they do not directly address affect, the work of Gopinath, Naficy, Niranjana, and Shukla may also be mined for insights into the affective connections formed through media.
3 Studies of mobility must, necessarily, be connected with the fraught histories of travel (and location and displacement) in contexts of colonialism and imperialism (see, for instance, the work of Kaplan 1996 and Grewal 1996).
4 Similarly, psychoanalytic theorists, ranging from Freud, to Lacan, to Laplanche and Pontalis and Žižek, also stress the sociopyschic bases of fantasy: far from being unanchored in the social, our fantasies are shaped by social logics. As Anne Allison points out, 'fantasy is not mere or random escapist fantasy, as the term is often used colloquially, but rather is constituted in relationship to the specific milieus in which people live and to which they refer even when constructing imaginary worlds … ' (2000: 124–5). Hence, rather than speak of mass-mediated fantasy as transcending the social, it makes more sense to conceive of fantasy as providing thoroughly social modes of living and experiencing the world.

Bibliography

Print

Allison, Anne (2000) *Permitted and Prohibited Desires: Mothers, Comics, and Censorship in Japan.* Berkeley CA: University of California Press.
Allison, Anne (2002) *Permitted and Prohibited Desires: Mothers, Comics, Censorship in Japan.* Berkeley CA: University of California Press.
Ahmed, Sara (2004) 'Affective economies', *Social Text* 79, 22 (2): 117–39.
Ahmed, Sara Claudia Castaneda, Fortier, Anne-Marie and Sheller, Mimi (eds) (2003) 'Introduction: uprootings/regroundings: questions of home and migration', in Sara Ahmed, Claudia Castaneda, Anne-Marie Fortier, and Mimi Sheller (eds) *Uprootings/Regroundings: Questions of Home and Migration.* London: Berg.
Aneesh, A. (2006) *Virtual Migration: the Programming of Globalization.* Durham NC: Duke University Press.

Appadurai, Arjun (1996) *Modernity at Large: Cultural Dimensions of Globalization*. Minneapolis MN: University of Minnesota Press.

Appadurai, Arjun and Breckenridge, Carol (1988) 'Why public culture?' *Public Culture* 1 (1): 5–9.

Clifford, James (1997) *Routes: Travel and Translation in the late Twentieth Century*. Cambridge MA: Harvard University Press.

Deleuze, Gilles and Guattari, Felix (1987) *A Thousand Plateaus: Capitalism and Schizophrenia*, trans. Brian Massumi. Minneapolis MN: University of Minnesota Press.

Ghosh, Amitav (1992) *In an Antique Land*. London: Granta Books.

Glick Schiller, Nina, Basch, Linda and Szanton Blanc, Cristina (1994) *Nations Unbound: Trasnational Projects, Postcolonial Predicaments, and Deterritorialized Nation-states*. New York: Gordon & Breach.

Grewal, Inderpal (1996) *Home and Harem: Nation, Gender, Empire and Cultures of Travel*. Durham NC: Duke University Press.

Grewal, Inderpal, Gupta, Akhil and Ong, Aihwa (1999) 'Introduction: Asian transnationalities: media, markets, and migration', *Positions* 7 (3): 653–66.

Gupta, Akhil and Ferguson, James (1997) *Culture, Power, Place: Explorations in Critical Anthropology*. Durham NC: Duke University Press.

Hall, Stuart (2000) 'Encoding/Decoding', in Paul Morris and Sue Thornton (eds) *Media Studies: a Reader*. New York: Washington Square Press.

Hannerz, Ulf (1996) *Transnational Connections: Culture, People, Places*. London: Routledge.

Harvey, David (1989) *The Conditions of Postmodernity: an Enquiry into the Origins of Cultural Change*. Oxford: Blackwell.

Ivy, Marilyn (1995) *Discourses of the Vanishing: Modernity, Phantasm, Japan*. Chicago: University of Chicago Press.

Kaplan, Caren (1996) *Questions of Travel: Postmodern Discourses of Displacement*. Durham NC: Duke University Press.

Kaplan, Caren (2003) 'Transporting the subject: technologies of mobility and location in an era of globalization', in Sara Ahmed, Claudia Castaneda, Anne-Marie Fortier, and Mimi Sheller (eds) *Uprootings/Regroundings: Questions of Home and Migration*. London: Berg.

Mankekar, Purnima (1994) 'Reflections on diasporic identities: a prolegomenon to an analysis of political bifocality', *Diaspora* 3 (3): 349–71.

Mankekar, Purnima (1999) 'Brides who travel: gender, transnationalism, and nationalism in Hindi film', *Positions* 7 (3): 731–61.

Mankekar, Purnima (2000) *Screening Culture, Viewing Politics: an Ethnography of Television, Womanhood, and Nation in Postcolonial India*. Durham NC: Duke University Press.

Mankekar, Purnima and Schein, Louisa (2004) 'Introduction: mediated transnationalism and social erotics', *Journal of Asian Studies* 63 (2): 357–65.

Massey, Doreen (1993) 'Power geometry and a progressive sense of place', in Jon Bird *et al.* (eds) *Mapping the Futures: Local Cultures, Global Change*. London: Routledge.

Massey, Doreen (1994) *Space, Place, and Gender*. Minneapolis MN: University of Minnesota Press.

Massey, Doreen (1999) 'Imagining globalization: power-geometries of time-space', in Avtar Brah *et al.* (eds) *Global Futures: Migration, Environment, and Globalization.* London: Macmillan.

Massumi, Brian (2002) *Parables for the Virtual: Movement, Affect, Sensation.* Durham NC: Duke University Press.

Morley, David and Robins, Kevin (1995) *Spaces of Identity: Global Media, Electronic Landscapes and Cultural Boundaries.* New York: Routledge.

Naficy, Hamid (1993) *The Making of Exile Cultures: Iranian Television in Los Angeles.* Minneapolis MN: University of Minnesota Press.

Ong, Aihwa (1999) *Flexible Citizenship: the Cultural Logics of Transnationality.* Durham NC: Duke University Press.

Film

Dilwale Dulhaniya Le Jayenge (1995) Aditya Chopra, director. Yashraj Films.

Hum Aapke Hain Kaun (1994) Sooraj R. Barjatya, director. Rajshri Productions.

Part III

Spectacle and the self

10 Form and power in an age of continuous spectacle

Nick Couldry

There was a time when it was impossible to say anything substantive in media research without launching into an exhaustive discussion on Althusser or Lacan. That time of compulsory theorising is over, to the relief of many, but that does not mean media research's relation to theory is now healthy. On the contrary, contemporary media research tends either to operate in a theory-free zone or in isolated capsules of theory saturation – Deleuzian, Manovichian, and so on – unconnected either to each other or to any wider space of debate. To change metaphors, we lurched in the late 1990s from an all-night party of theoretical excess to find ourselves at dawn in a 'post-theory' desert where even the effort of asking *why* we need theory, and *how* we might compare the relative merits of competing theories, seemed beyond us.

Luckily this book's editors are determined to prod us back into alertness. The stakes – both for media research and for wider social theory – are high, indeed they have rarely been higher. It matters what counts as 'good' media theory in an era when media logics are ever more closely embedded in the everyday stuff of politics and when everyday politics seems ever more closely dependent on the strategic use of spectacle by many actors (not only states) in a global sphere of conflict whose instabilities threaten us all.

The point, however, is not to construct large-scale theoretical systems in Parsonian style or to conjure up totalities and treat them as if they were real as in Hardt and Negri's provocative but ultimately unhelpful work *Empire* (2001). As Pierre Bourdieu and Stuart Hall have both argued,[1] theory is useful only if through its relative generality it enables us to engage better with the particular, that is, for better tools with which to practise our *suspicion towards* totalising claims, whether by academics, politicians, or media executives. It is here – in our choice of theoretical tools – that some difficult choices must be made, when we consider the entanglement of today's media forms with power.

The main choice I want to discuss is between Actor Network Theory (ANT) and ritual analyses of media, using Foucault's account of 'the order of discourse', briefly, as a bridge between them. Actor Network Theory – and the 'associology' that has recently emerged from it – for all its potential insight into media processes, lacks, I will argue, an interest in questions of social and media form, and so fails to deliver on Dorothy Smith's ambition (1987: 8–9) for a sociology that 'will look back and talk back' to the determinants of everyday life.

My point will be not to defend my own theory of media's ritual dimensions in detail – for that readers can look at my previous work (Couldry 2003a) – but to defend the type of theoretical choice it represents in answer to our task of understanding media power. At this 'metatheoretical' level I want also to make more explicit some philosophical underpinnings of the antipathy towards certain rhetorics of 'the social' that runs through my work on media rituals. That will lead me back to broader social theory, and to three forms of scepticism about the notion of 'society' – those of Latour and Laclau and the scepticism I find, against the grain, in the critical realism of Roy Bhaskar. I will argue for preferring the third over the first two. In conclusion, I recall the global political context in which our choices about theory come to matter.

Let me say a word about the word 'spectacle' in my title. I use it to refer to those things which in contemporary societies we are encouraged to view in large numbers and in viewing participate in an act of representative significance. Every era has had its distinctive spectacles but modern media make a decisive break in the history of spectacle (Thompson 1995: 134): whereas the spectacle of the old royal courts was 'representative' only by virtue of the high status of its performers and immediate audience, the representativeness of contemporary spectacle is inseparable from its dissemination to large and distant media audiences. '*Continuous* spectacle' in my title points to the intertextual and temporal intensity by which contemporary media spectacle creates, or appears to create, a 'media world' for our attention. This is not to deny Nicholas Mirzoeff's point that we also live in an age of '*anti*-spectacle' which on painful topics such as war and prisons 'dictates that there is nothing to see, and that instead one must keep moving, keep circulating and keep consuming' (Mirzoeff 2005: 16). We can, however, restate Mirzoeff's point by adapting Jonathan Crary's (1999) terminology: along with new 'regimes of attention' come new 'regimes of inattention', the relations between the two being important. None of this contradicts the more basic point that media contribute crucially to power in an age of continuous spectacle; indeed, the structured relations between regimes of attention/inattention suggest that from our involvements with spectacle emerge social forms of considerable significance. I will return to this point when I discuss ritual, but first I want to look at things from a very different angle, that of networks.

The limits of Actor Network Theory

My question is simple: how best to theorise – make broader causal, not incidental, sense of – how media act in and on the world. There are, of course, media specialists interested in media texts for their own sake but that approach is oriented by very different epistemological concerns. We are discussing here *only* media research for which social theory is at least in principle salient. Approaches to media formed within the paradigm of literary criticism are not relevant.

I begin with ANT, partly because it was important to me when I was starting down the path of media theory in the mid-1990s. At the time I just couldn't see how the classic elements of media research – the study of media texts, media institutions and the interpretations we make of those texts (vital though they all are) – could together be enough to explain the place of media in contemporary societies. We had also surely to confront the question of *belief*. Media institutions have as their main asset symbolic power: a concentration of symbolic resources – crudely, the power to tell and circulate stories about the world – that is historically unprecedented. But that symbolic power, however much its infrastructure depends on concentrations of economic and/or state power, is not reducible to them. It is sustained in part through belief, through legitimacy. How can that legitimacy be reproduced except through a stretched-out process that encompasses not just ceremonial moments but the full expanse of daily life? That was the starting point of *The Place of Media Power* (Couldry 2000).

And, although I drew on various inspirations – the late Roger Silverstone's (1981) work on myth and television, Stuart Hall's (1973, 1977) early work on media – there was one essay which freed things up for me more than any other: Michel Callon and Bruno Latour's 'Unscrewing the big Leviathan' (1980). There they showed that we can understand a particular node of power – and so the salience of the general accounts of the world made through it – not by imagining that node's power to be literally 'big' (which would be simply to repeat its own rhetoric) but by tracing all the local linkages that together, over time and under particular conditions, have generated the site from which such claims can circulate on a large scale. Scale, Callon and Latour say, is not a natural property of social space, but something produced by particular actors (using 'actors', of course, in the broad sense characteristic of ANT to include non-human actors).

Callon and Latour weren't thinking of media directly back in 1980, but that does not diminish the relevance of their insights for understanding media's symbolic power. How *better* to grasp the emergence in the twentieth century of legitimate media institutions which derive such broad authority to represent the world from very particular and local processes of production and decision making? Callon and Latour's tracking of how certain 'obligatory passing points', as they put it (1981: 287), become 'black-boxed' opened up for me a new demystified way of thinking about media power.

This is just the first of ANT's many advantages for media research. New research on the local television newsroom (Hemmingway 2007), online poker (Austrin and Farnsworth 2006) and the treatment of audience participants in game shows such as *Blind Date* (Teurlings 2004) is opening up important insights by building on ANT's interrogation of how networks are built, and how claims about the world come to be 'hard-wired' into everyday practice. Rather than discuss that new work, I want (schematically) to make some more general points about ANT's usefulness for media research.

First, ANT's general suspicion towards 'the social' encourages us to be equally suspicious about media institutions' claims to represent, or be proxy for, 'the social': more on this later. Second, Latour's analysis of networks' relation to the territories they cover captures beautifully why the complex issues of representation raised by media are always more than 'textual'. For, as Latour puts it in *We have Never been Modern*, talking about technological networks generally: '[they] are nets thrown over spaces, and retain only a few scattered elements of those spaces. They are connected lines, not surfaces' (1993: 118). So media texts, though they often seem to 'cover' a territory in their claims, retain only 'a few scattered elements' of the space they represent: this insight is fundamental for challenging functionalist claims about how media texts relate to 'society'. The idea that media make selections is of course familiar (as in theories of agenda setting or framing) but the misleading relationship between the *apparent completeness or saturation* of media discourse and the objects and worlds which media describes or shows is perfectly expressed by Latour's aphorism: media discourse crowds out the more particular perspectives from which its totalising nature can be grasped for what it is, just as a net appears to 'cover' completely the territory over which it is stretched. Third, ANT highlights the asymmetries of representation built into networks, and the difficulty of uncovering and renegotiating those asymmetries. As Latour and Woolgar put it in *Laboratory Life*, 'the result of the construction of a fact is that it appears unconstructed *by anyone*' (1979: 240, added emphasis). This remains a vital insight into the role of constructions in daily life, even if Latour sharply distinguishes it from social constructionism (2005: 90–1): luckily we do not need to pursue that point here.

In all these ways, ANT is a very useful tool for thinking about 'the fundamental asymmetry between shapers of events and consumers of events' (Hall 1973: 11) – an asymmetry of symbolic power that media do not so much create (it has long historical roots) as deepen, entrench, naturalise. Actor Network Theory helps us think about how particular asymmetries come into existence, and how they come to *remain* legitimate and (relatively) unchallenged. Actor Network Theory is equally useful for thinking about how *new spaces* of mediated story-telling are being generated, perhaps hard-wired into, everyday practice because of the networks of circulation and attention on which they rely: ANT accounts for such spaces in a way that does *not* presuppose media's everyday workings merge seamlessly into 'the social'. If ever new phenomena needed ANT to demystify claims about 'social' impact made on its behalf it is MySpace and Facebook.

But, like any set of tools, ANT has limitations. First, while it shares with Bourdieu an intense scepticism towards generalised notions of social space, it is less able than Bourdieu to map out the *stable* if complex relations between the relatively autonomous spaces of material and discursive production that Bourdieu calls 'fields': see Couldry (2003b) for detail. Second, while ANT may help us in thinking about how new practices emerge in the newsroom, or new mediated spaces online acquire the features of a 'territory', ANT is less equipped, by its very interests and preferences, to help us understand the consequences of the *representations* that media generate – how they work, and are put into everyday use. The latter problem may seem trivial, given how much we have already learned from ANT, but it is of fundamental importance. This becomes clear when we consider Latour's highly rhetorical defence of ANT in *Reassembling the Social* (2005). Latour is more insistent here than elsewhere that ANT is a complete new way of doing sociology (a 'sociology of associations' or 'associology') which in some ways replaces the old 'sociology of "the social"' – at least in relation to the more interesting things going on in the world. Latour concedes old-style sociology might still be able to make sense of the boring stuff, comparing it to physics before relativity theory! The problem with these grander claims is that they conflict with ANT's radically reduced ontology. In ANT there are things, persons conceived rather like things, and associations. That's it! Actor Network Theory looks, very acutely, at how associations are formed between persons and things (and, at a basic level, sustained) but has little or nothing to say about how actors interpret or think about the persistence of such associations and the institutions which result, or how actors reflect on their mutual relationships with each other and the wider space of networks.

The result is that, when Latour *does* come to deal with interpretations in one sense – the totalising interpretations of the social world he calls 'panoramas' (some are theoretical like Bourdieu's field theory, but he also means the claims of media, politicians, and so on) – he has little substantial to say about them (2005: 183–9). He points out, following ANT's usual argument, that such totalising claims about the world are only *local* constructions – we need, in media research, to hold on to ANT's radicalism here – but offers no way of sorting out good totalising constructions from bad ones, a vital task, we might think, in an age of continuous media spectacle. 'Panoramas' for Latour are all in one sense wrong (because totalising) but all in another sense potentially positive, since they contribute, he says, to our possibilities of thinking on a general level about the world. It is here, *unwittingly* (since the book's conclusion shows Latour wants to guard against this charge), that

ANT's political conservatism is revealed. Let me quote one passage at length:

> [panoramas'] role may become central since they allow spectators, listeners and readers to be equipped with a desire for wholeness and centrality. It is from these powerful stories that we get our metaphors for what 'binds us together', the passions we are supposed to share, the general outline of society's architecture, the master narratives with which we are disciplined ... so, no matter how much they trick us, [these panoramas] prepare us for the political task ahead.
>
> (2005: 189)

What 'political task' is this? The end of the book reveals it to be nothing more specific than living better together and keeping our eyes open for associations in and between unexpected places. This is fortunate, since, as Latour's discussion of panoramas reveals, ANT has no tools to help us to separate good representations of 'society' or 'world order' from bad ones, no tools to grasp how certain representations and claims about our world have a particular rhetorical and emotional hold on us. Why not? Because ANT is a theory of associations, not a theory of representation. Actor Network Theory is therefore agnostic on many of the key issues raised by contemporary media, but by default, and this is a disabling political quietism that is no less frustrating for being built 'from below' rather than imposed (like Niklas Luhmann's) from above.[2] The consequence is immediate: since media are practices of representation, ANT *cannot* even in principle offer a complete account of what media do in the world. Actor Network Theory cannot ground a full sociology of media, however useful and illuminating its 'associology'. While Latour may not care about this, we as media researchers must.

Are there alternatives?

Luckily, there are alternative paths for using social theory in media research not constrained by the self-imposed limits of 'associology'. I will spend most of this section reflecting on what is at stake in the 'ritual' approach to media developed in my work and others.

Foucault

First, however, it is worth recalling briefly the Foucauldian roots of ANT, which have been neglected as a resource for thinking about media. Foucault is important because he takes us back to the properties of discourse – not ignoring its material base in associations and interactions with objects, but in an analysis not *restricted* to the mere fact of those associations. Foucault was not, any more than Callon and Latour, focusing on media, but in

'The Order of Discourse' (1980) – his 1970 inaugural lecture at the Collège de France – he discusses some very general 'procedures' which 'permit the control of discourse'.

It is a matter of building on the principles Foucault establishes. He talks, for example, of the 'rarefaction of speaking subjects' (1980: 61). Some forms of this principle are less common (the intense ritualisation of certain speech settings, certain restricted 'societies of discourse'). But Foucault argues that, even in an apparent era of open discourse, there are hidden restrictions built into discourse's institutionalisation. In one sense Foucault's insights have already been adopted by a whole generation of discourse analysis (for example, Fairclough 1995) but there is still something exhilarating in Foucault's insistence on a *materialist* analysis of discourse, that undercuts the rhetoric of discourses themselves and explores the constraints built into various media discourses. By the rarefaction of speaking subjects, Foucault makes clear, he means not just the literal exclusion of particular people from speaking but also 'the gestures, behaviour, circumstances, and the whole set of signs which must accompany discourse' (1980: 62). There is more than enough here to provide a provocative starting point for analysing the gestural universe of celebrity culture.

And crucially (unlike ANT) Foucault develops his materialism into close attention to the patterns of discourse itself. 'Discourse analysis understood like this,' he writes, 'does not reveal the universality of a meaning, but brings to light the action of *imposed scarcity*' (1980: 73, added emphasis): that is, the scarcities, or limiting rules, that structure the surface of discourse. Such scarcity, working at the level of the categories and exclusions from which a universalising discourse is built, can be uncovered not by a generous reading of the text, but only by an investigation of its conditions of possibility. What better advice for deconstructing the mediated rhetorics of nation, society, community, 'the free world', and so on?

Ritual analysis

Having briefly recalled how much (*contra* ANT) we can learn about power's workings within discourse, I want to return to the question of social form raised earlier via work on media's ritual dimensions which draws on Durkheim's account of the social origins of religion. This move might seem paradoxical in this context, since Latour at least makes it very clear that the sociological tradition he wants to get distance from is precisely the Durkheimian (2005: 8–9). Latour, however, ignores the cost of this move, which is to put to one side the belief questions that media raise, and their links to the legitimacy of media power. Ritual analysis enables us to explore the cultural 'thickenings' (Löfgren 2001) around media that are so important to its authority – 'thickenings' that ANT, as a theory of association, not representation, is less well placed to grasp.

It is important to emphasise right away that ritual analysis is quite different from old-style ideological analysis, for it is precisely the simple notion of 'belief' implicit in classic Marxist ideological analysis (statements explicitly believed by people, yet false) that a notion of ritual *practice* moves beyond. Rituals work not so much through the articulation, even implicitly, of beliefs, as through the organisation and formalisation of behaviour that, by encoding categories of thought, naturalise them. As Philip Elliott put it: 'to treat ritual performance as simply standing for political paradigms is to oversimplify it. [Ritual performance] also expresses and symbolises social relationships and so, quite literally, mystifies them' (1982: 168). While this might sound like classic 1980s ideological deconstruction, Elliott here turns back from complete reliance on Steven Lukes's (1975) deconstruction of political ritual as pure ideology and acknowledges the force of Durkheim's theory of how social order is maintained through the embodiments of ritual practice. As Elliott and many other writers from Dayan and Katz to Michel Maffesoli have argued, there remains something very suggestive about Durkheim's account of totemic ceremonies for understanding contemporary political and media rhetoric. It is not a question here of relying on the historical accuracy of Durkheim's (1995) account of totemic ritual, or of accepting his claims about the origins of religion. The interest today of Durkheim's work lies in seeing how his proto-structuralist analysis of 'sacred' and 'profane' captures a generalisable pattern which links (1) those moments when we are, or appear to be, addressed as a *collectivity* and (2) certain categories of thought which have an organising force in everyday action. It is in this limited – but I hope precise – sense that I have borrowed from Durkheim to build a theory of the ritual dimensions of media (Couldry 2003a).

From this perspective, Durkheim can still teach us a lot about how to interpret the generalised claims that media make about the social world. But from that recognition we can head off in two very different directions. The first route (the 'neo-Durkheimian') argues that contemporary media reinstitute, through electronic means, the unity of the totemic ceremony (for example, Dayan and Katz 1992). The second approach – more compatible perhaps with today's greater scepticism towards totalising rhetorics of 'the social' – uses Durkheim merely as an entry point to a practice of deconstruction. Accepting that Durkheim draws our attention to the *constructions* encoded in ritual – the *claim* of media to invoke social order, to stand in for, and give us privileged access to, a social totality – this second approach aims to dismantle those constructions, drawing on anthropological insights about the organising role of ritual categories, the normative force of ritual boundaries and the expressive resonance of ritual practice, while rejecting any assumption that ritual really is the basis of social order. Indeed, this second approach rejects the very notion of 'social order' as a *normative* or *necessary* category while examining more closely the naturalisation of certain claims to social order in contemporary societies. The second approach is distinct both from ANT and from neo-Durkheimian functionalism: acknowledging (unlike ANT) those media representations which mobilise large emotions and encode large claims about 'the social' through their organisation and *formal* patterning but on the other hand (*like* ANT) refusing to take such media forms at face value and always remembering the material asymmetries which make them possible. Sensitised to the potency of ritual form by Durkheim, but inspired by a deconstructive spirit closer to Foucault, Bourdieu or Laclau, this approach to media power looks to media rituals' formal details as important sites where contemporary power is encoded and naturalised. As Maurice Bloch once put it, ritual *is* 'the use of form for power' (1989: 45).

Because it focuses on details of form, ritual analysis done properly (that is, with a substantive rather than purely nominal concept of ritual action)[3] gives us the tools to trace patterns not just in media discourse but also *in everyday actions oriented towards media*. It is vital to explore the linkages between the 'special moments' of media rituals (the final night of *Big Brother* or a person's entry on to the stage of *Jerry Springer*) and the wider hinterland of practice Catherine Bell (1992) calls 'ritualis*ation*' (for example, practices as banal as flicking through a celebrity magazine while you wait to get your hair cut). There are many terms in play in media ritualisation: not just celebrity, but the constructed categories of 'media'/'ordinary' people, things, places, times (and so on), and the category of 'liveness' (which indirectly affirms the priority of direct connection though media to social 'reality'). This approach is motivated *not* by a special interest in ritual or ceremony *per se* – there is no claim here that media rituals are emergent forms of secular religion! – but instead by a concern with the ways in which certain *claims of/to social order* (Wrong 1994) are naturalised in discourse and action. The subtle effectiveness of media power – the extraordinary fact that extreme concentrations of symbolic resources in particular institutions have remained legitimate for so long – requires theoretical tools of some subtlety for its analysis. Ritual and, just as important, ritualisation are just two of those tools.

More broadly, ritual analysis provides an account of what Bourdieu called 'the *production* of belief' that links us back into the local and detailed processes from which even the largest and grandest mappings of the social world derive (remember ANT) while drawing us outwards to explain the representations and formalisations on which much political and cultural staging relies. Consider the Live 8 concerts in early July 2005. In those events quasi-political actors (current and ex-music stars) orchestrated a process in which citizens could plausibly *act out* participation in political decision making – something very different from the political spectacle Murray Edelman deconstructed two decades ago (1988) as ideological rhetoric performed at a distance from audiences. The more participative Live 8 events bring out how *ritual* analysis – an attention to 'subjunctive'

or 'as if' language that is drawn upon, however elliptically, in action –
can supplement ideological analysis (important though the latter remains
of course in uncovering the explicit discursive contradictions around such
events). Only the former can explain how some of the Live 8 marchers (as
quoted by media) saw themselves as being 'part of the message' given to
governments and as a means to 'force' change in the very same political
establishment that (in the United Kingdom at least) had already *endorsed*
the spectacle in which they acted! We return here to the dialectic between
attention and inattention that I noted earlier.

At this point, given our wider aim of explaining social theory's role in
media analysis, it is worth reflecting on what the theoretical term 'ritual'
adds to the descriptive term 'spectacle'. This emerges in my one small
disagreement with Doug Kellner's excellent and courageous book *Media
Spectacles*. Early on in the book, when introducing his topic, Kellner writes
that 'media spectacles are those phenomena of media culture that *embody
contemporary society's basic values*, serve to initiate individuals into its
way of life' (2003: 2, added emphasis). But is this true? What are these
ideals and values Kellner talks about, and where is the evidence they are
so simply accepted and internalised by those outside media industries?
This is clearly a rhetorical concession by Kellner, but why concede *even
that much*? This small point limits Kellner's critique of contemporary
spectacles: since Kellner's argument starts by taking the normative force
of spectacles for granted, the only possibility of political resistance in our
era must be forms of counter-spectacle. But I would want to go further
and acknowledge forms of resistance that question the basic principles
and preconditions of media spectacle, and the inequalities and totalising
rhetorics on which that production is based. But to do this we need
a more detailed theorisation of how exactly spectacle works to encode
categories of thought and action: in other words, a theory of media
rituals – not for our own edification, but to deconstruct more fully both
the contents *and the form* of media's claims to represent the 'truth' of
populations.

Some right and wrong ways to deconstruct 'society'

I have argued that, if we take media representations seriously, we need
also to address the social forms constituted by and focused on those
representations. Analysing media rituals and ritualisation is one way of
doing this, providing insights not available to ANT. But within ritual
approaches there is, I argued, a fundamental choice between deconstructive
and reconstructive (or neo-Durkheimian) approaches. I will argue in
conclusion for the political value today of that deconstructive approach.

First, however, and in the spirit of making transparent the theoretical
choices involved, I want to explore some philosophical underpinnings
of this deconstruction. While my approach to media rituals seeks to

dismantle certain discourses about 'the social' and society – most obviously, functionalist discourses in the Parsonian or neo-Durkheimian tradition – surely there are languages of the social that we need to keep intact? Of the various deconstructions of 'the social' and 'society' on offer in contemporary theory (from Latour to Laclau to Bhaskar) which are more useful and which are less useful?

My previous critique of the 'myth of the (mediated) centre' (Couldry 2003a, 2006) was inspired initially by Edward Said, but it shares something important with Laclau and Mouffe's broader notion of hegemony whereby 'a particular social force assumes the representation of a totality that is radically incommensurable with it' (Laclau and Mouffe 2001: x).[4] What Laclau and Mouffe mean by 'contaminated universality' – a consistent confusion of the particular for the universal (2001: xiii) – is very similar to what I meant to capture by the notion of 'myth'. Media are *particular* institutions that benefit from a specific concentration of symbolic resources, even if one that is huge in scale: yet they represent their role as a relationship to/for *a totality* ('society', 'the nation', and so on). Media discourse is always contaminated by such claims to the universal (so too is government discourse, which incessantly speaks for the totality of the nation). Whatever the real pressures that exist towards centralisation in contemporary societies, the idea that such totalising rhetorics are fully explained, let alone made 'functional', by a particular centre *of value* is a delusion: as Laclau and Mouffe write, 'the mere idea of a centre of the social has no meaning at all' (2001: 139). I call this delusion 'the myth of the centre', on to which media build their own myth of privileged access to that centre ('the myth of the mediated centre'). And yet precisely such a myth was installed in the structural functionalism of Edward Shils (1975) and others in the mid-1970s and can be traced even today in discourse about media's relation to society.

Laclau and Mouffe's deconstruction of hegemony and universality seems even more useful for analysing media rituals and media power when we notice its historical dimension. As Laclau puts it in a passage I quote at the start of *Media Rituals*, contemporary societies 'are required by their very dynamics to become increasingly mythical' (1990: 67). The same point is made at greater length by Laclau and Mouffe elsewhere:

> advanced industrial societies … are constituted around a fundamental asymmetry … the asymmetry existing between a growing proliferation of differences – a surplus of meaning of 'the social' – and the difficulties encountered by any discourse attempting to fix those differences as moments of a stable articulatory structure.
>
> (2001: 96)

Laclau and Mouffe surely capture something here that helps explain the stampede by media industries in the past decade towards the apparently tautological aim of re-presenting to audiences their 'ordinary' 'reality'.

The more closely I look at Laclau and Mouffe's broader arguments about politics and 'society', however, the more uneasy I become. Any possibility of class-based identities is dismissed, not on grounds of historical contingency, but absolutely, because it is only a 'naturalist prejudice' that the economic underlies the cultural (2001: 67). 'Unfixity', we are told, 'has become the condition of *every* social identity', yet myths of society are deluded because they 'suture' an '*original* lack'; that lack, it seems, is endemic to the social itself – 'there is no sutured space peculiar to "society", since *the social itself* has no essence' (2001: 85, 88 n. 1, 96, added emphases). At work here in Laclau and Mouffe's argument is an absolutism of denial (an inverted universalism) which we should question. First, because it undermines their *historical* insight into the increasingly mythical nature of contemporary societies; for if the mythical nature of discourse about 'society' derives from the absolute gap between *any* discourse and what they call the 'field of discursivity', then it is difficult to see how contemporary societies can be any more mythical than all those that preceded them.[5] And, second, because if 'the social has *no* essence', then there is no stable basis for constituting a discipline around it. This is exactly the position of Latour, as we saw, yet the political aims and argumentative premises of Laclau and Mouffe seem very different. While Latour absolutely prioritises networks (in some sense) over things and people (or indeed representations), Laclau and Mouffe absolutely prioritise discourse (in some sense) over things or people. Laclau and Mouffe's prioritisation of discourse entails that everything, including 'the social', is subject to the conditions of discourse and in particular to one condition, discourse's 'openness' and non-totalisability. So Laclau and Mouffe tell us that the 'partial' character of articulation 'proceeds from the openness of the social, *as a result, in its turn*, of the constant overflowing of *every* discourse by the infinitude of the field of discursivity' and that objects cannot 'constitute themselves as objects outside any discursive conditions of emergence'; as a result, '"society" is not a valid object of discourse' (2001: 113, 108, 111, added emphasis).

Yet if the general terms 'society' and 'social' – and not just the value-loaded notion of a social 'centre' – are to be abandoned *entirely*, the idea of media research drawing on social theory is pure paradox, exactly as Latour would have us believe. At the very least, we are forced to make clear in what precise sense we draw on notions of 'society' and 'the social' when claiming that media research – whether on media rituals or anything else – may contribute something to 'social theory'. Here, I think, it is useful to draw on the 'critical realist' philosopher of science Roy Bhaskar, whose work,[6] for all its formidable difficulty of language, would seem to offer a nuanced position between Latour and Laclau, and between postmodernism and crude positivism.

Very briefly, Bhaskar's ontological starting point for the social sciences is that their subject matter includes 'both social objects (including beliefs) and beliefs about those objects' (1989: 101). Bhaskar is concerned to defend the importance in the social world of interpretations without lapsing into constructionism, and of concepts without falling into a 'conceptual absolutisation or reductionism (that concepts are not only necessary for, but exhaustive of, social life)' (1989: 185). Bhaskar rejects the absolutisation of discourse on which Laclau and Mouffe's arguments precisely rely as 'the linguistic fallacy', 'the definition of being in terms of ... language or discourse' (1989: 180). While Bhaskar's insistence that 'societies are real' (1989: 69) appears to be a naive positivism, it is far from that. For Bhaskar rejects the prioritising of either individuals or social groups in explanation – so ruling out both utilitarian liberalism and Durkheim's collectivist conception of society (1989: 73). The objects of social science for Bhaskar are above all 'the persistent relations between individuals (and groups) and ... the relations between those relations' (1989: 71). While society exists, society is not for Bhaskar a simple functional totality, but 'a complex totality', 'an ensemble of structures, practices and conventions that individuals reproduce or transform' (1989: 78, 76).

What matters here is that Bhaskar insists on the 'causal irreducibility of social forms in the genesis of human action' (1989: 91). And so, I suggest, should we – painful though it is to declare one's ontological commitments at such a high level of abstraction! The alternatives at the level of ontology – Latour's associationism (which runs the risk of turning into a strange vitalism of connections) and Laclau and Mouffe's discursivism – are hardly satisfactory. Nor is there any contradiction between a deconstructive spirit towards media rituals and critical realism as advocated by Bhaskar. On the contrary, it is difficult to see what other philosophical framework could provide the friction that a genuinely critical and deconstructive project needs.

Conclusion

We have never needed that deconstructive project more than now. We live in an intensely connected global mediaspace where media's capacity to saturate everyday life is greater than ever. Elements of decentralisation – the decentring of some transnational media flows, the intensified competition faced by national media sources – only make media spectacle a more important resource for all media actors, both political and non-political. Add in a conflict-ridden global politics and we can expect the resources of mediated ritualisation to be continually drawn upon by political, corporate and other actors, producing dangerous exclusions within the sphere of visibility (Butler 2004). There is something political at stake in achieving a *theoretical* grasp of how large-scale media forms work and aspire to the status of naturalised social forms.

The Retort Collective (2005) argue that political power is inseparable from media (symbolic) power in a world of spectacle far more dangerous than Guy Debord ever envisaged (see also Giroux 2006). If so, it follows that any challenge to political power must involve contesting *media power*: that is (following both ANT and ritualisation theory), questioning not just media's institutional power but our whole way of organising life and thought around and through media. (Here online resources will surely be crucial longer-term, whatever the dangers of believing the myths that currently circulate about the internet.)

The Retort Collective, from outside media research – they are sociologists, geographers, historians – set two very different challenges for media research. First, alongside paying attention to the major media spectacles of our time, we must analyse also the countless practices of 'mediation' that fall *outside* media's dominant flows and rhetorics, which silently challenge them by heading in a different direction and on a different scale: hence the importance of the expanding research into alternative media. Rejecting totalities means analysing new and different *particularities* and in sites beyond, or obscured by, the scope of those rhetorics.

A different challenge, implicit in the first, is to maintain, in the face of media's universalising 'panoramas', a deconstructive intent and a continual suspicion. It is of course tempting to argue – witness Simon Cottle's (2006) attempt to save media rituals from what he calls 'neo-Marxian' political critique – that, even if media events or rituals are social constructions, they are none the worse for that: what society can live without myths? Surely we should bracket out our usual questions (What type of myths? Whose myths? Myths constructed on what terms?), because, in the end, we have no choice but to accept media's role in focusing our world's mythical production? The 'end of history', perhaps, for critical media research? There is a pragmatic weight to such arguments, yet it is vital to resist such temptation. For it invites us, adapting Søren Kierkegaard,[7] to make the one error that, as media researchers, we had a chance of avoiding.

Notes

1 Bourdieu and Wacquant (1992); Hall (1996).
2 See Luhmann (1999).
3 Not all uses of the term ritual are helpful. For what I believe is an unhelpful usage see Cottle (2006) on 'mediatised rituals' and the response in Couldry and Rothenbuhler (2007).
4 Thanks to Mark Hobart for suggesting that I look more closely at the parallels between my position and Laclau and Mouffe's.
5 Butler makes a similar criticism directly of Derrida (1997: 150).
6 Bhaskar has generally been neglected in media research, so far as I can tell. For a rare discussion see Deacon *et al.* (1999).
7 Søren Kierkegaard wrote (1958: 167): 'Not to venture is shrewd. And yet, by not venturing, it is so dreadfully easy to lose that which it would be difficult to lose in even the most venturesome venture, and in any case never so easily, so completely as if it were nothing ... one's self.' Compare the unreferenced quotation from

Kafka in Laing (1971: 78): 'you can hold yourself back from the sufferings of the world ... but perhaps precisely this holding back is the only suffering that you might be able to avoid'. Kierkegaard and Kafka are writing about the individual self, but their logic is surely transposable to collective enterprises such as research.

Bibliography

Austrin, Terry and Farnsworth, John (2006) 'Fresh Connections: Illuminating Media Networks through Ethnography and Actor Network Theory in the Case of Mediated Poker', paper presented to the CRESC conference on 'Media Change and Social theory', St Hugh's College, Oxford, September.

Bell, Catherine (1992) *Ritual Theory, Ritual Practice*. New York: Oxford University Press.

Bhaskar, Roy (1989) *Reclaiming Reality*. London: Verso.

Bloch, Maurice (1989) *Ritual History and Power*. London: Athlone Press.

Bourdieu, Pierre and Wacquant, Loic (1992) *Invitation to Reflexive Sociology*. Chicago: University of Chicago Press.

Butler, Judith (1997) *Excitable Speech*. London: Routledge.

Butler, Judith (2004) *Precarious Life*. London: Verso.

Callon, Michel and Latour, Bruno (1981) 'Unscrewing the big Leviathan: how actors macro-structure reality and how sociologists help them do so' in K. Knorr-Cetina and A. Cicourel (eds) *Advances in Social theory and Methodology*. London: Routledge.

Cottle, Simon (2006) 'Mediatized rituals: beyond manufacturing consent', *Media Culture and Society* 28 (3): 411–32.

Couldry, Nick (2000) *The Place of Media Power*. London: Routledge.

Couldry, Nick (2003a) *Media Rituals: a Critical Approach*. London: Routledge.

Couldry, Nick (2003b) 'Media meta-capital: extending the range of Bourdieu's field theory', *Theory and Society* 32 (5/6): 653–77.

Couldry, Nick (2006) *Listening beyond the Echoes: Media, Ethics, and Agency in an Uncertain World*. Boulder CO: Paradigm Press.

Couldry, Nick and Rothenbuhler, Eric (2007) 'Simon Cottle on "mediatised rituals": a response', *Media Culture and Society* 29 (4): 711–15.

Crary, Jonathan (1999) *Suspensions of Perception*. Cambridge MA: MIT Press.

Dayan, Daniel and Katz, Elihu (1992) *Media Events: the Live Broadcasting of History*. Cambridge MA: Harvard University Press.

Deacon, David, Pickering, Michael, Golding, Peter and Murdock, Graham (1999) *Researching Communications*. London: Arnold.

Durkheim, Emile (1995 [1912]) *The Elementary Forms of Religious Life*, trans. K. Fields. Glencoe IL: Free Press.

Edelman, Maurice (1988) *Constructing the Political Spectacle*. Chicago: University of Chicago Press.

Elliott, Phillip (1982) 'Press performance as political ritual' in H. Christian (ed.) *The Sociology of Journalism and the Press*. Keele: University of Keele.

Fairclough, Norman (1995) *Media Discourse*. London: Arnold.

Foucault, Michel (1980) 'The order of discourse' in R. Young (ed.) *Untying the Text*. London: Routledge.

Giroux, Henry (2006) *Beyond the Spectacle of Terrorism*. Boulder CO: Paradigm Press.

Hall, Stuart (1973) 'The "Structured Communication of Events"', stencilled Occasional Paper No. 5, Birmingham: Centre for Contemporary Cultural Studies.

Hall, Stuart (1977) 'Culture, media and the "ideological effect"', in J. Curran, M. Gurevitch and J. Woollacott (eds) *Mass Communications and Society*. London: Arnold.

Hall, Stuart (1996) 'Introduction: who needs identity?' in S. Hall and P. Du Gay (eds) *Questions of Identity*. London: Sage.

Hardt, Michael and Negri, Toni (2001) *Empire*. Cambridge MA: Harvard University Press.

Hemmingway, Emma (2007) *Into the Newsroom: Exploring the Digital Production of Regional Television News*. London: Routledge.

Kellner, Douglas (2003) *Media Spectacles*. London: Routledge.

Kierkegaard, Søren (1958) *Fear and Loathing and the Sickness unto Death*. New York: Doubleday.

Laclau, Ernesto (1990) *New Reflections on the Revolution of our Time*. London: Verso.

Laclau, Ernesto and Mouffe, Chantal (2001) *Hegemony and Socialist Strategy*, 2nd edn. London: Verso.

Laing, R. D. (1971) *The Divided Self*. Harmondsworth: Penguin.

Latour, Bruno (1993) *We have Never been Modern*. London: Prentice Hall.

Latour, Bruno (2005) *Reassembling the Social*. Oxford: Oxford University Press.

Latour, Bruno and Woolgar, Steve (1979) *Laboratory Life*. Princeton NJ: Princeton University Press.

Löfgren, Orvar (2001) 'The nation as home or motel? Metaphors of media and belonging', *Sosiologisk Årbok* 1–34.

Luhmann, Niklas (1999) *The Reality of the Mass Media*. Cambridge: Polity Press.

Lukes, Steven (1975) 'Political ritual and social integration', *Sociology* 29: 289–305.

Mirzoeff, Nichlas (2005) *Watching Babylon*. London: Routledge.

Retort Collective (2005) *Afflicted Powers: Capital and Spectacle in an Age of War*. London: Verso.

Shils, Edward (1975) *Center and Periphery*. Chicago: University of Chicago Press.

Silverstone, Roger (1981) *The Message of Television*. London: Methuen.

Smith, Dorothy (1987) *The Everyday World as Problematic*. Evanston IL: Northwestern University Press.

Teurlings, Jan (2004) 'Dating Shows and the Production of Identities: Institutional Practices and Power in Television Production'. Ph.D. thesis, Brussels: Vrije Universiteit Brussel.

Thompson, John (1995) *The Media and Modernity*. Cambridge: Polity Press.

Wrong, Dennis (1994) *The Problem of Order*. New York: Free Press.

11 Spectacular morality

'Reality' television, individualisation and the remaking of the working class

Helen Wood and Bev Skeggs

Class themes haunt many of the debates about 'reality' television programming. In shows where media professionals are replaced with 'social actors' (Nichols 1991) discourses of class operate at a number of levels. *First*, 'reality' television is regularly spoken of as 'trash' television, locating participants and viewers at the bottom of a hierarchy of taste classification.[1] *Second*, 'reality' television is seen to represent a crisis in civic public culture because public and private spheres have been inverted and the 'ordinary' has been made central. As Roger Bromley (2000) notes, 'ordinary' is one of the many euphemisms to emerge, after thirty years of political rhetoric and academic theory claiming the demise of class, as a substitute for the term 'working-class'. Locating drama at the site of the 'ordinary' also suggests a greater purchase on the 'authentic' – a route informed by social-realist critique in documentary and film – which is often problematically associated with the working class. *Third*, there is overrepresentation of the working class on 'reality' television, precisely because of their cultural and economic situation: Mimi White (2006) in her analysis of the American 'reality' programme *Cheaters*, a programme set up to catch partners in acts of infidelity, admits that the $500 payment skews the class profile decisively, so much so that 'There is clearly a level of class exploitation at work' (p. 229). This simple fact is often minimised by an optimistic rendering of the democratising potential of 'reality' television, which underplays why the working classes make such good entertainment in the first place (paid or unpaid). *Fourth*, and connectedly, class raises its head because the access offered to television in the search for participants reinvents the mythologies of social mobility promoted by neoliberal political culture (Biressi and Nunn 2005), despite the fact that the gap between rich and poor widens, and social mobility rates remain stagnant (Aldridge 2004). *Finally*, many of the programmes are structured through class relations where the working class are exposed as inadequate and in need of training in middle or upper-class culture (a mutation of the Pygmalion narrative, e.g. *Ladette to Lady*, or differentiated within the working class by the traditional trope of rough versus respectable, e.g. *Holiday Showdown*, *Wife Swap*). And yet, notwithstanding the entry of 'reality' television into the heart of these glaring class-based realities, discourses and sensibilities, it has been possible for some authors in television and media studies to write about 'reality' television without an adequate theory of class relations.

This chapter argues for greater awareness of how class is being made and reproduced on television, drawing attention to new sociological theories of class. 'Reality' television programmes have a remarkable resonance with developments in inequality and injustice under neoliberal governments, primarily through the promotion of self-management as a form of pedagogy, made spectacular via melodrama. We detail how melodramatic techniques on 'reality' television visualise emotional engagement through blending verisimilitude of the ordinary with surface dramatic intensity, making particular class-based histories and values appear as either pathological or universal. Although the chapter is based on research about UK television and the British climate,[2] it should have significance for other similar political regimes.

Individualisation or individualised class relations?

It is now rather banal to cite how the explosion of 'first-person programming', a style of television relying on non-actors in various contrived situations, has managed to pad out the schedules of the multi-channel television era.[3] Critics have commented upon how the demands of a market economy within the television industry fuel this explosion (see Raphael 2004). Alongside the expansion of television channel schedules needing to be filled, we also see the development of particular types of programme that parallel neoliberal forms of governance: Laurie Ouellette (2004) describes how *Judge Judy*, a show in which participants submit testimonies of personal disputes to the authority of a television judge, offers lessons in self-government against the backdrop of increasing welfare cuts in the United States. The focus upon legal self-management accompanies the explosion of programmes on eating, dressing, looking after your finances, health, sex, etc., where television becomes a new governmental medium, offering to acculturate us into self-surveillance whilst delivering us to the market under the guise of model citizenship (Andrejevik 2004; Palmer 2003).[4]

The expansion of the television market economy and the more general 'turn' to governmentality (Rose 1989) generates a range of possibilities for applying television techniques, e.g. make-over, passing, competition, transformation, to any intimate area of human life. We have clothes and body transformations (*What not to Wear, Ten Years Younger*), diet programmes (*You are What you Eat*), family psychology interventions (*Family Forensics, Honey, We're Killing the Kids*), parenting programmes (*Supernanny, Nanny 911*), financial advice (*Bank of Mum and Dad*), programmes on improving sex lives (*Sex Inspectors*), ones which focus on health and hygiene (*How Clean is your House? Too Posh to Wash, Spa of Embarrassing Illnesses*) and even dog behaviour (*It's Me or the Dog!*). These programmes focus on the intimacies and intricacies of individual experience and relationships where work on parts of the self offers the possibility to change one's *whole* life. Indeed, there are relatively few places left for 'reality' television to penetrate as it pursues each new twist on tried and tested formulas.

Social theorists like Ulrich Beck (1992) and Anthony Giddens (1991) suggest that in a post-industrial society the individual is now compelled to make her/himself the centre of her/his own life plan and conduct. For Beck this is evidenced by the fact that everyone is now forced to consider their worth in relation to the labour market, which rearranges their relationship to the class structures of industrial society and throws into tension traditional roles within the industrial nuclear family. The increasing and encroaching forms of emotional labour required for self-management on 'reality' television and elsewhere (education, the welfare state) become part of our reflexive production of selfhood in line with the particular needs of the market (see Couldry forthcoming). For Giddens and Beck the emergence of 'life politics' uproots relations with structural inequalities such as those of class and gender, the narrative of selfhood takes over traditional affiliations, and class as a significant category disappears. Hence it is possible to see why, when discussions of 'reality' television are only spoken through discourses of neoliberalism, class might be replaced by life-politics, choice or reflexivity. In this sense 'reality' television and its exploration of the anxieties of the modern age, such as relationships, parenting, weight and sex, are emblematic of conditions of ontological insecurity in which our senses of identity and belonging are thrown into question, forcing the individual to struggle to constantly reorient themselves in relation to the personal risk relations with which they are faced. It is no surprise, then, that the constant reappearance of the 'first person' on television is registered as 'spectacular subjectivity' (Dovey 2000) in line with broader arguments about contemporary social life that suggest 'compulsory individuality' (Strathern 1992) or 'intimate citizenship' (Berlant 2000). Yet there is no reason why conditions of insecurity should automatically produce the disembedding or decline of class or other structural relations.

Steph Lawler (2006) and Roger Bromley (2000) point to a long US tradition of 'culture of poverty' debates whereby, once class is removed as a structural category, individuals can be blamed for the inequalities and injustices they experience: what Bromley calls 'causality transference'. In this way academic descriptions of the processes of individualisation might make class harder to see, but no less present. The problems of a class society become identified as the problems of working-class people, and we might say the way in which 'reality' television fetishises various social problems and locates them firmly as the responsibility of the individual is emblematic of a broader social change.

For instance, Chris Haylett (2001) reminds us how discourses from the New Labour government in the 1990s, via the establishment of the Social Exclusion Unit, suggests that inequality results from 'bad culture' and 'bad choices'. Current political rhetoric continues to reframe class away from an economic, and hence structural, classification to a cultural-moral site in which conduct, behaviours and taste become central to the way class is known and recognised. In the United Kingdom this is apparent in ASBOs and ABCs (Antisocial Behaviour Orders and Acceptable Behaviour Contracts under the Crime and Disorder Act 1998) which perhaps not surprisingly have provided good fodder for 'reality' entertainment: for example, *Asbo Fever, Asbo Night* and *From Asbo Teen to Beauty Queen*. This has been taken a stage further recently with the government's own launch of 'ASBO TV', a £12 million project funded by the Office of the Deputy Prime Minister, in which residents in one area of east London will be offered digital television with high-speed internet broadband complete with a local CC-TV channel in which they will be encouraged to compare characters they see behaving suspiciously with an on-screen rogues' gallery of local recipients of ASBOS. This is undertaken under the government's 'New Deal for Communities', established to regenerate poor districts (see Swinfold 2006).

More broadly, these trends speak to a considerable shift in modes of citizenship under neoliberalism. Consider the UK government's 'Respect Agenda'[5] in which a culture of rights becomes a culture of responsibilities through the monitoring of behaviour and manners. In this climate television programmes which may once have had a collective social emphasis now instance the particular: 'Thus a story which might once have raised civil liberty issues now finds itself interpreted as one of risk management' (Palmer 2003: 16). But this political shift is not 'just' restricted to crime and manners, for example the government launched the National Parenting Academy as part of the broader attack on antisocial behaviour – 'a single agency is to be created with whatever powers it needs to deal with problem families'.[6] Val Gillies (2005) charts how in many of the government's White Papers on education and parenting characteristics associated with children's failure and achievement are reduced to the psychological, detached from any social context. The plethora of parenting programming on 'reality' television demonstrates a similar decontextualised and psychologised polit-ical shift (e.g. *Supernanny, House of Tiny Tearaways, Nanny 911, Miss Beckles*), as we will proceed to demonstrate.

At the time of writing there is no foreseeable brake on the velocity with which 'reality' forms are multiplying. The desire to watch and be watched can be seen as part of the endless pursuit of the confirmation of selfhood among the loss of other more certain life trajectories: I see/I am seen, there-fore I am. Watching and being watched witnesses a shift from Foucault's (1979) panopticon (where the few see the many) to Mathiesen's (1997) synopticon (where the many watch the many). However, forms of selfhood, self-telling and self-display have historically been intricately woven into class processes. The autobiography was traditionally a technique of telling available only to aristocratic men, just as narrating one's life through a legal interlocutor in order to receive welfare was a subjective format for the working class (Steedman 2000). Even Beck (1992) notes that the narratives of choice that abound in consumer culture are not open to everyone equally. '[Choice] is, as sociologists of class know, a learned ability which depends upon special social and family backgrounds' (p. 98). Beck even refers to Basil Bernstein's (1971) discussion of middle-class elaborated and working-class restricted speaking codes to acknowledge that one must move to an elaborated code for self-expression. Self-reflexivity, therefore, even within the individualisation thesis, is acknowledged as a technique to which not all have access. All the new theories of mobility, reflexivity, prosthetic culture, choice, etc., concede that certain cultural resources are required for their actualisation.

Self-responsibility and self-management, the features identified by Giddens as necessary for the making of the 'new' reflexive self, hence become the mechanisms not by which class is replaced 'but precisely by which class inequality is produced' (Skeggs 2004: 60). If 'reality' television foregrounds the display of self-performance it must also offer a stage for the dramatising of contemporary class relations, and it is to these processes that we now turn.

Spectacular melodrama: the drama of the moment

In terms that echo some of the larger socio-political shifts outlined above, commentators have been concerned with the overall transformation of documentary television into 'staging the real' (Kilborn 2003) in a 'post-documentary culture' (Corner 2002) in which 'the real' is constituted through a contrived set of scenarios produced for entertainment, rather than any socially realist argumentation of benefit to public culture. Bill Nichols (1991) suggests programming that focuses on the personal and spectacular renders them inert as socio-political phenomena: 'Spectacle is more properly an aborted or foreclosed form of identification where emotional engagement does not extend as far as concern but remains arrested at the level of sensation' (p. 234). The characteristic motifs of depthless 'spectacles of particularity' in Nichols's presumption, however, fail to account for how political processes work at the level of sensation and emotion (see Deleuze 2003; Ahmed 2004), a process highly evident in our audience responses. But here we want to consider how the operation of spectacle in 'reality' television generates emotional engagement through melodramatic techniques.

By telling intimate stories 'reality' television draws on traditions of melodrama, as well as documentary. David Singer (2001) defines melo-drama as a 'cluster concept' with different configurations of constitutive factors, including pathos; overwrought emotion; dramatic intensity without the pathos (all characters expressing anger, frustration, resentment, disappointment etc.) moral polarisation; non-classical narrative structure and sensationalism. Our textual analysis suggests that dramatic intensity is regularly produced through what we have called 'the judgement shot', where, after crisis and chaos, expert advice is given or negative voice-over commentary provided and the participant is held in facial close-up. Often this is followed by a poignant symbolic image with ironic music, or the repeating and reselecting of various montage shots so that the dramatic significance is intensified. The long-held close-up is the modern equivalent of the theatrical melodramatic tableau – where the stillness and the silence of the actors enable the suspension of action and all attention is given to contemplation of the drama previously enacted. Once we started examining our material in detail for 'melodramatic moments' we became aware of the ubiquity of the use of the 'judgement shot' to produce dramatic tension. In this sense 'reality' television's relation to 'reality' is often more closely linked with 'emotional realism' (Ang 1985) where participants take part in what Helen Piper (2004) usefully calls a new category of 'improvised drama' more typically allied with the fictive traditions of melodrama than documentary. The use of melodramatic techniques to produce sensation should not surprise us; it is a tried and tested method for making the domestic and everyday more interesting. Peter Brooks maintains that:

> the melodramas that matter most convince us that the dramaturgy of excess and overstatement corresponds to and evokes confrontations and choices that are of heightened importance, because in them we put our lives – however trivial and constricted – on the line.
>
> (1995: ix)

These techniques follow a long tradition of 'women's television', as Rachel Moseley (2000) notes:

> Makeover shows ask the audience to draw on our repertoire of personal skills, our ability to search faces and discern reactions (facilitated by the close-up) from the smallest details – the twitch of a muscle, an expression in the eye – a competence suggested by Tania Modleski as key to the pleasure of soap opera's melodramatic form. These programmes showcase the threatening excessiveness of the ordinary ... These are, precisely, instances of powerful spectacular '*über*-ordinariness': an excess of the ordinary.
>
> (p. 314)

Thus the forms of excess and heightened drama, which according to Nichols (1991) in documentary forms generate a distancing effect, limiting modes of engagement, instead on 'reality' television offer resonance with our own intimate lives. Bringing together realism with melodrama, Christine Gledhill (1987, 2000) maintains, enables the techniques of film and television to increasingly intervene in 'private' life for the moral good of the nation. As 'reality' television uses documentary techniques to open out 'real' relationships, intimacy, and domesticity, it draws upon melodramatic traditions that give significance to and make daily lives sensational and intense, hence potentially more interesting to watch. Thomas Elsaesser (1987) notes in relation to these traditions, 'Even if the situations and sentiments defied all categories of verisimilitude and were totally unlike any thing in real life, the structure had a truth and life of its own' (p. 64). Historically the heroes and heroines of melodrama were not exceptional subjects but characters operating within social norms, making visible and sensational the differences between good and evil. The icon of the 'good home', for instance, has long been used to establish the 'space of innocence' and its virtuous victims. Melodrama was, and, we assert, still is, one of the main dramatic devices for making moral values visible across many domains of social life. For Brooks (1995) it represents the 'reaffirmation of society' of 'decent people'. Linda Williams (2001) proposes that melodrama has been insufficiently understood as a major force of moral reasoning that is not just limited to women's films or the domestic sphere but structures our understandings of the power of the nation more generally, generating a 'moral structure of feeling' (p. 26). In particular, and central to our argument, the reduction of morality to an individual dramatic performance enables social relations to be visualised and known through the psychologisation of character.

Ian Goode (2003) argues that it is the 'proximity to, and observation of behavior and character ... that drives the performative formats of "reality" television' (p. 108). In particular the construction of time on 'reality' television generates a sense of 'actuality', its reconstruction of time as an ontological claim to 'nowness' and possibly also 'hereness', rather than an epistemological claim to truth (Kavka and West 2004). This immediacy is part of the ahistorical emphasis that many critics of 'reality' television describe, its depthlessness apparently giving it no purchase on 'real' social issues. However, we would argue that it is *exactly* the lack of sociological understanding that repeats how the working class have been continually decontextualised, rerouting social problems to the level of the individual/psyche.

There are two important structural features of 'reality' television which are central to the way in which self formation now appears on television. First, by bringing together melodrama and realism, 'reality' television works with an aesthetics of depth below the surface (a variant of realism) where underlying forces govern surface phenomena which the characters will reveal: things happen to people which are beyond their own control. The realism expressed is a form of 'we are all governed by forces of happenstance', which relates in particular, Elsaesser (1987) argues, to working-class life. Yet at the same time we have noticed a shift in the subject positions offered to participants. Elsaesser's characters in melodrama are subject to forces beyond their control. But in 'reality' television, whilst participants are also subject to the unknowable, they are simultaneously faced with the impossible task of accounting for 'happenstance' (through the reiteration of reflexive talk to camera) and held responsible for the social positions they occupy. 'Reality' television thus retains a structural modicum of melodramatic fatalism whilst also effecting a shift into the individualised responsible self.

In this vein, many of the dramatic techniques used on 'reality' television rely on placing people in situations that are unfamiliar, in which they are likely to lack control, such as transformations through: swaps (wife, house, village, etc.), 'new lives in strange places' (*Get A New Life, No Going Back*), 'new' relationships (*What The Butler Saw*), 'new' jobs (*Faking It, The Apprentice*), 'new' clothes (*What Not to Wear*), 'new' culture (*Ladette to Lady, ASBO Teen to Beauty Queen*), all designed to generate insecurity, discomfort and humour for dramatic effect as we watch how the participant copes. Celia Lury (1998) identifies these techniques in consumer culture more broadly as evidence of 'prosthetic' culture, in which two central processes – indifferentiation (the disappearance of the distance between cause and effect) and outcontextualisation (where contexts are multiplied and rendered a matter of choice) encourage *experimental individualism*, in which the subject is increasingly asked to lay claim to features of the context or environment *as if* they were the outcome of the testing of his or her personal capacities. 'Reality' television visualises the impossibility of an ontological contradiction: we are rarely able to completely control events, but we are expected to do so as a measure of self-worth.

The second key structural feature to 'reality' television makes this contradiction even more intense, not just by the decontextualised immanent nature of much of the drama, but also by the way that the temporal version of 'everyday life' presented does not allow space for the type of modern self-reflexivity that Tony Bennett (2003) argues is necessary for the demonstration of depth and moral understanding. In discussing the literary construction of everyday life Bennett identifies two different architectures of the self, first, those who are said to live spontaneously at the level of everyday life, 'reproducing its habitual routines through forms of consciousness and behaviour that remain resolutely single-levelled' (p. 3) and those who have psychological and reflexive depth. The working class, he notes, have consistently been associated with the former, represented as incapable of acquiring the psychological depth needed for self-governance, hence their association with the 'mass'. If 'reality' television relies upon producing dramatic tension through immediacy and happenstance that outcontextualise and 'test' an individual's self-management, we need to ask: upon what resources can a participant draw to cope with the unexpected situations that develop?

Let us do this by comparing different programmes: *No Going Back* with *Wife Swap*. *No Going Back* is a documentary series made by Channel 4 about couples that decide to leave the 'rat race' and move abroad in pursuit of their 'dream'. In one episode of the 2003 series (first transmitted 5 November) Miranda and William Taxis buy a Tuscan farmhouse in need of renovation. Over the one-hour documentary we see two years of their lives, their struggles, their financial hardships, their children going to a new school, their community relationship with locals, and over and again their reflexive to-camera moments of exasperation, despair or joy. We see them working in different environments, making their case at Italian planning courts, even challenging the mayor over a proposed airport. In short we learn where they have come from and where they are going; on the Channel 4 web site we can see where they have ended – with an extensive complex of Tuscan holiday rentals. In many senses the focus in this series is still on the particular, in Nichols's (1991) sense: each episode consists of one couple's narrative of personal toil, rather than any socio-political commentary on what they are leaving behind, or why the narratives of escape might relate to any possible economic or cultural climate. But the way in which they can self-reflexively evolve renders this documentary as having a closer link with Bennett's more complete 'architecture of the self' than is available in, say, *Wife Swap*.

By comparison *Wife Swap*'s reliance upon melodramatic techniques calls on families to 'improvise drama' in relation to each other. The swap takes place over two weeks and we enter the drama immediately as the wives talk about how they feel about the ensuing set-up. In that sense their existence appears *for* the show and not *despite* it, therefore not a commentary on their 'everyday life' in which they can periodically demonstrate they are in control. In a *Wife Swap* from the same year (first broadcast 22 January 2003) Tracy swaps with Kate; both are working-class mothers, their difference generated by Tracy's aspiration to social mobility. The drama that unfolds is very much 'in the moment': the women are called to perform their differences from the outset. Tracy dedicates herself to her career and 'nice things' whilst Kate, a stay-at-home mum, dedicates herself to her six children. How the women have come to those positions is not part of the narrative; their differences speak only to how they can immediately make good drama. Most of the drama unfolds in home-based interactions and not on location with outside others. Their reflexive moments to camera are immediate reactions to the behaviour of others or the drama of the day rather than conscious renderings of their location with a particular narrative or history. The 'reality' is generated through the verisimilitude of the locations – the kitchens, dining tables, bathrooms, including the minutiae of their everyday lives, including eating, cleaning, parenting – which all have the familiarity of most people's domestic settings. The relationships are simultaneously familiar – as a subject position of 'wife', 'husband', 'child' – and totally unfamiliar, as they are detached and attached to others. The drama is generated through conflict and difference, edited and condensed into direct and immediate emotional statements: 'How can you treat me like this!' Comments are often a criticism of the relationship of the other wife – 'How can she let him behave like this?' 'Why does she do all the work?' 'How can she stand this?' etc. – detached from their 'life narrative' or their politics of a life, instead generated as a situational response: 'I'm not your wife,' 'I can't bear it.' The only substantive context is the domestic setting, which although recognisably familiar to the viewer is designed to destabilise and test the choices and capacities of the swapped participant.

The point is that in many modes of 'reality' television the focus is less on a documentary portrayal of a developing, contextualised, interesting life than on immediate situational melodramatic demonstration of domestic and relationship conflict and failure, where life is lived at the surface. The full story, then, is not the point, but the mundane decontextualised places of failure become the spectacular focus and overcoming them in the transformative programme style is the key to a better life. 'Reality' television participants therefore display class through access to or lack of the cultural and emotional resources required to move easily around the social spaces of unfamiliarity, offering instead people subject to forces beyond their control, detached from the comfort of their social position. Cultural difference is played out as dramatic pathology in the present, occluding all the structures, capitals, entitlements and exclusions that shape class relations from both the past and the present.

Forensic formats: metonymic morality

One of the most obvious ways in which these attempts operate to modify behaviour via responsibility on 'reality' television is through questions of taste. In *Changing Rooms*, *House Invaders*, *What Not to Wear* and *Would Like to Meet* participants are taught how to develop what the programme presenters define as taste, style, design and etiquette, all closely associated with long traditions of middle-class culture. In *What Not to Wear* the transformation of the self is complete only if the subjects conform to the *right* kind of (bourgeois) femininity, that is, clothing that excludes any form of excess (sexual, colour, frills, bodily exposure). For example, in one episode (first broadcast on 29 September 2004) the 'experts' make over Michalina. The camera focuses on her bright, brash clothing, droopy breasts, garish jewellery and heavy make-up whilst a 'humorous' derisory-tone voice-over makes sure the audience understand the perspective from which to judge the markers of classed bad taste. Similarly, Lisa Taylor documents how, in the gardening makeover programme, vulgar working-class tastes such as colourful bizzy-lizzy plants are uprooted to the horror of the owners, leading Taylor to suggest that 'the depth of personal [working-class] meaning must be sacrificed to the cleansing agency of design aesthetics' (2005: 119). These acts of transformation are examples of Bourdieu's (1979) 'symbolic violence' instantiated by legitimating middle-class taste in the name of 'lifestyle' and improvement. It is curious, then, that 'lifestyling' is often mooted as one of the indicators of the demise of class, when it is in fact one of the rhetorical techniques used to devalue working-class taste and culture (Palmer, 2004). Working-class taste, culture and values are eclipsed by the emphasis in these programmes on self-transformation – a better life is made through an individual's correct relationship with material goods.

Middle-class taste is not particularised but instead universalised and normalised as 'good' taste. Even in *Queer Eye for the Straight Guy* the queer eye is a middle-class one (Lewis 2007). This universalising of middle-class taste, behaviour, and culture via 'experts', and the future transformation that is projected in these programmes, echo a larger social shift in the late twentieth century whereby deindustrialisation, the eradication of apprenticeships and the decline of trade unions and the labour movement sidelined the working class as a central reference point in contemporary popular culture. According to Savage:

> the middle class then colonised the resulting empty social and cultural space, with the result that it has become the *particular universal* class. That is to say, although it was in fact a particular class with a specific history, nonetheless it has become the class around which an increasing range of practices are regarded as universally 'normal', 'good' and 'appropriate'.
>
> (2003: 536, emphasis added)

But the universalisation of middle-class values in 'reality' television does not stop at taste – it is also registered in the monitoring of modes of behaviour where working-class ways of life are constructed as *blockages* to appropriation of the right symbols of value and progressive ways of life. For example, in *Ten Years Younger* smoking, sun worshipping and unhealthy eating are the errant behaviours identified as blameful and shameful (Doyle and Karl 2007).

Modes of everyday life are often turned into spectacles of shame. In the programme *Honey, We're Killing the Kids* shame (not choice) operates as the catalyst. At the beginning, working-class parents stand in a white room in front of a large screen. Images of their children appear as they are now and then aged by computer graphics to the age of forty. The visual images of the children metamorphose into those of their parents, accompanied by a voice-over which increasingly and melodramatically mimes horror as the children visually become their parents, symbolising their future through the visual image of the already failed. Looking old and unhealthy (as the parents invariably do) are symptoms of life failure, offering a dramatic visualisation of a spectacle of shame. Looking back at the parents are the images of themselves: they are the problem here in the present. A family psychologist, Kris Murrin, is on hand to show them 'corrective' forms of behaviour, which focus on apparently neutral issues such as diet and healthy living, but also frequently stray into getting motivated and getting a job to be a good role model for your children. Her list of 'golden rules' includes: healthy food, daily routine, structured activities, respect, one-on-one time, stop smoking, 'you' time, give children responsibilities, family activities, children's learning, adult learning, challenge yourself and your kids, get kids motivated.[7] Again, although class is glaringly obvious as a broader social and economic set of circumstances, the issues are dealt with in terms of personal behaviour and psychology. This provides evidence to support Valerie Walkerdine's (2003) broader observation about how in the universalising of middle-class lifestyles a grammar of psychology replaces the grammar of exploitation. Pseudo-psychological experts abound in 'reality' television programmes, where even changing one's diet is the key to a happier life and the 'new you'. Failure is personalised at the level of the psychological, a result of lack of self-care detached from any economic, political or cultural differences and inequalities.

Mothering in particular emerges as one of the main sites of working-class failure, repeating the long tradition of pathologising working-class mothers (Lawler 2000). Jo, the 'expert' on *Supernanny*, enters participants' homes to outline the failures of the parents in disciplining their children and (usually) controlling children's sugary food intake. The focus on discipline is condensed on to the 'naughty step' as one of the many forms of advice, presented as 'useful tips'. Advice is also accompanied by instructions in speaking. A how to talk to children, to explain, to elaborate, and most definitely not to shout: a more thorough demonstration of the conventional middle-class elaborated-code standard of speech would be hard to find. As Deborah Cameron notes in a broader cultural shift to ideals of individualisation, communication is prized as a route improvement: 'Good communication is said to be the key to a better and happier life; improving communication "would improve everything else"' (Cameron 2000: 1).

'Good communication' as a trope appears in other ways, too. The mundane significance of the dining-room table is another motif by which behaviour is modified. Psychologists often introduce the dining table into family lives as a way of bringing the family together to talk. Talking and communicating are seen as one of the most obvious routes to parental responsibility, which stands against the images of the working class who eat 'TV dinners' as 'couch potatoes' and do not effectively interact. The television set in particular is representative of moral crime. In one episode of *Honey, We're Killing the Kids* a family are forced into opening up their dining room, saved for 'best', to the everyday eating habits of their household. It was clear to see how distressing this act of symbolic violence was to the mother whose 'fancy' dining room was a matter of pride and respectability.

In *Family Forensics* parts of the home that are seen (by the 'expert' psychologist) as diversions from a more modern, communicative and healthy way of life are actually cordoned off with crime-scene tape. The overrepresentation of the working classes in these programmes make them into reified abject objects for spectacular entertainment, just as they are in Home Office White Papers, where parenting practices become 'methods' (or Foucauldian techniques in the care of the self) that must be taught for the public good (Gillies 2005). What parents are actually being taught is the aspiration to and value of class mobility through the psychologising of class distinctions; as *Honey, We're Killing the Kids* visualised, failure to change is a failure of mobility mimicking education policy whereby 'the working classes are destined to transfer disadvantage to their children in a cycle of deprivation' (Gillies 2005).

'Reality' television programmes are therefore finding new force through a sub-genre that fetishises behaviour modification – social work television – where moral failure can be located in many intimate spaces of personal behaviour, making startling parallels with the many government behaviour modification initiatives. Presented through the auspices of lifestyle and psychology, seemingly unquestionable and universal ideals are standardised for the benefit of the nation's health. The uncomfortable presence of shame alerts us to the fallacy of discourses of 'choice': in *You are What you Eat* cameras take the opening-out of intimate behaviour to a new level, focusing on faeces as the visible evidence of a bad lifestyle. That eating take-away food might have a broader social and economic explanation as a working-class form of pleasure or a product of time necessity is not considered. Badly styled furniture in make-over programmes is a sign of lack of progress, wrinkles are the symptoms of the morally illicit pleasures of package holidays, raising your voice is a sign of lack of control and self-management. In short, each form of behaviour is given a negative value so that each part metonymically represents the 'whole' bad person: cultural differences visualised through the mundane and intimate details of everyday life that are presented as morally perverse, pathological and made spectacular.

Conclusion

In *Society of the Spectacle* Guy Debord (1931/1994) suggests that in societies where modern conditions of production prevail, through the autocratic reign of the market economy, spectacle is more than a collection of images, it *is* social relations among people, mediated by images. The fact that contemporary 'reality' programming represents an ahistorical and spectacular approach to social life does not mean that class is not present but it is precisely *because* class has ideologically shifted on to questions of moral visibility and individuality in political culture that makes it so easy to see. By denigrating the traditions of emotion and sensation[8] generated through melodrama on 'reality' television some critics have failed to register precisely the mechanisms by which class is being remade in the present. This is not to say that class is *not* made by other factors (economic, for instance) and across other sites (in political rhetoric and policy, as we have seen), rather 'reality' television is one of the sites where its making is made spectacular, reduced to psychologisation and shown to be loaded with moral value.

In a neoliberal society where a person's social worth is demonstrated by the capacity to self-manage, 'reality' television puts people in situations in which they can be *only* out of control, making them appear as completely incapable and inadequate; but rather than locating the forces that put them out of control as social, coping becomes instead a test of a person's individual capacity, and is marked on the body, dispositions, the house, the speech, the faeces, etc., through metonymic morality, where each part carries the value of the whole. Responsibility converts each mistake into a fault, which is the philosophical principle for attributing liability. If Williams (2001) is correct to suggest that melodrama carries a nation's moral values more generally, we suggest that 'reality' television is one of the most visible present political forms of generating inequalities in the moral economy of personhood.

Notes

1 See the McTaggart Lecture by Lord John Birt, ex-BBC Director, at the Edinburgh Festival, 26 August 2005.
2 The chapter draws on research conducted for the UK Economic and Social Research Council, entitled 'Making Class and Self through Televised Ethical Scenarios' (RES148-25-0040), which tracked the enormous explosion of 'reality' television across public and commercial channels. We selected ten programme series from an initial selection of forty-two self-transformation programmes (rather than psychological experiment and event type programmes, e.g. *Big Brother* or *The X Factor*) for textual analysis. Empirical audience research was also conducted with forty women of different generations, middle and working-class, white, black and Asian, settled and recent migrants, from four areas of south London.
3 In one week in November 2005 we counted ninety-two different 'reality' television programmes from UK terrestrial and free-view television packages. (The number would possibly be doubled if we were able to account for the entire availability across satellite and cable provision.)
4 See discussions in *Flow*, an online journal and discussion group for television studies, on 'Governmentality and citizenship', http://flowtv.org (accessed 21 October 2006).
5 See http://www.gov.org/respect (accessed 20 October 2006).
6 *The Scotsman*, 'Blair to unveil "parenting academy"', http://news.scotsman.com/latest.cfm?id=41952006 (accessed 10 January 2006).

7 From *Honey, We're Killing the Kids* website, http://www.bbc.co.uk/health/
tv_and_radio/honey/ (accessed 13 May 2007).
8 In Skeggs *et al.* (2008) we show how affect is translated into moral judgement.

Bibliography

Ahmed, S. (2004) *The Cultural Politics of Emotion*, Edinburgh: Edinburgh
University Press.

Aldridge, S. (2004) *Life Chances and Social Mobility: an Overview of the Evidence.*
Prime Minister's Strategy Unit, London: HMSO; http://www.strategy.gov.uk/
files/pdf/lifechances_social mobility.pdf.

Andrejevik, M. (2004) *Reality TV: the Work of being Watched.* Lanham MD:
Rowman and Littlefield.

Ang, I. (1985) *Watching* Dallas: *Soap Opera and the Melodramatic Imagination.*
London: Methuen.

Beck, U. (1992) *Risk Society: Towards a New Modernity.* London: Sage.

Bennett, T. (2003) 'The invention of the modern cultural fact: toward a critique of
the Critique of Everyday Life', in E.B. Silva, and T. Bennett (eds) *Contemporary
Culture and Everyday Life.* Durham NC: Sociology Press.

Berlant, L. (2000) 'The subject of true feeling: pain, privacy, politics', in S. Ahmed,
J. Kilby, C. Lury, M. McNeil and B. Skeggs (eds) *Transformations: Thinking
through Feminism.* London: Routledge.

Bernstein, B. (1971) *Class, Codes and Control* I. London: Paladin.

Biressi, A. and Nunn, H. (2005) *Reality TV: Realism and Revelation.* London:
Wallflower Press.

Bourdieu, P. (1979) 'Symbolic power', *Critique of Anthropology* 4: 77–85.

Bromley, R. (2000) 'The theme that dare not speak its name: class and recent
British film', in S. Munt (ed.) *Cultural Studies and the Working Class.* London:
Continuum.

Brooks, P. (1976/1995) *The Melodramatic Imagination: Balzac, Henry James,
Melodrama and the Mode of Excess.* New Haven CT and London: Yale
University Press.

Cameron, D. (2000) *Good to Talk? Living and Working in a Communication
Culture.* London: Sage.

Corner, J. (2002) 'Performing the real', *Television and New Media* 3 (3):
255–70.

Couldry, N. (forthcoming) 'Reality TV, or, The secret theatre of neoliberalism',
Review of Education Pedagogy and Cultural Studies.

Debord, G. (1931/1994) *Society of the Spectacle.* London: Verso.

Deleuze, G. (2003) *Francis Bacon: the Logic of Sensation.* London and New York:
Continuum.

Dovey, Jon (2000) *Freak Show: First-person Media and Factual Television.* London:
Pluto Press.

Doyle, J. and Karl, I. (2007) '"Shame on you": discourses of health, class and
gender in the promotion of cosmetic surgery within popular media', The Big
Reveal conference, Salford, May.

Elsaesser, T. (1987) 'Tales of sound and fury: observations on the family
melodrama', in C. Gledhill (ed.) *Home is Where the Heart Is: Studies in
Melodrama and the Women's Film*, London: BFI Books. pp 43–70.

Foucault, M. (1979) *Discipline and Punish: the Birth of the Prison.* New York: Vintage Books.

Foucault, M. (1990) *The Will to Knowledge: the History of Sexuality.* New York: Vintage Books.

Giddens, A. (1991) *Modernity and Self-identity.* London: Sage.

Gillies, V. (2005) 'Raising the "meritocracy": parenting and the individualisation of social class', *Sociology* 39 (5): 835–53.

Gledhill, C. (1987) *Home is where the Heart is: Studies in Melodrama and the Women's Film.* London: BFI Books.

Gledhill, C. (2000) 'Rethinking genre', in C. Gledhill and L. Williams (eds) *Reinventing Film Studies.* London: Arnold.

Goode, Ian (2003) 'Value and television aesthetics', *Screen* 44 (1): 106–9.

Haylett, C. (2001) 'Illegitimate subjects? Abject whites, neoliberal modernisation and middle-class multiculturalism', *Environment and Planning D: Society and Space* 19: 351–70.

Kavka, M. and West, A.(2004) 'Temporalities of the real: conceptualising time on "reality" TV', in S. Holmes and D. Jermyn (eds) *Understanding 'Reality' Television.* London: Routledge.

Kilborn, R. (2003) *Staging the Real: Factual TV programming in the Age of Big Brother.* Manchester: Manchester University Press.

Lawler, S. (2000) *Mothering the Self: Mothers, Daughters, Subjects.* London: Routledge.

Lawler, S. (2006) Introduction to special issue 'Class, Culture and Identity', *Sociology* 39 (5): 797–807.

Lewis, T. (2007) ' "He needs to face his fears with these five queers!" *Queer Eye for the Straight Guy*: makeover TV and the lifestyle expert', *Television and New Media* 8 (4): 285–311.

Lury, C. (1998) *Prosthetic Culture: Photography, Memory and Identity.* London: Routledge.

Mathiesen, T. (1997) 'The viewer society: Michel Foucault's "panopticon" revisited', *Theoretical Criminology,* 1 (2): 215–34.

Moseley, R. (2000) 'Makeover takeover on British television', *Screen* 41 (3): 299–314.

Nichols, B. (1991) *Representing Reality,* Bloomington IL: University of Indiana Press.

Ouellette, L. (2004) 'Take responsibility for yourself! *Judge Judy* and the neoliberal citizen', in S. Murray and L. Ouellette (eds) *Reality TV: Remaking Television Culture.* New York and London: New York University Press.

Palmer, G. (2003) *Discipline and Liberty: Television and Governance.* Manchester: Manchester University Press.

Palmer, G. (2004) 'The new you: class and transformation on lifestyle television', in S. Holmes and D. Jermyn (eds) *Understanding Reality Television.* London: Routledge.

Piper, H. (2004) 'Reality TV, *Wife Swap,* and the drama of banality', *Screen* 45 (4): 273–86.

Raphael, C. (2004) 'The political economic origins of reali-TV', in S. Murray and L. Ouellette (eds) *Reality TV: Remaking Television Culture.* New York: New York University Press.

Rose, N. (1989) *Governing the Soul: the Shaping of the Private Self*. London: Routledge.

Savage, M. (2003) 'A new class paradigm?' *British Journal of Sociology of Education* 24 (4): 535–41.

Singer, D. (2001) *Melodrama and Modernity: Early Sensational Cinema and its Context*. New York: Columbia University Press.

Skeggs, B. (2004) *Class, Self, Culture*. London: Routledge.

Skeggs, B., Thumim, N. and Wood, H. (2008) ' "Oh, goodness, I *am* watching 'reality' TV": how methods *make* class in audience research', *European Journal of Cultural Studies* 11 (1): 5–24.

Steedman, C. (2000) 'Enforced narratives: stories of another self', in T. Cosslett, C. Lury and P. Summerfield (eds) *Feminism and Auto/Biography*. London: Routledge.

Strathern, M. (1992) *After Nature: English Kinship in the late Twentieth Century*. Cambridge: Cambridge University Press.

Swinfold, S. (2006) 'ASBO TV helps residents watch out', *Sunday Times*, 8 January, http://www.timesonline.co.uk/tol/news/uk/article/786225.ece.

Taylor, L. (2005) ' "It was beautiful before you changed it all": class and the transformative aesthetics of the garden lifestyle media', in D. Bell and J. Hollows (eds) *Ordinary Lifestyles: Popular Media, Consumption and Taste*. Maidenhead: Open University Press.

Walkerdine, V. (2003) 'Reclassifying upward mobility: femininity and the neoliberal subject', *Gender and Education* 15 (3): 237–48.

White, M. (2006) 'Investigation *Cheaters*', *Communication Review* 9: 221–40.

Williams, L. (2001) *Playing the Race Card: Melodramas of Black and White from Uncle Tom to O. J. Simpson*. Princeton NJ and Oxford: Princeton University Press.

Wood, H., Skeggs, B. and Thumim, N. (forthcoming) ' "It's just sad": the mediation of intimacy and emotional labour in "reality" TV viewing', in J. Hollows and S. Gillis (ed.) *Homefires: Domesticity, Feminism and Popular Culture*. London: Routledge.

12 Variations on the branded self
Theme, invention, improvisation and inventory

Alison Hearn

... we arrived spectacular, tendering
our own bodies into dreamery,
as meat, as mask, as burden ...
　　　　　　Dionne Brand, *Inventory*

The reflexive project of the 'self', identified by Anthony Giddens as a hallmark of modernity, has become a distinct kind of labour under post-Fordist capital in the form of 'self-branding'. Self-branding involves the construction of a meta-narrative and meta-image of self through the use of cultural meanings and images drawn from the narrative and visual codes of the mainstream cultural industries. The function of the branded self is purely rhetorical; its goal is to produce profit. Different inflections of self-branding can be traced across several mediated cultural forms that directly address the constitution and celebration of the 'self' as such. The practice of self-branding is clearly expressed and delineated in current management literature as a necessary strategy for success in an increasingly complex corporate world. Many reality television shows invent narratives of self-branding and, simultaneously, produce branded personae. Web sites like 2night.com and universityparty.ca improvise on the theme of self-branding by taking photographs of young people at clubs and linking them to advertisements on line, blurring the distinction between private self and instrumental associative object, while social network web sites like MySpace and Facebook offer inventories of various selves.

The understanding of the self at work in this chapter takes seriously Michel Foucault's insight that 'nothing in man – not even his body – is sufficiently stable to serve as a basis for self-recognition or for understanding other men'(Foucault 1990: 153). Here the self is understood as something made or produced and conditioned by dominant notions of the 'body' and 'being'. Psychoanalytic concerns about unconscious identity formation are, for the most part, left to the side here, as are any claims about essential human nature. Indeed, this chapter assumes a dearth of orienting templates from which to produce a stable identity, arguing instead that current inflections of self-branding are the product of an economy and culture in the West intent on constant innovation and flexibility. This chapter hopes to explore the various kinds of work involved in creating a detachable, saleable image or narrative of self, which effectively circulates cultural meanings. This branded self either consciously positions itself, or is positioned by its context and use, as a site for the extraction of value. If we see the self as both a product and a reflexively constituted brand subject to transaction and exchange, we see a notion of self deeply marked by the discourses and practices of post-Fordist modes of capitalist production.

The idea of the self as a commodity, or form of property subject to market exchange, is not new; it was envisioned by John Locke in *The Second Treatise on Civil Government*. More recently Anthony Giddens offers a view of self-commodification as marked by 'the possession of desired goods and the pursuit of artificially framed styles of life' (Giddens 1991: 196) and writes of 'self-actualisation ... packaged and distributed according to market criteria' (Giddens 1991: 198). But what does it mean to suggest that the self has become a brand?

Branding is a distinct form of marketing practice, intended to link products and services with resonant cultural meanings through the use of narratives and images. In recent years the practices of branding have moved from attempting to discipline consumer taste directly to working more indirectly to install definite and highly circumscribed 'sets of relations between products and services' (Lury 2004: 1) and the consumers who use them. Branding does this by constructing a particular ambience, comprised of sensibilities and values, which may then condition consumer behaviour. A brand refers no longer to a simple commodity but to an entire 'virtual context' for consumption; it 'stands for a specific way of using the object, a propertied form of life to be realised in consumption' (Arvidson 2005: 244). In a world marked by increasing flexibility and flux, branding works to fix, albeit temporarily and tentatively, cultural meanings around consumption, producing aestheticised modes of justification for life under capital (Goldman and Papson 2006).

The material form of the brand as an image, logo, or trade mark is the first line of any marketing strategy. The brand or logo, dispersed via a variety of media forms, comes to stand as the face of a corporation, good, or service and functions as a central point of mediation between the brander and consumer. While the object of the logo or trade mark was initially intended to guarantee quality, it has now become the sign of a definite type of social identity, which summons consumers into relationship with it. The material brand is the ultimate image-commodity: a fetish object *par excellence*, pursued and paid for by consumers who wish to become a part of its fabricated world of purloined cultural meanings. Branders, as the apotheosis of Barthes's bourgeois myth makers, 'are addicted to borrowed equity; from babies to breasts, from heart-wrenching melodies to lame jokes, from leafy roads to grandiloquent clichés about the "road of life"'(Goldman and Papson 2006: 329); they steal images, stories, and language to constitute brand identities. This leads to another inflection of the brand as a specific cultural resource through which individuals and communities define themselves. Brands, both as trademarked image-objects and as sets of relations and contexts for life, become the ground and comprise the tools for the creation of self and community (Arvidson 2005; Holt 2002).

A third inflection of the term 'brand' defines it as a value-generating form of property in its own right. A brand is recognised as such by trademark licensing law and, since the 1980s, by corporate accounting practices, which consider the brand as a distinct, albeit intangible, commercial asset. Brands generate value for their corporate fathers in and through the practices described above, essentially monetising the symbolic meaning-making activities of consumers. Agencies such as Interbrand are dedicated to determining brand value (Lury 2004: 120) and measure brand equity by the extent to which consumers recognise, use, and live through the brand: 'the autonomous immaterial productivity of consumers is simply commodified as it unfolds "naturally"'(Arvidson 2005: 249).

The practices of branding comprise a rigorously instrumental set of commercial activities linked to the hegemony of post-Fordist corporate capital. In his book *Promotional Culture*, Andrew Wernick argues that all manner of communication under the contemporary cultural conditions of promotionalism have as their function 'some kind of self-advantaging exchange' (Wernick 1991: 181). So, while current branding techniques may no longer attempt to persuade consumers directly, their function remains fundamentally persuasive; they work to colonise the lived experience of consumers in the interests of capital accumulation. Indeed, the finely calibrated practices of corporate branding express the self-advantaging values of capital most pointedly, inscribing these values directly into branded experience. As 'managerial power becomes an immanent component of the very environment in which consumers act' (Arvidson 2005: 248) we are all, in some sense, 'branded' by the instrumental logics of corporate capitalist culture.

Andrew Wernick's work on promotional culture provides a useful starting point for the exploration of self-branding. Promotionalism, Wernick argues, is a dominant contemporary cultural condition. A promotional message is a 'complex of significations which at once represents (moves in place of), advocates (moves on behalf of), and anticipates (moves ahead of) the circulating entity ... to which it refers' (Wernick 1991: 182). Promotion entails a rearrangement of the relation between sign and referent; the sign comes to displace the material object to which it refers and, in this way, acquires a kind of agency. For Wernick promotion 'is a mode of communication, a species of rhetoric. It is defined *not by what it says but by what it does*' (Wernick 1991: 184). A culture marked by the ubiquity of promotional discourse is a truly postmodern one, signalled by a lack of trust in language. Here what matters most is not 'meaning' *per se*, or 'truth' or 'reason' (for these terms have been stripped of their referents and indentured into rhetorical service) but 'winning' – attention, emotional allegiance, and market share. Goods, corporations, and people are all implicated in promotionalism; not only are they commodified, but they must also generate their own rhetorically persuasive meanings. They must become 'commodity signs', which 'function in circulation both as ... object(s)-to-be-sold and as the bearer(s) of a promotional message' (Wernick 1991: 16).

The branded self is a commodity sign; it is an entity that works and, at the same time, points to itself working, striving to embody the values of its working environment. Here we see the self as a commodity for sale in the labour market which must generate its own rhetorically persuasive packaging, its own promotional message, within the confines of the dominant corporate imaginary. As such the branded self must be understood as a distinct kind of labour, involving an outer-directed process of highly stylised self-construction, directly tied to the promotional mechanisms of the post-Fordist market. Within promotional culture, the branded self may be seen as the 'significative supplement' (Wernick 1991: 190) of the commodity-self, transforming what it doubles and extends, producing a version of self that blurs distinctions between outside and inside, surface and depth. This 'persona produced for public consumption' reflects a 'self, which continually produces itself for competitive circulation' (Wernick 1991: 192) and positions itself as a site for the extraction of value. The branded self sits at the nexus of discourses of neoliberalism, flexible accumulation, radical individualism, and spectacular promotionalism.

Theme

Self-promotion is not new. One could argue that it has been around as long as there have been personal advertisements in newspapers, since ads for mail-order brides in the 1800s (Coupland 1996). Self-improvement books, such as Dale Carnegie's *How to Win Friends and Influence People*, have also been popular for many decades. The cultural forces and discourses that have given rise to the overt practices of self-branding as expressed in personal branding management literature are relatively recent, however, and have their root in the rise of the networked organisation and the entrepreneurial workplace.

The phenomenon of self-branding has developed against the backdrop of just-in-time post-Fordist industrial production processes and the rise of what David Harvey and others have termed 'flexible accumulation': a mode of production based on strategies of permanent innovation, mobility and change, subcontracting, and just-in-time, decentralised production (Harvey 1990). Flexible accumulation is heavily dependent on communication networks and on lateral flows of information and production, as opposed to hierarchical ones. Corporations increasingly act through 'the agency of small, independent production units, employing skilled work teams ... and relying on relatively spontaneous forms of cooperation with other such teams to meet rapidly changing market demands at low cost and high speed' (Holmes 2006: 5).

As a result of instantaneous communicative capacities, new technologies and mediatisation, the creation and deployment of ephemeral images comes to play a larger role in capital accumulation: 'investment in image-building ... becomes as important as investment in new plant and machinery' (Harvey 1990: 288). Flexible accumulation, then, relies heavily on the production and consumption of knowledge and symbolic products, emphasising packaging, image, design, and marketing over concrete material production (Goldman and Papson 2006; Harvey 1990). Here branding, as an 'institutionalised method of practically materialising the political economy of signs' (Goldman and Papson 2006: 328), becomes 'a core activity of capitalism' (Holt 2006: 300). Branding simultaneously produces sets of images and immaterial symbolic values in and through which individuals negotiate the world. It works to contain and direct the expressive, meaning-making capacities of social actors in definite self-advantaging ways, shaping markets and controlling competition. Within current branding practices, consumer behaviour and lived experience become 'both the object and the medium of brand activity' (Moor 2003: 42).

Luc Boltanski's and Eve Chiapello's research into the management literature of the 1960s and 1990s support the claims of David Harvey and others about the emergence of a new regime of capitalist accumulation, although from a very different, Weberian perspective. Boltanski and Chiapello argue that, in response to the economic and legitimation crises of the 1960s and early 1970s, capitalism has reconstituted its 'spirit' in the form of a networked organisation, marked by flexibility, subcontracting, casualisation, segmentation, speed-up, work intensity, and increased job competition or precariousness. This new organisation is accompanied by new value systems and new regimes of justification. In the contemporary networked organisation, activity becomes *the* standard of value for personal success:

> What is relevant is to be always pursuing some sort of activity, never to be without a project, without ideas, to be always looking forward to, and preparing for, something ...
>
> (Boltanski and Chiapello 2002: 9–10)

Perpetual activity on the part of workers is highly dependent on their flexibility and adaptability to change. The motivation for this activity must come from within and reflect personal innovation and autonomy.

Boltanski and Chiapello argue that the networked organisation and its attendant values of flexibility, communicative competence, and creativity are the result of capital's fun-house mirror recuperation of forms of cultural criticism from the 1960s, which attack capital's various modes of social and individual alienation. As Brian Holmes writes, 'the networked organisation gives back to the employee … the property of himself or herself that the traditional firm had sought to purchase as the commodity of labor power' (Holmes 2006: 6). Crucially, however, any attempt to overcome individual alienation in the workplace still happens in the workplace, on the ground of capitalist relations of domination (Virno 1996: 27). While individuals are expected to invest their soul in their work and to become 'the manager of their own self-gratifying activity' this may happen only so 'long as the activity turns into profit-producing activity' (Holmes 2006: 6). In true neoliberal fashion, the responsibility for self-fulfilment and meaningful community is downloaded on to the individual worker, as the world of alienated labour is ostensibly overcome.

As a result, we have seen the rise of what Paul du Gay and others have called an 'enterprise culture' in the workplace, which regards 'certain enterprising qualities – such as self-reliance, personal responsibility, boldness and a willingness to take risks … as human virtues and promote[s them] as such' (du Gay 1996: 60). Workers are expected to be 'entrepreneurs of the self'(du Gay 1996: 70), engaged in the 'continuous business of living to make adequate provision for the preservation, reproduction, and reconstruction of (their) own human capital' (Gordon 1991: 44). The workplace, now presumably full of non-alienated and self-directed workers, still requires containment and control by management, however. Distinct management strategies, such as team or family concepts and total quality management circles, are specifically 'concerned with the production and regulation of particular work-based subjectivities' (du Gay 1996: 59). They aim to keep workers invested in corporate functioning by addressing each worker's subjective sense of self and identity, soliciting them to express their uniqueness and tying that to corporate objectives.

There can be no doubt that the 'selves' that emerge from these management processes are deeply conditioned and constrained by the management processes that produced them. Participative management programmes remain authoritarian; 'one *has* to express oneself, one *has* to speak, communicate, cooperate … [t]he tone is that of the people who are in executive command' (Lazzarato 1996: 135). As David Harvey writes, the soul of the worker must be culturally legible, arguably in the form of a resonant image or brand, in order to be effective: 'the acquisition of an image … becomes a singularly important element in the presentation of self in labour markets' (Harvey 1990: 288).

The centrality of branding to capitalist accumulation occurs at the same time as the drive toward activity in any guise 'overcomes the oppositions between work and no work, steady and unsteady, paid and unpaid, profit-sharing and volunteer work' (Boltanski and Chiapello 2002: 9). Autonomist Marxist critics have referred to these conditions as the 'social factory', in which the human creative capacity or 'species being' is subsumed to the logic of capital and modes of capitalist accumulation extend well beyond the confines of the factory into all activities of human life (Hardt and Negri 2000; Lazzarato 1996). We might characterise all individuals at this historical moment, then, not as workers, on the one hand, or as autonomous individuals on the other, but as 'creative, nature-transforming agents on whose co-operative activity capital depends for the creation of surplus value' (Dyer-Witheford 2001: 164). Branding practices extract value from us, conditioned as we are 'by the logics of the world market, and ... socialised to be 'subjectively reconciled' to the situation, accepting it as if it were voluntarily chosen' (Dyer-Witheford 2001: 166). Nick Dyer-Witheford has named us 'global value subjects'.

Against this backdrop of neoliberalism, flexible accumulation, and the rise of a culture of promotionalism with the postmodern brand as life-defining resource, the personal branding movement in management literature arose in the late 1990s. Claiming to provide a 'communicative response to economic uncertainty'(Lair *et al.* 2005: 309), gurus of personal branding, such as Stedman Graham, Tom Peters, and Peter Montoya, offer ways to compete and gain power in the volatile work world of flexible capital. In this literature, success is dependent, not upon specific skills or motivation, but on the glossy packaging of the self and the unrelenting pursuit of attention. Here an improved self is not just a pleasant outcome of fulfilling work within a corporate setting but is explicitly defined as a promotional vehicle designed to sell: one that anticipates the desires of a target market. The most important work *is* work on the self. As Tom Peters writes:

> You're not a 'staffer' at General Mills, you're not a 'worker' at General Electric or a 'human resource' at General Dynamics ... You don't 'belong to' any company for life, and your chief affiliation isn't to any particular 'function' ... Starting today you are a brand.
>
> (Peters 1997: 83)

Unlike personal ads, which are highly circumscribed and formulaic types of self-promotion, the practices of personal branding are ongoing and involve a whole way of life. As Montoya writes: 'a personal brand [is] built on the person's true character, values, strengths and flaws' (Montoya 2002: 16). Workers are encouraged to distil their top ten qualities into a few outstanding attributes, or 'braggables', that might help them achieve 'top of mind' status in their target audience. As Chuck Pettis writes, 'You are a "product" with features and benefits, certain skills and special talents ... In creating your Personal Brand, Me Inc. ...

you want to use those skills and talents that are highly valued by your "customer"'(Pettis 2003).

Those in quest of a personal brand are encouraged to expose their braggables in every venue available to them by launching a full-on 'personal visibility campaign': 'When you're promoting brand *you*, everything you do – and everything you choose not to do – communicates the value and character of your brand' (Peters 1997: 83). Carefully crafted appearance and maximum image exposure, such as writing in newsletters or appearing on television, are crucial. Personal branders must also remain in control of their message at all times, even in private. Ultimately your personal brand is not only a pretty veneer; it is intended to be a rhetorically persuasive version of yourself. Like all branding practices, you are hoping to colonise a piece of real estate in the mind of your consumer, as You Inc.: 'Personal Branding is about taking control of the processes that affect how others perceive you, and managing those processes strategically to help you achieve your goals' (Montoya 2002: 7).

Gurus of self-branding are careful to dress up the practice in the rhetoric of self-care. As Stedman Graham writes, 'building a life brand is not about achieving status, wealth or fame. It's about taking responsibility for your own happiness and fulfillment. It's about creating a life of value by putting your gifts to their highest use' (Graham 2001: 22). The practices of personal branding can help in every area of life. Chuck Pettis describes his client, Will, who applied the steps of personal branding to his marriage by attempting to embody the desirables listed by his target audience, his wife. He sees his personal brand as a 'value added' to his relationship: 'Now I pick up my clothes,' Will states. 'My wife is the most important person in the world to me. Because she is the number-one customer in my organisation, I have to make sure she's 100 percent satisfied and happy with the product' (Pettis 2003). Gurus of personal branding simultaneously claim that a personal brand 'is not you; it's the public projection of your personality and abilities' (Lair *et al.* 2005: 325) *and* that it is a way to improve yourself and serve others, a means for achieving a 'transcendent self' (Graham 2001: 24).

As personal branding literature celebrates the freedom and radical individual empowerment involved in creating the personal brand, its numerous edicts and rules, and its relentless market discourse seriously delimit the field of possibilities within which any imagined 'authentic self' might be performed, reducing the self to a set of purely instrumental behaviours and circumscribing its meanings within market discourse. These practices are the epitome of a process Norman Fairclough has called 'synthetic personalisation' (Fairclough 1993). What is actually being sold in this literature, then, is expertise in crafting a potent *image* of autonomous subjectivity. As critics Daniel Lair, Kate Sullivan, and George Cheney write, 'a professional work world where personal branding predominates would ... be one with few enduring bonds and little trust but a great deal of political maneuvering, competition, and cynicism' (Lair *et al.* 2005: 335–6).

Invention

It is no coincidence that this description sounds just like an episode of *Survivor* (CBS, 2000) or *The Apprentice* (NBC, 2004). As I have argued elsewhere, reality television programmes invent narratives about how to become a notable self or celebrity at the same time as they offer a means to achieve a branded persona (Hearn 2006). Here the discourses of entrepreneurial self-branding and promotionalism are explicitly tied to the image economy of the culture industries. Reality programs entice individuals with the 'dreamery' of the television industry and ask them to share their unique virtuosity with the cameras for very little, if any, financial remuneration.

Autonomist Marxist critic Paolo Virno defines individual virtuosity as a capacity for improvised performance, linguistic and communicative innovation, which inevitably requires the presence of others. He sees virtuosity as a core component of immaterial labour, defined by Maurizio Lazzarato as 'the labor that produces the informational and cultural content of the commodity' (Lazzarato 1996: 133). Similarly, Lazzarato argues that the central component of immaterial labour is subjectivity, marked by communicative capacity, perpetual flexibility, innovation, and the continual self-(re)creation of subjects at work and through consumption. As the culture industries are, initially, where 'the virtuoso begins to punch a time card' (Virno 2004: 56), under post-Fordism the practices of the culture industries have become 'generalised and elevated to the rank of *canon*' (Virno 2004: 58). In so far as 'productive labour, in its totality, appropriates the special characteristics of the performing artist' (Virno 2004: 54–5), Lazzarato and Virno both argue that 'subjectivity ceases to be only an instrument of social control … and becomes directly productive' (Lazzarato 1996: 142). The culture industries, then, work to provide templates for effective performance, communicative, and image skills, all requisite for the production of the entrepreneurial branded self.

Reality television shows such as *American Idol* (Fox, 2002) and *America's Next Top Model* (UPN, 2003) have the story of self-branding as the central theme of their narratives and include explicit instruction on how to manage the demands of fame and effectively perform one's own celebrity brand. The body makeover shows are the literal enactment of Goffman's 'face work', involving the material construction of the body according to the dictates of celebrity culture, illustrated in shows like *I Want a Famous Face* (MTV, 2004) and *The Swan* (Fox, 2004). Transformation shows, such as *Extreme Makeover Home Edition* (ABC, 2004) or *What not to Wear* (the Learning Channel, 2003), offer instruction on how to achieve the appropriate wardrobe or home to gain attention and success on the more general market in social status. As one pleased contestant on *What not to Wear* states, 'I should always live as though there were television cameras outside my house!' To which the hosts reply, 'Not a bad idea!' Here the eye of the television industry, not the corporate boardroom, is the ultimate authorising force, the power behind the brand.

In this culture of promotionalism, or 'phantasmagoric capital', as Ernest Sternberg has called it, notoriety serves as a 'proxy indicator' of personal ability, and the 'capacity for calculated posing', or the construction of a clear brand identity, is often more important than possessing any specific skill set (Sternberg 1998). It can be argued that reality television provides a quick way for individuals to brand their own personae and get fame, which can be exchanged for cash down the line. American courts have recognised fame as a commodity since 1953, when the 'right to publicity' law was first introduced. The law recognises the fact that a celebrity image can 'enhance the commercial value to commodities or services with which they are associated' (Madow 1993: 128) and therefore treats the public persona or brand as a saleable commodity in its own right, ultimately alienable and descendible from the body that produced it (Madow 1993). Perhaps the best-known example of a celebrity brand functioning directly as a profit-producing, symbolic cultural resource on the open market is David Bowie's 1997 offer of 'Bowie bonds'. Here Bowie trades on his reputation directly, asking investors to bank on his brand equity, based on the past and future royalties of his music (Kadlec 2004).

While the right to publicity applies only to those considered 'celebrities', in it we can trace the roots of self-branding as a cultural practice. Here celebrity not only functions as cultural resource in and through which individuals construct their identities, it becomes a generalisable model of profitable self-production for all individuals. Participants on reality television, then, function both as image entrepreneurs, as they work to produce branded versions of themselves, and as unpaid labourers for the networks, which reap financial rewards as a result of lowered production costs. The immaterial labour involved in the construction of a personal image brand is simultaneously enacted in reality television's narratives and on their shop floors.

The notable thing about the kinds of personal brands generated on reality television is that they are not tied to any particular kind of work or specific skill set. Instead they are images of various types of everyday selves, generated inside the structural limits set by reality television's producers. Just as in the personal branding literature, the personae developed on reality television are often strategic choices made by the contestants, intended to persuade the camera, the producers, and the audience of the personal brand's viability. We might also see these character types as rendered from individuals' virtuosity; they are the result of communicative improvisation, which takes place inside a tightly controlled corporate context. In addition, and again, just as the personal branding literature dictates, the image-brands produced are consistent with the demands of the culture industries; they are 'synthetic, believable, passive, vivid, simplified, and ambiguous' (Boorstin 1961: 185). These highly structured narratives and the 'real' story of self-branding that underlie them simultaneously function as training for life under neoliberalism.

Improvisation

Websites like 2night.com and universityparty.ca actively capitalise on the improvisational communicative competences of partying young people, mining the theme of personal branding narrativised so inventively by reality programming. These sites hire photographers and send them out to clubs in various cities around the world. The photographers act as *paparazzi* and take pictures of the partiers. The photographs are posted online the next day, where anyone can download them for free.

Working within the genre of celebrity *paparazzi* candid shots, the tag line of 2night.com is 'Where the world sees you'. As the partiers go to the site to see themselves packaged in a celebrity format, the site capitalises on their attention, selling it to advertisers. On the web site the lines between the clubs, the advertisers, and the individuals are blurred, as they are all linked together in one promotional package. Much like the current trend in corporate advertising that encourages 'regular' (read unpaid) people to create their own ads, sites like 2night.com extract value from the unique virtuosity of partying men and women by packaging, branding them, and selling them back to themselves. These sites work to blur the distinction between product and consumer, private self and instrumental associative object, and, in this sense, are prime indicators of the extension of promotional and branding practices into all realms of experience.

Individuals captured on these sites are a part of a practice called 'ambient marketing', which involves recruiting spaces, bodies, and experience into rhetorical service. As marketer Adam Lury contends, 'everything is unpaid media if you want to use it in that kind of way' (Moor 2003: 45). Ambient marketing 'seeks to achieve a much more proximal relationship between consumer bodies and brands' (Moor 2003: 45), attempting to foreground the brand as the source of enriching life experiences. In this way the young people on these web sites contribute, through the simple act of socialising, to the bottom line of the experience economy (Pine and Gilmore 1999).

These web sites also point to the extension of image capital into all areas of life and to an embodied investment in its visual aesthetics. The fascination with the *paparazzi* format and the specific way of being seen that this format signifies reinforces the argument that fame and attention are now significant cultural values, which bring their own strict visual templates with them. These web sites trade on this recognition, and, in so doing, work to constitute the branded self as a transactional object, creating a strange new form of currency out of this dominant regime of exclusion, which I have elsewhere called 'the will to image' (Hearn 2004).

Inventory

The branded self is inflected differently again in the practices of social network sites like Myspace.com and Facebook.com. With MySpace accounting for 10 per cent of all advertisements viewed online (Hempel 2005) and Facebook receiving approximately 250 million hits a day (Bugeja 2006), it currently appears as though social network sites are the centre of both community and commerce in the virtual world. Both sites allow people to create their own unique virtual space. Users spend time crafting their public profiles, posting pictures and information about themselves and connecting with others doing the same. As Max Valiquette, head of the marketing firm Youthography, notes, 'everybody's got something, and that something needs virtual representation' (Halpern 2006).

In a questionnaire format focusing primarily on popular culture likes and dislikes, the profile pages of these sites encourage users to reveal intimate details of their consumer tastes. They also encourage the posting of as many personal images as possible. Christine Rosen has called these profiling practices 'egocasting' (Bugeja 2006). Participation on these sites also involves the formation of groups around shared interests and connections. Collecting or acquiring as many friends as possible seems to be a central goal. As one of my students told me, 'Facebook is addictive. It's a giant popularity contest to see how many friends you can accumulate. I have two hundred and sixty-one.'

Of course, the profiles that individuals create on Facebook or MySpace are clearly constrained by the structural features of the sites, most notably by the questionnaire formats, which focus on consumer tastes and activities. So, while a user becomes a 'digitised character actor' (Alexander 2007), carefully producing personal profiles and snapshots of their busy social lives, he or she also becomes a promotional object comprised of 'an inextricable mixture of what its author/object has to offer, the signs by which this might be recognised, and the symbolic appeal this is given in order to enhance the advantages which can be obtained from its trade' (Wernick 1991: 193). Users become Facebookers. Arguably these sites produce inventories of branded selves; their logic encourages users to see themselves and others as commodity signs, to be collected and consumed in the social market place. How else to understand the accumulation of hundreds of virtual 'friends' (usually people one barely knows) and the view that this constitutes 'popularity' than as the channelling of age-old human desires into the hollow, promotional terms of post-Fordist capitalist acquisition?

Beyond these theoretical claims, there is another, more concrete, inflection of self-branding at work here. Facebook and MySpace are coveted sites for web advertising, not only because they attract a youth demographic but because they are very 'sticky'. Users tend to visit often (Malik 2005). Given that 'millions of consumers, and especially young ones, now find online pals' content – be it photos, messages, or random musings – more compelling that that of 'professionals' (Fine 2006), corporate interests see a way to embed their brands in the minds of hard-to-reach teens by talking to them in 'their online vernacular' (Hempel 2005).

MySpace is practically synonymous with self-promotion; everyone from Paris Hilton to your next-door neighbour has a MySpace site and is working to draw attention to their 'special something'. Such is the power of these sites to attract attention and profit that 'parasites', such as Fakemyspace.com, have arisen, which allow a user to buy good-looking friends who will post on your wall twice a month for a set fee. Big Hollywood has found a way on to MySpace as well. Characters from Hollywood films are regularly assigned MySpace sites and interact with other users as though they were real people. The character Johnny Knoxville played in the film *The Ringer* garnered 11,000 friends in the time the space was up, even though there was never any guarantee that Johnny Knoxville himself was manning the site (Halpern 2006). Kevin Smith promoted his film *Clerks 2* by asking MySpace users to add him to their list of top eight friends. The first 10,000 users to do so were guaranteed a free DVD of the film and their name in the credits.

Mark Zuckerberg, Facebook's creator, has allowed corporations to trawl the site for organically generated groups who might serve as unpaid marketers for their particular brands. Apple Computers, Victoria's Secret and Electronic Arts all sponsor groups on Facebook, using the site to promote products and cultivate potential viral marketers or 'influencers' (Hempel 2005). Indeed, there are now sponsored Facebook groups for everything from local radio stations to Burger King: '[m]arketers pay for the ability to advertise their groups in "news feeds" alongside user updates on what's going on with their friends' (McArthur 2007: B3). Recognising its ability to generate vast amounts of social capital, Facebook has extended its own brand by inviting users to submit new platforms and add-ons to the site (Sun 2007). Just as with 2night.com and universityparty.ca, participants work to augment the market value of the brand through their social interactions.

The melding of egocasting with viral promotional tactics and ambient marketing produces another variation of the branded self. On sites like these the lines between private identity and public persona, corporate sponsors and individual users, producers and consumers are hopelessly blurred. In a universe where a fictional Hollywood character can be your 'friend' and the offer of a free burger is considered as significant as a relative's wedding, any meaningful distinction between notions of the self and capitalist processes of production and consumption has finally collapsed.

Recently the assiduously crafted gloss of privacy on these sites has been shattered as university administrators have logged in and busted students for everything from drinking to cheating. Facebook in particular has engendered its own moral panic, as pupils in Toronto were recently disciplined for writing derogatory comments about teachers on their profile pages (El Akkad and McArthur 2007: A1). In this era of hypervigilance, employers have begun using social networks sites as a quick and easy way to judge job candidates and run background checks. While employers can't ask personal or political questions in formal interviews, 'if it's on the web, they're entitled to make decisions based on it' (Medintz 2006). So, while individuals on MySpace and Facebook are busy acquiring friends and joining groups, exposing their every taste for marketers to exploit, potential employers are busy watching and assessing them. In the end, and not surprisingly, it all comes back to the smooth functioning of capitalist accumulation and to the effective reproduction of its labour power, no matter how socially dispersed or immaterial it might be.

Conclusion

The phenomenon of self-branding can be understood as labour in its simplest sense as 'the process by which people transform nature into objects of their imagination' (Burawoy 1979: 15). Indeed, the production of self must always involve some form of labour in order to create a public persona that might be of practical and relational use. Warren Sussman asserts that procedures of self-production have always reflected the dominant economic and cultural interests of the time. Invariably 'changes in culture do mean changes in modal types of character' (Sussman 1984: 285). We might argue that modalities of selfhood have shifted from preoccupation with 'character' in the nineteenth century to 'personality' in the twentieth. Now, in this era of flexible accumulation, we have seen the rise of what Brian Holmes has called 'the flexible personality': perpetually active, willing to innovate and change personal affiliations on a dime.

As Paolo Virno has written, in the precarious dog-eat-dog world of the flexible entrepreneurial workplace we no longer trust in any overarching system of values. In order to hedge against our 'stable instability' (Virno 1996: 17) we look to exploit every opportunity and grow increasingly cynical as we recognise that work is a game and that its rules do not require respect, but only adaptation. Along with this comes 'disenchantment' as we realise that there are no longer any identity systems worth believing in and 'no secure processes of collective interpretation' (Holmes 2006: 10) in which to invest.

The branded self is one of the more cynical products of the era of the flexible personality: a form of outer-directed self-presentation which trades on the very stuff of lived experience in the service of promotion and profit. Here the self is valuable only in relation to its flexibility, visibility, potential profitability, and ability to express and circulate resonant cultural meanings. Even when it might be argued that Facebookers and partiers on 2night.com are not consciously self-branding, they remain (as we all do) global value subjects. They are product, producer, and consumer, but they do not control the means of their own distribution. They remain captive to and conditioned by the controlling interests of global flexible capital.

This chapter has traced variations on the theme of the branded self across several mediated forms. It has considered the self as a strategic life brand intended to rhetorically persuade employers of its competitive viability, as a carefully crafted image invention designed to garner fame and profit, as an instrumental associative object exploited to sell ads even as it is in the thrall of its own image, and as a self branded through lists and inventories, which is sold and surveyed even as it attempts to form community and friendship. As an explicitly narrativised, image-based, and cynical form of labour the variations of the branded self described here confirm that the construction of the self is 'not some sideshow to the main event of global economic restructuring; rather it is an essential element in the very process of restructuring itself' (du Gay 1996: 69).

It is no accident that the discourses of branding borrow heavily from the language of radical individualism: the 'face' or 'identity' of a brand works to establish a 'relationship' with the consumer, corporations ask to be treated as though they are 'citizens' under the law and in the public mind. As we have seen, the degree to which a brand is able to embody human attributes is dependent on the degree to which it is able to insinuate itself into the lives of consumers in profound ways. Self-branding illustrates how flexible corporate capital has subsumed all areas of human life, including the very concept of a private self, so conveniently celebrated as sacrosanct by the ideologies of neoliberalism. Simply put, as the corporate brand becomes a commodity fetish, the self becomes reified, viewed as a brand in and for itself, a thoroughly promotional object, a simple means to a profit-producing end.

Bibliography

Alexander, Kevin (2007) 'Fast times at Make-believe High', *Boston Magazine*, January.

Arvidson, Adam (2005) 'Brands: a critical perspective', *Journal of Consumer Culture* 5 (2): 325–58.

Boltanski, Luc and Chiapello, Eve (2002) 'The new spirit of capitalism', chapter given at Conference of Europeanists, Chicago, 14–16 March.

Boorstin, Daniel (1961) *The Image*. London: Weidenfeld & Nicolson.

Bugeja, Michael J. (2006) 'Facing the Facebook', *Chronicle of Higher Education* 52 (21): 1.

Burawoy, Michael (1979) *Manufacturing Consent: Changes in the Labor Process under Monopoly Capitalism*. Chicago: University of Chicago Press.

Coupland, Justine (1996) 'Dating advertisements: discourses of the commodified self', *Discourse and Society* 7 (2): 187–207.

du Gay, Paul (1996) *Consumption and Identity at Work*. London, Thousand Oaks CA and New Delhi: Sage.

Dyer-Witheford, Nick (2001) 'The new combinations: revolt of the global value subjects', *CR: the New Centennial Review* 1 (3): 155–200.

El Akkad, Omar and McArthur, Kevin (2007) 'The hazards of Facebook's social experiment', *Globe and Mail* (Toronto), 1 May, p. A1.

Fairclough, Norman (1993) 'Critical discourse analysis and the marketization of public discourse: the universities', *Discourse and Society* 4 (2): 133–68.

Fine, Jon (2006) 'AOL: MySpace invader', *Business Week* 3969: 24.

Foucault, Michel (1990) *Language, Counter-Memory, Practice: Selected Essays and Interviews*, ed. Donald Bouchard. Ithaca NY: Cornell University Press.

Giddens, Anthony (1991) *Modernity and Self-identity: Self and Society in the late Modern Age*. Cambridge: Polity Press.

Goldman, Robert and Papson, Stephen (2006) 'Capital's brandscapes', *Journal of Consumer Culture* 6 (3): 327–53.

Gordon, Colin (1991) 'Governmental rationality: an introduction', in Graham Burchell, Colin Gordon and Peter Miller (eds) *The Foucault Effect: Studies in Governmentality*. Chicago: University of Chicago Press.

Graham, Stedman (2001) *Build your own Life Brand! A Powerful Strategy to maximize your Potential and enhance your Value for Ultimate Achievement*. New York: Free Press.

Halpern, Michelle (2006) 'Mass connection', *Marketing* 111 (3): 1.

Hardt, Michael and Negri, Antonio (2000) *Empire*. Cambridge MA: Harvard University Press.

Harvey, David (1990) *The Condition of Postmodernity*. Oxford: Blackwell.

Hearn, Alison (2004) 'Humiliating Images'. London, Ont.: University of Western Ontario.

Hearn, Alison (2006) ' "John, a twenty-year-old Boston native with a great sense of humour": on the spectacularization of the "self" and the incorporation of identity in the age of reality television', *International Journal of Media and Cultural Politics* 2 (2): 131–47.

Hempel, Jessi (2005) 'The MySpace generation', *Business Week* 3963: 86.

Holmes, Brian (2006) 'The flexible personality: for a new cultural critique', *Transversal*, <http://transform.eipcp. net/transversal/1106/holmes/en>, accessed 11 November 2006.

Holt, Douglas (2002) 'Why do brands cause trouble? A dialectical theory of consumer culture and branding', *Journal of Consumer Research* 29: 70–90.

Holt, Douglas (2006) 'Toward a sociology of branding', *Journal of Consumer Culture* 6 (3): 299–302.

Kadlec, Daniel (2004) 'Banking on the stars', *Time.com*, <http://www.time.com/time/innovators/business/profile_pullman.html> (accessed 25 May 2005).

Lair, Daniel J., Sullivan, Katie and Cheney, George (2005) 'Marketization and the recasting of the professional self: the rhetoric and ethics of personal branding', *Management Communication Quarterly* 18 (3): 307–43.

Lazzarato, Maurizio (1996) 'Immaterial labor', in Paolo Virno and Michael Hardt (eds) *Radical Thought in Italy: a Potential Politics*. Minneapolis MN and London: University of Minneasota Press.

Lury, Celia (2004) *Brands: the Logos of the Global Economy*. London and New York: Routledge.

Madow, Michael (1993) 'Private ownership of public image: popular culture and publicity rights', *California Law Review* 81 (1): 127–240.

Malik, Om (2005) 'The return of monetized eyeballs for highly trafficked websites: bubble-era buyouts are back', *Business 2.0* 6 (11): 55.

McArthur, Kevin (2007) 'For big brands a different kind of face time', *Globe and Mail* (Toronto), 28 April, sec. Report on Business, p. B3.

Medintz, Scott (2006) 'Talkin' 'bout MySpace generation', *Money* 35 (2): 1.

Montoya, Peter (2002) *The Personal Branding Phenomenon: realize greater influence, explosive income growth and rapid career advancement by applying the branding techniques of Oprah, Martha and Michael*. Santa Ana CA: Personal Branding Press.

Moor, Elizabeth (2003) 'Branded spaces: the scope of new marketing', *Journal of Consumer Culture* 3 (1): 39–60.

Peters, Tom (1997) *The Brand Called You*, New York: Fast Company.

Pettis, Chuck (2003) 'Building a personal brand identity: the case of Will and Lydia', http://www.brand.com/frame9.htm (accessed 28 July 2005).

Pine, Joseph and Gilmore, James (1999) *The Experience Economy*. Boston MA: Harvard Business School Press.

Sternberg, Ernest (1998) 'Phantasmagoric labor: The new economics of self-presentation', *Futures* 30 (1): 3–21.

Sun, Albert (2007) 'Facebook ask users for next big idea', *Daily Pennsylvanian*, 5 April.

Sussman, Warren (1984): *Culture as History: the Transformation of American Society in the Twentieth Century*. New York: Pantheon.

Virno, Paolo (1996) 'The ambivalence of disenchantment', in Paolo Virno and Michael Hardt (eds) *Radical Thought in Italy: a Potential Politics*. Minneapolis MN and London: University of Minnesota Press.

Virno, Paolo (2004) *A Grammar of the Multitude*. New York: Semiotexte.

Wernick, Andrew (1991) *Promotional Culture*. London, Thousand Oaks CA and New Delhi: Sage.

Part IV
Media labour and production

13 'Step away from the croissant'
Media Studies 3.0

Toby Miller

1   Will this get me a job?
2   Are games bad for you?
3   How do we get that show back on?

Questions posed by undergraduate majors

My goal in this chapter is to intervene in media studies as practised in Britain, the United States, and the white-settler colonies – Israel, Australia, Canada, and Aotearoa/New Zealand – and call for a different way of going about things.[1] Often politically isolationist and professionally intramural, media studies in these countries has been the provenance of Anglo-dominant, nativist social scientists and/or deeply impressionistic, olympian humanists. It is time that media scholars become more interdisciplinary and international. The ability to innovate as researchers will elude those wedded to monolingualism and disciplinarity. The study of media can be of value to the social world only if we engage, across disciplinary and national contexts, the key interrelationships that make our cultural condition at the nexus of money, law, policy, production, subjectivity, content, distribution, exhibition, and reception.

In the context of a book on media and social theory, this is to argue for a broader array of topics and techniques than the norm. I focus in particular on two issues: internationalism and labour. The international emphasis is an attempt to decolonise media studies by drawing on ideas and examples that derive from beyond the usual sources in the United States and Britain. The labour emphasis, by contrast, directs us back to the very origins of social theory: Adam Smith's ethnography of work, John Stuart Mill's account of the liberal individual, Karl Marx's observations on the fetishisation of commodities, and W. E. B. duBois, Rabindranath Tagore, and José Martí wrestling with subjectivities split between production, consumption, and citizenship. There would be no culture, no media, without labour (Wayne 2003: 33). Labour is central to humanity, but absent from media studies.

There is also a political point to be made here. Since the 1980s many oppositional formations have splintered: the collapse of dictatorship in Latin America and of state socialism in Europe, and the emergence of capitalism in China, compromised actually existing fascism and leftism, and explanations of them; Marxists were criticised by feminists, Third Worldists, and others who questioned class position as the principal axis of social suffering and critical agency; and feminists who posited a uniform female experience confronted critiques from women of colour, lesbians, the Third World, and the working class, who pointed to differentiated gender relations, strategic alliances with subjugated men, and multi-perspectival notions of oppression. Paradoxically, these emphases on difference emerged just as two new totalising, difference-crushing machines achieved hegemony: citizenship and consumption.

In his discussion of these questions, the eminent biologist Steven Rose argues that the 'psychocivilised society' promised by neuroscientific commerce is a paradoxical blend of individuation and control, with consumerism and government standing together against sociality (2006: 266). The questions begged are these: What would it mean to stand *for* sociality? What part might the media play in a new formation? Could we experience life as a work of art, to be enjoyed in a way that is not tied to income, and does not embroil us in commodity or religious relations? That would return us to Immanuel Kant's call for self-knowledge as an autotelic drive rather than an instrument, as an end in itself rather than a means towards some endlessly deferred or recurring achievement (Manninen 2006). Such self-knowledge could produce a wisdom that transcended marketing via focus groups or creative consultancies by cultural studies. It would be what Kant envisaged as *'man's emergence from his self-incurred immaturity'*, independent of religious, governmental, or commercial direction (1991: 54). In order to provide the conditions of existence for this work of art to come into being we need to account for the post-industrial standing of media workers (Rossiter 2006: 26–7) and reject a neoliberal embrace of casualised labour (Banks 2006).

The motivation for my critique comes from questions I often hear in classrooms, posed by the novitiate – new students who have an intuitive sense that something is wrong in their society and that the media have something to do with it, even as they follow consumerist norms in their everyday lives. In the United States these twenty-somethings boo when Health Maintenance Organisations are mentioned in movies; they don't like the fact that clothes they wear displaying their college logos were made in domestic and foreign sweatshops; they contest the representation of their gender or race on television; they receive letters from lawyers on behalf of copyright holders enjoining them to cease and desist from building web sites about their favourite music group and receive letters from advertising agencies for those same copyright holders urging them to continue what is seen as viral marketing; and when working eighteen–hour days as volunteer interns on a movie shoot they are being told to 'step away from the croissant' when their hungry elders are on set.

It is sometimes said that these young people stand at a bold new dawn of meaning. Cybertarian technophiles, struck by the 'digital sublime', attribute magical properties to contemporary communications and cultural technologies that obliterate geography, sovereignty, and hierarchy in an alchemy of truth and beauty. A deregulated, individuated media world supposedly makes consumers into producers, frees the disabled from confinement, encourages new subjectivities, rewards intellect and competitiveness, links people across cultures, and allows billions of flowers to bloom in a post-political cornucopia. It's a kind of Marxist/Godardian wet dream, where people fish, hunt, film, and write cheques from morning to midnight. In his survey of this work Vincent Mosco rightly argues that such 'myths are important both for what they reveal (including a genuine desire for community and democracy) and for what they conceal (including the growing concentration of communication power in a handful of transnational media businesses)' (2004). Yet, on reading scholarly work published in media studies, students routinely ask, 'What's this got to do with me?'

What *can* media studies offer young people? It has been dominated by three important topics: ownership and control; content; and audiences. Approaches to ownership and control vary between neoliberal endorsements of limited regulation by the state to facilitate market entry by new competitors and Marxist critiques of the *bourgeois* media for controlling the socio-political agenda. Approaches to content vary between hermeneutics, which unearths the meaning of individual texts and links them to broader social formations and problems, and content analysis, which establishes patterns across significant numbers of similar texts, rather than close readings of individual ones. And approaches to audiences vary between social-psychological attempts to correlate audio-visual consumption and social conduct, and culturalist critiques of imported audio-visual material threatening national and regional autonomy. These three components, fractured by politics, nation, discipline, theory, and method, are embodied in two varietals, which I am calling Media Studies 1.0 and Media Studies 2.0.[2] Both are ultimately to do with audiences. Media Studies 1.0 *panics* about citizens and consumers as audiences, whereas Media Studies 2.0 *celebrates* them. I investigate these histories here and make a case for a non-panicky, non-celebratory, and more internationalist Media Studies 3.0, taking electronic gaming and the international precariat movement as concluding examples of how we might do so with a labour focus.

Media Studies 1.0

So what is Media Studies 1.0? It derived from the spread of new media technologies over the past two centuries into the lives of urbanising populations, and the policing questions that posed to both state and capital. What would be the effect on cultural publics of these developments, and how would it vary between those with a stake in the social order versus those seeking to transform it? By the early twentieth century, academic experts had decreed media audiences to be passive consumers, thanks to the missions of literary criticism (distinguishing the aesthetically cultivated from others) and psychology (distinguishing the socially competent from others) (Butsch 2000: 3). The origins of social psychology can be traced to anxieties about 'the crowd' in a suddenly urbanised and educated Western Europe that raised the prospect of a long-feared 'ochlocracy' of 'the worthless mob' (Pufendorf 2000: 144) able to share popular texts. In the wake of the French revolution, Edmund Burke was animated by the need to limit popular exuberance via 'restraint upon ... passions' (1994: 122). Elite theorists emerged from both right and left to argue that newly literate publics were vulnerable to manipulation by demagogues. The founder of the 'American Dream' saw '[t]he mob mentality of the city crowd' as 'one of the menaces to modern civilisation', and he disparaged 'the prostitution of the moving-picture industry' (Adams 1941: 404, 413). These critics were frightened of socialism; they were frightened of democracy; and they were frightened of popular reason (Wallas 1967: 137). With civil society growing restive, the emergence of radical politics was explained away in social-psychological terms rather than political-economic ones, as the psy-function warmed itself by campus fires. In the United States, Harvard took charge of the theory, Chicago the ethnography, and Columbia the statistical manipulation of the great unwashed (Staiger 2005: 21–2).

The famous US Payne Fund studies of the 1930s investigated the impact of films on what a gaggle of sociologists labelled '"superior" adults' (this expression referred to 'young college professors, graduate students and their wives') versus children from juvenile centres. Researchers wanted to know 'What effect do motion pictures have upon children of different ages?' especially on what were known as the 'retarded'. These pioneering scholars boldly set out to discover whether 'the onset of puberty is or is not affected by motion pictures', specifically by what they called 'The Big Three' narrative themes: love, crime, and sex (sound familiar?). They gauged reactions through 'autobiographical case studies' that asked questions like whether 'All/Most/Many/Some/Few/No Chinese are cunning and underhand'. And they pondered 'demonstrations of satisfying love techniques' to see whether '[s]exual passions are aroused and amateur prostitution ... aggravated' by the screen. This research was undertaken, *inter alia*, by assessing 'skin response' through the use of such sensational machinery as the psychogalvanometer, attached to people in cinemas, and hypnographs and polygraphs, wired to them in their beds (Charters 1933).

The Payne Fund studies birthed what is now known as symbolic interactionism. They also inaugurated seven decades of obsessive social-scientific attempts to correlate youthful consumption of popular culture with antisocial conduct, emphasising audience composition and reactions to audio-visual entertainment: where they came from, how many there were, and what they did as a consequence of being present. As Bob Dylan put it, recalling the 1960s in Greenwich Village, 'sociologists were saying that television had deadly intentions and was destroying the minds and imaginations of the young – that their attention span was being dragged down'. The other dominant site of knowledge that Dylan encountered was the 'psychology professor, a good performer, but originality not his long suit' (2004: 55, 67). Such purveyors of normal science continue to cast a shadow across that village, and many others. The pattern is that, when cultural technologies emerge, young people are identified as both pioneers and victims, simultaneously endowed by manufacturers and critics with power and vulnerability. They are held to be the first to know and the last to understand the media – the grand paradox of youth, latterly on display in the digital sublime of technological determinism, as always with the superadded valence of a future citizenship in peril. Each technology and genre has brought with it a raft of marketing techniques, even as concerns about supposedly unprecedented and unholy new risks from the media recur: cheap novels during the 1900s, silent then sound film during the teens and 1920s, radio in the 1930s, comic books of the 1940s and 1950s, pop music and television from the 1950s and 1960s, satanic rock as per the 1970s and 1980s, video-cassette recorders in the 1980s, and rap music, video games, and the internet since the 1990s. The satirical paper *The Onion* cleverly mocked these interdependent phenomena of moral panic and commodification via a *faux* 2005 study of the impact on US youth of seeing Janet Jackson's breast in a Superbowl broadcast the year before ('US children ...', 2006).

Effects studies suffer all the disadvantages of ideal-typical psychological reasoning. They rely on methodological individualism, failing to account for cultural norms, let alone the arcs of history that establish patterns of text and response inside politics, war, ideology, and discourse. Each massively costly laboratory test of media effects, based on, as the refrain goes, 'a large university in the Mid-West' (of the United States), is countered by a similar experiment, with conflicting results. As politicians, grant givers, and jeremiad-wielding pundits call for more and more research to prove that the media make you stupid, violent, and apathetic – or the opposite – academics line up at the trough to indulge their contempt for popular culture and ordinary life, and their rent-seeking urge for public money. Media Studies 1.0 rarely interrogates its own conditions of existence – namely that governments, religious groups, and the media themselves use it to account for social problems by diverting blame on to popular culture. And it takes every new medium and genre as an opportunity to unveil its omniscience. Consider Dorothy G. Singer and Jerome L. Singer's febrile twenty-first-century call for centring media effects within the study of child development: 'Can we ignore the impact on children of their exposure through television and films or, more recently, to computer games and arcade video games that involve vast amounts of violent actions?' (2001: xv).

In addition to effects studies, many assumptions of Media Studies 1.0 inform the anti-media polemics of political economy, which focus on ownership and control rather than audience response, but also work from the nostrum that the media are all-powerful. The audio-visual sector is said to represent a turn away from precious artistic and social traces of authentic intersubjectivity, and towards control of individual consciousness. Because demand is dispersed and supply centralised, the media are said to operate via administrative logic. Far from reflecting already established and revealed preferences of consumers in reaction to tastes and desires, they manipulate audiences from the economic apex of production. Coercion is mistaken for free will, and culture becomes one more industrial process subordinated to dominant economic forces within society seeking standardisation. The only element that might stand against this levelling sameness is said to be individual consciousness. But that consciousness has itself been customised to the requirements of the economy and media production (Adorno and Horkheimer 1977). There are significant ties between the critical-theory tradition and political economy. The first is more philosophical and aesthetic in its desire to develop modernism and the avant-garde, the second more policy-oriented and political in its focus on institutional power. But they began as one with Adorno's work, which lamented the loss of a self-critical philosophical address at the same time as it lamented the industrialisation of cultural production. The two approaches continue to be linked via political economy's distaste for what is still often regarded as mass culture. We are all familiar with this account, thanks to the latter-day Frankfurters who continue to offer it to us, and their scornful critics from Media Studies 2.0, who continue to denounce its pessimism and snobbery in the name of populism.

Media Studies 2.0

So what about Media Studies 2.0? For some optimistic 1960s mass-society theorists, and many of us in cultural studies, popular culture represents the apex of modernity. Far from being supremely alienating, it embodies the expansion of civil society, the first moment in history when central political and commercial organs and agendas became receptive to, and part of, the popular classes; when the general population counted as part of the social, rather than being excluded from political-economic calculations. At the same time, there was a lessening of authority, the promulgation of individual rights and respect, and the development of intense but large-scale human interaction (Shils 1966; Hartley 2003).

This perspective has offered a way in to research of media audiences that differs from Media Studies 1.0 and its faith in the all-powerful agency of the media. For in Media Studies 2.0 the all-powerful agent is the audience. Media Studies 2.0 claims that the public is so clever and able that it makes its own meanings, outwitting institutions of the state, academia, and capitalism that seek to measure and control it. In the case of children and the media, anxieties from Media Studies 1.0 about turning Edenic innocents into rabid monsters or capitalist dupes have been challenged by a new culturalist perspective. This formation has, for example, animated research into how children distinguish between fact and fiction; the particular generic features and intertexts of children's news, drama, action-adventure, education, cartooning, and play; and how talking about the media makes for social interaction (Buckingham 2000).

Sometimes faith in the active audience reaches cosmic proportions. It has been a *donnée* of Media Studies 2.0 that the media are not responsible for – well, anything. This position is a virtual nostrum in some research into fans of television, who are thought to construct connections with celebrities and actants in ways that mimic friendship, make sense of human interaction, and ignite cultural politics. The critique commonly attacks opponents of commercial culture for failing to allot the people's machine its due as a populist apparatus that subverts patriarchy, capitalism, and other forms of oppression. The popular is held to have progressive effects, because it is decoded by people in keeping with their social situations. The active audience is said to be weak at the level of cultural production but strong as an interpretative community. All this is supposedly evident to scholars from their perusal of audience conventions, web pages, discussion groups, quizzes, and rankings, or by watching television with their children (Fiske 1989: 98–9). Consumption is the key to Media Studies 2.0 – with production discounted, labour forgotten, consumers sovereign, and governments there to protect them. The Reader's Liberation Movement is in the house (Eagleton 1982).

Consider the juncture of Media Studies 1.0 and 2.0 in games studies. A powerful binary situates at one antinomy (Media Studies 1.0) an omniscient, omnipotent group of technocrats plotting to control the emotions and thoughts of young people around the world and turn them into malleable consumers, workers, and killers; and at the other (Media Studies 2.0) all-powerful desiring machines called players, whose wishes are met by producers (Tobin 2004). In the latter group, new-media *savants* are fond of invoking pre-capitalist philosophers, thereby dodging questions of labour exploitation through wages by heading instead for aesthetics. High aesthetics and high technology are brokered through high neoliberalism. The dominant discourses on gaming fail to explain, for example, that the first electronic game, *Tennis for Two*, was produced at the US Department of Nuclear Energy (Consalvo 2006). And the fantasy that innovation comes from supply and demand mechanics is misleading. The state – specifically the military wing – is at the core. Media Studies 2.0 refers to ludology (but ignores the work of professional associations such as the Association for the

Study of Play or the North American Society for the Sociology of Sport) and narratology, returning to the non-materialist, non-medium-specific work of literary studies (but ignoring the critical work parlayed by the International Association for Media and Communication Research or the Union for Democratic Communication). Drawing on the possessive individualism of neoclassical economics, these reactionary game analysts study virtual environments as ways of understanding 'whole societies under controlled conditions' (Castronova 2006), ignoring or caricaturing the discourses of history and ethnography in the process.

The fundamental dilemma for the political claims of Media Studies 2.0 is this: can fans be said to engage with labour exploitation, patriarchy, racism, and neo-imperialism, or in some specifiable way make a difference to politics beyond their own selves, when they interpret texts unusually or chat about romantic frustrations? Have we gone too far in supplanting the panicky Woody Allen nebbishness of Media Studies 1.0 with the Panglossian Pollyanna nerdiness of Media Studies 2.0?[3] Virginia Postrel, then editor of the libertarian *Reason* magazine, and later a *New York Times* economics journalist, wrote a *Wall Street Journal* op-ed, welcoming Media Studies 2.0 as 'deeply threatening to traditional leftist views of commerce … lending support to the corporate enemy and even training graduate students who wind up doing market research' (1999). Ouch. Richard Hoggart, crowned by many Media Studies 2.0 true believers as the founder of cultural studies in Britain, has renounced such tendencies (2004).

A way ahead?

We need more *frottage* between Media Studies 1.0 and 2.0, breaking down the binary between them. We need Media Studies 1.0 to register struggle and Media Studies 2.0 to register structure. Media Studies 1.0 draws our attention to audience inoculation and corporate control, but it leaves out productive labour – the key place where value is made. Media Studies 2.0 draws our attention to patterns of uptake and response but, again, marginalises labour. Media Studies 1.0 misses moments of crisis and hope, presenting a subject-free picture with structure but no agency, other than psychological response, shareholder maximisation, and managerial rationality. Media Studies 2.0 misses forms of domination and exploitation, presenting an institution-free picture with agency but no structure, other than fan creativity and reader imagination. Both Media Studies 1.0 and Media Studies 2.0 are doggedly tied to nativist epistemologies that must be transcended. The nativism is especially powerful in the United States and Britain, where effortless extrapolations are made from very limited experience to support totalising theories and norms, due to the unfortunate hegemony of the English language, both domestically and abroad, and its long-term links to the warfare, welfare, and cultural bureaucracies

(Calhoun 2002; Simpson 1996; Hunter 1988). To transcend these pitfalls, we need Media Studies 3.0.

Media Studies 3.0 must blend ethnographic, political-economic, and aesthetic analyses in a global and local way, establishing links between the key areas of cultural production around the world (Africa, the Americas, Asia, Europe, and the Middle East) and diasporic/dispossessed communities engaged in their own cultural production (Native peoples, African and Asian diasporas, Latin@s,[4] and Middle Eastern peoples). Media Studies 3.0 needs to be a media-centred version of area studies, with diasporas as important as regions. It must be animated by collective identity and power, by how human subjects are formed and how they experience cultural and social space. Taking its agenda from social movements as well as intellectual ones, and its methods from economics, politics, communications, sociology, literature, law, science, medicine, anthropology, history, and art, it should feature a particular focus on gender, race, class, and sexuality in everyday life across national lines.

We can gain some tips on how to do this from the history of theorising culture. Culture has usually been studied in two registers, via the social sciences and the humanities – truth versus beauty. It has been a marker of differences and similarities in taste and status within groups, as explored interpretatively or methodically. In the humanities, cultural texts were judged by criteria of quality, as practised critically and historically. For their part, the social sciences focused on the religions, customs, times, and spaces of different groups, as explored ethnographically or statistically. So whereas the humanities articulated differences through symbolic norms (for example, which class had the cultural capital to appreciate high culture, and which did not) the social sciences articulated differences through social norms (for example, which people cultivated agriculture in keeping with spirituality, and which did not) (Benhabib 2002; Wallerstein 1989). This distinction fed into the Cartesian dualism separating thought from work, which presumed that the intelligent and the corporeal nature are distinct, with one focused on life as action, and the other on reason. That binary has played out throughout the study of the media and culture, for example through an opposition drawn between society and economy versus audience and meaning that haunts Media Studies 1.0 and 2.0.

But this binary opposition has long been unstable. Eighty years ago Thorstein Veblen described universities as 'competitors for traffic in merchantable instruction', recognising the importance of the 'industrial arts' (cited in Pietrykowski 2001). Knowledge and culture were bracketed together in a way that compromised this dualism. And the canons of judgement and analysis that once flowed from the humanities/social–sciences bifurcation over approaches to culture (and kept aesthetic tropes somewhat distinct from social norms) have collapsed in on each other. In Adorno's words, 'Whoever speaks of culture speaks of administration' (1996). Art and custom have become resources for markets and nations – reactions to the crisis of belonging, and to economic necessity. As a consequence, the media are more than textual signs or everyday practices, more than audience effects or interpretations. Whereas rights to culture did not appear in many of the world's constitutions until well into the twentieth century, contemporary ones routinely emphasise the topic. Cultural provisions are standard in post-dictatorship charters, for example those of Mexico, South Africa, Brazil, Portugal, Guatemala, Nicaragua, Paraguay, Perú, and Spain. The meaning is generally a double one, blending artistry and ethnicity. Concerns with language, heritage, religion, and identity are responses to histories structured in dominance through cultural power and the postcolonial incorporation of the periphery into an international system of 'free' labour (de Pedro 1991, 1999). Ministers of Culture deliver messages of cultural maintenance that are about economic development *and* the preservation of identity – means to growth and citizenship, based on the shared value placed on different cultural backgrounds, and the European Commission seeks to use culture to recognise difference, make money, and exercise diplomacy (2007). This is what George Yúdice (2003) refers to when he describes culture as a resource, and Rick Maxwell (2001) when he talks about being in the culture works.

Of course, there is no teleologically unfurling tale of progress towards social integration, with culture a magic elixir that produces harmony. Rather, culture has been a site of contestation, as per the civil rights movement, opposition to the American war in Vietnam, youth rebellion, China's Cultural Revolution, and Third World resistance to multinational corporations (Schiller 2007). The media are crucial components of this mosaic, as indices and generators of cultural stasis and change. This is where Media Studies 3.0 can draw on the venerable internationalism of political economy as one of its touchstones. Such critics of cultural imperialism and colonialism as Aimé Césaire, Amilcar Cabral, Frantz Fanon, Michèle Mattelart, Herbert I. Schiller, and Hamid Mowlana have animated both international political economy and cultural studies.

Following their example, I suggest that Media Studies 1.0 and 2.0's bifurcation and subsequent silencing of labour and culture, for all their sticky origins in Cartesianism, cannot hold: hence the capacity of labour to offer the second touchstone. Historically, the best critical political economy and the best cultural studies have worked through the imbrication of power and signification at all points on the cultural continuum. Blending the two approaches can heal the fissure between fact and interpretation, between the social sciences and the humanities, between truth and beauty, under the sign of a principled approach to cultural democracy. To that end, Larry Grossberg recommends 'politicising theory and theorising politics', combining abstraction and grounded analysis. This requires a focus on the contradictions of organisational structures, their articulations with everyday living and textuality, and their intrication with the polity and economy, refusing any bifurcation that opposes the study of production and consumption, or fails to address axes of social stratification (1997).

For instance, Arvind Rajagopal notes that because television, the telephone, the internet, and the neoliberal are all new to India, 'markets and media generate new kinds of rights and new kinds of imagination ... novel ways of exercising citizenship rights and conceiving politics' (2001). For Rosalía Winocur, women's talk-back radio in Latin America since the fall of US-backed dictatorships has offered a simultaneously individual and social forum for new expressions of citizenship, in the context of decentred politics, emergent identities, minority rights, and gender issues – a public space that transcends the subordination of difference and the privileging of elite experience (2002). And Mosco starts from the power of cultural myths, then 'builds a bridge to political economy' in his investigation of neoliberal *doxa* about empowerment, insisting on 'the mutually constitutive relationship between political economy and cultural studies' as each mounts 'a critique of the other' (2004). We can see similar intent animating such innovations as Sarai (sarai.net), the Free Software Foundation (fsf.org), and the Alternative Law Forum (altlawforum.org). These are exemplary instances of a Media Studies 3.0 that is in formation. They blend internationalism, political economy, ethnography, and textual analysis, and resist the binarism of Media Studies 1.0 and 2.0.

To understand the infrastructure of the media, we must address technological innovation, regulation, labour, and ownership, utilising ethnographic, political-economic, and public-policy research to establish how the media came to be as they are. To understand output, we must address production and undertake both content and textual analysis, combining statistical and hermeneutic methods to establish patterns of meaning. To understand audiences, we must address ratings, uses-and-gratifications, effects, active-audience, ethnographic, and psychoanalytic traditions, combining quantitative and qualitative measures to establish the audience's composition and conduct in the wake of media consumption. This incarnates a simultaneously top-down and bottom-up approach, undertaken always with an eye to labour issues.

Let me offer an example of a labour focus, from the history of the corporation Electronic Arts (EA). Based in Los Angeles, EA makes *The Sims* and the John Madden 'football' games. Electronic Arts was founded in 1982 by Trip Hawkins. He bought into Media Studies 1.0 and 2.0 simultaneously, dismissing broadcast television as 'brain-deadening', and embracing 'interactive media' as a development 'that would connect people and help them grow' (quoted in Fleming 2007). Hawkins's passion for complex board games melded with his excitement at the potential of the microprocessor. The company's name derived from a desire to emphasise art and technology under the sign of publishing, with developers initially promoted as authors. Its first games, such as *M.U.L.E.* and *Murder on the Zinderneuf*, were marketed with designers' names – rather like rock albums of the day. These shining young white design geeks were celebrated in a famous 1983 advertisement called 'We see farther'. But geek authorship was soon supplanted; by the mid-1980s, the 'authors' of key games were no longer dweebs in black polo necks but Doctor J. and Larry Bird, basketball celebrities brought in as endorsers and *faux* designers. Creators lost their moment of fame as authors. A stream of sports stories drew on promotions underwritten by others' creativity and money, displacing what were regarded as the esoteric pursuits of the first innovators. The labour process became fetishised as EA bought development studios and set up design teams on an industrial model. At the same time, the corporation sought to undermine the existing political economy of the industry by cutting the discount given to distributors of software, thereby building up revenues. Its next move was to deal direct with retailers, writing games for both personal computers and consoles and becoming a distributor itself. In addition to continuing with console options, it entered virtual worlds in the late 1990s, and awakened to female consumers, buying advertising space and time across fashion periodicals and girly television (Fleming 2007).

In 2004 the company became a public by-word for the worst labour practices across the sector when the blogger ea_spouse pseudonymously posted a vibrant account of the exploitation experienced by her fiancé and others at EA, eloquently ripping back the veneer of joyous cybertarianism from games development. As she put it, EA's claim to blend aesthetics and technology, as per their name and corporate trade mark, 'Challenge everything', belied both its treatment of workers and its products. Re labour, she wrote: 'To any EA executive that happens to read this, I have a good challenge for you: how about safe and sane labour practices for the people on whose backs you walk for your millions?' Re texts: 'Churning out one licensed football game after another doesn't sound like challenging much of anything to me; it sounds like a money farm.' Then she detailed the exploitation: a putatively limited 'pre-crunch' is announced in the period prior to release of a new game, such that forty-eight-hour weeks are required, with the alibi that months of this will obviate the need for a real 'crunch' at the conclusion of development; the pre-crunch goes on beyond its deadline; seventy-two-hour work weeks are mandated; that crunch passes its promised end; illness and irritability strike; and a new crunch is announced, whereby everyone must work between eighty-five and ninety-one-hour weeks, 9.00 a.m. to 10.00 p.m., Monday to Sunday inclusive, with the only (occasional) evening off being a Saturday, after 6.30. There is no overtime or leave in return for this massive expenditure of talent and time. The workers discern no measurable benefit from the crunch. So many errors are made from fatigue that time is needed to correct them.

In the middle of this crisis *Fortune* magazine ranked EA among the '100 best companies to work for'. It is No. 91 among corporations that

'try hard to do right by their staff' as measured by the Great Place to Work®
Institute in San Francisco. Electronic Arts calls itself 'a one-class society',
and its Vice-President of Human Resources, Rusty Rueff, operates with
the following (astonishing) dictum: 'Most creativity comes at one of two
times: When your back is up against the wall or in a time of calm.' In case
readers find this firing-squad analogy alarming, *Fortune* reassures them that
workers can 'refresh their energy with free espresso or by playing volleyball
and basketball'. Today, after the controversy begat a class-action lawsuit,
the firm ranks No. 62 in the magazine's 'List of Industry Stars' (Levering
et al. 2003).

ea_spouse's brave intervention (as we say in cultural studies) or outburst
(as they say elsewhere) generated febrile and substantial responses, such
as calls for unionisation, appeals to federal and state labour machinery,
confirmation that EA was horrendous but by no means aberrant, frustration
that the bourgeois press was disinclined to investigate or even report
the situation, denunciations of asinine managerialism and private-sector
bureaucracy (for example, 'The average game company manager is quite
possibly the worst qualified leader of people in the world'), and recognition
of how intellectual property rights make labour disposable ('I'm beginning
to think that EA is really nothing more than a licensing warehouse. [T]hey'll
always be able to recruit naive talent to slave away ... alienating talent is
not a big problem for them'). ea_spouse now runs a web site that is bom-
barded with horror stories by angry former idealists from all over the globe
who thought they were doing 'cool stuff' until they experienced web-shop
horror. Do you read about such matters in your friendly neighbourhood
media studies journal or textbook? I doubt it. Are such matters of interest to
young proto-cybertarians who think working for a games company would
be the greatest thing since the simultaneous orgasm? I think so.

We inhabit a world where flexibility is the mega-sign of affluence, and
precariousness its flip side; where one person's calculated risk is another's
burden of labour; where inequality is represented as a moral test; and youth
is supposed to respond to a calculated insecurity as an opportunity rather
than a constraint. But not everyone succumbs to Media Studies 1.0's sense
of helplessness or Media Studies 2.0's rhetoric of empowerment. Consider
the developing discourse of casualised workers, flexible labour among
cultural workers segmented through deregulation and new technology (Paul
and Kleingartner 1994; Dahlström and Hermelin 2007). In Western Europe
this group is renaming itself. The precariat/précaires/precarias/precari go
under the signs of 'San Precario' and 'Our Lady of the Precariat', who
guard the spirit of the 'flashing lights of life'. The movement embodies a
new style, a new identity, formed from young, female, mobile, international
workers in the culture industries, services, and the knowledge sector,
struggling for security against the impact of neoliberalism (Foti 2005). Since
2001 the Euromayday Network has organised Precariat Parades in twenty
European cities that feature 'contortionists of flexibility ... high-wire artists

of mobility ... jugglers of credit', along with apparitions by San Precario to protect his children against evil bosses ('Sign the call!' 2006). In 2005 San Precario appeared in the form of a worker uniformed and supplicant on his knees, with a neon sign on his head. Participants note the instability of working life today, and hale a new class of sex workers, domestic servants, and media creators at maydaysur.org. Their manifesto reads:

> Somos precarios y precarias, atípicos, temporales, móviles, flexibles.
> Somos la gente que está en la cuerda floja, en equilibrio inestable.
> Somos la gente deslocalizada y reconvertida.
>
> We are the precariat, atypical, temporary, mobile, flexible.
> We are the people on the high wire, in unstable equilibrium.
> We are the people displaced and made over.
>
> (Quoted by Raunig 2004)

The precariat suggests a complex connection between 'eslóganes de los movimientos sociales, reapropiados por el neoliberalismo', social movement slogans reappropriated for neoliberalism. It recognises that concepts like diversity, culture, and sustainability create spectacles, manage workers, and enable gentrification (Raunig 2004). Similarly, Espai en blanc 'afirma que vivimos en la sociedad del conocimiento y en cambio no existen ideas', affirms that we live in a society of knowledge and change where ideas don't exist (espaienblanc.net). Adbusters and cultural jamming (adbusters.org) work in cognate ways.

When the precariat and culture jammers declare a new 'phenomenology of labour', a 'world horizon of production' (Hardt and Negri 2000: 364), they are reoccupying and resignifying the space of corporate-driven divisions of labour in ways that Media Studies 1.0 and 2.0 have simply ignored. Antonio Negri refers to this interesting group as the cognitariat. They are comprised of the very students we teach – people with high levels of educational attainment and great facility with cultural and communications technologies and genres. They are the new breed of productive workers, who play key roles in the production and circulation of goods and services through both creation and co-ordination. They form a new proletariat – no longer one that is defined in terms of factories and manufactures versus a middle or ruling class of force and ideology. This proletariat is formed from those whose forebears, with similar or lesser cultural capital, were the salariat, and operated within systems of secured health care and retirement income. The new group lacks both the organisation of the traditional working class and the political *entrée* of the old middle class (Negri 2007: 264–5). It operates within a *culturalisation of production* (Wayne 2003: 21) that both enables intellectuals, by placing them at the centre of world economies, and disables them, by doing so under conditions of flexible production and ideologies of 'freedom'.

Such developments have special meaning for women, who traditionally occupy most service-sector employment but have been edged out by men as the sector has added in prestige and centrality with the decline of First World employment in primary and secondary industries (Martin 2002). There are wider public policy implications than labour itself. The scandal that engulfed British television in 2007 because of the way that the BBC as well as overtly capitalistic enterprises deceived viewers to cut costs and increase excitement, soon turned into a recognition of what happens to the ethos of public service when programmes are made on a project basis by businesses without any commitment to anything but profit and employees lacking any form of security or a sense of public purpose (Dyke 2007; 'Belief' 2007). The television executive Dawn Airey (2007) (once author of a television business plan orchestrated around 'films, football, and fucking') is now warning against 'the casualisation of the industry'. Similar debates have emerged over the exploitation of child workers in US reality television at the hands of subcontractors – who again eschew organised labour (Fernandez 2007, also see Tahiro 2002).

To summarise, Media Studies 1.0 is misleadingly functionalist on its effects and political-economy side, and Media Studies 2.0 is misleadingly conflictual on its active-audience side. Work done on political economy and effects has neglected struggle, dissonance, and conflict, in favour of a totalising narrative in which the media dominate everyday life. Work done on the active audience has overemphasised struggle, dissonance, and conflict, in favour of a totalising narrative in which readers and audiences dominate everyday life. We need Media Studies 3.0 to synthesise and improve what has already been achieved. Otherwise the questions with which I began will lie unanswered, leading to a group of angry young alumni and profoundly exploited new-media workers. Returning to those queries, here are some contingent replies:

1 If you know who owns and regulates the media, you'll know how to apply to work there, and minimise power imbalances once you've made it.
2 The question of media effects depends on who wants to know and why; the impact of games on those who make them is negative, because of exploitative work practices.
3 If you know how audiences are defined and counted, and how genre functions, you'll be able to lobby for retention of your favourite programmes.

Notes

1 Many thanks to the editors for their supportive and perspicacious comments.
2 These terms are also used at theory.org.uk.

3 The editors have asked me to explain these terms. Nebbishness refers to an unfortunate, solitary figure. It is derived from Yiddish. Pangloss refers to the optimistic philosopher in Voltaire's *Candide*, and Pollyanna to a classic of children's literature about a similarly sunny person.
4 This is the term increasingly used in Latin America and the United States in order to avoid gendered implications.

Bibliography

Adams, J. T. (1941). *The Epic of America*. New York: Triangle Books.

Adorno, T. (1996) *The Culture Industry: Selected Essays on Mass Culture*, trans. G. Finlayson, N. Walker, A. G. Rabinach, W. Blomster, and T. Y. Levin, ed. J. M. Bernstein. London: Routledge.

Adorno, T. and Horkheimer, M. (1977) 'The culture industry: enlightenment as mass deception', in Curran, J., Gurevitch, M. and Woollacott, J. (eds) *Mass Communication and Society*. London: Arnold.

Airey, D. (2007) 'Is the BBC a healthy institution ... or fundamentally sick at heart?' *Independent*, 20 July, p. 3.

Banks, M. (2006) 'Moral economy and cultural work', *Sociology* 40 (3): 455–72.

'Belief in the BBC' (2007) *Financial Times*, 20 July, 10.

Benhabib, S. (2002) *The Claims of Culture: Equality and Diversity in the Global Era*. Princeton NJ: Princeton University Press.

Buckingham, D. (2000) *After the Death of Childhood: Growing up in the Age of Electronic Media*. Cambridge: Polity Press.

Burke, E. (1994). 'The restraints on men are among their rights', in P. Clarke (ed.) *Citizenship*. London: Pluto Press.

Butsch, R. (2000) *The Making of American Audiences: from Stage to Television, 1750–1990*. Cambridge: Cambridge University Press.

Calhoun, C. (2002) 'The Future of Sociology: Interdisciplinarity and Internationalization', paper delivered to the Department of Sociology, University of Minnesota, at its centennial celebration, 29–30 March.

Castronova, E. (2006) 'On the research value of large games: natural experiments in Norrath and Camelot', *Games and Culture: a Journal of Interactive Media* 1 (2): 163–86.

Charters, W. (1933) *Motion Pictures and Youth: a Summary*. New York: Macmillan.

Consalvo, M. (2006) 'Console video games and global corporations: creating a hybrid culture', *New Media and Society* 8 (1): 117–37.

Dahlström, M. and Hermelin, B. (2007) 'Creative industries, spatiality and flexibility: the example of film production', *Norsk Geografisk Tiddskrift – Norwegian Journal of Geography* 61 (3): 111–21.

Dyke, G. (2007) 'This is the fault of politicians, not broadcasters', *Independent*, 20 July, p. 2.

Dylan, B. (2004) *Chronicles* I. New York: Simon & Schuster.

Eagleton, T. (1982) 'The revolt of the reader', *New Literary History* 13 (3): 449–52.

ea_spouse. (2004) 'EA: the human story', *Live Journal*, 11 November, ea-spouse.livejournal.com/274.html.

European Commission (2007) *A European Agenda for Culture in a Globalizing World*. Communication, Brussels.

Fernandez, M. E. (2007) '*Kid Nation* puts Hollywood labour tension into sharp focus', *Los Angeles Times*, 29 August, pp. A1, A14.

Fiske, J. (1989) *Reading the Popular*. New York: Routledge.

Fleming, J. (2007) 'We see farther: a history of electronic arts', *Gamasutra: the Art and Business of Making Games*, 16 February.

Foti, A. (2005). 'Mayday, Mayday: Euroflex workers, time to get a move on!' Republicart.net, 4.

Grossberg, L. (1997) *Bringing it all Back Home: Essays on Cultural Studies*. Durham NC: Duke University Press.

Hardt, M. and Negri, A. (2000) *Empire*. Cambridge MA: Harvard University Press.

Hartley, J. (2003) *A Short History of Cultural Studies*. London: Sage.

Hoggart, R. (2004) *Mass Media in a Mass Society: Myth and Reality*. London: Continuum.

Hunter, I. (1988) *Culture and Government*. London: Macmillan.

Kant, I. (1991) *Political Writings*, trans. H. B. Nisbet, ed. H. Reiss, 2nd edn. Cambridge: Cambridge University Press.

Levering, R., Moskowitz, M., Harrington, A. and Tzacyk, C. (2003) '100 best companies to work for', *Fortune*, 20 January.

Manninen, B. A. (2006) 'Medicating the mind: a Kantian analysis of overprescribing psychoactive drugs', *Journal of Medical Ethics* 32: 100–5.

Martin, S. (2002) 'The political economy of women's employment in the information sector', in E. Meehan and E. Riordan (eds) *Sex and Money: Feminism and Political Economy in the Media*. Minneapolis MN: University of Minnesota Press.

Maxwell, R. (ed.) (2001) *Culture Works*. Minneapolis MN: University of Minnesota Press.

Mosco, V. (2004) *The Digital Sublime: Myth, Power, and Cyberspace*. Cambridge MA: MIT Press.

Negri, A. (2007) *Goodbye, Mister Socialism: entretiens avec Raf Valvola Scelsi*, trans. P. Bertilotti. Paris: Seuil.

Paul, A. and Kleingartner, A. (1994) 'Flexible production and the transformation of industrial relations in the motion picture and television industry', *Industrial and Labour Relations Review* 47 (4): 663–78.

de Pedro, J. P. (1991) 'Concepto y otros aspectos del patrimonio cultural en la constitución', *Estudios sobre la constitución española: homenaje al profesor Eduardo Garcia de Enterria*. Madrid: Editorial Civitas.

de Pedro, J. P. (1999) 'Democracy and cultural difference in the Spanish constitution of 1978', in C. J. Greenhouse with R. Kheshti (eds) *Democracy and Ethnography: Constructing Identities in Multicultural Liberal States*. Albany NY: State University of New York Press.

Pietrykowski, B. (2001) 'Information technology and commercialization of knowledge: corporate universities and class dynamics in an era of technological restructuring', *Journal of Economic Issues* 35 (2): 299–306.

Postrel, V. (1999) 'The pleasures of persuasion', *Wall Street Journal*, 2 August.

Pufendorf, S. (2000) *On the Duty of Man and Citizen according to Natural Law*, trans. M. Silverthorne, ed. J. Tully. Cambridge: Cambridge University Press.

Rajagopal, A. (2001) *Politics after Television: Religious Nationalism and the Reshaping of the Indian Public*. Cambridge: Cambridge University Press.

Raunig, Gerald (2004). 'La inseguridad vencerá: activismo contra la precariedad y May Day parades', trans. M. Expósito, Republicart.net 6.

Rose, S. (2006) *The Twenty-first Century Brain: Explaining, Mending and Manipulating the Mind*. London: Vintage.

Rossiter, N. (2006) *Organized Networks: Media Theory, Creative Labour, New Institutions*. Rotterdam: NAi Publishers.

Schiller, D. (2007) *How to Think about Information*. Urbana IL: University of Illinois Press.

Shils, E. (1966) 'Mass society and its culture', in B. Berelson and M. Janowitz (eds) *Reader in Public Opinion and Communication*, 2nd edn. New York: Free Press.

'Sign the call!'. (2006) EuroMayday.org.

Simpson, C. (1996) *Science of Coercion: Communication Research and Psychological Warfare, 1945–1960*. New York: Oxford University Press.

Singer, D. G. and Singer, J. L. (2001) 'Introduction: why a handbook on children and the media?' in D. G. Singer and J. L. Singer (eds) *Handbook of Children and the Media*. Thousand Oaks CA: Sage.

Staiger, J. (2005) *Media Reception Studies*. New York: New York University Press.

Tahiro, C. S. (2002) 'The *Twilight Zone* of contemporary Hollywood production', *Cinema Journal* 41 (3): 27–37.

Tobin, J. (2004) 'Introduction', in J. Tobin (ed.) *Pikachu's Global Adventure*. Durham NC: Duke University Press.

'US children still traumatized one year after seeing partially exposed breast on TV' (2006) *The Onion*, 26 January.

Wallas, G. (1967) *The Great Society: a Psychological Analysis*. Lincoln NE: University of Nebraska Press.

Wallerstein, I. (1989) 'Culture as the ideological battleground of the modern world-system', *Hitotsubashi Journal of Social Studies* 21 (1): 5–22.

Wayne, M. (2003) *Marxism and Media Studies: Key Concepts and Contemporary Trends*. London: Pluto Press.

Winocur, R. (2002) *Ciudadanos mediaticos*. Barcelona: Editorial Gedisa.

Yúdice, G. (2003) *Los recursos de la cultura*. Barcelona: Editorial Gedisa.

14 Sex and drugs and bait and switch

Rockumentary and the new model worker

Matt Stahl

> Whoever does not adapt his manner of life to the conditions of capitalistic success must go under, or at least cannot rise.
>
> (Max Weber)

> It's more than an adventure, it's a job.
> (Indie musician Melanie De Giovanni, reversing the US army's 1980s recruiting slogan to describe touring with a rock band)

I

Non-fiction narratives of cultural production and producers are undergoing a considerable expansion in a variety of media. This chapter proposes a social-theoretical framework for the analysis of this efflorescence through an examination of the documentary representation of popular musical careers, against the backdrop of recent analyses of organisational change in neoliberal work regimes. The developing interactions of neoliberal political-economic change, the social division of labour, and the labour process are of increasing interest to social scientists and theorists (e.g. Boltanski and Chiapello 2005; Sennett 1998, 2006; Reich 2001); this chapter focuses on the figure of the creative worker as agent and pedagogue of such change.

The rhetorical work of documentary, argues Nichols (1991: 140), is to gain assent to statements about and orientations for action in the social world. Growing numbers of analysts from various quarters suggest that entertainment firms present models of flexibility and risk management – neoliberal reorganisation *avant la lettre*[1] – and that the working conditions and career trajectories of creative workers are at the cutting edge of this shift. I argue that while contemporary rockumentary exhorts us to attend to and value a vision of autonomous freeholders that appears to offer a radical challenge to the norm of alienated work, the model of work that emerges tends to follow along the lines of that now favoured by the neoliberalising state and private sector. The task here is to draw attention to rockumentary's narratives of work in the contemporary political economy, to its productive relationship with forms of economic subjectivity consonant with ongoing processes of neoliberalisation.

Cultural conceptions of work and the working subject are an essential component in any political-economic regime (Biernacki 1995; Read 2003: 98), and rockumentaries such as 2004's *Dig!* are consent-seeking vehicles of such cultural conceptions. Weber's *Protestant Ethic and the Spirit of Capitalism* (1958) and Macpherson's *Political Theory of Possessive Individualism* (1962) analyse the changes in conceptions of ethics and human nature that attended the emergence of fully fledged capitalism. But changes *within* capitalism continue to promise and depend on significant socio-cultural change. On a finer scale than the two magisterial works cited above, Warren Susman argues that the shift from a nineteenth-century producer society to a twentieth-century consumer society depended in large part on a shift from an understanding of the self in terms of 'character' to one framed in terms of 'personality'. The conception of the self as expression of 'character', he argues, set up self-sacrifice, in the name of 'duty, honour, [and] integrity', as a chief value. The new vision of the self as 'personality' required those hoping to succeed in the new regime 'to be unique, be distinctive, follow [their] own feelings, make [themselves] stand out from the crowd, and at the same time, appeal – by fascination, magnetism, attractiveness – to it' (1984: 280). The promulgation of this new conception of the self took place, Susman shows, not only through the advice manuals that form his main body of evidence, but also through representations in the mass media and the embodiment of 'personality' by media figures such as Douglas Fairbanks (p. 283).

My hypothesis is that the cultural producer is currently playing an important role in the production of significant refinements in the contemporary understanding of work and the working subject. This is taking place on two interrelated levels. First, with the ongoing expansion of communication channels of all kinds, the demand for cultural products has grown substantially and the number of producers and amount of production have followed suit, generating new forms of cultural labour, work opportunities, and spaces of positions. Second, at the same time, the amount of media devoted to the *representation* of cultural producers engaged in the work of cultural production has undergone a commensurate increase. This latter level is the focus here.

The growing accumulation and popularity of media concerning cultural production and producers can be understood to illustrate 'the central place of symbol creators in fantasies and beliefs about what "good work" might involve in modern capitalism' (Hesmondhalgh 2002: 71). Indeed, studies of job satisfaction and of perceived prestige in various occupations demonstrate that autonomy of the kind enjoyed by recognised and recognisable 'symbol creators' in a range of cultural industries is the most desirable and highly esteemed (Sennett 2006: 111–12; Foley and Polanyi

2006: 179). As Pierre-Michel Menger writes, '[a]rtistic careers ... seem to situate themselves at the top of the ladder of professions, in regard to almost each of the determinants which are traditionally considered in psycho-social studies of job satisfaction. ... Freedom to organise one's work,' he continues, 'isn't that, after all, the condition *par excellence* of authentic artistic accomplishment?' (2002: 52).

Of all the arenas of professional symbol creation susceptible to media narrativisation, however, popular music appears to be of most interest to producers and audiences. Books, movies, and television shows that focus explicitly on the labour processes and careers of music makers are all accumulating rapidly. There are several factors at work here. Popular music increasingly saturates social and media worlds; moreover, low barriers to entry render music making increasingly comprehensible to and practicable by growing publics. The apparent capacity of many music makers to resist alienation – their apparent achievement of significant degrees of self-actualisation, self-determination, personal authenticity and autonomy in their work – sets popular music making apart as an example of 'good work' to which, because of lowered barriers to entry, virtually anyone may aspire.

I have argued elsewhere that the top-rated US television show *American Idol* (Stahl 2004) operates aggressively in this connection. But where *American Idol*'s is a massive popular audience, and where it has engendered an institutionalised entertainment industry treadmill (with tens of thou-sands of aspirants showing up to audition for each season), contemporary rockumentary appeals to a more rarefied audience, often invoking an individualised, aspiring-elite subject in response to a more social network-centred (rather than institution-centred, as in the case of *American Idol*) career narrative. The subject of the rockumentary, in fact, may often be more properly understood as comprising both the musical act *and* the filmmaker, so important are they to each other and to the trajectories of professionalisation, upward mobility, innovation, and reputation they represent. Thus, at the same time that *American Idol* cultivates a reserve army of institutionally oriented proletarian peddlers of entertainment labour power on the absurdly remote promise of stratospheric stardom, media devoted to the workaday world of autonomous professional cultural producers engaged in extra- or quasi-institutional cultural production can be seen as appealing more rationally to the interests of those who them-selves are aiming a bit lower, for less institutionalised, more autonomous, *moderately* elite status (such as that enjoyed by the elite consultants studied by Barley and Kunda 2004).

Richard Sennett distinguishes between the positions of elite and mass workers in the new economy precisely along these lines. 'The new elite,' he writes, 'has less need of the ethic of delayed gratification, as thick networks provide contacts and a sense of belonging, no matter what firm or organisation one works for. The mass, however, has a thinner network of informal contact and support, and so remains more institution-dependent' (2006: 80). This 'new elite' can be recognised also in the population labour analyst Robert Reich once labelled 'symbolic analysts' but whom he now prefers to call 'creative workers', who, he argues, comprise the 'the highest paid 25 percent' of American workers (2001: 69). Rock music makers are 'creative workers' par excellence; it is on the basis of what they share and don't share with growing numbers of professionals that the social dimensions of rockumentary's contemporary proliferation (as, among other things, advice manuals) can best be understood.

Perhaps most significant for an understanding of rockumentary's role in the propagation of new cultural concepts of work and the working subject, then, is the notion that stories of music makers – as opposed to narratives of cultural production in other sectors – offer profoundly legible social scripts for the navigation of the new economy's upper quarter. In contrast, for example, to those of film or television production, popular music's production processes are increasingly familiar and easier to 'read' in terms of Manichean social relations, making rockumentary an ideal medium for the promulgation of new conceptions of work and the working subject. If it is imperative for neoliberalisation that workers at all strata increasingly understand themselves in the same terms as have artists for generations, and that firms look to the cultural industries for new models of flexible organisation, then stories of creative workers that simplify and highlight essentials of the social relations in the world of cultural production will be of great interest. In rockumentary the struggles between 'artist' and 'impresario', 'artist' and 'producer' or 'artist' and 'record label' are never thematically or rhetorically far from those between 'labour' and 'capital', 'worker' and 'manager', or 'resistance' and 'control'.

At the core of most stories of popular music making – fictional as well as non-fictional – is the problem of autonomy. Both fictional and non-fictional narratives tend to emphasise popular music performers' humble origins; they tend to imply, when they don't say outright, 'You can do it too!' to the viewer. (Much non-fiction hip-hop film, in fact, is explicitly 'how to' media.) Most important, however, virtually all of them employ a frame which implicitly or explicitly defines performers in opposition to businesspeople, a frame that Keir Keightley (2003) has traced to the rock 'n' roll movies of the 1950s and 1960s. This frame is crucially important. Keightley (2001: 131–41, 2003) denotes it with the term *authenticity*, a concept familiar to popular music scholars. Toynbee's work on the subject suggests that *cultural* concepts of authenticity in musical work have *political-economic* repercussions – it is the expectation of fans that artists express themselves in their own ways, on their own terms, that fortifies producer autonomy. According to Toynbee, 'popular music takes on a diminished commodity form just because people insist on an authentic relation to it. Such a discourse ... helps to push back industrial control over music activity' (2000: 6), thereby expanding musician autonomy in meaningful ways.

Also of consequence are three additional social aspects of the professional music-making occupation which will be explored further below. First, as Hirsch (1972) pointed out, entertainment industries depend on a steady stream of marginal innovation for continued profits. Second, for many music makers, autonomy is a by-product of the bargaining power that derives not just from fan expectations but also from being a monopoly supplier of what economists call 'imperfectly substitutable' talents for particular kinds of innovation. Third, copyright law preserves statutory authors from the kind of appropriation to which virtually all other working people are subject: authors own the product of their labour (Rose 1993; Fisk 2003: Ellerman 1992).[2]

Rockumentary typically concerns a particular kind of work relation in which the worker experiences, in combination, significant and real degrees of autonomy, self-actualisation, and de-alienating control over the process and produce of labour, an extremely privileged position for which, remarkably, no professional credential or inherited privilege is required, and to which, with profoundly democratic resonance, almost anyone can reasonably aspire. In section II I will argue that, in its presentation of the quotidian lives of rock musicians, contemporary rockumentary – here represented by 2004's *Dig!* – proposes a model of professional work that promises to foster autonomy, self-actualisation and de-alienation in the contemporary political economy. In section III I will contrast what the film purports to say about how to live and work with my own analysis of the film, against the backdrop of a recent analysis of the anticipatory role of the artist in the new economy.

II

In the early 1990s, just out of college, filmmaker Ondi Timoner moved to Los Angeles to make her way into the film industry, bringing with her a documentary about a woman in a Connecticut prison she'd made while a film student at Yale. Her hope was to shop her student film for production as a full-length feature, but all she found were industry sharks offering Faustian bargains. Reflecting on these encounters, Timoner, also an amateur musician, conceived a project that would focus on indie rock music in order analogically and allegorically to explore, she said, 'what happens when art and industry meet' (McConvey 2004). During a mid-1990s trip to San Francisco she was introduced to Anton Newcombe, the songwriter and lead singer of the Brian Jonestown Massacre. He, in turn, introduced her to his favourite band, the Dandy Warhols, of Portland, Oregon. Both bands agreed to let her film them. On and off, over the course of seven years, she, her brother, and her husband (partners in her Interloper Films) shot some 2,000 hours of film from which *Dig!* was produced. *Dig!* premiered at the

Sundance film festival, where it garnered a top prize and set Timoner apart as an up-and-coming young director.

Dig! concerns the diverging fortunes of the two bands, whom we encounter at the start of the film as friends and socio-musical equals. (The Dandy Warhols had just signed to a major label, and it appears that the Brian Jonestown Massacre is close behind.) Their trajectories split as Newcombe's unpredictable temper causes the Brian Jonestown Massacre to miss crucial opportunities, and as the Dandy Warhols find success and rock stardom in Europe, largely as the result of a European cellphone company's choice of one of their songs for use in a television commercial. Toward the end of the film, Newcombe begins stalking the Dandys, who seem less and less inclined to indulge him in a Beatles/Stones or Oasis/Blur-style rivalry, friendly or otherwise. The last scenes of the film feature the Dandy Warhols cannily spending their video budget on building a multi-purpose performance/recording space for their own use and to rent, and Newcombe being hauled away in a police car following an attack on an audience member at an LA gig.

Many of the recent crop of rockumentaries from which I have selected *Dig!* depend to a great extent for their claims of 'representing reality' (Nichols 1991) on extensive use of filmmaking techniques first pioneered under the banner of 'direct cinema' – the name chosen by its founders for a late 1950s/early 1960s documentary movement, most often referred to as 'American *cinema verité*'. It was precisely these filmmakers – Albert and David Maysles, Donn A. Pennebaker, and Richard Leacock – who produced several of the first major US rock documentaries, including the Maysles' *The Beatles' First US Visit* (1964) and *Gimme Shelter* (1970), and Pennebaker's *Dont Look Back* (sic) (1967), and *Monterey Pop* (1969). Citing the statements of these collaborators, Allen and Gomery argue that direct cinema was essentially a liberal-democratic, reformist medium. According to Leacock, he and Pennebaker and the Maysles brothers formulated an approach that 'presented you with data to try to figure out what the hell was really going on', letting self-evident 'facts' 'speak for themselves' (Allen and Gomery 1985: 233). To this end, recalled Leacock, they subjected themselves 'to a rather rigid set of rules. If we missed something, never ask anyone to repeat it. Never ask any questions. Never interview' (Levin 1971: 196). The conviction held by these filmmakers that the 'truth' of a given situation could be discovered and recorded by a sensitive camera-wielding observer reveals the basic assumption behind direct cinema's reformism: presented with 'factual' representations of the world, viewers could and would make rational judgements and participate in public life on that basis. Indeed, documentary scholar Bill Nichols argues that documentary constitutes arguments about the world that call on us to respond affirmatively. The 'voice of the documentary,' he writes, 'is a proposition about how the world is – what exists within it, what our relations to these things are, what alternatives there might be – that invites consent' (1991: 140); the latter is given as we incorporate documentary's truths into our stances toward the social world.

While Timoner did not rigorously follow the rules developed by these filmmakers, *Dig!* shares their reformist bent. In the film, for example, Timoner employs the form's conventional critical-journalistic stance toward social institutions. The film clandestinely pursues its subjects into conversations and dealings with music industry executives, exposing, as did the American *verité* pioneers, private spaces and private dealings. Timoner repeatedly makes it plain that she understands herself to be working in this tradition. In a panel discussion on rockumentary at the London Film Festival, for example, Timoner invokes the footage-to-finished film ratio of *Dig!* as characteristic of film: 'We were around so much and there's nearly 2,000 hours of footage, so it's true *verité*, you know?' (London Film Festival 2004).

American *verité* of the 1960s focused to a great degree on cultural workers; contemporary rockumentary hews closely to that model, telling stories about institutions, labour processes and careers in the popular music industry. Taken as a genre, contemporary rockumentary is a form of documentary that focuses on the subjective experience of a particular form of work in and at the margins of contemporary capitalist cultural industries.[3] Timoner set out to make a film that would throw into relief creators' struggles over authenticity and autonomy at the boundary of the recording industry. Her statement that with this film she hoped to 'inspire other people to explore their own creativity and their hearts, to see if they are following their lives right' (Bunbury 2005) suggests the degree to which modes of organisation and concepts of work and the working self rooted in the cultural industries and the experiences of creative workers can be understood popularly to be quite relevant to a much broader range of working people.

Timoner's conviction with respect to inspiring people with her microscopic examination of these two west-coast bands is especially appropriate in the context of contemporary rockumentary. Keightley argues that rock in the post-1960s and 1970s era has undergone a process of 'miniaturisation'. 'Rock,' Keightley writes 'no longer occupies the centre of popular music, no longer commands the singular attention and respect it once did ... the scale of its ambitions and audiences [has been] reduced' (2001: 140). Contemporary rockumentary participates in this miniaturisation. The epic concert films of Pennebaker and the Maysles brothers, as well as their more intimate portrayals of Dylan and the Beatles, on the other hand, participated in spectacularisation and myth-making. The empiricist ethos of American *verité* presented the heroic status of the Beatles, the Rolling Stones, Bob Dylan, and others tautologically. Rock's miniaturisation has taken place alongside what Nichols (1991: 56) calls an increase in 'reflexivity' in documentary practice, a retreat from American *verité*'s conceit of 'unmediated' presentation of 'the facts' towards a greater acknowledgement of interaction between subjects and filmmaker(s), a more conscious consideration of the role of the filmmaker in shaping the proceedings, as well as a more critical consideration of the ethics of representation.[4] The evolution of the rockumentary in this context is unmistakable: what is most of interest to audiences, it assumes, is an exhaustive, often maudlin, rumination on intimate details of the working and personal lives of musicians, in the often manifest presence of sympathetic participant-observer.

A striking example of the miniaturisation of the rockumentary gaze is Sinofsky and Berlinger's 2004 film *Metallica: Some Kind of Monster* (made in fact by two filmmakers who had apprenticed to Albert Maysles for a combined total of twenty years) in which the thrash metal band is depicted spending months in meetings with a therapist. Together, group and therapist work through the communication and personality conflicts that, while they once yielded productive tension, had begun to hinder the group's productivity. According to Jason Newstead, former Metallica bassist, the group began having trouble writing their next album around the time filming began. As interpersonal difficulties began to hinder the creative (or 'innovation') process, he recalled, 'the managers suggested that we have a psychotherapist come in, a man that meets with pro ball teams, big-ego, big-dollar guys that can't get along but have to make some kind of entity flow, so everybody else can make the money' (Sinofsky and Berlinger 2004).

This concern with productivity deepens the complexity of the rocku-mentary's presentation of the self-actualising, de-alienating fantasy of rock and the 'good work' fantasy of creative work and returns us to a point to which I alluded earlier, that is, the composite nature of the subject of the rockumentary. The rockumentary subject increasingly comprises both the filmmaker and the band/musician; considering both aspects of this com-posite will bring into relief the ways in which rockumentary rhetoric and pedagogy operate with respect to professional work in the new economy.

In incorporating many of the elements of post-*verité* documentary that Nichols characterises as reflexive, *Dig!* can be understood to be as much 'about' the filmmaker as it is 'about' the two subject bands. The film concerns the fortunes not of two groups of cultural producers but of three. All three come together in the mid-1990s under the auspices of a relatively dense constellation of shared cultural dimensions of habitus: 1960s music and fashion, youthful urban misbehaviour, 'resistant' indie cultural production. The divergence that takes place is not, as is suggested by the film's reviews, between two bands over different attitudes towards the music business. It is, rather, between two groups of cultural producers drawn to homologous forms of indie cultural production but characterised by non-overlapping orientations, expectations, and resources, beyond their shared interests. A common value of 'hold[ing] on to their integrity in the face of commodifying their art' (Timoner 2004) may have suffused their initial moments of cultural camaraderie, but these two groups – Newcombe and his bandmates on the one side, and the Dandy Warhols and Timoner on the other – put these cultural signifiers and practices to work in different ways and to different purposes.

In many places in the film and its special features, Dandy Warhols leader Courtney Taylor and Ondi Timoner assert that Taylor and the Dandy Warhols provide Newcombe with a 'foil' of commercial success against which the latter could understand himself as musically and ethically pure. More can be learned from this film by reversing that framework. Without reducing the tangle of issues here either to purely psychological or to purely sociological arguments, I suggest that Newcombe's apparent madness provides the Dandys with an irrational Other whose flagrant self-sacrifice on the altar of authenticity reciprocally makes plain the soundness and reasonableness of the Dandys' moderate approach, and allows Timoner to avoid dealing with the possibly thornier problem of trying to reconcile her initial critical and conventional *verité* stance with a less dramatically exciting but perhaps more narratively and ethically challenging story of *successful* rather than *failed, frustrated, ill starred* or *self-sabotaged* collaboration with capital. This makes possible the presentation of a pedagogical, even disciplinary, model orientation to work and the economy that subtly reinforces the ties between authenticity-inflected cultural production and neoliberal/entrepreneurial subject positions.

Timoner befriends both bands and films them relaxing, fighting, playing gigs, on tour and dealing with businesspeople. She practically becomes a band member herself, wielding her camera on-stage, sharing drugs at band parties. Trajectories diverge as Newcombe's volatile, occasionally violent, character becomes more and more of a problem for the Brian Jonestown Massacre and the filmmaker and as the Dandy Warhols' self-proclaimed status as 'the most well adjusted band in America' adds to the rapidly deepening contrast between the two bands. The theme begins to shift markedly from 'what happens when art and industry meet' to 'what happens when an artist with a personality disorder fixates on a particularly rigid construction of authenticity, alienates friends and collaborators and destroys business relationships'. Newcombe is increasingly the focus of dramatic amateur psychological analysis, colourful diagnosis, and pseudo-clinical portraiture, while Taylor and the Dandy Warhols are, in comparison, normalised and flattened with respect to their own origins, personal lives, and career and social trajectories.

For an example, let us look at how Newcombe's drug use is portrayed in contrast to that of the Dandys and the filmmakers. According to Nina Ritter, one of the A&R reps who appears in the film as an authority on music and the music industry, 'You walk[ed] into [Newcombe's home studio] and it just felt like death was everywhere. It was just a smack-house. It was reeking of death.' According to Timoner, 'Anton cultivates a certain edge, he denies a home, he denies self-comforts, he self-medicates, he denies himself psychotropic drugs which may help him stabilise because he cultivates and maintains that edge' (Timoner 2004). Newcombe's drug use is pathologised.

The Dandys' drug use, conversely, is a subject of wonder and admiration for the filmmakers. Early in the film we are introduced to Zia McCabe, the Dandy Warhols' keyboardist, as she is driving the filmmakers around during an interview. Voiced-over commentary of David and Ondi Timoner provided in the *Dig!* DVD special features accompanies this moment:

Ondi Timoner.	We were crashing with Zia...
David Timoner.	Yeah.
Ondi. ...	who was cutting up various drugs for us in the evening.
David (chuckles).	But they were the most functional people who also cut up drugs, it was really together.
Ondi.	It was incredible, yeah, like, warm breakfast in the morning but ecstasy at night, you know?

(Timoner 2004)

This admiration betrays a shared productivist orientation between Timoner and the Dandys that acts not (or not simply) as a *moderator* of excess but rather as a *component* of excess. There is an undercurrent throughout this film that suggests that there is *destructive* rock excess and there is *productive* rock excess; the excess of Newcombe and his bandmates is contrasted to that of the Dandy Warhols and their new documentarist friends. In the contemporary political economy, the former derails and disturbs, the latter aligns and smoothes the way. Destructive excess is pathological, a failing strategy. Productive excess, *Dig!* suggests, plays an important role in forming the kinds of professional networks that are crucial for the success and upward mobility of promising young cultural producers and, increasingly, aspirants in a range of fields (Sennett 2006: 80; Reich 2001: 142). The Brian Jonestown Massacre is portrayed as a doomed 'heroin band', wantonly destroying support systems and resources; the Dandy Warhols, argued by one critic to exemplify 'generation Y industriousness' (Sinagra 2004: 60), are a turbo-charged 'ecstasy band', productively cementing friendships and expanding networks, in part through intense 'partying'.

The film's shift toward the pathologisation of Newcomb forestalls questions that are more pertinent with regard to the interests of aspiring or upwardly mobile 'creative workers' concerning the disavowed but hoped-for outcome: 'what is happening when art and industry meet *and get along really well'*. What is going on when self-actualisation, de-alienation, resistance, authenticity, and so on – including, in this case, sex and drugs and rock and roll – slot happily into industrial structures? The shift away from an account of adjustment and profit toward one of pathology and dissolution happens, I believe, for two reasons. First, Newcombe's behaviour and pronouncements *do* make extremely compelling cinema. The second reason, of interest here, is that poring over the struggles of music makers while eschewing the political economic nitty-gritty of their social practices and relations allows documentarists to make apparently instructive, even critical, films that elide the ways in which the 'good work' of cultural production reproduces aspects of the 'bad work' to which it is contrasted, that support widespread perceptions of creative work as somehow essentially exceptional to the run of work in capitalism.[5]

III

Pierre-Michel Menger, in his *Portrait de l'artiste en travailleur : métamorphoses du capitalisme*, argues that:

> [f]ar from the romantic, contentious or subversive portrayals of the artist, from now on the creator must be seen as a model figure of the new worker, a figure through which are seen transformations as decisive as the break-up of the salaried world, the growth of autonomous professionals, the magnitude and undercurrents of contemporary disparities, [and] the individualization of work relationships.
>
> (2002: 8)

Dig! and its genre-mates have a curious relationship with the dynamic Menger explains. If Timoner's statements, as well as those of reviewers of her film (but also the pronouncements of Sinofsky and Berlinger and reviewers of *Metallica*), are to be taken at face value, documentary explorations of the worlds of rock musicians have much to offer average viewers with respect to 'following their lives right'. But beyond the focus on Newcombe, what answers does the film actually offer?

Dig! teaches that creative workers' excessive commitment to authenticity and autonomy is a failing – indeed, insane – position, but it avoids laying out how *exactly* – with a moderate, negotiated commitment to authenticity and autonomy – success *can* be achieved. Timoner and the bands expressed an initial commitment to autonomy and authenticity. The Dandys and Timoner accustomed themselves to the negotiations required by capital as they established themselves as promising (i.e. profitable, worthy of investment) players in the Los Angeles entertainment scene, construing that success as having been achieved 'on their own terms'. Both entities ally in framing the Brian Jonestown Massacre's failure, and not the mechanics of their success, as the topic of the film. Let us turn to Menger's analysis to help elucidate the nature and conditions of the Dandys' and Timoner's success in the context of the cultural constellation of which *Dig!* forms the heart.

Recall Hirsch's seminal (1972) argument about the cultural industries' need for continuous marginal innovation. Lately, Hirsch (2000),

Reich (2001), Menger (2002), as well as analysts in other fields have stressed the expanding importance of innovation across industrial and service sectors. Artists are widely understood by definition to be innovators, and in that capacity (as well as many others, as Menger points out) can be usefully understood as new model workers, particularly of Reich's 'creative' sort. Menger argues that one way of understanding the manner in which workers are increasingly interpellated by employers hoping to enjoy the benefits of creative worker innovation in the context of cultural industry-style flexibility is to conceive of a dual process of segmentation on perpendicular axes. On one axis segmentation occurs horizontally; each person is separated from his or her neighbours as, for example, a bearer of a unique set of 'competences'. On the other axis the segmentation is vertical; each person is subject to incremental rankings of quality and value.

Both segmentation processes have long been exemplified in the relations of creative production; when applied as a model to work in general, however, they produce a devastating combination. The first, horizontal, is commonly understood among analysts of the cultural industries as having to do with 'product differentiation'. In the broader work world, it can be understood as the individualisation of work, skill sets, and career trajectories such that, for example, solidarity seems counterproductive. It is with vertical segmentation, however, that horizontal segmentation reveals the potentially perilous depths of its promise. '[O]n the ocean of this infinite differentiation of work and talent,' writes Menger, 'comparisons operate indefinitely to evaluate, rank, sort, orient preferences' (p. 31). It is on this vertical axis, where minute distinctions in quality become magnified to form increasingly unbridgeable gaps, that *Dig!* indicates (albeit through a glass darkly) some of the processes at work.

There are many problematic dynamics that accompany the exportation of forms of ranking characteristic of the world of artistic production to the general world of work that *Dig!* obliquely communicates. Menger argues that one of the exported mechanisms through which disparities are magnified is what he calls the 'matching up' of talents at similar levels:

> The talented are matched among themselves within projects or within organizations that expect to draw advantages from the grouping of those who within each one's specialty belong to groups of equivalent reputation, in order to increase the productivity of the competencies of each member of the team and to increase the chances of success and profit.
>
> (p. 44)

What we don't see taking place *between* scenes shot over the course of seven years is the process of professionalisation Timoner and her partners are undergoing as they develop their business. *Dig!* did not just come out of nowhere to win a prize at Sundance; for years Interloper Films had been producing commercials, music videos, and other work for a range of clients. Timoner explains to *American Cinematographer* that the film's use of multiple formats (Super-8 to 16 mm to 35 mm, with very different associated costs) reflected the increasing success of the Dandy Warhols (Pizello 2004: 28). This it no doubt did, but at the same time it reflects the changing fortunes of this young filmmaker and her crew.

Perhaps more tellingly, this match-up appears to have evolved 'organically', 'naturally', as the two groups of producers increasingly accepted each other as professional equals on related, indeed linked, trajectories. It is, in part, the mechanics of this match-up that are obscured as the narrative centres more and more on the Brian Jonestown Massacre's dissolution and shies away from a more reflexive consideration (more consonant with contemporary trends in documentary, that is) of the Dandys' and Timoner's own professional trajectories. Despite this skewed focus, however, Timoner understands herself to have produced a film that will help people 'follow their lives right'. Surely she's not suggesting that a drug and alcohol-fuelled descent into mental illness and isolation is the answer, but that is the focus of three-quarters of the film. If you want *actually* to learn something about how following your creativity and your heart can bring material success according to *Dig!*'s underlying doctrine, however, learn to think like the risk-embracing, productivity-maximising cultural entrepreneurs obscured by the smokescreen of Newcombe's crash-and-burn (see also Reich 2001 and Sennett 2006).

IV

In the worlds of art and cultural production, autonomy and risk have long been two sides of the same coin, acceptable to creative workers as a dual reality because of the kinds of monetary and non-monetary rewards on offer. Contemporary rockumentary narrates the trajectories of entrants in the fields of popular music, promulgating cultural concepts of work and the working subject as essentially autonomous. *Dig!*, *Metallica*, and other films offer social scripts for the adaptation of 'manner[s] of life', to use Weber's (1958: 72) phrase, in accordance with the proliferation of autonomy as a desideratum in the organisation of work and as ascendant aspect of the working subject. The risk embraced by rockers is framed as chosen voluntarily, it is part of the package of possible outcomes of which some – stardom, for example – appear extraordinarily desirable.

The combination of autonomy and risk embraced by artistic workers, however, is quite different from that increasingly imposed on workers in other sectors. Autonomy was once associated with the choice of whether or not to enter into employment: a choice made possible for many people, prior to the emergence of fully fledged capitalism and the consumer society, through their access to alternative means of self-provisioning (i.e., productive property, from vegetable gardens and access to common land, to rent and profit-producing capital enterprises) (Perelman 2000). Most people in the modern Anglo-American world do not have access to the sort of productive property on which such autonomy could be based. However, a new kind of worker autonomy is of increasing value to capital (Barley and Kunda 1992; Kraft 1999; Honneth 2004; Stahl 2006), useful in eliciting consent and legitimating the redistribution of corporate risk while the corporation itself maintains possession of the material means of making a living. In this context the increasing autonomy of work at the cutting edge is coupled with increasing risk of vulnerability to exploitation and social exclusion (Beck 2000). Following Marx, most working people – no matter how innovative, no matter how autonomous – still have nothing to sell but their skins.

The same is not true for those popular music makers who can claim the mantle of authorship: they are the recognisable owners of potentially productive property in the form of their songs and performances. Their autonomous work in the context of risk characteristic of art worlds is thus not analogous to that of the preferred new worker. The autonomous work of rock 'n' roll *authors*, while it may not produce immediate income, does produce unique intellectual properties. These properties constitute a potential basis for entry into the class of *rentiers*, those who make money from property and investment.[6]

Thus *Dig!*'s bait-and-switch: first the bait, consisting in the lure of real autonomy, the making of rock music presented as an ideal form of work; then the switch, that is to say, the substitution of a form of autonomy which is the obverse of that represented in the contemporary rockumentary's typical career narrative. What for musicians and cultural producers is the challenging and fulfilling experience of creativity for other workers turns out to be the exhausting demonstration of continual innovation and value-adding. Hence the flip side of original, unique self-expression is consequential individualisation, horizontal segmentation and vertical ranking – 'flexibility' as consignment to radical insecurity.

Notes

The author wishes to thank Jane Stahl, Jason Toynbee, David Hesmondhalgh, Keir Keightley, Heide Solbrig, Sophia Snow, Michael Mascuch, and Will Straw for their assistance.

1 E.g. Keightley (personal communication 2007); Lash and Urry (1994: 123); Hirsch (2000); Lampel *et al.* (2000).
2 The proprietary nature of authorship is a base assumption of this chapter. Let me clarify here that, while many music makers grant exclusive licence of their works to record companies – ceding virtually all rights – in US law that period is limited to thirty-five years, after which an author – no matter what the licensing contract says – may exercise an inalienable right to a 'second bite at the apple' through the right of 'termination of transfers' (Hull 2005: 301).

3 Other examples of contemporary rockumentary include: *I Am Trying to Break Your Heart* (featuring the band Wilco, 2002), *End of the Century* (Ramones, 2004), *Meeting People is Easy* (Radiohead, 1999), *Drive Well, Sleep Carefully* (Death Cab for Cutie, 2004), Shane McGowan: *If I should Fall from Grace* (2003), *The Flaming Lips, the Fearless Freaks* (2005), *Strong Enough to Break* (Hanson, 2006), *Shut Up and Sing* (the Dixie Chicks, 2006). The list lengthens constantly.

4 While my analysis touches on ethical issues in documentary representation, this is not my analytical perspective here. For a trenchant consideration of these issues see Coles (1997).

5 This mode of filmmaking would also appear to suit contemporary rock musicians because it satisfies on the one hand a need to maintain closer relations to the smaller audiences characteristic in an era of miniaturised careers, and on the other a desire to show how adept rock musicians are at remaining 'authentic' and autonomous in the face of sweeping political-economic change.

6 In Grant Gee's *Meeting People is Easy* (1999) a member of Radiohead remarks that they 'are coming up with bands now that own hotels and, you know ... have investment companies and more businesses. There's this documentary done recently about Pink Floyd, and when it was shown to Pink Floyd they refused to have it released because it basically showed them going in and out of business meetings and boardrooms and discussing moving money around.'

Bibliography

Allen, R. C. and Gomery. D. (1985) *Film History: Theory and Practice*. New York: Knopf.

Barley, S. R. and Kunda G. (1992) 'Design and devotion: surges of rational and normative ideologies of control in managerial discourse', *Administrative Science Quarterly* 37: 363–99.

Barley, S. R. and Kunda, G. (1992/2004) *Gurus, Hired Guns, and Warm Bodies: Itinerant Experts in a Knowlege Economy*. Princeton NJ: Princeton University Press.

Beck, U. (2000) *Brave New World of Work*. Malden MA: Polity Press.

Biernacki, R. (1995) *The Fabrication of Labor: Germany and Britain, 1640–1914*. Berkeley CA: University of California Press.

Boltanski, L. and Chiapello E. (2005) *The New Spirit of Capitalism*, trans. Gregory Elliot. New York: Verso.

Bunbury, S. (2005) 'Rock gone wild', *The Age*, 10 April, http://www.theage.com.au/news/Film/Rock-gone-wild/2005/04/07/1112815672469.html (accessed 2/05/06).

Coles, R. (1997) *Doing Documentary Work*. New York: Oxford University Press.

Ellerman, D. P. (1992) *Property and Contract in Economics: the case for Economic Democracy*. Cambridge MA: Blackwell.

Fisk, C. (2003) 'Authors at work: the origins of the work-for-hire doctrine', *Yale Journal of Law and the Humanities* 15 (1): 1–70.

Foley, J. and Polanyi, M. (2006) 'Workplace democracy: why bother?' *Economic and Industrial Democracy* 27 (1): 173–91.

Hesmondhalgh, D. (2002) *The Cultural Industries*. London: Sage.

Hirsch, P. (1972) 'Processing fads and fashions: an organization-set analysis of cultural industry systems', *American Journal of Sociology* 77: 639–59.

Hirsch, P. (2000) 'Cultural industries revisited', *Organization Science* 11 (3): 356–63.

Honneth, A. (2004) 'Organized self-realization: some paradoxes of individualization', *European Journal of Social Theory* 7 (4): 463–78.

Hull, G. (2005) 'Termination rights and the *real* songwriters', *Vanderbilt Journal of Entertainment Law and Practice* 7 (2): 301–21.

Keightley, K. (2001) 'Reconsidering rock', in S. Frith, W. Straw and J. Street (eds) *The Cambridge Companion to Pop and Rock*. New York: Cambridge University Press.

Keightley, K. (2003) 'Manufacturing authenticity: imagining the music industry in Anglo-American cinema, 1956–1962', in K. Dickinson (ed.) *Movie Music, the Film Reader*. New York: Routledge.

Kraft, P. (1999) 'To control and inspire: US management in the Age of Computer Information Systems and Global Production', in Mark L. Wardell, Thomas L. Steiger and Peter Meiksins (eds) *Rethinking the Labour Process*. New York: SUNY Press.

Lampel, J., Lant, T. and Shamsie, J. (2000) 'Balancing act: learning from organizing practices in cultural industries', *Organization Science* 11 (3): 263–9.

Lash, S. and Urry, J. (1994) *Economies of Signs and Space*. London: Sage.

Levin, G. R. (1971) *Documentary Explorations: Fifteen Interviews with Film Makers*. Garden City NY: Doubleday.

London Film Festival (2004) 'Rockumentary debate live online', http://www.lff.org.uk/news_details.php?NewsID=39 (accessed 2 June 2006).

Macpherson, C. B. (1962) *The Political Theory of Possessive Individualism: Hobbes to Locke*. Oxford: Clarendon Press.

McConvey, J. (2004) 'The good, the band, and the ugly', http://www.eyeweekly.com/eye/issue/issue_10.07.04/film/dig.php (accessed 2 June 2006).

Menger, P-M. (2002) *Portrait de l'artiste en travailleur: métamorphoses du capitalisme*. Paris: Éditions du Seuil et la République des Idées (trans. Jane Stahl).

Nichols, B. (1991) *Representing Reality: Issues and Concepts in Documentary*. Bloomington IN: Indiana University Press.

Perelman, M. (2000) *The Invention of Capitalism: Classical Political Economy and the Secret History of Primitive Accumulation*. Durham NC: Duke University Press.

Pizello, C. (2004) 'Production slate: sex fiends and rock 'n' roll rivals: battle of the bands', *American Cinematographer* 85 (10): 26, 28–30.

Read, J. (2003) *The Micro-politics of Capital: Marx and the Prehistory of the Present*. Albany NY: SUNY Press.

Reich, R. (2001) *The Future of Success*. New York: Knopf.

Rose, M. (1993) *Authors and Owners: the Invention of Copyright*. Cambridge MA: Harvard University Press.

Sennett, R. (1998) *The Corrosion of Character: the Personal Consequences of Work in the New Capitalism*. New York: Norton.

Sennett, R. (2006) *The Culture of the New Capitalism*. New Haven CT: Yale University Press.

Sinagra, L. (2004) 'Almost famous: two indie bands struggle to survive the industry and each other', *Village Voice* (New York NY), Tuesday 5 October 2004, p. 60.

Sinofsky, B. and Berlinger, J. (2004) *Metallica: Some Kind of Monster*. Yorktown Heights NY: Third Eye Motion Picture Company.

Stahl, M. (2004) ' "A moment like this": *American Idol* and narratives of meritocracy', in Chris Washburne and Maiken Derno (eds) *Bad Music: the Music we Love to Hate*. New York: Routledge.

Stahl, M. (2006) 'Non-proprietary authorship and the uses of autonomy: artistic labor in American film animation, 1900–2004', *Labor: Studies in Working Class History of the Americas* 2 (4): 87–105.

Susman, W. (1984) *Culture as History: the Transformation of American Society in the Twentieth Century*. New York: Pantheon.

Timoner, O. (2004) *Dig!* Los Angeles: Interloper Films.

Toynbee, J. (2000) *Making Popular Music: Musicians, Creativity and Institutions*. London: Arnold.

Weber, M. (1958) *The Protestant Ethic and the Spirit of Capitalism*, trans. Talcott Parsons. New York: Scribner.

15 Journalism

Expertise, authority, and power in democratic life

Christopher Anderson

American journalism, it is safe to say, enters the twenty-first century beset on all sides. Journalists' tenuous role as experts in determining 'all the news that's fit to print' is under fire. At the same time, bloggers, online journalists, and other ordinary citizens and writers are attacking the very idea that there is any sort of journalistic expertise at all. As the editors note in the winter 2005 issue of *Neiman Reports*, 'with the arrival of the internet, the ability of non-journalists to publish their words and link them with those of other like-minded scribes has forever altered the balance of power between those who control the means to publish and those who believe they have something important to say' (*Neiman Reports* 2005). Empowered by new digital technologies, and emboldened by the internet, the very idea that there might be an occupational monopoly on 'telling the news' seems, to many observers, dubious at best.

I would argue that many of these debates regarding the occupational identity and public relevance of the journalism profession – Are bloggers journalists? Do online journalists practise traditional forms of journalism? If not, what are the key differences between older and new journalistic practices? (*Neiman Reports* 2003, 2005) – can be helpfully reframed as a series of questions regarding *journalistic expertise*. Within various academic disciplines there has been a growing interest in questions of expertise, an interest building upon, though not entirely displacing, earlier scholarship in the sociologies of knowledge, the professions, and discourse analysis (Eyal 2002). Additionally, a growing scholarly debate seeks to analyse a normative relationship between expertise and democracy (Dzur 2004; Collins and Evans 2002). Applying this perspective to journalism, then, we might wonder: does journalistic expertise exist? If so, what is it? Who has it and where is it found? Why is journalistic expertise, along with other systems of expertise, under such concerted assault today, and what are the consequences of this assault for the normative values of democracy, public life, and social justice?

To date, very little has been written about the problem of journalistic expertise in either the communications or sociological literature. While quantitative literature overviews can often obscure as much as they reveal, in this particular case, the discrepancy is large enough to be telling: a search of the Web of Science journal archive for articles on 'scientific expertise' uncovers 120 articles, while a similar search for 'journalistic expertise' finds none. The difference is even more stark if we utilise Google Scholar: 7,240 entries on scientific expertise can be compared to fifty-five on journalism. The situation is similar to the one discussed by Ekstrom in his overview of the epistemology of television news; although 'journalism, in its various forms, is clearly among the most influential knowledge-producing institutions of our time ... [it] has not received much attention within the sociology of knowledge. Studies focusing on scientific institutions are considerably more common' (Ekstrom 2002: 259).

Despite this comparative neglect there have been a number of studies, many of them written under the broad rubric of the sociology of culture, that have analysed journalism as a profession, a form of 'sacred knowledge', and a discursive practice. If one of the major foundations of the sociology of expertise is its attempt to synthesise these various fields – the sociology of the professions, the sociology of knowledge, and more Foucauldian, discursive perspectives, all of which have contributed to the academic study of journalism – than it would seem possible to piece together an analysis of journalistic expertise by constructing a similar scaffold. One of the primary goals of this chapter, then, is to 'stock my analytical toolbox', both with the aim of developing a larger metatheory of journalistic expertise, and with the hope of clearing a path for future research on the institutions and practices of twenty-first-century journalism.

This chapter begins with an overview of three major threads of journalism scholarship, beginning with the critical studies of the 1970s and early 1980s, continuing through the greater emphasis on culture and discursive construction in the early 1990s, and finishing with an overview of current 'field approaches' to journalism research. All three of these approaches have, in different ways, investigated the relationship between journalistic objectivity, professionalism, discourse, and expertise. The section after next more explicitly poses the question of journalistic expertise and draws the three research perspectives already outlined into a discussion around this central problematic. The final section briefly revisits the normative question posed above – why is journalistic expertise, along with other systems of expertise, under such concerted assault today? – drawing on the proposed framework in order to sketch out a response.

Three strands of journalism studies: professions, discourse, and fields

This chapter, then, has both a theoretical and a practical focus. I use one strand of social theory – the sociologies of the professions and knowledge, along with various theories of cultural authority – to understand how technological developments are challenging our understanding of what journalism is and how it operates. In the pages that follow I dissect *journalistic authority*, i.e., the power possessed by journalists and journalistic organisations that allows them to present their interpretations of reality as accurate, truthful, and of political importance. By 'authority' I refer to a cultural form of power, that is, to a form of domination considered largely *legitimate* by those who both exercise and are subject to it (Starr 1984). The source of this journalistic authority primarily stems from the expert position of journalists and journalistic organisations within what Bourdieu has called 'the field of cultural production'. In most advanced capitalist democracies journalists positions are due in large part to the outcome of an occupational struggle that sociologists have labelled the professional project. Occupations engaged in the professional project struggle to gain and maintain a legitimate jurisdiction over certain discursively, culturally, and epistemologically constructed forms of expertise. By analysing the position of various social actors within the journalistic field, the professional struggles between them, and the construction of various forms of journalistic expertise, I believe we can gain a deeper insight into the maintenance of, and challenges to, journalistic authority.

Each of the strands of journalism studies I discuss below addresses some, though not all, of these multiple components of journalistic authority. Therefore, an overview and synthesis is in order.

The first strand of journalism studies: organisational analysis, objectivity, and the professions

Journalism is an institution and social practice that proudly claims to possess special insight into the shape and meaning of the endless torrent of events that constitute our lived universe. The first research thread analysing journalistic knowledge in this sense – as a process by which knowledge about the outside world is produced – crested in the late 1970s, part of broader critical (and largely non-Marxist) tendencies within journalism scholarship. Research in this vein began with Epstein's analysis of television news (1973), continued on through Carey's overview of journalism's 'whiggish history' (1974), and culminated with Tuchman's description of journalistic objectivity as a strategic ritual (1978); Gans's detailed analysis of the daily processes by which news decisions were made (2004); Schudson's social history of nineteenth-century newspapers (1978); and Gitlin's critique of the process by which the national media shaped the image and social behaviour of the 'new left' (1980). The major development in journalism scholarship in the 1970s can be seen as the deconstruction of the idealised image of the journalist that saw him or her as the transparent relay of external events. Indeed, contrary to the usual tendency of scholars to locate this clutch of analysis in different communications 'sub-disciplines', I argue that they would be better analysed together, united as they are in their sceptical attitude toward the epistemologies of journalism and their desire to link these knowledge-producing practices to broader professional systems. In this context I follow Ekstrom's definition of epistemology, looking at it 'not as a philosophical inquiry into the nature of true knowledge but to the study of knowledge producing practices and the communication of knowledge claims' (Ekstrom 2002: 259).

Breathing the same constructivist air that would produce, around the same time, a similar critique of science and the scientific establishment (Feyerabend 1975; Collins 1975), these critical sociologists directed their attack at a target far more helpless and exposed than the natural sciences. Benson has convincingly pointed to the indebtedness of many of these scholars to the work of Goffman, Garfinkel, and Alfred Schutz (Benson 1999); and Tuchman herself writes, in a chapter entitled 'News as a constructed reality', that 'news work transforms everyday occurrences into news events ... all of [my] concepts stress that men and women actively construct social meanings' (Tuchman 1978: 184). Although Gans's theoretical position is less constructionist than Tuchman's, his detailed study of the way story selection is 'centered on the unwritten rules journalists apply ... and the roles that information sources, audiences, and people who exert pressure to censor news play in the total process' (Gans 2004: 73) can be seen as an in-depth analysis of a process of symbolic goods production which inevitably selects, omits, and ignores various aspects of reality. Schudson and Carey, by calling the 'natural history' of objectivity into question, challenge the idea of journalistic transparency on a broader historical level, and Gitlin, in his explicit discussion of the skewed manner in which the national media framed the New Left, produced a model of content analysis which has come into common use among media scholars and activists alike. Of course, apart from Tuchman, these authors may have not seen the epistemological critique of journalism as their main goal; Gitlin in particular has expressed his view that *The Whole World is Watching* is primarily 'not a book about how the media distorted the reputation of a social movement, but rather a book about the *dance* between the media and the movement, about a *complicated relationship* of mutual dependence and about a political consequence' (Reese 1994, emphasis added). Nevertheless, in any overview of sociological scholarship on the media from the late 1970s the epistemological critique is unavoidable and, in some ways, all the more powerful due to its assumed, taken-for-granted status.

The critical studies of the late 1970s sought to do more than simply dissect the journalist's construction of reality, however; they were also part of what Thomas Haskell has called the 'relentless critique of professionals and professionalism' (Haskell 1998). Schudson's original dissertation, entitled *Origins of the Ideal of Objectivity in the Profession: American Journalism and Law, 1830–1940*, was the most explicit in this regard, although some of the original sociological focus was muted with the later revision of what became *Discovering the News*. Gans notes that *Deciding What's News* was written 'during the emergence of a pervasive critique of professionalism', and that 'the book is a study of a national profession, and what I have to say … may provide clues about how other national professions function' (Gans 2004: xiv). Although *The Whole World is Watching* never formally addresses issues of professionalism, Gitlin's book can certainly be seen as an exemplar of the sort of pervasive critique mentioned by Haskell and Gans. Tuchman, for her part, explicitly places her project in the border zone between the sociology of the professions and the sociology of knowledge (Tuchman 1978: 5).

If the critique of journalism's construction of reality paralleled, perhaps unwittingly, other critiques of science and scientific knowledge, journalism studies' turn towards the 'professionalisation frame' found resonance with developments in sociology more generally. By the late 1970s the sociology of the professions was enjoying something of a renaissance as scholars began to turn away from the prevailing neo-structuralist, Parsonian understandings of the professions, adopting a more Weberian or Marxist critique of professional power. Taking their cue from Everett C. Hughes, many of these sociologists 'passed from the false question "Is this occupation a profession?" to the more fundamental one "What are the circumstances in which people in an occupation attempt to turn it into a profession and themselves into professional people?"' (Hughes 1963: 655). The major moment of division came in the 1970s and early 1980s as study of *the profession* as an idealised structural-functionalist category was replaced by the more Weberian study of *professionalisation* and the *'professional project'* (Larson 1977).

By emphasising journalism's attempt to translate that epistemological expertise ('special knowledge and skills', in Larson's terminology) into political authority and economic rewards (the 'professional project'), along with its daily construction of knowledge about the world, the sociological studies of the late 1970s emphasised journalistic expertise as *both* an epistemological and organisational process by which the journalist constructs the public's knowledge of reality *and* a structural claim of professional power in which journalists marked their status as experts who possessed an authoritative insight into the shape and meaning of public life. And yet it is unclear as to the degree to which this analytical linkage succeeds. On the one hand, the basic idea contained in the critical news studies literature – that news is 'constructed' rather than 'a reflection of the world outside' – is now so commonplace within journalism scholarship that Schudson, by 2005, could label the battle effectively over and, indeed, argue that the new 'radical' position might be one that admitted that journalistic reporting actually bore some relationship to reality (Schudson 2005). On the other hand, the sociologists seemed less successful in their attempts to trace the social process by which claims to journalistic expertise become institutionalised within political and social life. Schudson, drawing most explicitly on the sociology of the professions, and aided by the historical nature of his enquiry, was perhaps the most successful in linking large-scale economic and political developments to journalistic authority (although his model provides little guide for those doing less historical work). With their primary emphasis on the bureaucratic constraints imposed on journalists by their employers, and their tendency to limit their research to individual media organisations, Gans and Tuchman fall victim to the more general critique mounted against organisational studies – that they substitute the elaboration of the specific for an analysis of larger structures. Gitlin, whose use of the theoretical concept of hegemony was perhaps the most direct sociological attempt to transcend the organisational studies perspective and link journalistic processes with larger systems of political and economic power, has since admitted that 'I could have done the analysis in *Whole World* without ever using the word 'hegemony' (Reese 1994) and has expressed general dissatisfaction with the hegemony concept.

In sum, with the possible exception of Schudson, what I have called the first thread in journalism studies is far more successful in documenting the organisational processes by which journalists construct reality than it is at analysing and explaining the social and political authority which accrues to journalists through the knowledge claim which they make. What seems to me to be the fundamental problem – how journalists translate one order of scarce resources (their expertise in constructing the news) into another (social and political power) – goes unanswered, despite the first thread's provocative allusions to professional systems, political culture, and hegemony. As a second thread of journalism scholarship emerged in the early 1990s the analysis of the sources and foundations of journalistic authority would become much more explicit.

The second strand of journalism studies: culture, narrative, and discursive communities

How, Barbie Zelizer asks in *Covering the Body*, do 'half-jumbled wisps of conversation become full blown news stories ... told with a knowing and certain voice?' (Zelizer 1992: vii). What factors give journalists the power to present their versions of reality as accurate and authoritative? Zelizer's research programme seeks to analyse the underlying mainsprings of journalistic authority – 'the ability [of journalists] to promote themselves as authoritative and credible spokespersons of "real life" events' (Zelizer 1992: viii) – discounting the usefulness of the 'professionalism lens' in analysing this authority and seeing, rather, journalistic power as grounded primarily in a discursive and cultural framework. If the first strand of journalism studies seeks to demonstrate the constructed nature of reality in journalism, and link this to the professional power of journalists, the second strand, consisting of more culturalist approaches, attempts to demonstrate the *constructed nature of journalists themselves* and their relationship to systems of social authority.

For Zelizer, the notion of the construction of the journalist begins with an attack on what she labels the journalistic 'professionalisation paradigm'. Communication scholars, she argues, must either view journalism as a 'failed profession' or abandon the professionalisation notion entirely:

> Unlike classically defined professions, such as medicine or law, journalism has not required the trappings of professionalism: many journalists do not readily read journalism handbooks, attend journalism schools, or enroll in training programs. Codes of journalistic behavior are not written down, codes of ethics remain largely nonexistent, and most journalists routinely reject licensing procedures. Journalists are also indifferent to professional associations.
>
> (Zelizer 1992: 6)

Zelizer thus prefers to speak of journalists as an 'interpretive community' whose authority stems from cultural, symbolic, and narrative sources inside and outside professional space. While practising journalists may see themselves as professionals, she argues elsewhere, this self-conception is not one shared by most of the academic community engaged in the analysis of journalism; 'many quarters of the academy have long dismissed professionalism as a fertile way of thinking about journalistic authority' (Zelizer 2004: 78). In her case study of media coverage of the John F. Kennedy assassination Zelizer looks at how one group of previously disparaged journalists (television reporters) inserted themselves into the journalistic profession via both their coverage of the killing and, more important, the stories they later told each other about the killing. 'Journalists use narratives to maintain their position and stature as an authoritative interpretive community,' Zelizer argues. 'They function as a community that authenticates itself through its narratives, and whose authority has cultural dimensions designed to consolidate journalists into a cohesive group' (Zelizer 1992: 197). The fundamental link between journalistic expertise and journalistic power, Zelizer maintains, is discursive boundary construction (Zelizer 1992: 196).

Covering the Body thus marks a major step forward in understanding the connection between journalism's authority and its expertise; indeed, the discursive perspective is remarkably conducive to the analysis of newer, more digital forms of journalism, as Zelizer herself notes (Zelizer 2004: 178). Not content to simply demonstrate the malleability of journalistic standards of objectivity or the discrepancies between the image of the Kennedy assassination presented by the media and the 'actual events themselves', Zelizer moves quickly on to what I have identified as the more interesting question: how journalistic expertise is both codified and publicly legitimated.

Nevertheless, I feel there are at least two problems with Zelizer's perspective as articulated in *Covering the Body* and in her subsequent work. First, she fails to link the discursive construction of journalistic *expertise* with the more politically and economically based positioning of the journalist as occupational *expert*. She ignores, in short, forms of power not grounded in narrative. Second, Zelizer unconvincingly (and, in my opinion, unnecessarily) distances herself from the 'professional project' perspective advanced by Larson and others (see p. 252 above), and especially Andrew Abbott. Indeed, the modification of the analysis of professions that began with Larson and others would accelerate a decade later in the work of Abbott, whose book *System of the Professions: an Essay on the Division of Expert Labor* (1988) was published several years prior to *Covering the Body*. Perhaps Abbott's most important advance is his argument that study of the professions must begin with a focus on professional work rather than the occupational group as a distinct object of analysis. The key aspect of professional behaviour can thus be seen as the link between knowledge and work, a link Abbott refers to as jurisdiction (Abbott 1988: 19). Continuing along the path outlined by Hughes, Abbott views the professional field as a terrain of struggle, though in this instance as a struggle over *jurisdiction* rather than the structural emblems of professionalism. Claiming jurisdiction, a profession asks society to recognise its cognitive structure through exclusive rights; 'jurisdiction has not only a culture, but also a social structure' (Abbott 1988: 59).

Following Abbot, then, *Covering the Body* can be read as the analysis of a specific type of professional project – as an attempt by network television reporters to gain for themselves professional stature and authority and to negotiate a special position within the hierarchy of modern journalism. The fact that this struggle on the part of television journalists was, by Zelizer's account, primarily waged through *narrative* (or, as Abbot 1988 would have it, through 'cultural work') links *Covering the Body* to particular analyses of professionalism, rather than the reverse.

That said, it is the lack of consideration of authority-affecting factors other than narrative that forms the basis for a second critique of Zelizer. Cultural/narrative explorations of journalistic expertise, in addition to their focus on the relationship between authority and discourse, need to focus more specifically on various other types of power. While Zelizer, and those engaged in similar work, rightly draw our attention to the discursive aspects of authority (stories, symbols, self-descriptions), they have less to say about other factors that might contribute to the reality-shaping abilities of journalists: state power, questions of hegemony, concentrations of economic capital, ethnic and class-based exclusions, and legal decisions. Cultural narratives are important aspects of journalistic legitimation and contestation. But they are not the only ones. A third and most recent strand of journalism studies attempts to correct this overemphasis on the cultural aspects of journalism by grounding its analysis of the profession in the tradition of 'field research' pioneered by French sociologist Pierre Bourdieu.

The third strand of journalism studies: the journalistic field

In the past few years a growing scholarly concern with the analysis of the journalistic 'field' has marked the return of an explicitly sociological take on journalism, in contrast to the more 'culturalogical' approaches of Zelizer and others. Inspired in part by Bourdieu and Ferguson's polemical *On Television* (1999), but drawing greater intellectual sustenance from the work of Bourdieu's students (Champagne 2005), a 'field approach' to journalism studies attempts to bridge the gap between micro-level, organisational analysis of the newsroom and more macro-sociological overviews of the relationship between journalism and society (Benson 1999), revamping our understanding of the professions by a focus on work rather than formal organisational membership. In terms of the specific problems of expertise raised above, a field approach can help us better formulate the model of social space in which the professional struggle over journalism occurs and can serve as a limiting framework for Zelizer's theory of discourse and narrative.

Much confusion surrounds the Bourdieuean concept of the field, and I would like to clarify my own use of the term in the pages that follow. My conception is that the field serves as an analytical model of social space in which action and social struggle are structured. As Bourdieu writes:

> To think in terms of a field is to think relationally ... I could twist Hegel's famous formula and say that the *real is relational*: what exists in the social world are relations – not interactions between agents or intersubjective ties between individuals.

> In analytic terms, a field may be defined as a network, or a config-uration, of objective relations between positions. These positions are objectively defined, in their existence and in the determinations they impose on their occupants, agents, or institutions, by their present and potential situation in the structure and distribution of species of power (or capital) whose possession commands access to specific profits that are at stake in the field, as well as by their relation to other positions.
> (Bourdieu and Wacquant 1992: 96)

It is not my goal here to judge the applicability of Bourdieu's field concept to the entirety of social life (though Bourdieu certainly feels that such an application is possible). Less still is it my goal to convert the human world into an 'obdurate social structure' (Gitlin 2004) whose unthinking 'field of forces' resolves, once and for all, pressing sociological questions of structure and agency. I *do* maintain, however, that the field concept is useful if we want to place the professional struggle over various forms of occupational expertise within a specific social spaces, including the social space of journalism. We have already critiqued both the classic organisational studies of journalism and Zelizer's discursive model for ignoring these very questions. Where, after all, does the 'struggle over jurisdiction' described by Abbott occur? For Abbott the key spatial metaphor is that of the system, or 'occupational ecology' (Abbott 1988). A more useful model, I contend, might be that of the field.

Just as the field approach to journalism helps mitigate some of the thornier issues relating to the structural components of the professionalisation project, so Abbott's analysis can help answer some of the questions often posed to Bourdieu, at least with regard to the professional and culture-producing fields (of which journalism is one). Critics often ask Bourdieuan scholars: how do fields come into being? Abbott's answer, which I believe would be applicable to Bourdieu, seems to be that a professional field begins when an occupational group or groups attempt to seize jurisdiction over a form of expertise via cultural work. The journalistic field emerges, in this instance, when an occupational group ('journalists') attempt to claim for themselves a monopoly on the provision of everyday public knowledge, later redefined as journalistic expertise. Likewise, a second critical question directed at Bourdieu asks where do fields 'begin' and 'end'. Abbott's answer, at least with regard to the professions, is that such a question must be posed in terms of 'who is doing the professional work'. 'The central phenomenon of professional life is thus the link between a profession and its work ... to analyse professional development is to analyse how this link is created in work, how it is anchored in formal and informal structure' (Abbott 1988: 20). Thus the journalistic field includes all those individuals and organisations engaged in the 'work of journalism' and not simply those formally certified as doing so. A fusion of the Bourdieuean field perspective and the professionalisation perspective advanced by Larson and Abbott thus resolves a number of difficulties with regard to the positioning of journalistic experts in social space. Bourdieu structuralises Larson, while Abbott directs our attention to Bourdieu's oft-neglected theories of agency.

We can now step back and examine the three strands of journalism studies, their relationship to larger questions of journalistic authority and expertise, and ways in which they can be synthesised.

Of experts and expertise

I have, at various points, referred in passing to the distinction between experts and expertise. As Eyal notes:

> One should distinguish between the group of experts, on the one hand, and expertise, on the other. They require two different modes of

analysis. Gouldner and the sociology of professions have focused on the group of experts. They analyzed 'professionalization' as the process whereby a group of experts lays claim to jurisdiction over a certain area of human experience and legitimates this claim by means of some form of rational knowledge. The emergence of a form of expertise, on the other hand, requires an analysis of discourse.

(Eyal 2002: 657)

Applying this distinction to journalism, we can synthesise the major theoretical arguments of the three threads above by positing that expert professionals – in this case, journalists – seek, via professional struggle, to monopolise a form of journalistic expertise, which is itself discursively constructed out of various journalistic practices and narratives. If the primary object of our analysis is journalistic authority, the source of this authority should be conceptualised as arising from the position of journalists and journalistic organisations within the field of cultural production. This position, in turn, must be analysed as the outcome of an occupational struggle – the professional project. Occupations engaged in the professional project attempt to acquire and maintain a legitimate jurisdiction over discursively and epistemologically constructed varieties of expertise.

All three of the dominant modes of journalism analysis since the 1970s have emphasised or de-emphasised particular aspects of this basic paradigm. While the critical sociologists examined journalistic practices on an organisational level – practices that helped, in part, define the nature and content of journalistic expertise – they paid less attention to the discursive foundations of that expertise and failed to adequately address well the relationship of these practices to the larger macro-structures in which journalists' professional authority operated. Zelizer, on the other hand, devoted most of her attention to discourse, primarily the ways in which rhetoric and narrative serve to draw expert boundaries (Gieryn 1983), although she failed to distinguish between journalistic experts and journalistic expertise, and paid even less attention to larger societal structures than the first strand of journalism studies. Most recently, field analysis deserves praise for its fusion of the micro-level of journalistic practice (as knowledge producing behaviour) and larger political and economic structures; nevertheless, this perspective has a limited understanding of the professional project (a legacy of Bourdieuean structuralism) and most likely shares, with the professionalisation perspective, a unitary conception of journalistic expertise.

Bringing together the three threads above, drawing on their strengths while avoiding their weaknesses, we might summarise the jurisdictional struggle over journalism as follows: journalism – as a system of knowledge production, a structural claim to expert status, and statement of cultural authority – must be seen as an outwardly directed assertion of legitimate control over the news-gathering process. Professional journalists should thus be envisioned as attempting to establish a *jurisdiction* over journalistic expertise, all the while attempting to control the cultural discourse that both defines them in relation to others and defines the very nature of their expertise. The conflict with the bloggers, in this instance, could be explained as a conflict over journalistic jurisdiction, a conflict similar to the one between professional journalism and the public relations industry early in the twentieth century (Abbot 1988: 224; Schudson 1978: 133). Within this narrative, professional journalists could be seen as engaging in an attempt to sharply delimit the boundaries of their jurisdiction, battling bloggers for occupational control of news-gathering and redefining the core of their abstract 'journalistic knowledge' in an attempt to solidify their control over the production of news. From this theoretical perspective all changes to the knowledge-producing practices of journalism, as well as to its cultural claims, would be subsumed into a zero-sum struggle over the jurisdiction of news-gathering.

There is, nonetheless, a problem with this narrative: it does not entirely jibe with reality. Or rather, it tells only part of the story, failing to engage with the full historical complexity of various journalistic boundary disputes. For in fact, journalism's occupational identity is grounded as much in *opposition* to the professional project as it is in the type of competitive struggle discussed by Abbott and Larson.[1] Within much of the journalistic profession there remains a deep cultural opposition to the entire notion of the 'journalism school', for example, and many of the most celebrated journalists have entered the news profession as outsiders. On a sociological level, the current connection between journalists and bloggers might be seen as a contradictory and uneasy partnership in addition to or alongside a more competitive relationship.

These facts do not demonstrate that the pathway towards journalistic status is as open as the mythology of journalism claims; we have seen, historically and more recently, very real struggles over the boundaries of the journalistic profession. However, they do point to the fact that journalism is, an *anomalous* profession. By using social theory to map out an ideal theoretical paradigm through which to describe the competition over cultural authority that professionalism provides, as has been done in the pages above, we are in a better position to grapple with the tensions and complexities of the specific case of journalism (Anderson and Schudson 2008).

Professionalism, expertise, and democracy

Deep conflicts about the authority of expert professionals in a democracy are nothing new; indeed, as Hallin points out in this volume, radical social movements of the 1960s and 1970s mounted some of the sharpest challenges to notions of professional autonomy, a challenge that impacted both journalism and other expert domains (also see Hoffman 1989). Only in recent years, however, has the status of expertise become the subject of major theoretical debate. Collins and Evans argue that the time has come for sociologists of science to 'develop a normative theory of expertise' (Collins and Evans 2002: 237). Drawing on Tocqueville and Dewey, Dzur contends that we need to develop a theory of 'democratic expertise', noting that 'with technocratic rather than democratic professionals a democratic polity is weaker, citizens are less engaged and competent, and professions themselves are vulnerable' (Dzur 2004: 11). Schudson, in contrast, has inveighed against the tendency to see expertise as a 'permanent embarrassment to democracy', arguing instead that 'democrats should incorporate a more forgiving view of the role of expertise' (Schudson 2006: 491). Why is expertise being so widely challenged today? What are the consequences of this challenge for the normative values of democracy, public life, and social justice?

One of the more ironic developments since the 1960s has been the gradual 'de-ideologisation' of the populist critique of professional power. When it comes to criticism of professional journalism, disgust with the mainstream media is now as much a trope of the American right as it is a talking point of left. 'The populist persuasion', of course, does not correspond neatly to divisions between traditional political categories (Kazin 1989); hatred of the 'Mainstream Media' ('MSM') by activists of the right usually stems from a critique of the liberal attitudes of individual journalists and a claim that media institutions take a liberal position on social issues. This kind of bipartisan critique, of course, further feeds into professional journalism's self-conception as an objective, reasonable entity under assault from extremists of both sides. The unspoken arrogance of such a view only inflames the partisans further.

A second recent development, more structural than ideological, has been the general decline in the autonomy of numerous professional groups under pressure from the market and, in recent years, from the state. This is, of course, a Bourdieuean point (Bourdieu and Ferguson 1999), open to its own criticisms on both normative and empirical grounds. Nevertheless, there is little doubt that in the United States (at least) economic, political, and legal pressures are conspiring to undermine the already tenuous autonomy of professional journalists. The collapse of the newspaper industry and the consequent diminishing of the employment prospects of entry-level and veteran journalists; the existence of systematic and widely applied news propaganda projects carried out at the highest levels of government; and court decisions reaffirming the lack of a journalistic 'professional privilege' have all served as concrete blows to the autonomy of the reporter.

What about technology's role in challenges to concentrated forms of professional power? Although this is not the place to revisit the endless (and endlessly exasperating) debate between 'technological determinists' and 'social constructionists', it may not be too much to argue that the decentralised nature of the internet carries within it deep anti-authoritarian affordances (Graves 2007). 'Web 2.0' challenges to centralised domains of cultural authority have not only rocked the foundations of journalism but also authorities in academic knowledge collection (Lih 2004), medicine (Boulos and Wheeler 2006), and even patent law (Noveck 2008). Combined with the political and structural attacks on expertise already discussed, digital innovation may be only the latest, and most potentially far-reaching, blow to traditional notions of specialised expertise – including the expertise of the professional journalist.

Are these wide-ranging attacks by bloggers, politicians, and various social movement organisations on professional expertise and concentrated networks of cultural authority something to be celebrated or feared? Do they herald the promise of new forms of citizens' democracy or represent the final overthrow of established systems of rational truth seeking and hierarchical control? There isn't the space here to conduct a full-scale normative evaluation of the sociological trends just sketched, so I will content myself with four brief remarks. To begin with, it should be clear that the once bright hopes of the radical left – that attacks on unequal systems of cultural authority would lead to a corresponding 'flattening' of unequal concentrations of political and economic power – are unfounded. Anti-professionalism is not the sole province of either the left *or* the right; attacks on elites can be used for progressive purposes, or in the service of reactionary goals, or both. This is nor to argue, of course, that cultural anti-authoritarianism has *no* political consequences; it is simply to state the obvious fact that the anti-authoritarian movement of the past fifty years affects the world in ways that do not easily map on to traditional political concerns.

More specifically, the degree to which we should praise the 'populist insurgency' clamouring at the gates of traditional journalistic structures is heavily dependent on the actual content of journalistic expertise itself. In short: is journalistic knowledge an 'expert' domain of knowledge at all? Is it, in other words, *hard* to be a journalist? Very little has been written about 'what journalists know and how they know it' within the journalistic studies literature. An understanding of exactly what it is journalists know, and what it is they think they know, is essential for a deeper understanding of attacks on journalistic professionalism.

On a more structural level, much of our evaluation of the populist penetration of what might be called the 'journalistic field' turns on the degree to which we value the autonomy of such fields in the first place. Should journalism be autonomous? *Is* journalism autonomous? To the degree that it is not (or should not be), we are then faced with a second question: is democratic penetration of journalistic systems to be less feared than market or state penetration? There is little doubt that the market is deeply embedded in the American system of cultural news production and that, at least traditionally, social democratic European systems have seen the state exercise a degree of control over journalism. Is the entry of so-called 'citizen media makers' into the journalistic sphere simply a reflection of the market? Or the state? Or neither? To what degree can it balance these forces? To what degree is it simply complicit in them?

Finally, we should be open to the possibility that what we are witnessing at the dawn of the twenty-first century is a *transformation* of the bases of cultural authority rather than an *elimination* of that authority altogether. At least theoretically, the internet opens up space for the generation of new systems of networked authority, as evidenced by collaborative projects like Wikipedia and the Community Peer Review Patent Project. This, of course, raises up an entirely new series of questions concerning the actual content of authority, the degree to which it can be decentralised, and the manner in which it can or should be made compatible with democratic norms. There is little doubt that empirical investigations into the nature of cultural authority should be high on the agenda of media researchers in the years to come. Hopefully, the theoretical spadework done in this chapter will help frame this empirical research, and will enrich our understanding of journalism – one of the key knowledge-producing institutions of the modern era.

Note

1 I thank Michael Schudson for his clear articulation of this point.

Bibliography

Abbott, A. D. (1988) *The System of Professions: an Essay on the Division of Expert Labor*. Chicago IL: University of Chicago Press.

Anderson, C. and Schudson, M. (2008) 'Objectivity, professionalism, and truth-seeking', in T. Hanitzsch and K. Wahl-Jorgensen (eds) *The Handbook of Journalism Studies*. Mahwah NJ: Erlbaum.

Benson, R. D. (1999) 'Field theory in comparative context: a new paradigm for media studies', *Theory and Society* 28: 463–98.

Boulos, P., Maramba, I. and Wheeler, S. (2006) 'Debate: Wikis, blogs, and podcasts: a new generation of web-based tools for virtual collaborative clinical practice and evaluation', *BMC Medical Education* 6: 1–8.

Bourdieu, P. and Wacquant, L. J. D. (1992) *An Invitation to Reflexive Sociology*. Chicago IL: University of Chicago Press.

Bourdieu, P. and Ferguson, P. P. (1999) *On Television*. New York NY: New Press.

Carey, J. (1974) 'The problem of journalism history', *Journalism History* 1: 3–5, 27.

Champagne, P. (2005) 'The double dependency: the journalistic field between politics and markets', in R. Benson and E. Neveu (eds) *Bourdieu and the Journalistic Field*. New York NY: Polity Press.

Collins, H. M. (1975) 'The seven sexes: a study in the sociology of a phenomenon, or the replication of experiments in physics', *Sociology* 9: 205–24.

Collins, H. M. and Evans, Robert (2002) 'The third wave of science studies: studies of expertise and experience', *Social Studies of Science* 32: 235–96.

Dzur, A. W. (2004) 'Democratic authority and professionalism: sharing authority in civic life', *The Good Society* 13: 6–14.

Ekstrom, M. (2002) 'Epistemologies of TV journalism: a theoretical framework', *Journalism* 3: 259–82.

Epstein, E. J. (1973) *News from Nowhere: Television and the News*, New York NY: Ivan R. Day.

Eyal, G. (2002) 'Dangerous liaisons between military intelligence and Middle Eastern studies in Israel', *Theory and Society* 31: 653–93.

Feyerabend, P. (1975) *Against Method: Outline of an Anarchistic Theory of Science*. London: New Left Books.

Gans, H. J. (2004) *Deciding What's News: a Study of CBS Evening News, NBC Nightly News, Newsweek, and Time*. New York: Pantheon.

Gieryn, T. (1983) 'Boundary work and the demarcation of science from non-science: strains and interests in professional ideologies of scientists', *American Sociological Review* 48: 781–95.

Gitlin, T. (1980) *The Whole World is Watching: Media in the Making and Unmaking of the New Left*. Berkeley CA: University of California Press.

Gitlin, T. (2004) 'Reply to Rodney Benson', *Political Communication* 21: 309–10.

Graves, L. (2007) 'Emergence or Affordance? Blogging Culture and the Question of Technological Effects', paper presented at the International Communications Association conference, San Francisco CA.

Haskell, Thomas (1998) *Objectivity is not Neutrality*. Baltimore MD: Johns Hopkins University Press.

Hoffman, L. (1989) *The Politics of Knowledge: Activist Movements in Medicine and Planning*. Albany NY: State University of New York Press.

Hughes, E. C. (1963) 'Professions', *Daedalus* 92: 655–8.

Kazin, M. (1989) *The Populist Persuasion: an American History*. Ithaca NY: Cornell University Press.

Larson, M. S. (1977) *The Rise of Professionalism: a Sociological Analysis*. Berkeley CA: University of California Press.

Lih, A. (2004) 'Wikipedia as Participatory Journalism', paper presented at the Online Journalism Conference 2004, Austin TX.

Neiman Reports (2003) 'Weblogs and journalism', from *Neiman Reports* 57 (3).

Neiman Reports (2005) 'Editor's introduction', from *Neiman Reports* 59 (4).

Noveck, B. (2008) 'Wiki-Government', *Democracy Journal* 7 (Winter 2008).

Reese, S. (1994) 'Todd Gitlin on *The Whole World is Watching*', http://courses.communication.utexas.edu/jou/reese.s/todd_gitlin.doc (retrieved 3 May 2006).

Schudson, M. (1978) *Discovering the News: a Social History of American Newspapers*. New York NY: Basic Books.

Schudson, M. (2005) 'Four approaches to the sociology of news', in M. Gurevitch and J. Curran, *Mass Media and Society*. London: Arnold.

Schudson, M. (2006) 'The trouble with experts – and why democracies need them', *Theory and Society* 35: 491–506.

Starr, P. (1984) *The Social Transformation of American Medicine*. New York NY: Basic Books.

Tuchman, G. (1978) *Making News: a Study in the Construction of Social Reality*. New York NY: Free Press.

Zelizer, B. (1992) *Covering the Body: the Kennedy Assassination, the Media, and the Shaping of Collective Memory*. Chicago IL: University of Chicago Press.

Zelizer, B. (2000) 'What is Journalism Studies?', *Journalism* 1 (1): 9–60.

Zelizer, B. (2004) *Taking Journalism Seriously: News and the Academy*. Thousand Oaks CA: Sage.

16 Media making and social reality

Jason Toynbee

Consider the long-running argument in media scholarship about the comparative importance of the two 'moments' of communication: reception and production. We know that each position has a distinct theoretical approach. So, broadly speaking, audience research (located in cultural studies) is premised on relativism and constructionism, whereas work on production (the political economy tradition) draws on a materialist view of the world. These intellectual approaches are not only intellectual, of course. Behind them is a division of labour such that academics in the field tend to work on just one moment. As a result intellectual partisanship and professional self-interest reinforce each other, and positions become embedded. Now in one sense this is just another story of specialism in the academy. But what marks out media studies is that even as they occupy their 'own' moment, specialists frequently claim it as *the* moment, that it trumps the other in significance, and encompasses the fullest meaning of the media. In other words, there is a kind of hegemonic thrust in each of these two branches.[1]

I say this at the outset because I take a partisan position myself in this chapter.[2] I begin by arguing for the precedence of production, and then examine what that precedence means for media making. In putting the case I draw on ideas from critical realist philosophy and social theory, a body of work which has hardly been taken up in media studies.[3] What critical realism brings to this undertaking is explanatory power, a metatheoretical setting of the media in society that helps to clarify the premises of rival approaches in media studies as well as differences and convergences among them. More than that, realism contributes to understanding how the media are implicated in human oppression, and its converse, the struggle for emancipation. It has a political dimension in other words.

Critical realism and the precedence of production

Realists assert the existence of things independently of the means of knowing them. Behind this bald statement, however, lurk several philosophical tendencies and, associated with them, distinct realist ontologies, or theories of existence. In what follows I will draw on the critical realism (CR) of Roy Bhaskar and others, which, apart from its cogency, can be recommended because it deals directly with the problems of *social* realism (see Bhaskar 1998). One of the key issues here is that society is 'concept-dependent', as Bhaskar puts it (1998: 38, 45, 49). In other words it involves discourse. What we think and say (and, critically, what the media represent to us) contribute to the constitution of the social.[4] In this sense CR, just like cultural studies, has a cultural constructionist conception of human life. What radically demarcates CR from cultural studies, however, is that it posits a social existence which extends beyond discourse and experience to include causes and powers we cannot directly apprehend, and most often do not consider.

Let's see what this might mean for understanding the significance of the media moments. A cultural studies approach to the audience begins and ends with lived experience. Look at the growing body of ethnographic work in audience studies. Much of it suggests that a high degree of conscious activity is involved in watching television. Such conditions also seem to apply to new media. (See Livingstone 2004 for a survey and discussion of the literature.) This is undoubtedly an important and compelling strand of research. In CR, however, the experience of actors is only a part of social being. Underneath, as it were, are real structural-causal factors which may not be directly experienced. That being the case it is surely better to start with a procedure which can tap those factors than with a method like ethnography whose scope is necessarily limited to the experiential.

CR has just such a procedure – the transcendental argument. A transcendental argument is one in which the following question is asked. 'What are the pre-conditions for the possibility of *x*, where *x* is a more or less widely accepted phenomenon?' If we take the media as *x*, then it quickly becomes apparent that the presence of the audience, just as much as production, is a necessary condition for media to be possible. Remove either of the moments and we no longer have anything that would qualify as the media. Looking more closely, it becomes clear that what is at stake here are *relations* between moments. In other words, production and reception acquire their constitutive character as media moments through their mutual orientation.

However, to take the next step, and make the case for the *precedence* of production, involves more concrete analysis than the relatively abstract question of the *existence* of media moments. In taking that step I would suggest that we cross a line from the level of metatheory to that of substantive sociological enquiry. (For a useful discussion of this distinction see Sibeon 2004: 12–23.) If this is so then a transcendental argument will have less purchase. Quite simply, to examine a phenomenon concretely is to show its many aspects (Lawson 1998a: 170), and thus to pose a multiplicity of preconditions for its existence. That makes it harder to pinpoint which ones are decisive. What to do then? How should we approach the problem of assessing the significance of production against the other media moments?

The response of empiricism – the dominant tradition in the social sciences – would be to seek event regularities of the sort 'when *x* happens then *y* happens', and in this way demonstrate a law governing a particular social process or event. But critical realism is sceptical about this method. For in the 'open systems' which constitute social reality one cannot produce closed experimental conditions like those created in the natural sciences. And without isolation of variables there can be no satisfactory testing of their correlation. Anyway, as Roy Bhaskar suggests, empiricism does not even try to explain what it demonstrates. To present correlations is to do little more than posit what may well be contingent regularities while ignoring the really important issue of the causes which generate observable events (Bhaskar 1998: 45–6).

There has of course been an empiricist case made for the priority of production, namely in so-called 'effects' research. In its most politically significant (and pernicious) strand, regularities are posed between the broadcasting of violent television programmes and violent behaviour among viewers. The latter is said to be an effect of the former. Now my sense would be that many readers of this book will be unsympathetic to such a position. Critique of crass empiricism of the sort involved in effects research is quite extensive in media studies, and is taken up in political economy as well as in cultural studies. But I think it is still worth sketching a specifically CR critique of 'effects', both because it interrogates empiricism quite rigorously and because it suggests an alternative approach to understanding the significance of production.

What's wrong with effects research is that it does not acknowledge the openness of media in society, considered as a system. There is simply no way of isolating the watching of media violence among a complex of putative causes of violent behaviour among research subjects. Thus any correlation shown between the two (media and violence) may be contingent. More than this, even if one were to accept a causal link, there are no means to establish the direction of causality between correlates. In a study claimed as the first to show long-term effects from childhood watching to violent behaviour in adulthood, the authors can say only that 'it is more plausible that exposure to television violence increases aggression than that aggression increases television-violence viewing' (Huesmann *et al.* 2003: 216). Plausibility, of course, depends on some conception of social causality *outside* the event regularity that is supposed to do the explanatory work.

As an account of the primacy of production, then, empiricism fails. But the appeal to plausibility, just mentioned, does at least point a way forward. What's needed is some notion of the salience of social causes. Even if one cannot *prove* the crowning significance of a particular factor among many, it might be possible to begin to understand how social phenomena exist through illuminating contrast. This is the proposal of Tony Lawson. He suggests that social science:

> aims to identify single sets of causal mechanisms and structures. And these are indicated where outcomes or features of different groups are such that, given the respective causal histories and conditions of these groups, their observed relation is other than might have been expected.
>
> (1998b: 150–1)

Lawson calls these types of indicative social phenomena 'contrastive demi-regularities', or 'demi-regs' for short (1998b: 151–62). Demi-regs are good enough regularities through which one can plausibly infer that significant causes are at work. The point about the contrastive dimension is then that it gestures towards explanation through alternatives. In other words it raises the question 'What factors are at work in this case rather than that one?' This would seem to be an approach well suited to considering the salience of media production, just because different kinds of producer roles are at stake in different kinds of communication.

Fortunately, there is already a contrastive analysis of communication we can draw on, namely John Thompson's discussion of 'face-to-face interaction', 'mediated interaction' and 'mediated quasi-interaction' (1995: 81–118). The first type (everyday talk) is fundamentally dialogical. The second (telephone conversations, exchanges of letters and the like) is dialogical but also mediated. In the third category (mass media) there are two distinguishing factors. First, 'symbolic forms are produced for an indefinite range of potential recipients' rather than specific others. Second, communication is generally one-way. 'The reader of a book, for instance, is primarily the recipient of a symbolic form whose producer does not require (and generally does not receive) a direct and immediate response' (p. 84). Of course, as Thompson goes on to argue, indirect responses to media do occur. Indeed, they are central to the very nature of the media as a social phenomenon (pp. 98–118). Still, for our purposes his typology establishes good enough demi-regs. In contrasting the three types of communication we can say that what distinguishes the mass media from other forms of symbolic communication is the temporal primacy of production, premised on monologue from one to many.

This may seem laboured. But I make the argument carefully because I take seriously the objection from cultural studies to what seems to be implied by the conclusion just reached. Broadly, cultural studies has it that the audience makes use of media texts in such a rich variety of ways that the *prima facie* case for the precedence of production is negated. Audiences make texts their own. This is a strong suit. But the realist response would be simply that, *unlike in the case of dialogue*, however broad and deep the interpretation is, it is an interpretation based on a given – the text as produced – and there are no direct means of shaping the next text from producers.[5] In other words, media producers can make decisions about the nature of communication without recourse to the opinions of those who attend. Further, the fact that media monologue is organised on a one-to-many basis implies hierarchical producer–audience relations: a privileged few have the capacity to speak and show to the many.

Media structure/social structure

If, as I have just been arguing, producers have precedence to the extent that they control the form and content of the media monologue, perhaps the first questions to ask are, how is production organised and what shapes its output. To address them we can turn to CR social theory, at the heart of which is a view of society based on structure and agency. We will deal with agency in the next section. Here the focus will be on structure.

As Douglas Porpora (1998) puts it, social structures exist as 'systems of human relations among social positions'. A Marxist conception, where system is mode of production and social positions are classes, would fit this bill. So would systems of patriarchy and racial exclusion; they all depend on positions in socially significant relation (1998: 343). Crucially, structures are casual mechanisms. That is, they are not merely heuristic devices, or means of understanding the world, rather they belong to the world, and have real causal powers.[6] Thus workers work and capitalists exploit their workers by dint of the capital–labour relation. Similarly, television producers make programmes and people watch them as a consequence of the media relations that we examined in the previous section.

It is worth reflecting on what this media structure does and does not entail. As we saw, producers can control the form and content of media texts without recourse to the audience. Further, media are organised on a one-to-many basis. Together these factors would seem to offer producers large amounts of power over audiences. Certainly, much of the work on media production (as well as the first wave of studies of the audience in the 1930s and 1940s) has endorsed a strong view of media power. But the question is, does monological media structure, considered purely on its own terms, justify the strong view?

In the first place, producers do have the *facility* to try to persuade audiences of things – this is implied in the monological structure of the media. We can usefully refer to speech act theory in order to tease out what such a facility involves. J. L. Austin calls 'perlocutionary' those utterances in ordinary language which are intended to 'produce certain consequential effects' among the audience (1975: 101). Effectively, all utterances have a perlocutionary dimension, and by extension so do media texts. Journalists want their audience to be informed, rock musicians want theirs to be transfixed, and so on and so forth.

Immediately, though, we need to make some qualifications. As Austin points out, perlocution can 'misfire', leading to unintended consequences, or it can just fail to achieve any effects at all. In fact there are many and complex variations on these themes (pp. 103–32). The implication for media production is that power over the audience is relatively weak. Mediated interaction then further weakens this power. Quite simply, it is hard to get feedback about what effects you are having on audience members, owing to your spatial/temporal dislocation from them.[7] That makes it difficult to adjust production and so reduce misfires. And there is something else: the monological and perlocutionary structure of the media explains nothing about interest and content, in other words what might influence producers to make specific texts with a view to getting audiences to think, or do particular things. These points are absolutely crucial. Media producers *qua* producers have relatively little power over audiences, and no particular interest in persuading them of anything, except perhaps that the media are to be trusted. Even in this last case it is difficult to infer very much without some notion of the social animus of the media. To derive such a notion, we need an account of the *complex* of social structures which impacts on media production, and which in turn media production acts back upon.

In CR social reality is stratified. At the top are experiences (the *empirical* domain), which form a subset of all the events that occur yet may not necessarily be experienced (the *actual* domain). Both categories are in turn the product of causal mechanisms which in society, as we have seen, take the form of social structures. (This is the domain of the *real*.) (Collier 1994: 42–5; Sayer 2000: 11–12.) But stratification does not end with these three nested domains of the empirical, actual and real. Structures themselves may provide the basis for other structures. The notion of basis is crucial in CR. It indicates a 'without which not' condition such that, for instance, the commercial media could not exist without a capitalist mode of production. The parochial social relations of media making depend on this material base – for example, the structure of competition for status among symbol makers which Bourdieu (1996) identifies in the 'field of literary production' in nineteenth-century France. But we can also note a higher economic level, namely specific media sectors with their own particular organisation and imperatives. These of course depend on the capitalist mode of production too. Above the social and economic we have semiotic structures, through which are generated actual media practices and texts. Semiotic structures depend on the kinds of social structure just mentioned, but also on biological and physical mechanisms lower down in stratified reality – for instance the seeing, hearing, touching, motor and cognitive mechanisms of human beings.

Upward causality is not monolithic, however. In other words, lower-level structures constrain, enable and influence higher ones, but they do not fully determine them. CR explains this through 'emergence', whereby higher-level strata have a certain autonomy in relation to lower ones (Bhaskar 1998: 97–9). Thus the social depends on the biological embodiment of human beings yet exists as a distinct level of reality with its own tendencies. The key point is that, in all instances of emergence, two or more elements from a lower level are *reconfigured*, so that a new entity is formed at a higher level with powers that are proper to it (Elder-Vass 2005). Frequently, emergence is associated with the acting back of higher upon lower levels. For example, in the case of speaking, psychosemiotic mechanisms, emergent from the neurological processes of the brain, direct the larynx and tongue to produce meaningful sound.

Critically, emergence enables a depth ontology but without reductionism, that is, the explanation of higher levels purely in terms of lower and more fundamental ones. Against reduction, emergence offers an understanding of reality in which the future resonates with possibilities. What's more, in the context of this chapter, it enables us to treat media making as a relatively autonomous structure and practice, though one that is always shaped and constrained by the powers of other mechanisms below and above it.

So far we have been examining the vertical stratification of reality. But, as is already starting to become clear, shaping and constraining are also the product of the 'horizontal' conjunction of generative structures at any level. In some cases the powers of a particular structure will cancel out, or predominate over, the powers of another. In other cases mechanisms will work conjointly in a positive way. It follows that we must refer to a particular historical conjuncture of structures at different levels – some negative, others positive in their effect – in order to explain the *actual* production of media, at the level of events.

To do that work we need to shift analytical gear again, from metatheory to substantive sociological analysis. Here I would simply argue for a class/race/gender model, such that the capital–labour structure has great salience, but so do sex-gender and racialised identity relations. These are the big three structures which have a major impact on media making. Nevertheless, bearing in mind the multiple horizontal and vertical causality we have been discussing, we know that outcomes will be produced in complex and relatively inconsistent ways: demi-regs rather than law-governed patterns. And, of course, the large structures do not exhaust causality. Other significant structures interact with the big three. Some are politically charged (just like class, sex-gender and race), that is, they are structures of domination which work against the possibility of human emancipation (see Bhaskar 1991). In other cases, for instance the structure of the media themselves, structural relations involve little or no politics *per se*, in which case the political will be more or less completely overdetermined by the conjunction of other mechanisms in which political interests are at stake.

The concrete question of how, in a particular historical conjuncture, the media then take on a political complexion and represent, or sometimes resist, dominant interests brings us back to the more familiar terrain of critical media studies. Here we can identify a continuum, I think.

At one end is political economy, which examines relatively specific forms of causality, namely from the structure of the media sector within the capitalist economy to the decisions made by media producers. At the other end is ideology critique, which is concerned to show at a meta-level how the whole ensemble of power relations determines the broad ideological landscape, including media representation. In the late 1970s Peter Golding and Graham Murdock (1979) argued persuasively that analysis of the media based on ideology – the emerging cultural studies tradition of Stuart Hall and others – failed to take account of the concrete linkages between mode of production, sectoral organisation of the media and professional codes of media makers. In the absence of such a focus, the ideological approach had to rely solely on inference from textual analysis for its account of how power relations become inscribed in media output. This was in effect 'circumstantial evidence' about media power (p. 224). My point would be that, via a CR social ontology which brings together structures (and not only economic structures), ontological depth and horizontal conjunction we avoid having to choose between macro- and micro-causality, between inference from text and from causal linkage. Instead we can use both approaches. Indeed, we *ought* to use both because the complexity of media–society relations and the fallibility of knowledge call for multiple perspectives (Sayer 2000: 51–5).

Agency, intention and autonomy

The argument of the last section was that media making has a perlocu-tionary dimension which, of itself, is both weak and empty. The need was then to establish how in their complex conjunction social structures overdetermine media making. But this still leaves out the critical issue of the way media production *emerges* from society, how its practices are relatively autonomous. In approaching that problem we need to consider the agency of producers. Roy Bhaskar has a theory of structure and agency which can help with this. He develops it through a critique of classical sociology (1998: 31–7).

In the first place he agrees with Durkheim that social structure pre-exists the individual, being 'always already made'. However, he also accepts Weber's proposal that society exists only through the activity of individuals. Peter Berger had argued that these two views could be reconciled; individual and society are simply moments in a single 'dialectical' process. But for Bhaskar this is an 'illicit identification'. For if one accepts the 'always already made' condition 'it is no longer true to say that men *create* society. Rather one must say: they *reproduce* or *transform* it' (1998: 33–4). This is the basis of Bhaskar's 'transformational model of social activity' (TMSA). Activity and social structure are mutually constitutive yet ontologically distinct. On one side, social structure consists in relations between people, and depends on their activities, activities which reproduce or (less often) transform it. On the other side, human practice depends on society, such that there can be no meaningful action without social structure. A key point follows. Structure enables and imposes limits on what people can do, yet by the same token it never fully determines actions. Agency is emergent from structure – and vice versa.

Bhaskar goes on to articulate this structure – agency duality, showing that each side consists in a second duality. 'Society is both the ever-present *condition* (material cause) and the continually produced *outcome* of human agency. And praxis is both work, that is, conscious *production*, and (normally unconscious) *reproduction* of the conditions of production, that is society' (pp. 34–5). How does this double duality map on to the making of media? So far we have been considering media structure as a set of relations between producers and audience. In order to understand how media texts get made we need to move in closer and consider production itself. Let's take the example of situation comedy. On the *structure* side, relations between genre conventions, as well as the division of labour, enable sitcoms to be made (condition). Yet these same relations exist only through their continued practice by script writers, actors, directors and so on (outcome). Over on the *action* side, the production team put together shows for their own reasons, such as the desire to make people laugh (production). But to produce a sitcom also involves reiterating the genre structure and division of labour (reproduction).

Clearly, structure can be transformed as well as reproduced. We know that transformation is extremely difficult in the big social structures like capitalism and patriarchy. The interests of the powerful in preserving the *status quo* become deeply embedded. However, in situation comedy, and media making more generally, transformation happens all the time. One of the most illuminating strands of media studies research in the last twenty years has been concerned with that problem; the hybridisation of genres, changing narrative conventions, emerging styles in popular music and so on. The TMSA helps to make sense of this process along the following lines: a change in production yields a new outcome which then becomes a condition for the next moment of production, which yields a new outcome ... and so it goes. In effect, transformation in the structure of a genre is achieved through many cycles of the TMSA, each yielding an incremental shift in structural relations.[8]

Whether or not producers reflect on such processes of generic change, they clearly have intentions when they work. How far are intentions effi-cacious, though? Bhaskar's response is unambiguous. Any theory of agency worth the name must pose reasons as the cause of action (1998: 90–7). People think they act intentionally and for reasons, and there is every reason to conclude that they are right. Reasons include beliefs and desires, as well as calculations about the consequences of actions. Nevertheless, intention is sometimes thwarted by 'sources of opacity in social life' which make reasoned action less effective, namely unconscious

motivation, tacit skills, unacknowledged conditions and unintended consequences (1991: 75). It seems to me that this formulation of agency as
intentional, yet also limited by the opacity of social being, is incredibly
useful in understanding media production.

For there is a major contradiction about it. On the one hand, production
tends towards a kind of institutional autonomy (in this connection see
Matt Stahl's analysis of rock music in the present volume). That is, the
agency of producers is recognised and enshrined by the media industries
for the functional reason that symbol making is highly variable, intuitive
and therefore not amenable to detailed administration.[9] On the other
hand, a number of strategies are used to pull producers back under the
discipline of the market and ideological control, from the 'soft' supervision
of cultural brokers to the brutal use of short-term contracts and the
lure of deferred payment. In this difficult situation coping discourses
tend to develop. At one end of the spectrum – among rock musicians,
for example – romantic notions arise of the artist embattled against
commerce. This is a refusal of the nature of cultural labour. At the
other end – among television journalists, for instance – are codes of
media professionalism which confer integrity on producers despite their co-
optation by industry (see Daniel Hallin's chapter in this book). All these
involve some kind of denial of the structural conditions of media making,
or else a shying away from the consequences of production practice,
namely that you always embed external influences in 'your own' creative
artefacts.

So there is a peculiar combination of strong agency, structural constraint
and high opacity among media practitioners. This is key in explaining
how media making can be instrumental, in other words subject to market
control or more broadly influenced by powerful social forces, and yet
at the same time can exist as a zone of relative autonomy and counter-
intuitive expression. It is precisely such a contradiction, and the ambiguity
which follows from it, that legitimate media power in capitalist formal
democracies. To the extent that the media are trusted and granted
perlocutionary 'rights' by audiences it is because they don't see producers
as mere puppets of advertisers or the ruling class. And at least sometimes,
or to some extent, they are right about this.

Production is about the world

None of the above tells us what media making is about though. To say that
production is perlocutionary and has an ideological component (serving the
interests of power) is to stop short of the problem of reference. Generally,
outside of critical work on political communication, media studies has
tended to avoid this issue. It is not an oversight, of course, but rather part
of a political project. The whole thrust of textual analysis has been away
from understanding media in terms of their reference to things, and towards

the notion that media construct discourses, images, ways of thinking.[10] Certainly, there is progressive intent here: media makers and audiences should be freed from the tyranny of reductionism. Or, to put this view in its strongest form: saying that media texts are about the world is to connive with the powerful who want to fix things as they are, and deny the creative imagination of the people.

Actually, the anti-reference tendency extends well beyond media studies. It is, for example, strongly represented in Bourdieu's work on literary production. In an essay on 'Flaubert's point of view' Bourdieu argues that the key to understanding it is to appreciate how the novelist placed himself between realist authors and writers of genre literature. At stake here is a strategy based on position taking in the field: not this style, not that form of words, not those themes (Bourdieu 1996: 87–91). As Bourdieu goes on to say, what makes Flaubert's work so original 'is that it makes contact, at least negatively, with the totality of the literary universe in which it is inscribed' (1996: 98).

But this is surely to turn cultural production into something completely self-referential. Form and theme are significant only to the extent that they can be related homologically to the structure of the field. Imagine carrying the homological method across to, say, popular music. We would have no way of understanding songs in terms of their reference to people, places, emotions, relationships ... even power; no inkling that vocal style might have significance because of its sensuous performance of the human body. The rejection of reference is mistaken, then. More, I would suggest it is politically dangerous, because we lose any sense of the truth or adequacy to reality of media texts.

In order to reinstate the problem of reference we can turn once again to an argument about the nature and consequences of media structure. It is this: just as perlocution is entailed by producer–audience relations, reference is entailed by producer–world relations.[11] Media makers tend to be objective, because their work is oriented outwards, in the direction of people and things. A game show is about a game between contestants; the news is about current events of a certain kind; a feature film has a fictional story about people in recognisable social and geographical locations. In his essay 'In defence of objectivity' Andrew Collier makes a case for the 'essential other-directedness of human mental acts and processes' (2003: 138). But if this is true of experience in general, it is emphatically so with the media, which are offered to us just as means of showing and telling about the world *beyond mere hearsay*. Indeed, the objectivity of media is a significant public value, enshrined in codes of media practice, and embedded in the everyday hermeneutics which people in the audience bring to bear on media texts.

Of course, critical researchers have rightly been suspicious about the ease with which media producers can undermine the objectivity that is posed by media–world relations. And I entirely agree that the influence of systemic social power is constantly directed towards subverting the media's witness in the interests of the powerful. What's more, that influence frequently prevails. But in this context to deny the possibility of reference is both mistaken in fact, and an act of political conservatism. For without at least some understanding of the world via the media we surely cannot hope to transform its iniquitous structures of power. The point here is not that the media could ever provide us with certain knowledge. This would be the case even in a hypothetical world where there was no systemic pressure on media producers to distort objective accounts of the world. For all ways of knowing (CR social theory as much as media artefacts) are socially produced and historically changing. In CR, then, epistemological relativism is a necessary consequence of a realist ontology.

Yet that relativism does not mean all ways of knowing should be equally good. For whenever we encounter knowledge or reference to the world we have to make a decision about its adequacy. Thus judgemental rationality is the necessary counterpart to the fallibility of knowledge (Bhaskar 1991: 153–4). And that in turn means we need to hold media makers and owners to account for what texts get made. A politically engaged media studies must be concerned with how far and how adequately the media refer to the world – not only in news and current affairs, but in music, drama, even reality television.

As I started to think through what a realist take on media texts might involve a couple of years ago I feared that some dourly serious and reductive analytical work would be called for. But I shouldn't have worried. For reality is complex and always changing, while the media's reference to it is necessarily provisional, given the fallible, perspectival nature of knowledge. Realist textual analysis thus has the character of being serious as life itself, while at the same time being preoccupied with the camp, the piteous, the polemical, satirical, absurd, fantastic …. The list of objective qualities you might need to consider is a long one.

Conclusion

I began by announcing an argument for the precedence of production. Through bringing to bear CR social theory, the chapter would examine the implications of that precedence for media making. Now I think we are in a position to draw some conclusions. There are four of them.

1 Precedence means that production comes first in time in that well known series of producer–text–audience. To make a text is to limit the terms and conditions of its meaning at time 1 so that when the text is interpreted by the audience at time 2 it will be with some of its perlocutionary meaning intact. The logic of this is both inexorable and fuzzy; inexorable because, once composed, media texts are objects with real causal powers. The fuzziness arises because these

causal powers are opaque to some extent – unintended meanings may arise both at production and, particularly, at reception. What such fuzzy logic suggests for media studies is that we ought to recognise the temporal/causal chain, in other words that things start with production located within a specific conjuncture of social relations. Yet that precedence of production does not mean that it is more important as a research topic than the audience. How could it be so? The perlocutionary structure of the media poses not only causes but also effects, namely the audience interpreting texts. It follows that specialisation within media studies is legitimate only for the practical reason that there is a limit to the number of things you can know about in any depth. In general, media researchers ought to be considering the critical problem of media-in-society, even and especially when they are focusing on their 'own' media moment.

2   The monological (one-way) and hierarchical (few to many) structure of the media does not necessarily entail powerful media. Misfires and failures ensure that meanings often do not get through, and media organisations find it hard to measure the perlocutionary hit rate among the audience. As for the hierarchical aspect, this can be understood only in the context of power relations in society: the media are located in a complex nexus of social structures which exert and reproduce power, though never, given the openness of the social system, in predictable and regular ways. In sum, powerful interests influence and inflect media making, and this is the central problem we need to address when we consider the question of media power.

3   The agency of producers, and the special autonomy they have as cultural workers in capitalist formal democracies, produces a contradiction. On the one hand autonomy merely legitimates the authority of the media among the audience. On the other hand it is substantive, and means that producers are sometimes and to some extent able to make texts independently of market pressures or other forms of external influence. More generally, autonomy constitutes a form of emergence on which is premised the possibility of all kinds of structural transformation. While genre structures frequently change (CR's transformational model of social activity can help to show us how), social structures are difficult to transform. Still, the possibility of and need for radical social change persist, and critical media studies should therefore keep a constant eye on how media producers make a difference to our understanding of that possibility and that need.

4   Producer–world relations pose the essentially objective character of the media. However, if producers treat things in the world, then by the same token they can make falsely objective texts. This may be inadvertent or, more rarely, intentional (i.e. some form of deception). In either case it is often the result of the influence of powerful interests. Because of this capacity of the media to both represent and distort

reality there is a need for textual analysis which will itself be driven by an ethic of objectivity.

None of the above points are new, of course. They have all been made before in media studies. However, I think that CR gives them a more rigorous standing – and perhaps enables a synthesis of positions which can take us beyond the war of the media moments to a new kind of critical media studies. In any event, that surely has to be the goal as reality bites, and jolts even those among us who still dream that in media, as in life itself, we simply dream.

Notes

1 I have not mentioned textual analysis, which forms a third would-be hegemonic position in media studies. There is no space to discuss it properly as a position here, although there certainly will be discussion of texts and textuality.
2 Many thanks to David Hesmondhalgh for help with this chapter, both in discussion beforehand and in editing as I clawed my way to a final version.
3 However, see Raymond Lau's important article (2004) on news production for a pioneering example.
4 This means that the realist claim for the existence of the world independently of means of knowing it needs to be modified in the case of the social, as opposed to the natural, world. On the one hand, society indeed has a dimension of 'existential intransitivity', that is, it exists as an object of enquiry (and becomes manifestly intransitive as we examine it in the past; no amount of reinterpretation changes what went before). On the other hand, knowledge production has consequences for the constitution of society, and vice versa, hence there is 'causal interdependency' between discourse and the social (Bhaskar 1998: 47–8; see also Sayer 2000: 10–11).
5 Market apologists argue that the market and market research feed back the opinions of the audience to production units. Still, even if one grants the market with such a feedback effect (and there are many reasons to doubt its efficacy), this is in no way comparable to the communicative conditions of dialogue.
6 If this sounds worryingly metaphysical, then, as Andrew Sayer suggests, we can find reassurance in the fact that 'many mechanism are *ordinary*, often being identified in ordinary language by transitive verbs, as in "they *built up* a network of political connections"' (2000: 14).
7 A related issue is the event–regularities problem in empiricist research which we discussed earlier. Media-commissioned audience research suffers from this as much as academic empiricist work.
8 For a discussion of stylistic change in reggae music, and the role of Bob Marley in it, which uses the TMSA see Toynbee (2007).
9 Of course, this tendency varies enormously in degree and kind across the media industries. There are also economic factors at play to do with offloading risk on to producers.
10 Tobin Nellhaus (1998) points to the basis of this trend in cultural theory's wholesale adoption of Saussurian semiology. Saussure's 'signified' has no object. Conversely, reference is central to Pierce's semiotics (pp. 2–3). Nellhaus goes on to develop a compelling synthesis of CR social ontology and the Piercian system of semiotics in this article.
11 The two are linked in that reference is the aim of perlocution. Audiences should get to see, hear, feel and understand things in the world.

Coventry University Library

Bibliography

Austin, J. (1975) *How to do Things with Words*, 2nd edn. Oxford: Clarendon Press.

Bhaskar, R. (1991) *Philosophy and the Idea of Freedom*. Oxford: Blackwell.

Bhaskar, R. (1998) *The Possibility of Naturalism: a Philosophical Critique of the Contemporary Human Sciences*, 3rd edn. London: Routledge.

Bourdieu, P. (1996) *The Rules of Art: Genesis and Structure of the Literary Field*. Cambridge: Polity Press.

Collier, A. (1994) *Critical Realism: an Introduction to Roy Bhaskar's Philosophy*. London: Verso.

Collier, A. (2003) *In Defence of Objectivity and other Essays: on Realism, Existentialism and Politics*. London: Routledge.

Elder-Vass, D. (2005) 'Emergence and the realist account of cause', *Journal of Critical Realism* 4: 315–38.

Golding, P. and Murdock, G. (1979) 'Ideology and the mass media: the question of determination', in M. Barrett, P. Corrigan, A. Kuhn and J.Wolff (eds) *Ideology and Cultural Production*. London: Croom Helm.

Huesmann, R., Moise-Titus, J., Podolski, C-L. and Eron, L. (2003) 'Longitudinal relations between children's exposure to TV violence and their aggressive and violent behaviour in young adulthood, 1977–1992', *Developmental Psychology* 39 (2): 201–23.

Lau, R. (2004) 'Critical realism and news production', *Media, Culture and Society* 26 (5): 693–711.

Lawson, T. (1998a) 'Abstraction', in M. Archer, R. Bhaskar, A. Collier, T. Lawson and A. Norrie (eds) *Critical Realism: Essential Readings*. London: Routledge.

Lawson, T. (1998b) 'Economic science without experimentation', in M. Archer, R. Bhaskar, A. Collier, T. Lawson and A. Norrie (eds) *Critical Realism: Essential Readings*. London: Routledge.

Livingstone, S. (2004) 'The challenge of changing audiences, or, What is the audience researcher to do in the Age of the Internet?', *European Journal of Communication* 19 (1): 75–86.

Nellhaus, T. (1998) 'Signs, social ontology and critical realism', *Journal for the Theory of Social Behaviour* 28 (1): 1–24.

Porpora, D. (1998) 'Four concepts of social structure', in M. Archer, R. Bhaskar, A. Collier, T. Lawson and A. Norrie (eds) *Critical Realism: Essential Readings*. London: Routledge.

Sayer, A. (2000) *Realism and Social Science*. London: Sage.

Sibeon, R. (2004) *Rethinking Social Theory*. London: Sage.

Thompson, J. (1995) *The Media and Modernity*. Cambridge: Polity Press.

Toynbee, J. (2007) *Bob Marley: Herald of a Postcolonial World?* Cambridge: Polity.

Index

eBooks

eBooks – at www.eBookstore.tandf.co.uk

A library at your fingertips!

eBooks are electronic versions of printed books. You can store them on your PC/laptop or browse them online.

They have advantages for anyone needing rapid access to a wide variety of published, copyright information.

eBooks can help your research by enabling you to bookmark chapters, annotate text and use instant searches to find specific words or phrases. Several eBook files would fit on even a small laptop or PDA.

NEW: Save money by eSubscribing: cheap, online access to any eBook for as long as you need it.

Annual subscription packages

We now offer special low-cost bulk subscriptions to packages of eBooks in certain subject areas. These are available to libraries or to individuals.

For more information please contact webmaster.ebooks@tandf.co.uk

We're continually developing the eBook concept, so keep up to date by visiting the website.

www.eBookstore.tandf.co.uk

Crime and Media A Reader

Chris Greer, City University, London

Routledge
Taylor & Francis Group

This engaging and timely collection gathers together for the first time key and classic readings in the ever-expanding area of crime and media. Comprising a carefully distilled selection of the most important contributions to the field, *Crime and Media: A Reader* tackles a wide range of issues including: theoretical perspectives; research methods; media influence; crime news and fiction; media, criminal justice and social control; and new media and surveillance technologies. Specially devised introductory and linking sections contextualize each reading and evaluate its contribution to the field, both individually and in relation to competing approaches and debates. Accessible yet challenging, and packed with additional pedagogical devices, *Crime and Media: A Reader* will be an invaluable resource for students and academics studying crime, media, culture, surveillance and control.

Contents
Part 1: Understanding Media and Society Part 2: Researching Media Part 3: Crime, Newsworthiness and News Part 4: Crime, Consumption and Creativity Part 5: Effects, Influence and Moral Panic Part 6: Cybercrime, Surveillance and Risk

September 2008

HB: 978-0-415-42238-3: £80.00
PB: 978-0-415-42239-0: £23.99

Routledge books are available from all good bookshops, or can be ordered by calling Taylor and Francis Direct Sales on +4401264343071 (credit card orders)

Routledge
Taylor & Francis Group

Handbook of Public Communication in Science and Technology

Massimiano Bucchi and Brian Trench

Handbook of
Public Communication of
Science and Technology
Edited by Massimiano Bucchi
and Brian Trench

Comprehensive yet accessible, this key *Handbook* provides an up-to-date overview of the fast growing and increasingly important area of 'public communication of science and technology', from both research and practical perspectives. As well as introducing the main issues, arenas and professional perspectives involved, it presents the findings of earlier research and the conclusions previously drawn. Unlike most existing books on this topic, this unique volume couples an overview of the practical problems faced by practitioners with a thorough review of relevant literature and research.

The practical handbook format ensures it is a student-friendly resource, but its breadth of scope and impressive contributors means that it is also ideal for practitioners and professionals working in the field. Combining the contributions of different disciplines (media and journalism studies, sociology and history of science), the perspectives of different geographical and cultural contexts, and by selecting key contributions from appropriate and well-respected authors, this original text provides an interdisciplinary as well as a global approach to public communication of science and technology.

Contents

Introduction 1. Popular Science Books 2. Science Journalism 3. Science Museums and Science Centers 4. Cinematic Science 5. Of Deficits, Deviations and Dialogues: Theories of Public Communication of Science 6. Health Campaign Research 7. Genetics and Genomics: The Ethics and Politics of Metaphorical Framing 8. Survey Research and the Public Understanding of Science 9. Scientists as Public Experts 10. Public Relations in Science: Managing the Trust Portfolio 11. Environmental Groups and other NGOs as Science Communicators 12. Public Participation and Dialogue 13. Internet: Turning Science Communication Inside-Out 14. Risk, Science and Public Communication: Third-Order Thinking about Scientific Culture 15. Public Communication of Science and Technology in Developing Countries 16. Communicating the Social Sciences 17. Evaluating Public Communication of Science and Technology

April 2008   Hb: 9780415386173 £95.00

VISIT www.routledge.com   TELEPHONE: 01264 343071

Routledge
Taylor & Francis Group

Science in Society

Massimiano Bucchi

The world around us is continually being shaped by science, and by society's relationship to it. In recent years sociologists have been increasingly preoccupied with the latter, and now in this fascinating book, Massimiano Bucchi provides a brief introduction to this topical issue.

Bucchi provides clear and unassuming summaries of all the major theoretical positions within the sociology of science, illustrated with many fascinating examples. Theories covered include Thomas Kuhn's theory of scientific change, the sociology of scientific knowledge, actor-network theory, and the social construction of technology. The second half of the book looks at recent public controversies over the role of science in the modern world including:

- the Sokal affair, otherwise known as the science wars
- debates over public understanding of science, such as global warming and genetically modified food
- the implications of the human genome project.

This much needed introduction to a rapidly growing area brings theory alive and will be essential reading for all students of the sociology of science.

Contents

Introduction Prologue 1. The Development of Modern Science and the Birth of the Sociology of Science 2. Paradigms and Styles of Thought: A 'Social Window' on Science? 3. Is Mathematics Socially Shaped? The Strong Programme 4. Inside the Laboratory 5. Tearing Bicycles and Missiles Apart: The Sociology of Technology 6. Science Wars' 7. Communicating Science 8. A New Science? References. Index of Names

February 2004   Hb: 9780415321900 £75.00 Pb: 9780415322003 £21.99

VISIT www.routledge.com   TELEPHONE: 01264 343071

Taylor & Francis Group

3rd Edition

Theories of the
Information Society

Frank Webster

Coping in an era of information flows, of virtual relationships and break-neck change poses challenges to one and all.

In *Theories of the Information Society* Frank Webster makes sense of the information explosion, taking a sceptical look at what thinkers mean when they refer to the 'Information Society' and critically examines the major post-war theories and approaches to informational development. This third edition brings the book right up to date with both new theoretical work and, social and technological changes (such as the rapid growth of the Internet and accelerated globalization), reassessing the work of key theorists in light of these changes.

This book is essential reading for students of contemporary social theory and anybody interested in social and technological change in the post-war era. It addresses issues of central concern to students of sociology, politics, communications, information science, cultural studies, computing and librarianship.

Contents

1. Introduction 2. What is an Information Society? 3. Post-Industrial Society: Daniel Bell 4. Regulation School Theory 5. Network Society: Manuel Castells 6. Information and the Market 7. Information and Democracy: Jurgen Habermas 8. Information, Reflexivity and Surveillance: Anthony Giddens 9. Information and Postmodernity 10. The Information Society?

August 2006   Hb: 9780415406321 £90.00 Pb: 9780415406338 £22.99

VISIT www.routledge.com   TELEPHONE: 01264 343071

12, 195